D0932503

MUNICIPAL MANAGEMENT SERIES

Developing the
Municipal Organization

THE MUNICIPAL MANAGEMENT SERIES

EDITORS

Stanley Piazza Powers

University of Nebraska
at Omaha

F. Gerald Brown

University of Missouri—
Kansas City

David S. Arnold

International City
Management Association

Developing the Municipal Organization

Published for the
Institute for Training in Municipal Administration
by the
International City Management Association

MUNICIPAL MANAGEMENT SERIES

David S. Arnold
EDITOR

Managing the Modern City

Principles and Practice of Urban Planning

Municipal Finance Administration

Municipal Personnel Administration

Municipal Police Administration

Municipal Fire Administration

Municipal Public Works Administration

Management Practices for Smaller Cities

Community Health Services

Case Problems in City Management

Effective Supervisory Practices

Municipal Public Relations

Policy Analysis in Local Government

Developing the Municipal Organization

Managing Municipal Leisure Services

Foreword

The publication of this book by the International City Management Association provides recognition of the changes that have taken place in urban government in this country since the publication of the predecessor volume, *Supervisory Methods in Municipal Administration,* just sixteen short years ago. These changes in society and government have been in the nature of a revolution and have had an enormous impact on the ability of municipal government to adjust to and cope with radically different demands and expectations.

To even the casual observer these changes are obvious. To the government practitioner they represent almost a new way of professional life. A brief and not exhaustive list might include the following.

Intergovernmental Relations. The emergence of the federal government's role directly impacting on cities in the social areas such as Model Cities; job training and economic aid; revenue sharing; mass transit systems; and regional council review of federal grant applications.

Citizen Participation. Economic opportunity and maximum feasible participation; public hearing requirements for highways; and just the growing recognition by the public that you *can* fight City Hall.

Affirmative Action. Equal employment requirements; racism; sexism; economical housing; and integration.

Environment: Growing recognition that the highway and automobile are not kings anymore (Who would have thought twenty years ago that freeways are no longer a sign of progress?); air, water, land, and noise pollution; and environmental impact reporting standards.

Labor Relations. Growing strength of public employee unionism; strikes; and mandatory requirement for labor negotiations and contracts.

Growth Control. After all these years of encouraging and facilitating growth we are now devising ways to either stop it or at least to slow it down.

Regional Government. The rapid growth of councils of governments and the almost overwhelming growth of regional control agencies.

New Management Techniques. Organization development; team building; behavioral science; and even concepts of working more closely with elected officials.

All of these plus many other changes should be sufficient to point up the present and emerging problems facing urban administrators.

The keynote of course is change—change from our physically-oriented values of a few years ago to the human values of government today. How do we understand it? Adjust to it? Cope with it?

That's what this book is all about. It has been written for the urban administrator at all levels, from the city manager to the first-line supervisor, so that each person can understand the nature of this very real change.

The great difficulty that most of our urban administrators are going through today is that our education and experience have too often been inadequate for facing today's urban problems. Many of the old traditions are gone, and new methods are required. We now are seeking ways to identify those traditions that should be kept, and to learn about and use new methods of management and supervision.

An easy way to quickly understand the change

that this book represents is to compare it with the table of contents of its predecessor book. For example, *Supervisory Methods in Municipal Administration* did not even mention the word "change" whereas the current volume refers to it repeatedly. Working with citizens, or citizen participation, had only ten pages devoted to the subject in the old book. This new volume has an entire chapter. Labor relations was given only three pages in the old book whereas the current volume devotes two full chapters, which represents a tenfold increase in space. The present volume gives increased coverage to individual and group behavior and substantial emphasis on "organization development," a term which was not in popular use sixteen years ago.

I believe that the key importance of this book is to put into practice the changes in public administration theory that have been developed in the last two decades. I have recently read such books as *Beyond the Stable State,* by Donald A. Schon, *The Intellectual Crisis in American Public Administration,* by Vincent Ostrom, *Managerial Psychology,* by Harold J. Leavitt, *The Exceptional Executive,* by Harry Levinson, and *Organization Development: Its Nature, Origins, and Prospects,* by Warren Bennis, among others. They provide a pretty clear picture of how theorists view the shifts and needs for today's public administrator. But, of course, all of us who are practicing public administrators never seem to have the time to read what our intellectual peers are writing; even more difficult is our ability to translate that theory into practice. Again ICMA (as in the last forty years) has come to our rescue by putting together the kind of practical, usable, and understandable training volume that will permit us to develop the requisite skills for today's and tomorrow's administrator.

Thomas W. Fletcher

President
National Training and Development Service
for State and Local Government

Washington, D.C.
April 1974

Preface

In 1958, in the predecessor book, *Supervisory Methods in Municipal Administration,* the authors noted that "Changes in American society in the last fifty years have complicated greatly the work of the supervisor; for that matter, the work of all persons in administration." With the passage of sixteen years these changes have multiplied and have become much more complex and inter-related. One of the major purposes of this book is to help sort out some of these changes. In the broadest terms it is a book about bureaucracy, but not about bureaucrats in the pejorative sense; about organization technology, but not about technical aspects of operations research; about people in organizations, but not about the Organization Man.

Supervisory leadership, techniques, and perspectives within the framework of the work group were the broad areas of content for *Supervisory Methods in Municipal Administration.* Its creative approaches to the processes and psychology of work were a significant contribution to the training of thousands of local government employees in the United States and Canada. The book has been widely used by university continuing education agencies and by city, county, and regional training groups as well as in the more formal setting of college and university classes.

We have now come to the point where a new look is needed at the development of people in organizations in both the formal and informal structures and systems that enable cities, counties, and other local governments to get work done. In this evolutionary process the most striking trend is a psychological blending, a behavioral approach if you will, of people, struc-ture, systems, and technology into a process that is sometimes loosely identified as organization development but might more accurately be called organization development and renewal. The title of this book, *Developing the Municipal Organization,* was chosen deliberately to emphasize this change in coverage. The book has been written and edited to serve local government administrators, especially chief appointed executives, department heads, division and section heads, and supervisors. The book also will serve teachers and students who wish to gain fuller understanding of the complexities of the administrative and organizational processes that underlie the traditional concerns of organization and management.

This book, like others in the Municipal Management Series, has drawn on the first-hand experience of governmental administrators, teachers, and consultants. Each of these volumes incorporates the latest developments in research, teaching, and application.

The titles in the Municipal Management Series have been prepared especially for the Institute for Training in Municipal Administration. The institute offers in-service training specifically designed for local government officials whose jobs are to plan, direct, and coordinate the work of others. The institute has been sponsored since 1934 by the International City Management Association.

This book is the work of many hands. We want first to acknowledge our debt to Frank P. Sherwood, and Wallace H. Best, authors of the predecessor volume, *Supervisory Methods in Municipal Administration.* Their pioneering efforts provided the foundation for this volume. We are grateful for the encouragement and support from staff members of the Industrial Relations Center, University of Chicago, especially Wallace G. Lonergan, director of the center, and for the support of the staff of the Center for Management Development, School of Administration, University of Missouri—Kansas City, especially Louise Gammon, Gilda Bormaster, and Robert J. Saunders, director of the center.

Of particular value to us was a detailed commentary of almost all the chapters in the book provided by five staff members of the National Training and Development Service for State and Local Government, who reviewed the manuscript and offered many helpful suggestions for improvement. The NTDS staff members who provided this review were Thomas C. Clary, Frederick E. Fisher, Roy G. Gregg, Robert A. Luke, Jr., and William J. Silver.

The editors are especially grateful to the authors we were privileged to work with, to Emily Evershed for final edit and preparation of the Index, and to Herbert Slobin for preparation of many of the illustrations.

STANLEY PIAZZA POWERS

Assistant Professor
Director, Governmental Organization
    Development Division
Department of Public Administration
University of Nebraska at Omaha

F. GERALD BROWN

Assistant Professor
Coordinator of Public Administration Programs
Center for Management Development
School of Administration
University of Missouri—Kansas City

DAVID S. ARNOLD

Director, Publications Services
International City Management Association

Washington, D.C.
April 1974

Table of Contents

Figures

Illustration credits: Figure 5—2: Reprinted by permission from THE MANAGERIAL Grid, by Robert R. Blake and Jane Srygley Mouton (Houston: Gulf Publishing Company, 1964), p. 10. Figures 9—8 and 9—9: Robert K. Burns, THE LISTENING TECHNIQUES (Chicago: Industrial Relations Center, University of Chicago, 1958), p. 4. Figures 9—10 and 9—11: Robert K. Burns, THE QUESTIONING TECHNIQUES (Chicago: Industrial Relations Center, University of Chicago, 1958), p. 4. Figure 14—1: A PROPOSAL FOR AN INTEGRATIVE MUNICIPAL INFORMATION SYSTEM, I, Kansas City, Missouri, October 31, 1969. Figure 14—2: John E. Dever, "A Comprehensive Management Information System," PUBLIC MANAGEMENT, May, 1973, p. 13. Figure 14—3: Herbert Simon, THE SHAPE OF AUTOMATION (New York: Harper and Brothers, 1965), p. 62. Figure 14—4: Planning-Programming-Budgeting Systems for State and Local Governments, A Seminar on New Concepts of Financial Planning, Management and Control, sponsored by the state of Washington, February 14-15, 1968. Figure 14—5: Kenneth L. Kraemer, Integrated Municipal Information System Project, U.S. Department of Housing and Urban Development, Figures 15—3 and 15—4: Based on U.S. Veterans Administration form 4546, August 1958. Figure 15—5: United States Air Force, "How To Develop a Better Method," Management Course for Air Force supervisors, AFP 50-2-7 (Washington, D.C.: Government Printing Office, 1955), p. 20. Figure 15—6: U.S. Veterans Administration form 10-2993, October 1959. Figure 15—7: Department of the Army, TECHNIQUES OF WORK SIMPLIFICATION, DA Pamphlet 20-300 (Washington, D.C.: Comptroller of the Army, 1951), p. 19. Figure 19—1: University of Missouri-Kansas City/Mid-America Urban Observatory, ORGANIZED CITIZEN PARTICIPATION IN KANSAS CITY, MISSOURI, 1971, taken from Appendix 2.

Developing the
Municipal Organization

Part One

Organization Policies, Concepts, People, and Systems

Introduction

Because in the administration it hath respect not to the few but to the multitude, our form of government is called a democracy.

THUCYDIDES

THIS IS A BOOK about the municipal government as an organization. It begins with a chapter on the legal basis, formal structure, and political environment of municipal government and then proceeds in subsequent chapters to examine many sides of organization, including structure, people, systems, and technology. Most of this examination is internal—that is, how the organization reacts and interacts with its employees and with the social system and work processes. In the concluding chapters the organization is dealt with externally with respect to labor relations, public information, and the emerging role of citizen participation.

The above quotation from Thucydides expressed the thought well over two thousand years ago that administration respects the "multitude," and that means all of us. The democratic ideal of the Greeks provided part of the framework for development of governmental institutions in the United States. Chapter 1 sets forth the historical perspective for the formal development of local government structure and summarizes current legal, political, and organizational realities that condition the way work gets done by the municipal organization. The author points out that we are moving away from the traditional organization built on a formal hierarchy and toward new ways of getting work done with varied and flexible approaches. These ap-

proaches are covered in subsequent chapters from several different perspectives.

Such changes do not occur of course by chance. As industralization and urbanization set in, from the midnineteenth century on, many social and economic changes took place that all of us are familiar with. Since World War II, however, a new dimension has been added—the impact of technology which has brought new heights in the national standard of living and profound sociopsychological changes in work and the way people regard work.

Chapter 2 enables us to take a closer look at organization models in the structural sense. Historically, organizations have been built along military lines with clear-cut ranks and levels. With the Industrial Revolution, industrial managers naturally turned to the forms they were familiar with in setting up their own organizations to meet the expanding requirements of society. By far the most important person in this development was Frederick Winslow Taylor, known generally as the father of scientific management. In broad terms the other major development was the human relations movement which stressed the needs of people and their psychological investment in the work process.

In recent years, as this book points out in several chapters, efforts have been made to reconcile the obvious extremes of the two approaches—scientific management and human relations—and bring their useful features together through the findings of behavioral psychology. This is a trend of considerable importance in understanding the purposes of this book. This effort is known loosely as organization development. Borrowing somewhat from the field of medicine, its advocates talk about a healthy organization that is whole and self-renewing. To make this as specific as possible, it is worth quoting directly from Chapter 2:

Its most significant characteristic is the attempt to take a total organization point of view—to build in both the imperatives of law, policies, and structure and the needs and aspirations of workers, to provide for nonquantifiable goals while recognizing that much work still is measured numerically, and to develop in workers the motivation and capacity for both on the job.

Chapter 3 begins to look more closely at the people in organizations. We return to the pioneering work of Taylor, and considerable attention is given to Taylor's projects with respect to worker reactions and work results. Then the human relations movement is described in some detail on the basis of the experiments conducted at the Hawthorne Works of the Western Electric Company. These studies were extremely important in showing for the first time the influence of the way people relate to each other within a work group and the effects of the work situation or environment.

The balance of Chapter 3 moves on to others who have a more comprehensive understanding of the human personality—its needs, hopes, aspirations, fears, strengths, and weaknesses. Their work has helped us gain enormously in understanding how and why people react the way they do in work situations, especially in groups. The author notes that Chapter 3 has been built "on the assumption that man's positive (or 'good') tendencies are stronger than other forces in his personality and that organization and management should function accordingly." This is the point of view of the editors of this book, but it is not a universal point of view. Those of a more conservative persuasion are inclined to be skeptical of man's capacity and incentive for self-improvement even in organizational surroundings that encourage self-help.

The last chapter in Part one is an unusual effort to look at the municipal organization as a system that is self-contained with public policy and other inputs feeding into the municipal organization through the technological process of work and the social process of the organization with the output of services to the public. The feedback is completed when the goals are returned to the public policy side. The chapter is somewhat theoretical, but it has a very practical purpose. Chapter 4 is intended to help you keep the technological process of work and the social process of the organization pulling together to get the work done so that services can be delivered to citizens. This is as realistic a statement as anyone can make as to why we are here. The manager who overemphasizes one to the detriment of the other does so at his peril. The manager who thinks and acts in terms of the whole job and the whole organization is the effective manager.

1

The Realities
of Local Government

Forces of urbanization have been moving relentlessly across the land since the industrialization which followed the Civil War. This is not a new phenomenon. The fact is, we are an urban nation and have been for at least half a century.[1] Urban problems can no longer be assigned simply to the big cities. Central cities, their suburbs, and independent cities alike have begun in the past few years to recognize the demands of organized urban life. Urban change has accelerated to the point where national domestic policies are now concerned with the problems of the cities.

As a nation we have come through the decade of the sixties when we measured urban problems by crisis proportions. We risk triteness in recounting the forces associated with the dimensions of our urban problems. Race relations, population explosions, ecology, transportation snarls, water and air pollution, housing, poverty, equal opportunity, welfare, and many other matters have been subjects of national concern in publications of every variety for the past several years. Cities continue to wrestle with the problems of growth and decline, the building of suburbs, which are in a real sense evolving into "the city," and the decay of the central cities.

We have become a relatively affluent society in which the gap between the affluent and the poor has been filled with alienation and dissatisfaction. Local government has borne the brunt of this dissatisfaction on the part of alienated people seeking redress of their grievances against the social system and its institutions. All of this is viewed in the context of municipal interests of a generation ago which contrast with the agenda of new concerns for local government today. Local government is in the vortex of change, and the local government practitioner is an agent of that change.

In reflecting the society that has created them, local governments are changing institutions, filled with incredible stresses and tensions as new demands are placed upon them. For many years the functions of local government were centered around the physical building of streets and roads, and the operating of water and sewage facilities, and around efficiency in the management of these functions. In response to a new agenda of concerns, municipal functions have developed around Model Cities, human relations, housing, and social and economic development, for example, which go far beyond the programs associated with physical planning and local government structures.

The Local Government Practitioner

In responding to these new demands and changing concerns, local government operates within a complex set of realities, with form and structure built out of laws which still often reflect the concerns and problems of a society or community of a generation ago. Whatever local government does is the result of the political process and ultimately is tested in that process. Political control is a fact of life, with practical effects on how the organization performs its tasks as well as what tasks the organization performs.

The local government practitioner lives and works within the context of these realities. For him, the effects of political control may more nearly represent reality than the organization itself. Because of this, reality may never be fully rational or irrational, never totally human or totally technological, never completely black and white or fully compromising. The local government professional is considered a problem solver, yet he frequently feels stymied because of "outside forces." These outside forces may be government form and law, local customs and prejudices, or politically expedient decision making. All of these outside forces determine to a large extent the professional's ability to use the technology and resources at his disposal.

The local government supervisor is charged with running an efficient and economical operation—in other words, getting the job done. Yet his boundaries are frequently set by a framework of policies built within the confines of antiquated city charters and state laws which preclude efficiency and prohibit responsive change. Moreover, he may work in an organization in which his relationships with superiors do not allow him to significantly influence policy making or to sense the value of his own efforts.

The successful supervisor/manager must be a creative planner and problem solver, though he may frequently spend most of his working hours fighting small administrative and technical "fires" in lieu of more creative work. The supervisor has that difficult organizational assignment of linking the policies and goals established by top political and administrative leadership with organizational muscle. This is the real challenge of being a supervisor.

Although the supervisor must still see that the chuckholes are filled, the garbage is collected, the water is pumped, and the equipment is running, he must, today, have a sophisticated understanding of a much more complex government organization. He must be able to cope with the growing interdependence of functions not only within his own department but throughout the organization. If he is a technician, he needs some understanding of the departments meeting human and social needs. If he is concerned with human needs and social action, he must also understand the problems of the more mechanical services and their delivery. The supervisor provides the most important link of all: he is at the interface between citizen and service. If policy is correctly carried out and service is performed well, the government has in that instance been effective in the eyes of the citizen.

In this chapter we will not discuss and develop in detail the complexities of the supervisory role. That will be done in other sections of this book. Our intent here is to provide the overview, so that the reader can begin to establish his own perspective of how and why the supervisory role is developing within the rapidly changing framework of local government.

We want, in this chapter, to focus our attention on reality and some practical effects of theories. Our first task will be to examine some of the historical and legal constraints which are the heritage of local government. This will lead us to a pragmatic consideration of some implications of government form and structure for managers and supervisors. Finally, we will consider some of the problems created by the tensions of incorporating the new functions of city government with the old, and some likely requirements of managing the local government organization in the future.

Historical Perspective

Modern local government is truly a product of the twentieth century. It has grown out of an age of reform which began to sweep across the land in response to misplaced and misused political power and obvious inability of local government structures to cope with growing problems of urban life.

Prior to the twentieth century, local government structure generally was established within a weak mayor form of government. Major features were a large city council, frequently with upper and lower chambers, and numerous separately elected officials who were in many instances operating department heads. The lack of centralized administrative authority made the absence of coordination and control over local government functions a major attribute.

Within this structural context a significant concern of local leaders often was the exercise and keeping of political power. Local governments, especially in the larger cities, were under the control of political machines, and the excesses and abuses of political power produced a sordid tale of dishonesty, graft, corruption, and municipal failure.[2] Although the abuses of political power through machine control by no means explain entirely the need and precedent for municipal reform, let us look further into the nature of machine politics.

THE POLITICAL MACHINE

The term political machine has taken on rather sinister connotations over the past fifty to seventy-five years. However, some current writers remind us that the machine was no more totally sinister than is present-day local government totally effective.[3] During the period of industrialization and urbanization which followed the Civil War, the political machine began to gain its prominence. During the second half of the nineteenth century, urbanism and machine politics were frequent companions.[4]

The political machine was the institutional backbone of city government during the period in which the bricks and mortar of our older cities were put into place.[5] The mainstays of the political machine were the precinct or the election district and its leader and his ward organization. The precinct leader was usually a small jobholder in local government who was convinced that his allegiance to the machine and its activities would benefit him personally. If the precinct leader was successful it did, and he was rewarded with progressively better jobs, greater remuneration, and perhaps, more significantly, a greater share of personal control over the life and activities within his precinct and within his ward.[6]

In return for the personal rewards which he received, the precinct leader performed several functions for the segment of citizens he served and for the total political machine. He was in charge of a small area—perhaps only one or two blocks. If a citizen had a problem he knew who to turn to—his friend the precinct leader. Social or welfare needs, a problem with the law, or difficulties with local government services were easily resolved for the citizen at the neighborhood political clubhouse. If action from the city government was required, that, too, could be achieved with dispatch. The neighborhood political leadership knew how to invade the local government bureaucracy laterally to achieve results without red tape.[7] For the citizen the end result was immediate access to services. In return, he paid his personal price by supporting the incumbent machine with his vote on election day.

The glue which held the organization together was the patronage and political favoritism it could bestow, in particular the jobs dispensed by the machine in return for loyalty, which was effectively repurchased with every paycheck. Thus the machine had a constant pool of loyal servants with which to staff the city organization. Withdrawal of political favors was a formidable disciplinary force for the machine boss to use at will.

Few would argue that the machine model promoted efficiency and honesty in city government. In fact, while it created easy access to local services for the citizen it also created confusion and the opportunity for corruption to flourish. There are those who would argue, however, that the classical political machine was responsible for much of the progress of our cities during a period of growth and expansion, regardless of the cost, and would lament quite nostalgically its virtual complete passing from the local government scene.

Not all cities were in fact governed by corrupt or self-serving political machines, but at the turn of the century most cities were visibly ineffective. Incoherent, cumbersome, decentralized structure—a boon to the would-be spoilsman—gave rise to a mood for improvement and reform. The dual conditions of corruption and misused political power plus generalized concern about structural ineffectiveness gave impetus to the reformer's movement. The degree to which experimentation with structure was sanctioned by the citizenry around the turn of the century is perhaps a good barometer of the true conditions of local government.[8] It it these structural inadequacies that we will now look at, since they help explain why cities are governed as they are today.

STRUCTURAL DEFICIENCIES:
PRELUDE TO REFORM

The lack of centralized executive authority was of prime importance to reformers, since without it accountability and control were almost impossible to achieve. The morass of council administrative committees, independently elected minor officials, and many appointed independent boards and commissions created a patchwork set of relationships which were difficult for even the most informed citizens to monitor. The would-be spoilsman had little difficulty invading such a structure. The goals of honesty and efficiency were thwarted by decentralized responsibility.

Structural reform, therefore, first focused on straightening out the tangled executive, legislative, and administrative relationships, centralizing the executive authority in a strong mayor, streamlining the legislative body into a unicameral house, and shortening the election ballot to a minimum number of officials, whose qualifications could be screened by the voter. In order to protect local government structure from future invasion by political bosses, municipal elections were taken out of the realm of party politics and the ballot was made nonpartisan. The election of councilmen at large was proposed, and often adopted, to break up the political party organizations which focused on precincts and wards.

Another area of significant concern for the reformers was the problem of how services were to be delivered to the citizenry once political favoritism and the spoils system had been eliminated. The reformers turned their attention to the need for local government organization and became interested in the management methods of private business. Effective management of the public's business was considered essential. Replication of private business's successful administrative tools for budgeting, accounting, personnel, purchasing, engineering, administrative planning, coordination, and control was seen as the path to the ultimate goal of efficient delivery of services and effective administration of public business.

For the structural deficiencies, the reformers devised a series of mechanical solutions supported by theoretical concepts. As specific op-

portunities occurred, the theoretical ideas of the reformers were put to work; out of this grew certain new forms of government.

New Forms of Government

STRONG MAYOR FORM

In 1897, under the auspices of the National Municipal League, the first model city charter was drafted, and was proposed to that organization the following year. This charter set forth a strong mayor form of government with centralized executive powers. It was hoped that a strong executive would use the new appointive powers given to him to surround himself with competent and qualified department heads. It was reasoned that, if such appointments were made on the basis of specific functional expertise, the management and delivery of municipal services would be removed from political spoilsmen and made more businesslike. The ballot was shortened and legislative powers were centralized in a unicameral city council. Independently elected officials were eliminated. National Municipal League influence, through the league's endorsement of the strong mayor form of government, was to remain potent until its model city charter was changed to incorporate the council-manager plan in 1915. Many cities to this day have some variation of the strong mayor form of government.

COMMISSION FORM

In 1900, in keeping with the spirit of experimentation of that time, another form of local government was created when the governor of Texas appointed a commission of five businessmen to govern and administer the city of Galveston following the disastrous hurricane of that year. The commission form went even further toward simplification of structure in that it unified the administrative and legislative functions of local government. Both functions were placed in the hands of a group of commissioners who were the only elected officials of the city. As a group of five, the Galveston commissioners collectively made local government policy and law; as individual commissioners they administered those policies by managing specific areas of municipal affairs. Consistent with the policy of reform, elections were nonpartisan and the commissioners were elected from the city at large. The commission form had a conspicuous but short-lived popularity as its variations spread from Galveston to over five hundred communities by 1917. Today, however, it is rare.

COUNCIL-MANAGER PLAN

The most significant structural advancement was yet around the corner. Experience was accumulating with the new approaches of unified and integrated structure, nonpartisan elections, and shortened ballots. In 1909 the National Short Ballot Organization was formed by Richard S. Childs, who enlisted the aid of Woodrow Wilson and other influential persons to promote the elimination of structural factors which were conducive to the spoils system. Childs was an articulate and indefatigable campaigner who believed there were universal principles of good government which, if found, could be applied from city to city. Childs saw the political machine as a threat to all cities and felt that local government structure was the key to the citizen's protection against prostitution of the political process.[9]

But perhaps a greater contribution was Childs's concern for a structure that provided for management of city functions. The major weakness of the commission form of government had been its total unification of legislative and executive powers in the same group of commissioners. Commissioners were required to make policy in which they had a vested interest as administrators. Thus, the integration of functions had gone a step too far. Further, seldom were persons trained in administration brought to city government by the elective process.

In 1908 members of the Staunton, Virginia, city council had been baffled by a series of engineering problems and an unwieldy set of administrative committees from the bicameral city council. Staunton had begun, pragmatically, an experiment which culminated in the creation of a "general manager" position which was superimposed on the existing governmental structure. Despite the cumbersomeness of the Staunton experience, its potential was recognized immediately by Childs.

Richard Childs combined the integrated structure and nonpartisan short ballot features of the commission form of government with the concept, borrowed from private business, of the "general manager" or "company president" (as in the Staunton experiment) and created the commission-manager or council-manager plan. The "city manager" in Childs's model was to be appointed on the basis of his competence and his administrative talents by a small city commission of no more than five members, which would make policies to be administered by the manager. The city council would deal only with the manager, who would in turn be in complete charge of the city government organization. The manager would have power to hire and fire department heads and to administer city affairs without interference by the city council. Should the manager fail to perform to the satisfaction of the council he could be dismissed forthwith.

Childs's model of commission-manager government was yet to be tested. In 1910 Childs drafted his model for consideration by Lockport, New York, but Lockport failed to gain permission from the state legislature to implement it. The first city to adopt the full-scale commission-manager plan was Sumter, South Carolina, in 1912. Several other cities followed suit. In 1914 Dayton, Ohio, became the first city of major size to adopt this form of government.

Council-manager government has been hailed as the most significant contribution made to local government by this country. Its popularity and significance may be seen in its widespread use throughout the United States and Canada. The growth of the plan was slow until 1945. Since then, however, some sixty-five places annually, on the average, have adopted the council-manager form. By 1973 a total of 2,390 places were governed under the plan.[10] Of perhaps equal significance, however, is the fact that the theoretical concepts for both governing and administering a local government found in the work of Childs and his colleagues have served as the framework for numerous variations of government form and structure to the present day. Council-manager government has provided the practical bridge between policy making and the management and delivery of local government services.

The Rise of Professionalism

Almost synonymous with the growth of council-manager government was the growth of professionalism in the local government service. The earliest city managers generally had an engineering background and therefore had ties to a profession. Within a few years they were seeking similar professional ties within their newly adopted vocation. In 1914 eight of the then thirty-one city managers in the country met in Springfield, Ohio, to exchange ideas and form an association.[11]

The rapid growth of the technical expertise increasingly required to perform municipal functions and the employment of specialists to fill local government jobs further increased the professional character of local government. Professionalism was significantly enhanced by the establishment of the civil service concept or merit system for municipal employment. Throughout this growth of professionalism, the city manager and his professional organization, the International City Managers' Association, have played a key role. The adoption of the City Manager's Code of Ethics by the International City Managers' Association in 1924 was an important and extremely significant step toward establishing the professional climate of local government service.

In 1969 the International City Managers' Association made a subtle change in its name and became the International City Management Association, adopting a broadened set of goals and membership categories to reflect the stature which it had achieved as the major professional organization for the local government executive career service. Changes and variations which had occurred in local government structure as a response to new conditions of urbanism made such a change advisable to the membership.[12] The creation of councils of governments, regional planning groups, and other units of local government which provided for general management administrators with duties and responsibilities not significantly unlike those of a city manager definitely signaled a new plateau of acceptance of the local government professional.

Legal Constraints

We have reviewed briefly the historical process of the early part of this century which, in effect, remade city government form and structure. The efforts of reformers were concentrated on new ways to govern cities and on numerous campaigns to establish legal powers to complete their work.

Much legislative effort was required to commit to law the protective devices which were to ensure that the "rascals" would be kept out and that honest men would govern. The concern with honesty and efficiency led also to the establishment by state law and city charter of numerous administrative mechanisms which formed the framework of local government bureaucracy. Frequently, for example, detailed requirements for operating personnel, accounting, and purchasing systems were set out in minute detail. While these protective devices were potent weapons in the arsenal of the reformers of a previous era, many are now the onerous burden of a bureaucracy which prohibits response to new conditions and concerns. For example, in some states local government units are required by state law to publish semiannual financial statements that include every warrant, to whom paid, and for what purpose issued. While such a procedure once provided full financial disclosure, it now proves only the increased volume of local government business.

A different example may be found in personnel systems which serve to prohibit local governments from responding creatively to hiring minorities. Such laws frequently result in accusations that local governments are discriminatory or unresponsive in their employment practices. The setting of personnel policies in city charters minimized public risk taking as defined by the problems of an earlier generation. However, to seek reform today of those same laws requires amendments to city charters and state laws which frequently may be made only through a long and cumbersome process.

Local governments are creatures of the state in a legal sense. They may be formed and disbanded only as permitted by state law. They hold only the powers granted to them by their creators. Local government powers may be broad or narrow or somewhere in between. But basically, in most states, a local government unit can do only those things and assume only those powers which have been specifically granted by the state. More significantly, not all cities within the same state may do the same things, since powers may be assigned to a given city or classes of cities by special laws or by population, assessed valuation, or other distinguishing characteristics.

The state constitution determines how the city's powers may be granted. For example, in some states, cities are granted powers of home rule. They may frame their own charters and form their own governments by the decision of their electorate. In other states, home rule is not allowed. In the latter states, city government form and structure is determined by general laws of the state legislature or, in a few instances, by city charters granted by act of state legislatures. In any case, in most states there are optional forms of general government law which a city of a certain size and certain characteristics may adopt. Such optional forms of government will generally include strong or weak mayor-council government, the commission form of government, or council-manager government.

Thus, we can see that cities adopt their form of government and gain their powers to make laws and perform functions from the state constitution, from general state laws, or from city charters adopted by the city or granted by the state legislature.

The basic unit of local lawmaking is the city ordinance. The city council is empowered under the state constitution and its laws to pass ordinances pertaining to matters within its powers. Thus, the policies and programs of the city will be established in most instances by city ordinances. As the city ordinances are passed by the city governing body, they may also be changed or revoked by it. It is the city ordinance which provides the force of law behind city programs and the legal boundaries within which administrators must operate. Ordinances also provide the penalties for failure to live within the expectations of the ordinance.

The influence of schools of political and administrative thought, current around the turn of the century, played a significant part in the way local government was organized and set into law. The scientific management of Frederick Winslow Taylor and the organizational theory of Max Weber are particularly apparent in the work of Richard Childs.[13] The major goals of all three men were to establish legalistic, rational, formal systems of organization which were based on incontrovertible "principles."

The contribution of Taylor's scientific management was its assumption that facts could be ascertained and that principles could be established from the facts. From the principles (and a devotion to the systematic study of management job performance), ultimate efficiency could be achieved and any organization could determine the "one best way" to accomplish a given task. It was maintained that a virtually complete rational system could be created by scientific inquiry. Thus, the emphasis was on developing fail-safe mechanisms based on principles which could produce the desired goals of efficiency and economy.

Max Weber contributed his emphasis on establishing a legal, rational system of organization which was designed to parcel out authority according to the specific place occupied by the worker in a hierarchical structure. Weber's legalistic model was made operational by prescribing boundaries and rules within which the bureaucrat was to function.[14]

Richard Childs's contribution was a consistent political philosophy that applied the approaches of Taylor and Weber to municipal governance. He attempted to ascertain principles of good government and to prescribe a legal-rational organizational model to assure their implementation.

With local government coming out of an era of low public trust and emphasis on governmental structure, all that was left for the reformer was to find the universal principles of good government structure, the mechanisms to make those principles and that structure operational, and the means to commit these to law. Thus we have numerous city charters and a body of municipal law, formed in the early part of the century, which establish severe legal constraints on the powers of city government.

Today the role of local government is

changing. The critical issue of trust has subsided, and problems of building physical facilities have been greatly relieved by success in utilizing the technological advances of the past half century. Traditional functions still must be maintained, but the emphasis has shifted to matters of social concern. The problems of human rights, equal opportunity, alienation, and maintenance of a sense of community all make significant requirements of the departments charged with building and maintaining physical structures.

With the changing roles of local government has come a time of experimentation. The nature of growth in metropolitan areas with central cities and suburbs, the development of the megalopolis, and other evidences of our increasing urbanization have led us to experiment with a new sense of freedom. Clearly, some of these forms do not reflect the early principles established by the reformers.

There is a constantly growing problem of intergovernmental relations and the need for coordination. Therefore, we now see the emergence of councils of governments and regional planning groups, together with experimentation with decentralization of large urban governments, and, conversely, in a few places the consolidation of governments. There is increasing concern also about developing both political leadership and the form and structure which will encourage and enhance such leadership. Experimentation with the chief administrative officer under the strong mayor is an example.

New trends are developing in writing municipal charters and local government laws. The preoccupation with prescribing minute administrative detail is absent. The basic trust issue seems to have been put to rest, at least temporarily, in favor of giving local government suficient latitude for developing new tools to pursue and achieve its objectives. A framework is developing in which a local government can respond quickly and decisively to urgent issues.

Managers in Organizations

HIERARCHIES AND RELATIONSHIPS

We have seen how local governments came to be organized as a result of the reformers' emphasis on honesty and efficiency. With replication in local government of a successful business management model came the organization chart and with it the bureaucracy necessary to carry out complex organizational missions. Externally, local governments began to take on the bureaucratic look of any well-managed corporation.

A look at the typical organization chart of a city government shows a clear hierarchy of departments, in which supervisors and managers theoretically know where they fit in the total structure. Supposedly, lines of authority and responsibility are clear. Managing such an organization is theoretically mechanistic. If the "mechanic manager" could keep all of the cogs and wheels properly lubricated and meshed, the "machine's" efficiency would be guaranteed. Further, with clear accountability to the democratic process, the work of designing an effective local government structure would be complete. However, in this chapter we are talking about realities, and so we must carry our concern a few steps further. Organizations are populated by human beings, and we now have the perspective, provided by some fifty years of experience with local government structures, to view the effects that human beings have had in making their structures work.

Today we have the benefit of additional knowledge of how individuals behave in organizations, which indicates that the mechanistic view of organizational life, established from the works of Taylor and Weber, does not go far enough. Not all of the answers to effective administration of public business are found in the formal organizational apparatus that is installed. From the works of Mayo, Roethlisberger, and those who have followed in the development of the behavioral science view of organizations, we recognize that there is a social system as well as a technical system within the organization.[15] The generalist manager of an organization ought to be equally concerned with informal aspects of the social system. The interpersonal relations between generalists and specialists as well as the interpersonal relations among the specialists will determine to a large extent the way work gets done and the ultimate effectiveness of the organization.

The bureaucratic structure of local government places authority at the top of the hierarchical pyramid, and the supervisor receives his share of that authority by delegation downward from the manager and department heads. The supervisor in such a system must know how much authority he has or must request, from up the line, additional authority to perform his tasks. When the unique problem which does not fit the delegated authority is fed into the system, it must travel up and down the bureaucratic line until an appropriate fit is made.

Frequently, such a request may have to be reviewed by several persons in the hierarchy as it seeks its way into the hands of the person with sufficient authority to take action. The supervisor and the manager depend on the system. If the system can predict all future demands that will be placed on it, then the formal structure may be adequate to handle the situation. Since local government functions are infinitely more complex than that, this is often not the case. The most distressing problems in local government seldom can be solved by a routine approach. Rather, they require unique and creative responses. Yet creative problem-solving behavior may come into conflict with the established rules, constraints, and controls of the formal organization. To move outside of formal rules and procedures is risky. To accept such a risk and solve the problem may not be valued behavior in the rule-centered organization. The bureaucracy may create a dependency of individuals which stifles the creative and adaptable response for problem solving. In such a system, the ingenious human mind will develop personal strategies for coping with the system which may clearly be in conflict with organizational objectives.

As we shall see later, local government problems today often are not clearly within the range of a single department or work unit. They have implications requiring the skills or the policies of several work units either within the same department or perhaps across departmental lines. In such cases, collaborative relationships may be required to achieve solutions within a relatively short period of time. This places a high premium on effective interpersonal relations. If organizational relationships which promote collaboration have not been established, effectiveness may be lost by disclaiming ownership of the problem and passing the buck to another point in the organization.

Conflict between departmental units and entire departments may be a serious problem in such an organization. In a highly rigid, departmentalized structure, the behavior which managers and supervisors may see as most valued is a highly competitive, win-lose behavior. The competition for resources and the lack of trust generated by the personal strategies required for survival in this system may interfere with the establishment of collaborative relationships at some later time when problem solving requires them. In such an organization, conflict may be subverted and never openly acknowledged unless it is arbitrated by higher authority. All of which may simply serve to reinforce a noncollaborative problem solving and departmentalized functioning of city government. A vicious circle is established which serves the competitive needs of the organization's social system rather than the problem-solving needs of the public's business.

Thus, the answer of the reformers, while an important contribution, has proved to be partial. Legal structure and organizational form have been essentially a matrix around which people organize their relationships to each other, to work and pursue diverse goals. The historical use of the council-manager form by the Pendergast machine in Kansas City, Missouri, showed that structure could not by itself guarantee honesty, let alone the other two goals of the reformers' trilogy—efficiency and economy.

ADMINISTRATORS AND POLITICS

Of real significance in the practical workings of city government is the recognition that the dichotomy established by reformers between politics and administration has long since given way. Political scientists have been concerned with this theoretical construct of public administration for years. Much has been written which acknowledges and justifies the demise of the concept of a clear dichotomy. In spite of a structure which denies that the administrator or the politician will perform in the other's sphere of activity, it does, in fact, happen in many legitimate ways.

It is accepted ethical behavior that the professional administrator will not participate in the support or election of candidates to office, for this is a partisan political activity. However, the administrator is involved politically when publicly supporting programs established by his governing body. Many city managers and department heads have been campaigners for issues subject to referenda once they have been adopted by the city council. In recent years we have also seen administrators publicly supporting national issues such as revenue sharing, as well as other state and local government issues. Obviously the support of such issues has political overtones and tends to place the administrator somewhere in the spectrum of political activity in the community. Our purpose here is not to condemn such duality of behavior but rather to acknowledge that it is the case, and it is likely that the public administrator will continue to find himself being drawn into these types of political issues.

As administrators define problems, prepare alternative solutions, and control the information which is used to select the most viable policy direction, they are participating in the policy making (political) process.

Of great concern to the administrator are the unofficial and informal incursions of political leaders or elected officials into the administration of city programs. No rules have been established as to how this matter may be handled. Although such a state of affairs was decried by those who established nonpartisan local government and the professionalism of local government administration, it is bound to happen and must be recognized as a part of reality. The "purist manager" would argue that a matter of principle has been violated by the city council if such an event occurs; the "pragmatist manager" will draw his lines less sharply. As administrators' roles continue to change in such a way as to blur even further the line between policy and administration, we can expect policy makers—city councilmen especially—to assume a more active interest in the administration of programs. The challenge to the administrator is to develop a creative rather than defensive response to the partnership of the elected or appointed official.

The Fact of Political Control

Concern for the efficient and economical delivery of services notwithstanding, the central issue for any form of local government is its democracy. No matter how perfect or rational the administration of any local government or its programs, it must constantly be tested in the political process. It is at this point that the city organization may face what appears to be a totally irrational world. Public administrators offering much needed programs have frequently been defeated in quest of their goals because they were not in tune with public sentiment. Political control is a fact of life in our local government and should be understood not only by those who are responsible for direct relationships with political leaders but also by those who perform the organization's work.

POLITICIANS AND ADMINISTRATORS:
A PARTNERSHIP

In the pursuit of change and improvement the public administrator and the political leader form a unique partnership for building a political process which produces productive political control. Timothy Costello has described the basic premise of the political leader's role: "The primary, but not ... exclusive, mission of a mayor (or any elected official) is to enhance his likelihood of reelection while keeping open as many other options as possible."[16]

Whether this is sound political theory, we don't know, but anyone interested in effecting change in municipal government should take it as fact. Proposed changes that are perceived as serving that goal are supported by efforts to implement them. Other changes have to fight their own battles, except those that would jeopardize the goal, and those, of course, are opposed.

Apart from the self-interest of the elected official, the goal does serve the democratic process of keeping the governing body sensitive to the values and wishes of the electorate. From a management point of view it is essential that an elected official maintain his option to gain reelection (or higher office), in order to assure full command of his administration during his term. "Lame ducks don't make changes."[17]

Thus, we can see that a "good" municipal program must also be politically viable if it is to stand its test in the political process. Viability, to the elected leader, will in all likelihood be measured to some degree by the standards suggested by Costello. It is the public manager's duty to keep his organization sufficiently open to political leadership and the citizen so that the goals of the political leadership are not aborted. The ultimate decisions will be made by elected officials and will reflect their perceptions of political realities. Administrators must maintain their openness to this kind of reality. Without it the political leader and the administrator may come to an unnecessary collision course, and an otherwise productive partnership will inevitably come to an end.

INSTITUTIONAL POLITICAL CONTROL

Political control may be exercised in numerous ways. We have institutionalized many of its forms and incorporated them systematically into structure. Public administrators who are dedicated to the political process may tend to think of control exercised in this manner as legitimate, which of course it is in the sense of legal and institutional processes. Mayoralty or councilmanic elections, referenda on bonds or levies, council meetings where resolutions and ordinances are voted and policy directions determined, or the action of a city council in hiring or firing a city manager represent institutionalized ways of exercising political control over the government.

INFORMAL POLITICAL CONTROL

However, there are other ways in which political control is attempted or accomplished. Such ways may be more subtle, informal, and perhaps less rational when viewed within the total governmental system. Although they may be outside the institutional framework, it is naive to assume they do not exist, since they do represent the political process at work. Political control exercised in this manner may represent the greatest challenge to the professional administrator, for here he must determine when his professional ethics require him to stand on principle and when such a stand is nothing more than a vain attempt at self-vindication.

Examples of political control of this sort may be found in informal relationships between those of relatively different status and powers, impromptu confrontations between a citizen or group of citizens and a local government official or employee, or an informal request of a local government leader to an administrator in the organization for specific actions. The local government organization's ability to handle such informal political control, ethically and with political responsiveness, is in a real sense a practical test of its ability to survive.

ORGANIZATIONAL RESPONSIVENESS

Political control is really the problem of keeping the government responsive to its citizens. In recent years, with the impact of urbanization, our cities have become the focal point for expressions of dissatisfaction and frustration. The urban crisis we hear so much about is in part the lack of responsiveness and relevance of local government to the citizen's sense of frustration over unmet needs. The question when put in this fashion is, "Who does the city serve?" Thomas Bradley has spoken of it thus:

The term urban crisis these days has come to mean the grand backlog of urban needs in our major cities. Our cities suffer from physical decay. Many of their inhabitants are ill housed, ill fed, unemployed, poorly educated, racially and residentially separated so that there is no real communication between them, and accordingly there is no communication between large segments of our population and the leadership at city hall. The sad part of the situation is there seems to be no evidence that we are going to improve the lot of those I have just described to you. Lack of adequate public transportation today results in clogged highways and our air filled with pollutants from these very same automobiles. We plan our airports, and before they are constructed they are out of date. We talk about pollution and we find the government is pouring, in some cases, 75 per cent of the pollutants into the air, dirtying our water, failing to provide for disposal of our human wastes. All but the insane would quickly agree that our urban centers are fast becoming uninhabitable and sometimes unmanageable. We know what the problems are; what we seem to be lacking is the kind of commitment to deal with these problems and the kind of leadership required to get the job done.[18]

The focus of dissatisfaction and frustration at the local level may be expected when one contrasts the accessibility of local government with that of the state or federal government. Not only is the citizen able to reach city hall physically to register his discontent, but he also experiences immediately the impact of the quality of city services. If city services are not adequate to meet his perceived needs, or if they fail to provide the quality of service he deems desirable, the city government fails and is at fault. This is complicated by the fact that the city must call frequently upon its citizenry, perhaps at least once a year, to register opinions formally on candidates, bonds, levies, or other electoral issues. Reaction to unpopular local decisions or action may be swiftly registered by a disgruntled citizen.

If local government is immediately accessible to the citizen through the institutionalized political process, elections and representation, the question may still be raised as to the accessibility of local government services through the organization or bureaucracy. The question may well be put, "How capable is the local government organization in responding to a citizen's personal needs?" Much of the success of the political machine of another era was its ability to invade the bureaucracy and produce immediate service for the citizen. The political machine was less interested in formal and institutionalized ways of exercising control and thrived on establishing its own strategies, which were much more flexible and less likely to involve the citizen in the proverbial red tape. To the individual citizen the successful local government is one which is able to respond to him personally. In spite of the complexities of managing services for larger local governments and larger numbers of persons, the individual citizen is not likely to be convinced or committed to his local government if he feels it does not serve him personally.

CITIZEN PARTICIPATION

The impact of the recent frustration and dissatisfaction which has been aimed at city government may well be the establishment of a higher degree of constituent participation in local government affairs. This is frequently a threatening proposition to the public administrator and the elected official alike. Citizen participation in the decision-making processes may be seen as interference with the technical performance of duties by professionals and subversion of the legally established powers and prerogatives of the elected official. It seems likely, however, that a participatory style of community involvement is here to stay. Indigenous community groups, forming around particular program or service interests, are now a familiar occurrence. Minorities especially find such groups appropriate for the expression of their concerns. Some federal programs, such as Model Cities, have required this process to be institutionalized as a part of community life.

The extent to which citizen participation will become a viable vehicle for overcoming the sense of alienation and frustration which many citizens have expressed remains to be seen. The same is true of the extent to which public decision making and the administration of public programs will be effected. Nevertheless, the public administrator must be prepared to work creatively with, and with real commitment to, involved citizens' groups.

Organizational Tensions: The Old and the New

Local government organization is taking on a new look with the adoption of social service functions. In recent years many local government organizations have added new departments or new divisions within established departments. Alongside the traditional functions of public safety, parks, public works, water, sewers, waste collection and disposal, aviation, and a variety of proprietary functions, there have been added programs on human relations, community development, health, Model Cities, employment opportunities, youth, aging, housing, welfare, and economic opportunity. Certainly not all local governments have accepted all of these functions, but they are characteristic enough of the new social concerns of local government management to warrant attention.

There are characteristic differences between the "hard" technologies of the traditional line functions and the "soft" technologies of the so-called "people services." These differences may result in organizational tension unless the specialists engaged in the various activities are sensitive to them. In today's local government, interdependency of departments is unquestioned. What one department does is important to other departments, and the success of the total organization will determine its image with the citizens. The "soft" technology departments which are serving human needs will inevitably be concerned with how, where, why, and when the development of physical facilities takes place. Further, line departments, if they are to be effective, must also serve people, and their conception of what serves people will be important to the social agency. If such an interdependence is not recognized, the organization may find itself in the embarrassing position of being at odds with itself.

It is erroneous to view the new functions of local government as simply "people-oriented," for every department of the effective local government organization must be people-oriented. It is much more helpful to look at the implications of the different technologies which the departments use to serve people and the considerably different results which they must achieve. Therefore, we shall look at some of the contrasts between the two broad groups.

The advent of the "soft" technologies has been the result of a new concern with human process issues. Frequently, of major importance is not just what is done, but rather how it is done, by whom, and for what reasons. This concern for process may be easily recognized in the work of human relations units or in the citizen participation components of Model Cities or city planning functions. While the product of their labors must certainly be more than just talk and may result in the determination to build a facility or establish and locate a program, the process through which that product is achieved is of equal importance in its final acceptability. Such motivational questions are not easily established objectively. Honest men can disagree, and the problem of hammering out a consensus or working through the difficult problems of human misunderstanding may be painful and time-consuming.

The kinds of process questions which make up the work of social service programs are intimately tied to the political process of a community; therefore, such departments must be aware that their responsibilities are "politically

loaded." Issues of equality, opportunity, and responsiveness are desired by all concerned, but the issues of racism, poverty, and equal opportunity are emotionally charged. All of these issues may mean different things to different people. Within the city organization, as with the community at large, the search for policy directions will go on.

In contrast, the more traditional line department may concentrate on more easily defined end products or services. Such departments have the benefit of a rational, factual technology built on firm foundations of experience and professional standards that transcend city boundaries. Local government has succeeded well in developing and utilizing the knowledge and technology accumulated over past years for building streets, roads, bridges, and water and sewer facilities, for example. The technology is in place. Once decisions are made to provide facilities, they may be acted on with dispatch. Further, even in such areas as public safety, parks, and recreation we have gone far in developing standards for judging on a rational basis when and where physical facilities are needed.

Thus armed with traffic counts, cost-benefit ratios, or statistical experience factors provided by the "hard" technologies with which they work, traditional line departments will likely be less patient with exploring the cross-currents of influence and opinion to interpret the effects of building public facilities that respect neighborhood identity, city ecology, or human relations. There may be little patience with attempts to allow for community decision making. From the technological point of view the establishment of such physical facilities may be seen as relatively routine—an objective matter determined from rational data. At such a point conflict may emerge between social service departments and traditional line departments.

Within the organization the focus of the differing technologies may produce further tensions around staff functions and internal decision making. The issues of allocation of resources, administration of personnel merit systems, hiring practices, and evaluation of effectiveness will be viewed differently by functions with different technologies.

In a rational sense human service departments, like more traditional operating departments, are line functions with responsibility for programs. Staff agencies, such as budget, finance, and personnel departments, whose purpose is to provide expert counsel, advice, and service to operating departments, may not be geared to the new demands of social service units.

The social service product is not countable or finite and cannot be evaluated on a cost-benefit basis. It follows that allocation of resources and budget must be determined more by commitment to abstract program goals which are based on social values and which reflect those values dominant in the community represented by the governing body.

The Management Team

All local governments must rethink the way they are organizing and managing to get their jobs done. This is not easy when local government structure is locked in by the forces of law and structural change is prevented by tradition and local custom. New roles and tasks, and a more highly educated, sophisticated, and aware citizenry are demanding a higher quality and larger quantity of local government services.

In spite of these formidable constraints, local government managers may be becoming more adaptive in managing the internal affairs of their organizations. There is growing support for the prediction that the end of the traditional, hierarchical bureaucratic organization is in sight and that we are moving toward new ways of organizing to get work done. Warren Bennis, a leading exponent of this point of view, describes the phenomenon as follows:

"The bureaucratic machine model" was developed as a reaction against the personal subjugation, nepotism, cruelty and capricious and subjective judgments that often passed for managerial practices during the early days of the industrial revolution. Bureaucracy emerged out of the need for more predictability, order and precision. It was an organization ideally suited to the values and demands of the Victorian Empire, and just as bureaucracy emerged as a creative response to a radically new age, so today, new organizational shapes and forms are surfacing before our eyes.[19]

If the way we work in organizations is changing, then we can find some indication of the skills and abilities that management will need from the characteristics of the effective organization of the future. Once again, Bennis describes this new organization:

Organizations will no longer be rigid, pyramidal, hierarchical kinds of organizations. As a matter of fact, rather than organization charts, I believe we are going to have project charts or problem solving charts, because I see the organization having characteristics like these.

We will be working more and more in temporary systems where people from diverse special fields and professions come together for a time, solve a problem, disband and then regroup to become a part of a new problem solving team. So I see organizations in continuing organic flux, reacting to and also reacting on the environment, adapting, innovating, bringing people together, then regrouping them to solve new problems.[20]

Surely, with this view of organization the premium on management skills will be the ability to adapt to new problem-solving techniques. The organization will require managers who can carefully and appropriately identify problems and can combine problem-solving task forces from various departments in a collaborative approach toward specific objectives. Effective management will bring together the resources and particular skills of all its members, from chief administrative officer to supervisor.

With the increasing complexities of urbanism, the nature of work is changing also. While the supervisor may be responsible for a more traditional, routinized set of functions, he is implicated, nevertheless, in the broader context of the organization's work, which is less tied to muscle and more concerned with intellectual and communicative skills. The supervisor is a part of a management team.

Further, organizational effectiveness is determined not simply by the success of a given division of a particular department; rather it is the organization's consistent record of problem solving and effective delivery of services throughout all its functions which will determine its success. Little is gained by the organization whose management is not effective at all levels.

The chief administrative officer in a local government is faced with a constantly expanding role. As the demands of managing the organization are increasing, so also are the demands of community leadership. Others have documented extensively the changing role of the city manager. Today's city manager is certainly not a back room technician. He spends numerous hours relating to the legislative body and community groups, building community consensus, and dealing with the intricacies of intergovernmental relations. The social issues of the times which beset city government require a new type of policy leadership.

The advent of a problem-solving organization suggests that top management's role will be less concerned with the development and maintenance of a rule-oriented organization and more concerned with the development of the human resources of a sociotechnical system. The chief administrative officer's role must still be one of leadership, development, and control of the organization, but he will be less concerned with making rules and procedures and more concerned with building and maintaining an organizational climate in which people can function fully. The climate of the organization must be one of openness and trust, in which the information essential for getting the best decisions and problem solutions can be shared from no matter what level of the organization. Such a climate must eliminate the defensiveness and parochialism prevalent in the organization where risk taking is defined in terms of "letting the boss hear what we think he wants to hear," and where "bad news" is never fully communicated.

In the new organization the chief administrative officer will be less concerned with making the lonesome, tough decisions which have characterized his position and be more concerned with providing leadership in which tough decisions can emerge as a result of the best use of minds and skills. This is not to suggest that decision making for managers is a thing of the past. On the contrary, management problems which are complex and require the skills of technical specialists will also require a higher degree of participation of those specialists than has been the case. Management decisions will be made not on the basis of position but rather on the requisite skills, expertise, and information.

Summary

We have established the context in which local government form and structure was built in the early days of this century. We have surveyed the unique problems of misplaced political trust and the quest for efficient delivery of local government services. Government form and structure designed for a previous generation is the heritage which has determined the nature of our present local government organizations.

Local governments are institutions caught in the vortex of rapid change. Managers and supervisors must deal with infinitely more complex problems which do not necessarily fit the precedents of previous times. In such an environment it is not easy to maintain the perspective necessary to handle constructively the demands of changing roles.

Local government management is facing a new age demanding creativity. Not only are new functions and services being added to its responsibilities, but a more educated, sophisticated, and aware citizenry is being served.

Political control is a fact of life which the public servant must reckon with. Various means of political control will reflect the changing needs and desires of citizens. The local government manager must be prepared to respond creatively in an organization that is capable of providing the citizen with easy access to the services which he requires and wants. And, certainly, the citizen who seeks to participate in the affairs of government which affect him most must find a response which will encourage and develop his commitment to local government.

¹Daniel P. Moynihan, ed., TOWARD A NATIONAL URBAN POLICY (New York: Basic Books, Inc., Publishers, 1970), p 7.

²For an account of political abuse at the turn of the century, see Lincoln Steffens, THE SHAME OF THE CITIES (New York: McClure, Phillips & Co., 1904).

³Edward N. Costikyan, "Cities Can Work," SATURDAY REVIEW, April 4, 1970, p. 19.

⁴John Porter East, COUNCIL-MANAGER GOVERNMENT: THE POLITICAL THOUGHT OF ITS FOUNDER, RICHARD S. CHILDS (Chapel Hill: University of North Carolina Press, 1965), p. 16.

[5]Costikyan, "Cities Can Work," p. 19.

[6]Frank R. Kent, THE GREAT GAME OF POLITICS (Garden City, N.Y.: Doubleday, Doran & Company, Inc., 1930), p. 28.

[7]Costikyan, "Cities Can Work," p. 20.

[8]Orin F. Nolting, PROGRESS AND IMPACT OF THE COUNCIL-MANAGER PLAN (Chicago: Public Administration Service, 1969), pp. 1—2.

[9]Ibid., p. 5.

[10]International City Management Association, THE MUNICIPAL MANAGEMENT DIRECTORY (Washington, D.C.: International City Management Association, 1973), p. 8.

[11]Nolting, COUNCIL-MANAGER PLAN, pp. 49—50.

[12]Ibid., p. 81.

[13]East, COUNCIL-MANAGER GOVERNMENT, p. 36.

[14]Ibid., pp. 102—104.

[15]See Elton Mayo, THE HUMAN PROBLEMS OF AN INDUSTRIAL CIVILIZATION (New York: The Macmillan Company, 1933); and F. J. Roethlisberger and William J. Dickson, MANAGEMENT AND THE WORKER (Cambridge, Mass.: Harvard University Press, 1939).

[16]Timothy Costello, "The Change Process in Municipal Government," in EMERGING PATTERNS IN URBAN ADMINISTRATION, ed. G. Brown and T. P. Murphy (Lexington, Mass.: D. C. Heath & Company, 1970), p. 13.

[17]Ibid.

[18]From an unpublished speech by Councilman Thomas Bradley, 10th District, Los Angeles, at the Fourth Annual Urban Problems Seminar, School of Administration, University of Missouri—Kansas City, Kansas City, Mo., 29 April 1970.

[19]Warren Bennis, "Organizations of the Future," in CURRENT PERSPECTIVES FOR MANAGING ORGANIZATIONS, ed. Bernard M. Bass and Samuel Deep (Englewood Cliffs, N.J.: Prentice-Hall, Inc., 1970), p. 528.

[20]National Association of Manufacturers, Industrial Relations Division, WHAT'S WRONG WITH WORK? HOW TO RELEASE HUMAN POTENTIAL AND IMPROVE PRODUCTIVITY (New York: National Association of Manufacturers, 1967), pp. 42—43.

2

Management Concepts and Organization Models

WHEN MANAGEMENT ATTEMPTS to improve the municipal organization, it generally does what it has been doing for the past forty or fifty years, only much more vigorously. Improvement of the management of municipalities continues for the most part to concentrate on budgeting, personnel, operations, and methods. Concerns center around tightening the hierarchical structure of the organization, injecting a higher degree of order into the situation, placing more stringent controls over employees, emphasizing employee roles, and eliminating waste and inefficiency. In short, the tendency is to stress the classical approaches to management improvement.

Little attention generally is paid to the sociopsychological variables present in any management situation. The good employee is the conforming employee: the yes-man and follower, who takes his orders, no matter what his personal feelings, and carries them out to the letter. The burden of enlightened decision making falls on top management, and the burden is extremely heavy. In the complex sociotechnological situations of municipal organizations, enlightened leadership along traditional lines calls for supermen, but there just aren't that many supermen.

Problem solving calls for innovation and creativity, while organizations center on conformity and obedience. Nevertheless, faith continues in classical theory. Innovative and creative ideas are to come from the man at the top and are to be carried out and implemented by those at lower levels of the organization. While lower levels may question the quality of those decisions among themselves, feedback is cut off by conformity and obedience. Talent at lower levels—talent that might have been used to create an innovative approach to a problem, finds itself bogged down in trying to make an inappropriate solution work.

Pressure on managers and department heads to perform as supermen, providing answers for all problems, forces many very close to the breaking point. As pressure builds at the top, it is increased on the lower levels of the organization. The result is usually a copout. We do the best that we can under the circumstances. Less-than-desirable solutions to problems become acceptable, and less-than-desirable performance is viewed as success. "After all, we can only do so much."

As most municipal organizations are structured and operated today, it is probably a tribute to management and other employees that they do as well as they do. In effect, however, this turns out to be a holding action. The question becomes one of how much longer municipal organizations can operate well. There is no easy answer to the question, but it would appear to be, "Not much longer." Unresolved or partially resolved problems have a way of compounding themselves. Occasionally, time resolves these problems, but management cannot count on this. The usual condition is that the problems expand or go underground, to surface at a later date in a much more severe form.

The evidence is accumulating that there are better ways to manage municipal organizations.

While management theory today is in transition, it seems clear that a melding of classical and modern theory can create a management system that works well.

Various approaches to management have been developed in municipal and other organizations with a certain degree of success. These approaches will be outlined and discussed. In the process, some of our preferences (or biases!) will emerge. This is unavoidable. It is hoped that you will take from this book those things that you feel will fit in with your knowledge, skills, and work environment.

The improvement of municipal organizations will depend largely on how well management puts it all together. As pointed out in Chapter 1, any approach to municipal management must consider the realities of the particular situation. Every municipal manager, department head, and supervisor wants to do a "good" job of managing. While definitions of good management vary, intentions are, generally speaking, universal. Circumstances, situations, goals, objectives, policies, procedures, people resources, and financial resources, however, frequently are tangled, so that good management seems impossible.

New approaches to effective management, such as planning-programming-budgeting, systems analysis, management by objectives, management information systems, small group interaction, democratic and participative management, and, occasionally, a revival or modification of POSDCORB,[1] all promise significant management improvement. As managers and supervisors struggle with these and other methods they frequently find them causing as many problems as they solve.

Coupled with these analytical methods is the pervasiveness of technology. The interaction forces us to think often in a framework that is man/system/data/machine-oriented. Management thus increasingly is called on to fill a role never contemplated during the Industrial Revolution.

Despite this complexity, there has never been a time when the promise of enlightened management has been more evident. More talent and effort are being focused on the study and development of effective management practices in all types of organizations than ever before. Never

before has there been greater awareness of management problems. Never have managers been more sophisticated in their approaches to management problems, and never have they had a more sophisticated work force to manage.

Greater knowledge on the part of management and workers, coupled with a more sophisticated technology, provide the opportunities for accomplishment that heretofore were only visions. The municipal organizations that develop these opportunities will make meaningful contributions to the "good life" in cities.

Municipal Organization Structure

Traditionally, municipal organizations have been structured along hierarchical lines into the various functions to be performed by the organization. This type of organization places a chief administrative officer at the top of the hierarchy. He works with the institutional subsystem and transmits policies and other actions at the institutional level to the managerial and technical levels. While he may be known by any of several titles, he will be referred to in this chapter as either the manager or the chief executive.

Following this hierarchical pattern, functions have been divided into police, fire, public works, finance, etc., each presided over by a department head. This pattern has served local governments reasonably well in the past. The rub comes in what happens in these departments and how they interact with each other as parts of the managerial and technical subsystems within the larger system of the city government. Frequently, each department has become the personal fiefdom of the department head. So strong are some of these fiefdoms that one almost needs a visa just to visit from one department to another, let alone *work with* a department.

Attempting to tie these various fiefdoms together into a unified, well-functioning organization, the chief executive may respond in many different ways. Depending on the press of duties in other areas of the organization, and his own management style, the executive may have both a close and a distant relationship with each of his department heads, or a close relationship with some and a distant relationship with others. The executive may see some department heads daily, others weekly, some monthly, and a few others only when all hell breaks loose.

Influencing all of these relationships will be the executive's relationship with the city council or mayor. It is an unwritten law that the appointed executive must always help the council or mayor appear in a good light, or at least do nothing that might make either look bad. Many executives may spend a large portion of their time tending to this chore. In such situations little time is spent with department heads and even less time with others in the organization. Rivalries develop between departments, and when they reach crisis proportions the executive may try to reconcile the differences. The usual procedure is to see the department heads, either together or separately, and try to reason with them or, as a last resort, order them to settle their differences. (Occasionally the expedient practice is to forget the whole business and hope the department heads will settle the dispute themselves.)

The department heads, in turn, usually attempt to explain the problem from their frame of reference, to deny their guilt in the problem, and to vow that they are trying and will continue to try to work it out. The confrontation, whether the department heads are seen together or separately, usually results in a form of withdrawal, with each keeping a wary eye on the other, looking for a vantage point from which to continue the battle.

In this process, another unwritten law is that the department head always helps the executive look good. As one goes farther down in the organization the law is less rigid, with midlevel and first-line supervisory people sometimes taking delight in making the department head look bad.

This thumbnail description of certain kinds of behavior in a municipal organization may not fit yours—you will know if it does, however—yet such conditions do exist in municipal organizations. Typifying such a municipal organization will be a high degree of competition with other departments, a win-lose approach to conflict resolution, destructive interdepartmental relationships, one-sided problem solving, rejection of

other points of view, perspectives of other departments as rivals and competitors, and suspicion of other departments.

Within the departments similar kinds of conditions will usually exist. Discussions will be limited to surface facts, competitiveness will be high, people will guard and hoard information, feelings will be denied, members of the department will undercut other members, there will be very little awareness of group processes, department resources will be underutilized, conflict will be resolved on a win-lose basis, there will be resistance or apathy to departmental goals, and individual members of the department will be characterized by self-enhancing behavior.

Not all of these behaviors will be exhibited in their most severe degree, but in too many organizations all of them will be present in some form. It is not a pretty picture. Both the social climate within the organization and the hierarchical structure may be at fault.

If the foregoing sketch is descriptive of municipal organizations, how does a manager deal with such behavior? For the most part, management has been muddling through, working from crisis to crisis, occasionally breaking out of such a pattern, and sometimes tightening controls through structural changes such as centralization or decentralization, or through systems analysis and a host of other management tools. Most of these maintain the hierarchical pattern and rarely get at behavioral problems. Rivalries continue to exist, trust stays at a low level, and crises and problems are solved only on a short-term basis.

In other instances, a management team approach is brought into play. Usually this team is composed of special assistants to the chief executive and sometimes key department heads. The team proceeds to make decisions and attempts to force these down through the organization, frequently with little success. Under this system, instead of one person making decisions for the organization a small group makes the decisions. The result is generally not very different.

In other instances, the chief executive may try a form of management by objectives. This approach may vary from a situation where the chief executive outlines broad objectives for various departments to a situation where objectives are set by individual departments or department heads. Success may or may not be forthcoming.

In other situations, the chief executive may decide that what the organization needs is more internal participation. He may decide that communication is the big problem and that more staff meetings aimed at getting department heads to communicate more effectively are needed. With this in mind he schedules periodic staff meetings. These generally turn into "Yes, boss," sessions, or, in another extreme, serve as arenas for department heads to slug it out with each other. The results generally contribute to a higher degree of dysfunctional behavior.

In some instances, these and other approaches work well; this will be discussed in later chapters. When new approaches continue to fail, or result in a minimum amount of success, however, management has a tendency to drift into management by neglect. Narrow interests are developed and pursued, and other areas of the organization are neglected until the problem solves itself, no longer exists because of time and change factors, or reaches a condition in which it can no longer be neglected. At this point, a short-term solution is generally found and the organization drifts back to some form of mediocre stability.

Historical Perspective

Forms of organization developed historically from two sources: the military and the Church. While one might think two such organizations would have little in common, a quick look at history shows this is not so. Both were founded on absolute loyalty and faith. Both aimed for maximum control over those enlisted in their ranks, and both sought power to maintain this control. Both were organized by hierarchy with levels of command and authority and a supreme commander at the top. Most organization charts follow a similar pattern.

With the advent of the Industrial Revolution, it was natural that industrialists would turn to existing models to form their own organizations. As the Industrial Revolution advanced and technology became more sophisticated, widespread attention focused on efficiency within the hierarchical system. As engineering developed into complex technology, the efficiency built into machinery became apparent and a few creative engineers began to look at these principles in terms of the organization.

The Classical Approach

Most widely known among these men was Frederick Winslow Taylor, a steel production engineer, who came to be known as the father of scientific management. Taylor applied engineering principles to the work situation. He broke every job down into its basic components, then came up with the "one best way" to perform it. Once a job was looked at in this manner, time periods for performance could be set as well as quality control.

His view of workers was that man was basically lazy and, given a choice, would not work unless he had to. This idea was expanded somewhat along the lines of Adam Smith's economic man concept, which assumed that the basic motivating force in man was economic. With this in mind, Taylor set piecework rates based on time-and-motion studies.

Thus was born the time study or social engineering approach to management, which is still in practice in some form or another in many organizations. Frank and Lillian Gilbreth aided the movement with their studies, undertaken about the same time.

This approach was originally termed scientific management. Today, refinements of this approach are known as the mechanical/rational approach to management, since the approach deals primarily with systems and things. Taylor's work and his contributions to scientific management are reviewed in some detail in Chapter 3.

Max Weber, in his work on bureaucracy, outlined roles in the hierarchical structure and also outlined ways in which the various levels of the structure should act and react. Conflict between the demands of the organization and the people within it was to be settled in favor of the organization. Taylor, Weber, and others built their theories around depersonalizing processes which fitted the individual to the organization.

Continuation of this mechanical/rational approach to management centers on such tools as systems analysis, program evaluation and review technique (PERT), planning-programming-budgeting system (PPBS), critical path method (CPM), among others. While some consideration is given to human factors, the approach largely involves rational decision making, technology, and mechanisms for control. It equates management with engineering and accounting, and, through role definition, manipulation, rewards and punishments, and sometimes outright coercion, attempts to adjust people to organizational imperatives.

THE HUMAN RELATIONS APPROACH

The human relations approach to management was an outgrowth of a mechanical/rational research project conducted in the late twenties at the Hawthorne, Illinois, works of the Western Electric Company to determine the effect of lighting on worker performance. The research team, which came from Harvard University, was headed by Elton Mayo and F. J. Roethlisberger. In the conduct of their experiments, the team found that production increased whether lighting was increased or decreased. They concluded that the increase in production was a result of the increased attention given workers in the experiment. The Hawthorne studies of Mayo and Roethlisberger are covered in more detail in Chapter 3.

From this beginning, the human relations approach focused on meeting the needs of people involved in the organization. The approach emphasized the significance of the human group and the idea that affiliation, acceptance, and belonging are some of man's strongest needs. Kurt Lewin, a pioneer in modern social psychology, writing along these lines, stressed the importance of *participation* in motivating people, as well as the promise of democratic decision making.

Others investigating the subject over the years pointed up still other facts of human behavior. Positive feelings and likings were stressed by J. L. Moreno as being fundamental to effective group action. Carl Rogers, building on his concept of client-centered therapy, branched off into the need for understanding, empathy, and self realization. Abraham Maslow built on his concept of the hierarchy of needs, with self-accom-

plishment as the strongest motivating force in man.

THE TOTAL ORGANIZATION POINT OF VIEW

The above is only a brief sketch of the mechanical/rational and human relations approaches to management. Each is dealt with in more detail in later chapters of this book. Most management theorists and management theories, however, fall within one or the other of these broad schools of thought. Over the years, something close to an adversary relationship has arisen between the two schools. While each has been willing to admit that the other's theory has a place in management, each has also accused the other of causing more problems than it solves.

An emerging trend in recent years has been the effort to reconcile the obvious extremes of the mechanical/rational and human relations points of view and integrate their useful features with the findings of behavioral psychology. This effort is known losely as organization development. Its most significant characteristic is the attempt to take a total organization point of view—to build in both the imperatives of law, policies, and structure and the needs and aspirations of workers, to provide for nonquantifiable goals while recognizing that much work still is measured numerically and to develop in workers the motivation and capacity for growth on the job. Those who hold the total organization point of view state that some progress has been made, even though such development lies largely in the future.

The focus of organizational development is on groups in the organization and the development of a system that takes into consideration not only goals and objectives but also the values of individuals and groups in the work force. There is agreement that old forms of organization are no longer adequate and that depersonalizing human beings is neither ethically nor morally justifiable. What is needed is a repersonalizing of management processes, and it is felt that this can probably best be accomplished through organizations composed of small, interdependent, interacting groups. Furthermore, these kinds of organizations are necessary, both to fulfill human needs and to get the work done.

Organizations are formed to accomplish goals and objectives through people with the greatest benefit and satisfaction to all concerned. "Satisfaction to all concerned" includes the clientele of the organization, the persons directly involved in the organization, the fiscal and material resources available, and the larger society. Operating under this premise, competitiveness, rivalries, and mistrust must be dealt with before reaching crisis proportions.

Richard Beckhard has identified many of the characteristics necessary for an organization operating under this premise in his description of the healthy organization:

1. The total organization, the significant subparts, and individuals manage their work against *goals* and plans for achievement of these goals.
2. Form follows function (the problem, or task, or project determines how human resources are organized).
3. Decisions are made by and near the sources of information regardless of where these sources are located on the organization chart.
4. The reward system is such that managers and supervisors are rewarded (and punished) comparably for:
   a) Production performance
   b) Growth and development of their subordinates
   c) Creating a viable work group.
5. Communication laterally and vertically is *relatively* undistorted. People are generally open and confronting. They share all the relevant facts, including feelings.
6. There is a minimum amount of inappropriate win/lose activity between individuals and groups. Constant effort exists at all levels to treat conflict and conflict situations as *problems* subject to problem solving methods.
7. There is high "conflict" (clash of ideas) about tasks and projects, and relatively little energy spent in clashing over *interpersonal* difficulties because they have been generally worked through.
8. The organization and its parts see themselves as interacting with each other, *and* with a *larger* environment. The organization is an "open system."
9. There is shared value, and management strategy to support it, of trying to help each person (or unit) in the organization maintain his (or its) integrity and uniqueness in an interdependent environment.
10. The organization and its members operate in an "action-research" way. General practice is to build in *feedback mechanisms* so that individuals and groups can learn from their own experience.[2]

John Gardner approaches the healthy organization from a self-renewing point of view. He outlines five conditions that must be present if the organization is to be capable of renewing itself and thus maintaining its health:

1. The organization must have an effective program for the recruitment and development of talent.
2. The organization must provide a hospitable environment for the individual.
3. The organization must have built-in provisions for self-criticism.
4. There must be fluidity in the internal structure of the organization.
5. The organization must have some means of combating the process by which men become prisoners of their procedures.[3]

There is little in these descriptions of the healthy organization to identify them with the traditional hierarchical form, which, with its competitiveness, power bases, subordinate levels, interdepartmental rivalries, role definition, etc., works against the conditions necessary for organizational health.

Creating the healthy organization is not an easy job. (Methods and approaches for accomplishing this are discussed in detail in later chapters. One stumbling block is that most of us have been trained—perhaps conditioned would be a better word—to accept, or at least tolerate, the traditional hierarchical structure. Recent psychological research indicates that children can grasp organizational concepts at a remarkably early age. From this, one might infer that we are thus early conditioned to respond to organizational pressures for conformance.

A second complication involves outside interests. By developing strong interests outside the organization some persons are able to raise their own tolerance level for hierarchical forms. In a sense they abandon hope for fullfilment within the organization, probably out of frustration, and seek a meaningful life in other pursuits. (This is discussed in more detail in Chapter 3.)

A third stumbling block arises from the fact that few hierarchical forms actually work as outlined on the organization chart. Participants in training sessions, when discussing their own organization charts, usually point out that, while that is the way the organization is structured, "It really doesn't work that way." The hierarchical form prescribes roles for persons at various levels within the organization. These roles frequently have a depersonalizing effect, and little provision is made to deal with this. As a consequence, an informal organization develops through which relationships are repersonalized.

In short, the hierarchical form has worked because of conditioning for tolerance, outside interests, and circumvention. If this sounds ambiguous, it is only because organizations are fraught with ambiguities, and these ambiguities are what cause many of the problems.

If the hierarchical form works primarily by circumvention and informal contacts, it would make sense to recognize this and formalize the informal. But this is difficult. In a system where recognition is tied strongly to rising through the levels of the hierarchy, change can be threatening—not only to those in positions of power but also to those striving for such positions.

Changing the hierarchical form to reflect the informal organization involves a shift in official relationships and a sharing of power and authority. Despite the democratic ideals of our society, one rarely thinks of gaining power to share it. One gains power to wield it. We justify this by assuring ourselves, and others if they ask, that we wield or intend to wield power altruistically, for the benefit both of the organization and of society. To share power is to risk the chance that the person with whom it is shared might not be as altruistic and might use power for personal advantage. We, of course, would never do this.

Where power is not shared, however, it is generally taken away, through circumvention from the informal organization, through work slowdowns, both intentional and unintentional, through strikes, and, in the extreme, through revolution. In actuality, we frequently have a tendency to overestimate just how much power we do have. Prisoners in Nazi work camps during World War II were able to slow down production by as much as 90 percent through the simple expedient of asking for directions on every task. Other groups have used similar tactics successfully.

Alternatives

The foregoing does not mean that municipal organizations have been entirely static over the years. It is more likely that a process of evolution has been at work and that we are at another stage in that evolutionary process.

THE TANGLED FABRIC

Two of the early innovators were Luther Gulick and Lyndall Urwick.[4] In the mid-thirties they outlined a municipal organization structure built largely around purpose departments, process departments, and geographical location. Examples of purpose departments might include police, public works, health, and parks. Process departments might include finance, personnel, statistical services, or other departments organized primarily to provide services to purpose departments.

Purpose departments were depicted vertically on the chart and process departments were depicted horizontally to illustrate the coordination necessary for effective functioning of the organization. A geographical dimension was added to account for the question of centralization versus decentralization. The chart thus formed what Gulick termed the "tangled fabric" of the organization. A further dimension pointed out that certain departments performed both vertical (purpose) and horizontal (process) functions. Thus, the health department (vertical) might, in addition to providing community health services, also provide health services within the organization to municipal employees in various departments.

Another example might be the municipal library that provided services to the community as well as research and other services to both vertical and horizontal departments within the organization.

According to Gulick:

From the standpoint of coordination it would seem that the heads of departments should visualize and understand the network in which they belong, so that they may proceed intelligently and energetically not only to carry out the work under their direction, but to see that that part of their work which falls within the overlapping purpose, or process, or regional area of another department may be fitted together harmoniously. Such an approach may serve to dispel the feeling of exclusive ownership and jealousy so common in government departments[5]

While Gulick was designing a structure

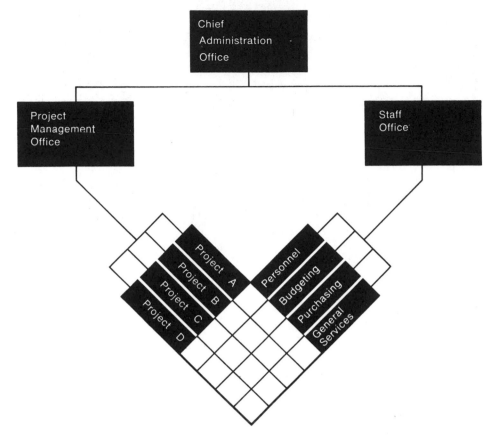

FIGURE 2—1. *Simple model of a matrix organization.*

primarily along functional lines, he was not unaware of jealousies and other forms of dysfunctional behavior that arise in organizations.

Many municipal organizations are structured along this tangled fabric approach, or a modification of it. The structure is similar to the matrix organization, except that Gulick's model focused more on a global framework while the matrix model focuses on a project framework.

THE MATRIX ORGANIZATION

The matrix organization takes on a slightly different form, as illustrated in Figures 2—1 and 2—2. In the simple model (Figure 2—1) the principal difference from the tangled fabric model is that purpose departments are divided into projects and listed under a project management office. The various projects extend "horizontally" through the model and obtain needed services from "vertical" process departments organized under a staff office.

Projects are considered to be temporary. As objectives are accomplished the project group either takes on new projects or is disbanded, with members joining other projects in the organization. In some instances project objectives may be expanded or redefined, thus extending the life of the project group.

The complex matrix model (Figure 2—2) involves permanent purpose departments as a third dimension in addition to staff services and projects. In such a model a project group might involve itself with a number of departments as well as call on staff for various services. Gulick and Urwick pointed out that their tangled fabric model might be better drawn in three dimensions, thus providing for the contingencies included in the complex matrix model.

Matrix models have not been widely used except in some unusually large organizations engaged in complex technical undertakings—for instance, the development and manufacture of guided missiles. Many cities have adopted a modified form of the structure based on the tangled fabric model.

The matrix model is particularly effective in reducing the organizational tendency to spend large sums of money and time on survival. It is especially amenable to accelerating change and to management by objectives. At a time when society is increasingly mobile and temporary, matrix management has much to recommend it. The model assumes that many of the major tasks of the organization are not fixed. With this in mind, it provides flexibility to deal with changing demands on the organization.

As with the tangled fabric model, the matrix model depends on constructive interaction within and among groups in the organization. Power plays and rivalries can play havoc with the model and will generally bring about negative results. It takes a healthy organization to maximize its effectiveness.

THE CONSOCIATED MODEL

At the Minnowbrook Conference on The New Public Administration, held at Syracuse University in 1968, Larry Kirkhart presented his consociated model of organization structure. The consensus at the conference was that all elements within the model are now being used in various organizations to varying degrees, but that everything about present public administration, in the technical sense, works to make further development of this type of organization difficult. Present classification systems, certification systems, incentive systems—practically any systems in public administration—are based on assumptions fundamentally opposite from those of the consociated model.

Basically, the consociated model has the following characteristics:

1. The basic work unit is a project team, interdependent with other teams, funded by a lump sum budget, and provided with tailor-made technology.
2. Leadership is based on the situation under a

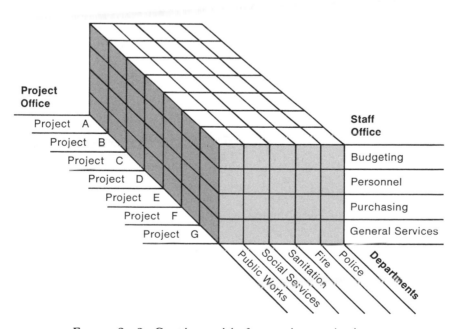

FIGURE 2—2. *Complex model of a matrix organization.*

nonpermanent hierarchy, thus permitting diverse authority patterns among the various project teams.

3. The total organization operates on strict time limitations with focus on the work to be accomplished.

4. Diverse subunits work on the same problem or goal.

5. High interpersonal competence and trust is developed through team-building training during formation of each project team and prior to initiating each project.

6. Clientele served is represented in the organization.

7. Careers are associated with professional reference groups and the organization is considered primarily as a place of employment.

8. Record keeping is computer based.

9. Professional roles are based on social and technical skills, permitting ambiguity and trust, and generating a minimal degree of social stratification.[6]

No attempt was made to depict the consociated model in chart form. In such a form it might have similarities to the matrix organization and would need some form of linking or overlapping to tie the total organization together. Since an important element is a high degree of interpersonal skill and trust, item 5, team-building training, is a key dimension. (This subject is discussed in more detail in Chapter 11.)

While Kirkhart is enthusiastic about his model, he does not expect traditional organizations to be willing to adopt it in its entirety. He does point out that certain parts of the model, or an adaptation of the model, will be adopted gradually; in time, perhaps, the model will be adopted in its entirety.

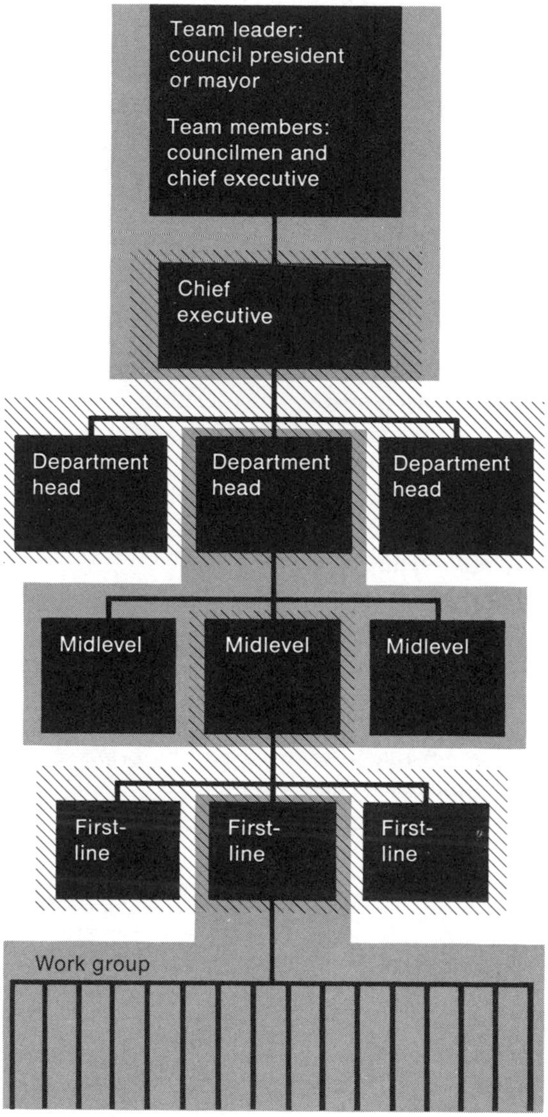

THE SYSTEM FOUR MODEL

Of the many writers on organization structure and design, Rensis Likert has done the most to work out the details of and to experiment with organization structure. Likert calls his model System Four Management. Likert's approach consists of small, interacting groups drawn from various levels within the organization. The leaders of groups at one level form the groups at the next level. In this manner, each group leader

FIGURE 2—3. *Overlapping team concept for municipal organizations.*

is a leader of a group at one level and a member of a group at the next highest level.

In this way, leaders function as linking pins, facilitating interaction among the various groups and promoting an open style of communication. Interaction and communication are facilitated upward, downward, and laterally. In addition, for special purposes or tasks temporary groups may be established consisting of members of the same group or members from different groups at different levels. Once the purpose of the temporary group has been served or the task accomplished, the group disbands.[7]

Two points are important here. The first is that there is minimum change in the structure of the organization. Basically, the hierarchical structure remains. The second point is that the social environment of the organization is changed and interpersonal relationships are facilitated and encouraged.

Under this approach each level in the organization constitutes a team. Such an organization is depicted in Figure 2—3, which shows five levels of teams within the organization.

The first-level team includes the council president or mayor as team leader and the councilmen and the chief executive as team members. Linkage with the broader community is provided by the elected officials, and with the organization by the chief executive.

The chief executive, as linking pin, is team leader at the next lower level of the organization, with department heads as team members.

At the third level each department head performs as a team leader, with his midlevel supervisory personnel or those persons reporting directly to him as team members, thus providing the link with this level of the organization.

At the fourth level each midlevel supervisor functions as a team leader among those first-line supervisors who report to him.

At the fifth level each first-line supervisor functions as a team leader, and his work force makes up the membership of his team.

The first-level team then provides linkage with the total community through the election process, and with the organization through the chief executive. The second level builds on this and provides a horizontal as well as a vertical linkage. The next three levels provide vertical and horizontal linkage with each department.

A further dimension is added, similar to the project management mentioned earlier, through temporary teams organized for special projects or tasks. Membership in these teams may come from a vertical, horizontal, or diagonal slice of the organization. An example might be a team composed of members from the welfare, recrea-

tion, police, fire, and public works departments working together to solve a problem dealing with a slum or a substandard area of the city. Membership on the team might also include elected officials and members of one or several citizen groups. In addition, membership might come from any level within the departments mentioned, depending on the talent needed for the project. Each member of the team would provide, in addition to his input to the task, a linking-pin function between his department and the project team.

Other examples could be illustrated by the involvement of municipal boards and commissions, other governmental jurisdictions, and citizen participation groups.

Advantages of System Four Management. System Four Management's advantages are numerous, and may be stated as follows:

1. One of System Four's main advantages is that it breaks the organization into small groups, thus facilitating relationship building and open communication. Consensus building in large groups is extremely difficult. In smaller groups consensus will be reached earlier, consequently commitment to follow through will be established at the beginning of a project or program.

2. Small groups permit greater use of available talent. As an example, integrating the work of process and purpose departments within an organization has always been a problem. Purpose departments have long feared the control that process departments might exercise by withholding necessary services. In linking such departments horizontally and vertically, these kinds of conflicts can be dealt with more effectively. In addition, departments have better access to each other's practices and methods, thus enhancing the possibilities for work improvement.

3. Contradictions are minimized, since policies at each level can be determined by groups responsible for carrying them out.

4. Policies throughout the organization are more consistent, since they are arrived at through the thinking and involvement of all levels in the organization.

5. Dysfunctional conflict is minimized, since

conflict areas may be recognized at an early stage in their development and dealt with at a small-group level.

6. Over the long run, since dysfunctional conflict is minimized, less energy is dissipated in conflict resolution. Conflict focuses more on ideas and less on individuals.
7. Greater satisfaction for all persons in the organization is generated, thus creating a higher level of morale and commitment.
8. The organization becomes much more responsive to demands placed on it from both internal and external sources.

Disadvantages of System Four Management. Following are the disadvantages of System Four Management:

1. Without a high element of trust among employees, groups may turn into battlegrounds.
2. Certain emotionally insecure people might find it difficult to function effectively in small, open groups.
3. Groups might turn into therapy sessions. A certain amount of this in a group can be useful, but carried beyond a point this might produce highly dysfunctional behavior.
4. Certain individuals might dominate the groups through their own forcefulness, possibly producing dysfunctional behavior.
5. Communication might take the form of charisma, producing what has been called "groupthink," where decisions are reached not because they are necessarily the best decisions but out of respect and admiration for the employee who is most personable, forceful, and persuasive.
6. Linking pins may abdicate their leadership role, thus producing a laissez-faire leadership situation, leading again to dysfunctional behavior. Blake and Mouton in their Managerial Grid refer to this as country club management.[8]
7. Some employees may be so conditioned to strong, autocratic leadership that they are lost without it.

SOME COMPARISONS

Of the four organization models examined here, the first two, Gulick and Urwick's tangled fabric model and the matrix model, appear to have their roots in traditional organization. Both deal primarily with work purposes and processes and secondarily with human factors. Each has been made to work satisfactorily at varying times and under varying circumstances. Neither is totally or inherently "bad," yet each lacks certain dimensions necessary for adequate performance.

The consociated model takes on a futuristic shape. While many facets are in operation in various organizations now, it is highly improbable that any organization has adopted all of the model. Kirkhart himself says that it is doubtful that many organizations will adopt the consociated model in its entirety for some time in the future.[9] Nevertheless, it is evident that organizations are moving in this direction. It will take time and some rethinking of management processes to get there.

Likert's System Four Management model holds much promise for the organization of the future because it avoids rigidities. It softens structure for effective functioning of the organization. No charter changes are necessary for a municipality to begin functioning under a System Four Management model.

Additionally, System Four provides a framework for effective interaction between purpose and process departments and among all departments, allows for project management along the matrix model where appropriate and necessary, and encourages continued improvement in management methods.

It is no mere cliché to say that any well-functioning organization requires a great deal of teamwork. No group can function as a team without training, practice, and experience. Management must not only understand teamwork and cooperation but must also believe and practice teamwork. Well-functioning organizations are put together by the people who work in them, not by executive fiat.

An Example of the Misuse of Management. The president of a large firm, having read an article describing System Four Management, decided that this was just what his organization needed. He spent several nights drawing up an elaborate chart with linking pins and circles, similar to the chart in Figure 2–3. With chart in hand, one bright morning he announced that henceforth the firm would be managed under System Four.

To say the change was greeted with suspicion is an understatement. While cooperation was ranked almost as high as patriotism and motherhood, few of the department and division heads felt they could afford to cooperate with each other. "Too much to lose that I've fought so hard to gain." After about six months of frustration and mild chaos the president sent out the following memo:

To All Department Heads:

It has come to my attention that System Four is not working in this organization because certain department heads refuse to communicate with each other. In the future, all department heads will resolve their differences and begin communicating or be subject to dismissal.

Needless to say, differences were not resolved, communication was not improved, and no one was fired. The point is that individuals cannot be ordered to improve in personal relationships and cooperation. This is largely a decision they have to make for themselves. Imposing a system for interpersonal cooperation and communication from above will not make it work.

The model is not revealed wisdom. It must be tailored to the organization and the employees. It may be a sad statement, but many individuals do not know how to cooperate in a manner which they and others can accept. If they did, they would probably be cooperating. Opportunities must be afforded for practice and experience that develop skills for cooperation.

Conclusion

The management concepts and organization models described in this chapter are broad areas of inquiry for systematic planning, development of alternatives, selection of approaches, implementation of programs and projects, and continual evaluation. Overlaps and ambiguities are inevitable in a subject as new (in the historic sense) and developmental as management and organization. The term "model" is categorical for many, but that is not the intent in this book. Hopefully, the concepts and models set forth here and elsewhere in this book will help you in doing a better job of continual growth and development.

---

¹The acronym POSDCORB translates into Planning, Organizing, Staffing, Directing, Co-Ordinating, Reporting, and Budgeting. Luther Gulick, "Notes on a Theory of Organization," in PAPERS ON THE SCIENCE OF ADMINISTRATION, ed. Luther Gulick and Lyndall Urwick (New York: Institute of Public Administration, 1937), p. 13.

²Richard Beckhard, ORGANIZATION DEVELOPMENT: STRATEGIES AND MODELS (Reading, Mass.: Addison-Wesley Publishing Co., Inc., 1969), pp. 10—11.

³Ibid., p. 11. Quoted from John W. Gardner, "How To Prevent Organizational Dry Rot," HARPER'S MAGAZINE, October 1965, pp. 20—26.

⁴Gulick and Urwick, PAPERS ON THE SCIENCE OF ADMINISTRATION, pp. 15—29.

⁵Gulick, in ibid., p. 21.

⁶Larry Kirkhart, "Toward a Theory of Public Administration," in TOWARD A NEW PUBLIC ADMINISTRATION: THE MINNOWBROOK PERSPECTIVE, ed. Frank Marini (Scranton, Pa.: Chandler Publishing Company, 1971), pp. 159—61.

⁷Rensis Likert, THE HUMAN ORGANIZATION (New York: McGraw-Hill Book Company, 1967), p. 50.

⁸Robert R. Blake and Jane S. Mouton, THE MANAGERIAL GRID (Houston, Tex.: Gulf Publishing Co., 1964).

⁹Kirkhart, "Toward a Theory of Public Administration," pp. 158—64.

3

The Human Side
of Organization

Any ORGANIZATION MUST CONTROL some aspects of employee behavior to meet goals and objectives. Such control may range from the discipline imposed in a highly structured work environment to the self-discipline in an open environment. While control may exhibit itself in many ways, it is nevertheless control. When we speak of management, then, we are speaking of control of human behavior as well as control of physical resources. Early concepts of management focused on control for the accomplishment of objectives, with little thought to satisfaction. Modern concepts of management focus on control with satisfaction to the persons involved and to their objectives, as well as satisfaction to the organization and its objectives.

All theories of organization have, as a prime ingredient, a concept of human nature. While there are many variations of concepts of man, such concepts generally develop from three basic propositions: (1) man is basically "bad" and must be controlled for his own good and the good of society; (2) man is basically neutral and can become either "good" or "bad," depending on how he is shaped or conditioned; and (3) man is basically "good" and needs only an environment which will permit this basic goodness to arise.

It is doubtful whether any organization theory looks at these concepts as a pure state of man. For example, if man is entirely bad then it is not likely that man also can develop any concept of goodness or explain those persons who are not all bad. If he is entirely neutral, it is difficult to explain those persons who refuse to be shaped or conditioned. If man is basically good, then how do we account for those who insist on being bad?

Each of these concepts of man is tied to one of three predominant theories of organization: (1) mechanical/rational, generally stemming from Frederick Winslow Taylor and his formulation of scientific management and from Max Weber and his formulation of bureaucracy; (2) humanistic management, growing out of the famous Hawthorne studies conducted by Roethlisberger and Mayo; and (3) integrationist management, growing out of the work of Douglas McGregor and others. Figure 3—1 summarizes these concepts by organization characteristics.

Mechanical/Rational Theory

Scientific management as developed by Taylor was based on a concept of man as basically bad. Indeed, Taylor's motivation appears to have stemmed from an obsession with what he termed "soldiering" by workers who were naturally lazy and indifferent. Taylor, an engineer in the iron industry in Pennsylvania, wrote that "one of the very first requirements for a man who is fit to handle pig iron as a regular occupation is that he shall be so stupid and so phlegmatic that he more nearly resembles in his mental make-up the ox than any other type."[1]

Taylor's indictment was not restricted to the worker, but was extended to include management as well. Management, through its greedy behavior, contributed as much to the situation as did the workers through their laziness. Greed and laziness were not to be restricted to classes but were rooted in human nature itself. Since management controlled the means of production, it was management's responsibility to control the workers.

Taylor also felt that laziness was not just an individual trait: in groups, workers got together to restrict production to as little as they could get by with. Such action was detrimental not only to the worker's welfare but to the welfare of society as a whole. Restricting production deprived both the worker and society of the maximum material benefits available from the Industrial Revolution. Greater efficiency and productivity would provide greater shares for all.

Prior to Taylor, management's control of production largely amounted to determining the environment in which machines would be placed, what would be produced, and who would be hired. Workers for the most part controlled their own tools and work methods. Work methods were learned by watching someone else do the job and following up through trial and error. Taylor felt this was very inefficient. He contended there was one best way to do any job and that it was management's responsibility to find this way.

Taylor's methods and results were described in a paper presented to the American Society of Mechanical Engineers in 1895. Entitled "A Piece Rate System,"[2] the paper centered on a differential piece rate but contained elements of Taylor's scientific approach to management. Under the differential piece rate system, the job was first analyzed and broken into its various elements; each element was timed and a total time set for the job. Two rates were then set—one lower than the previous rate for reaching "ordinary" production and one higher than the previous rate for reaching the new rate of production.

For example, if the previous rate had been $2.50 for five pieces, and Taylor's methods made it possible to produce ten pieces in the same amount of time, the worker was paid $3.50 for producing ten pieces. If he produced only five pieces, or anything less than ten, he was paid

only $2.00—actually less than the previous rate. While the worker might be able to earn more money, the employer could hardly lose since he would be no worse off if the worker produced as few as four pieces in the alloted time under the differential rate.

While the differential rate might discriminate against a worker who could not make the differential, Taylor's response amounted to "So what!" Those who could not make the differential would soon quit. The process would weed out the slow workers. Over a period of time the employer would end up with only workers who could make the differential rate, and both employer and employees would be better off. Taylor contended that where the rate was set by scientific job analysis, any worker who really wanted to could attain that level of production.

While the paper on piece rates contained many elements of scientific management, it was not until 1903, when Taylor published his famous paper entitled *Shop Management,* that his total approach to scientific management was outlined. Scientific management centered on seven factors, sometimes referred to by Taylor as principles and frequently as laws. These included:

1. Analyze the work and standardize: machinery, materials, and tools
2. Standardize the purchase of materials.
3. Standardize the storage of materials.
4. Analyze the job to: determine the various elements, study the time for each element, and set a standard task time for each element.
5. Select the right man for the right job.
6. Train him to do the job in the best way.
7. Pay a higher than ordinary wage for meeting the differential.[3]

For its time, there was much to recommend in Taylor's approach. In later writings Taylor pointed to plants where machines, tools, and materials were in such disarray as to make it a miracle that any production was accomplished at all. Materials were stored in inconvenient areas and in inefficient ways. Purchasing was handled in a haphazard manner resulting in excessive spoilage, overruns, and failure to get the best price. Workers were underutilized and were per-

Organization characteristic	Concept of man—organization theory		
	"Bad"— mechanical/ rational	"Neutral"— humanistic	"Good"— integrationist
Social objective	Control	Shape	Develop
Social method	Technological design	Social conditioning	Facilitating growth
Motivating force	Reward and punishment	Reward and punishment	Self-actualization
Organization design	Hierarchical structure	Hierarchical structure	Small group structure
Leadership style	Authoritarian	Benevolent/ authoritarian	Consensus
Organization climate	Closed	Combination of closed and open	Open

FIGURE 3—1. *Concepts of man and organization theories by organization characteristic.*

mitted to perform the job in any way they wished. No provisions were made for training. Productivity was low, and wages were low.

Taylor argued that workers and management had a stake in efficiency and productivity. Rather than facing each other as adversaries, they should be working as partners. While such cooperation is necessary, Taylor insisted that it be enforced cooperation. Workers could not be trusted to cooperate even in their own best interests.

It is only through *enforced* standardization of methods, *enforced* adoption of the best implements and working conditions and *enforced* cooperation that this faster work can be assured. And the duty of enforcing the adoption of standards and of enforcing this cooperation rests with the *management* alone.[4]

While Taylor has been maligned by many—though worshiped by some—criticism stems largely from his concept of human nature. Where his methods were implemented, there was a general increase in productivity. Many of his innovations remain in use today, including operations and methods research, centralized purchasing, warehousing, establishment of a personnel department (Taylor termed it a department of labor), and of on-the-job training.

Looking at scientific management in terms of Figure 3—1, it is evident that his concept of management centered on a mechanical/rational approach. Work was a mechanical process that could be analyzed and the best way found for its performance.

Controls were to be present not only in the work process but in the social process as well. When workers were paid for individual production, economic gain would provide a means to overcome social pressures from less productive workers. In addition, less productive workers would be naturally weeded out of the organization.

The motivating force would be provided through economic reward for high productivity and economic punishment for low productivity. Workers would thus ensure behaving in the best interests of their employers by behaving in their own best interests.

A hierarchical structure would weld the organization together, with each level planning the work of the level below it.

Leadership would be largely authoritarian and would center around work rules derived from technology. Decision making would be vested in the hierarchy, with little necessity for lower levels to be bothered with decisions. Since both management and the worker would be concentrating on their common interests, management could be trusted to make the right decisions.

How Well Did Scientific Management Work?

Scientific management was vigorously opposed by the union movement. It was branded as dehumanizing. So far as labor is concerned it is a cunningly devised speeding-up and sweating system.

"Scientific Management" is a device for the purpose of increasing production and profits, and tends to eliminate consideration for the character, rights and welfare of employees.... "Scientific Management" puts into the hands of employers at large an immense mass of information which may be used unscrupulously to the detriment of the workers, and offers no guarantee against abuse of its professed principles.[5]

To implement scientific management took time and a rather large capital outlay in improved machinery, tools, and materials. At the end of two years, at the Watertown Arsenal near Boston, Taylor and his associates had just begun to install the differential piece rate in the machine shop division. Other departments had not yet been touched by the project. Analysis of the work generally resulted in a new plant layout. In addition, new tools had to be purchased, and materials and their flow had to be standardized. Though this phase could be handled with reasonable precision, it took time and a fairly large expenditure of money.

Analyzing the job was generally less scientific, and quite subjective measures were used in determining time factors for various elements. It was usually necessary to initiate new accounting and timekeeping methods, usually much more intricate than previous ones. As was the case with the Watertown Arsenal project, this work could take more than two years, with a high capital outlay and little to show in results.

To run machines at double or triple their ordinary speed required machinery that was in first-class condition. Materials capable of being handled at these speeds were also necessary, as well as an effective flow system. To neglect these factors was to court disaster. It is also understandable that if workers were to operate at such an increased pace they, too, would have to be in top physical as well as mental condition—although Taylor contended that his methods actually made the work easier and less fatiguing.

If the foregoing factors were frequently neglected, matching the man to the job, and training, were practically nonexistent, even in those projects initiated and followed through by Taylor himself. While hiring practices became more centralized under management, selection consisted mostly of hiring the number needed from those who showed up at the employment door. Training consisted of a few instructions and a demonstration of how the job was done. Then the worker was more or less on his own.

The uproar over scientific management reached all the way to Washington, resulting in investigations by the Interstate Commerce Commission, the United States Commission on Industrial Relations, and several other federal agencies. These investigations led to a prohibition against stopwatches and piece rates in all federal installations. This ruling was in effect until 1949, although scientific management in several other forms continued in governmental and other organizations.

Scientific management made impressive contributions in work methods, including plant layout, centralized purchasing, large-scale warehousing and storage, and standardized machines, tools, and equipment. The pioneering efforts in work processes made possible the giant corporation of the twentieth century.

One little-noticed contribution stemmed from the accounting procedures necessary to keep track of production rates and costs for setting piece rates and determining production times. Prior to Taylor such information had generally been unavailable to management. Any judgment of efficiency depended on observation. Profit-and-loss statements were rarely available until six months after the close of the year and frequently a year or eighteen months later.

The bad points of scientific management stemmed largely from a pessimistic assumption about human nature and a lack of consideration of human emotions. While there has always been an adversary relationship between workers and employers, which Taylor was well aware of, this relationship was accentuated under scientific management.

Minor Chipman, a management consultant retained by workers at the Watertown Arsenal to study their complaints, concluded that scientific management lacked three elements of fundamental importance: (1) an adequate method of industrial education, (2) adequate recognition of the principles of democracy in industry, and (3) an adequate conception of and sympathy with the sociological and economic aspirations of the workers. Education he specified as an absolute necessity when adapting to new forms of organization and new methods of work. Arguing that conflict was inevitable when change was forced on men regardless of their wishes, he wrote:

"The breaking up of crafts under scientific management is also breaking up certain of our social formations. Industrial training must be more than the mere training for a particular piece of intensive production work. It must give the worker an adequate conception of his place in the whole process of manufacture."[6]

Notice that these criticisms are not against organizing the work, facilities, and materials, nor are they against developing better work methods. All three revolve around treatment of the worker. Taylor's methods, though not completely scientific, did bring about increased production. His problems appear to have stemmed more from his personality and his obsession with "systematic soldiering." Taylor's biographer, Frank B. Copley, brings this to light when he quotes one of Taylor's workmen:

"I often thought Mr. Taylor would have made more rapid progress if he had been more tactful and not so willing to combat in such an intense way anyone who did not agree with him. A remark that always impressed Mr. Shartle and myself was one he sometimes used when we opposed him or discussed a proposition with him. 'You are not supposed to think,' he would say, 'There are other people paid for thinking around here,'" To this Mr. Shartle adds, "I never would admit to Mr. Taylor that I was not allowed to think, We used to have some hot arguments just over that."[7]

Copley points out that Taylor himself was always ready to serve as subordinate or superior and both gave and received much in loyalty to and from his subordinates and gave loyalty to his superior. His feeling was that a man owed more loyalty to his immediate supervisor or his immediate subordinates than to any enterprise or institution. Loyalty and effort should be given both ways. Copley writes:

In every case, giving must be reciprocal. But let every man, whether employer or employee, be ready to be the first to start the game. The one who starts it first is in a position to exact giving from the other fellow. And if the other fellow fails, in due season, to respond, then fire the hog, be he your employer or your employee. In every case be ready to give too much rather than too little, and in every case give the other fellow plenty of chance to respond. Be careful, however, not to weaken yourself by your giving; never give so much as to unfit yourself for giving more. This, as we understand it, was the philosophy that Taylor did his best to practice.[8]

In regard to training, Taylor himself wrote:

"No man should expect promotion until after he has trained his successor to take his place. The writer is quite sure that in his own case, as a young man, no one element was of such assistance to him in obtaining new opportunities as the practice of invariably training another man to fill his position before asking for advancement."[9]

Management is still learning this lesson.

THE RIGHT MAN FOR THE RIGHT JOB

Taylor was convinced that there were different classes of men and that a type or kind of work could be found for which each class was best suited—some to be common laborers, some to be skilled workmen, some to be clerks, some to be foremen, some to be plant supervisors, some to be technical experts, and some to be top management. He further felt that it was the duty of technical and management elites to discover the most productive labor methods, instruct workers in their use, and demand levels of performance. If a man could not meet the level of performance for the job, and if the method and level of performance had been scientifically set, then the man had been placed in a job for which he was unfit and should be placed in a job for which he was better fitted and could be trained.

In this process, he contended, workers and employers could not behave as adversaries but must respond to laws of work and production. While dividing men into classes, Taylor contended not that one class was better than another in that one had inherent "goodness" and the other inherent "badness," but that all were basically bad if enforcement measures were not brought into play. His feelings were that he had scientifically discovered this and that one could not argue with the findings of scientific management.

The Human Relations Movement

The human relations movement received much of its impetus from the work of Elton Mayo and Fritz Roethlisberger at the Hawthorne Works of the Western Electric Company, just outside Chicago. In 1923, Western Electric began a series of studies to measure the fatigue attributable to lighting conditions in the plant and the effect of fatigue on production. After approximately three years the investigators found no statistical relationships between lighting and fatigue or between lighting and production. The research was part of a time study and scientific management approach to improved production. By this date, scientific management had been accused of causing fatigue among workers, and fatigue factors were under investigation by many in the management field.

Eager to pin down such a relationship, Mayo and Roethlisberger, then at the Harvard Graduate School of Business Administration, were called in to continue the research. This led to a series of studies beginning in 1927 and lasting more than five years.

The studies first concentrated on measuring the effect on output of certain changes in physical working conditions. In order to control changes, a test room was set up, somewhat isolated from the main body of workers. At first no changes were made with the exception of putting the workers in the test situation in an attempt to establish production norms for the group. During this period output rose.

Other experimental changes in the study included such factors as method of pay, number and duration of rest periods, refreshments during rest periods, and hours and days of work. With each change, output continued to rise. After eleven such experimentally induced changes,

the group returned to original conditions in the experiment and output rose to a point higher than at any other time. This was the twelfth period in the experiment and lasted twelve weeks. At the end of this period, rest pauses and refreshments were restored and output rose once again to even greater heights.

It was apparent that the itemized changes imposed during the study, though they might account for minor variations in output, could not explain the increasing level of output with each change. The steady increase in production appeared to ignore whatever experimental changes were introduced. Reports indicated that average weekly production had increased from about 2,400 units per worker to 3,000 units per worker. In an early period of the experiment, before hours were reduced and rest periods initiated, production had amounted to less than 2,500 units per worker. When these same conditions were restored, average weekly production reached more than 2,900 units per worker. Average hourly output was higher during this period than in earlier periods even though experimentally induced conditions were basically the same as at the start of the project.

As examples of the outcome of the experiment, Mayo selected the following passages from a report to company officials:

There has been a continual upward trend in output which has been independent of the changes in rest pauses. This upward trend has continued too long to be ascribed to an initial stimulus from the novelty of starting a special study.
The reduction of muscular fatigue has not been the primary factor in increasing output. Cumulative fatigue is not present. . . .
There has been an important increase in contentment among the workers under test-room conditions.
There has been a decrease in absences of about 80 per cent among the workers since entering the test-room group. Test-room operators have had approximately one-third as many sick absences as the regular department during the last six months.
Output is more directly related to the type of working day than to the numbers of [working] days in the week. . . .
Observations of operators in the test room indicate that their health is being maintained or improved and that they are working within capacity. . . .
The following conclusions from former reports are reaffirmed: . . . (n) The changed working conditions

have resulted in creating an eagerness on the part of operators to come to work in the morning.... (s) Important factors in the production of a better mental attitude and greater enjoyment of work have been the greater freedom, less strict supervision, and the opportunity to vary from a fixed pace without reprimand from a gang boss.[10]

Mayo also pointed out that "the operators have no clear idea as to why they are able to produce more in the test room; but as shown in the replies to questionnaires... there is the feeling that better output is in some way related to the distinctly pleasanter, freer, and happier working conditions."[11] Perhaps this statement had a profound effect on many who followed in the human relations school who mistakenly assumed that only happier working conditions were all that was necessary to increase worker output.

Neither the wage increases nor all the changes in physical conditions could explain the increases in output or the higher morale and satisfaction of the workers. It was concluded that, in the attempt to set up a test condition with all factors constant, where a single variable could be changed and the effect measured, the researchers had introduced the largest change of all—a change in human attitudes and sentiments. Moreover, they had brought about a radical change in the method of supervision and the social relationships of workers involved.

Previously the workers had been under strict supervision. In the experiment, however, an official observer and other experimenters assumed most of the supervisory functions; the atmosphere became more relaxed. Workers were allowed to talk freely; changes in conditions were discussed with them in advance instead of being arbitrarily announced. Roethlisberger, one of the chief researchers, later wrote:

In the endeavor to keep the major variables in the situation constant and the girls' attitude cooperative, the investigators inadvertently altered the social situation of the group. Thus, as a consequence of setting up an experiment to study the factors determining efficiency of the worker, they abrogated most of the rules intended to promote and maintain efficiency.[12]

In addition, workers involved in the experiments received more attention. The fact that they were studied became a source of pride. Important visitors came through the test room, and the workers received considerable attention from top management. As a consequence, the workers became a close-knit group. They cooperated not only with the experimenters but with each other. They began to enjoy interpersonal relationships at work and began to associate socially outside the work environment.

The conclusions were that human relations between workers and their supervisors and among workers are important influences on workers' behavior, at least as important as monetary incentives and physical working conditions. This discovery has been hailed by many commentators as the "great illumination." It pointed up many of the weaknesses of the efficiency gospel that arose from Taylor's work and the conceptions of human behavior in scientific management.

It was apparent that an enlightened policy toward production and carefully worked out work methods and processes were not enough. The administration of a carefully worked out plan, no matter how logical and efficient on a take-it-or-leave-it basis, generally puts the individual in opposition to himself. Even with a large will to cooperate, the individual finds it difficult to persist in action for an end he cannot at least dimly see and understand.

In summing up the findings of more than 21,000 interviews with employees at the Hawthorne Works, Mayo came to the following conclusion:

Human collaboration in work, in primitive and developed societies, has always depended for its perpetuation upon the evolution of a nonlogical social code which regulates the relations between persons and their attitudes to one another. Insistence upon a merely economic logic of production—especially if the logic is frequently changed—interferes with the development of such a code and consequently gives rise in the group to a sense of human defeat. This human defeat results in the formation of a social code at a lower level and in opposition to the economic logic. One of its symptoms is "restriction." In its devious road to this enlightenment, the research division had learned something of the personal exasperation caused by continual experience of incomprehension and futility. It had also learned how serious a consequence such experience carries for industry and for the individual.[13]

Thus, management thought moved from a concept of human character as basically lazy or "bad" to a concept that man is rather neutral and that the circumstances of the situation largely influence and determine behavior. Mayo and Roethlisberger based many of their concepts of human behavior on the works of Janet concerning obsessive thinking and the Freudian concept of compulsion neurosis, as well as on the work of other psychologists of the time. While psychological study of the individual is important, it can do little more than touch the fringes of human behavior. Mayo pointed out that the individuals who make up a working department are not merely individuals. They constitute a group within which individuals have developed routines of relationship to each other, to their superiors, to their work, and to the policies of the organization. Social maladjustment in such a group is more likely to be due to something in these routine relationships of one person to another than to some primary irrationality in the individual.

Man as Basically Good

The concept of human nature as basically good may be found in the work of Kurt Lewin and Douglas McGregor. Evidence may be gained from a summary of Lewin's theories as they relate to the individual's needs and interests in an organization:

1. The willingness of a man to cooperate in a program of activities depends upon how he perceives the environment and his own place in it. This is what Kurt Lewin has called "his life space."

2. The way a man perceives his own situation or life space is largely determined by his membership in primary groups and by the way he interacts with others in these primary groups. Lewin refers to these groups as the "social field of force."

3. When a worker finds that he is developing conflicting motives in a situation, he is likely to become frustrated. The result of such a situation is low morale and substandard achievement.

4. A worker will resist introduction of technical or procedural changes in the work situation because they are inconsistent with the old way of doing things. The new goals and the paths leading to them will also meet with resistance because they are inconsistent with those already set up.

5. The most effective way to modify the way a man perceives a situation is by using the primary groups of which he is a member. When workers resist production goals, the most economical way to handle the problem is to support the primary groups by bringing them into planning.

6. When groups have a democratic and permissive atmosphere and the members participate in setting their own goals, they will have higher morale. Such groups will have a greater commitment to the organization than groups led by authoritarian leaders. Finally, the level of participation will affect the group's level of achievement.[14]

Lewin's ideas generally support the contention that effective cooperation within the work group rests on consensus—that leadership rests on the consent of those being led.

Similar methods for managing work groups and understanding human behavior have been expounded in the Theory Y approach of Douglas McGregor. McGregor contrasts this theory with what he calls Theory X. Theory X may be summarized under three premises concerning human nature:

1. The average human being has an inherent dislike of work and will avoid it if he can....
2. Because of their dislike of work, most people must be coerced, controlled, directed, and/or threatened to get them to put forth adequate effort toward achievement of organizational objectives....
3. The average human being prefers to be directed, wishes to avoid responsibility, has relatively little ambition, and wants security above all.[15]

In his Theory Y approach, McGregor develops six major premises for a more effective method of management.

1. The expenditure of physical and mental effort in work is as natural as play or rest. The average

human being does not inherently dislike work. Depending upon controllable conditions, work may be a source of satisfaction (and will be voluntarily performed) or a source of punishment (and will be avoided if possible).

2. External control and the threat of punishment are not the only means for bringing about effort toward organizational objectives. Man will exercise self-direction and self-control in the service of objectives to which he is committed.

3. Commitment to objectives is a function of the rewards associated with their achievement. The most significant of such rewards, e.g., the satisfaction of ego and self-actualization needs, can be direct products of effort directed toward organizational objectives.

4. The average human being learns, under proper conditions, not only to accept but to seek responsibility. Avoidance of responsibility, lack of ambition, and emphasis on security are generally consequences of experience, not inherent human characteristics.

5. The capacity to exercise a relatively high degree of imagination, ingenuity, and creativity in the solution of organizational problems is widely, not narrowly, distributed in the population.

6. Under the conditions of modern industrial life, the intellectual potentialities of the average human being are only partially utilized.[16]

In writing about Theory Y, McGregor stressed that the manager or supervisor should restrict his authority to essentials. The preferences of the individual must be given equal weight with the preferences of the organization. Work objectives and the means of reaching them must be determined in consultation with all persons involved. Managerial and staff activities are defined as services rather than controls.

Hierarchy of Human Needs

Bearing some similarities to McGregor's Theory Y management is Maslow's hierarchy of human needs. According to Maslow, man's highest need is for self-actualization involving accomplishment and self-development. This need is insatiable and is never completely met. Other needs, in their broad categories and in a descending order, include a need for uniqueness, a need for belonging, and a need for survival. This hierarchy works from the bottom up. That is, one first focuses on survival needs and once these are met progresses to the satisfaction of belonging needs. Once these are met, one then works on the need to be unique and finally on self-actualization.[17]

While such needs may be separated for the purpose of explanation, in actual practice the distinction is not nearly so clear. The human being usually works on some form of self-actualization no matter what other needs he is concerned with at the moment.

SURVIVAL NEEDS

Man must satisfy three kinds of needs just to survive. The most obvious is physiological: the need for food, drink, shelter, sleep, air, and sex.

Next is the need for personal safety: protection against injury, illness, accidents, attack, extremes of hot and cold weather, and other dangers.

Finally, there is the need for activity. People must do something. The human organism has been designed for activity, and either body or mind, usually both, must reach some minimum involvement. Inactivity, with rare exceptions, leads to decay, disintegration, and even death.

Once physiological, safety, and activity needs—all necessary for survival—are met, a person feels a sense of self-accomplishment. He may even have a certain feeling of relief. At this level, however, these feelings generally are of short duration. What seemed so important diminishes in importance. A person moves up in the hierarchy and begins to set goals in terms of belonging needs.

BELONGING NEEDS

Not many people are strong enough to stand alone—at least not for long. Each needs love, affection, and a sense of belonging. He needs the support of others and the security of numbers. In this manner, people obtain gratification merely from being part of a family, work group, organization, or political party.

The price for belonging, however, usually is conformity to accepted codes of behavior. Consequently, as people attempt to belong they also feel a need to conform. Heightened by the normal processes of acculturation, a person's need to conform may frequently be so strong as to lead to bitter self-punishment when he deviates from accepted codes. Such deviation may be accompanied by an overwhelming sense of guilt that can be difficult to overcome. In its extreme manifestations, belonging may be carried to the point of denying individuality. Conformity then becomes utter submissiveness to authority or complete dependence on others.

THE NEED FOR UNIQUENESS

Every human wants to be unique, but this desire appears to conflict with his desire to belong. Although a person may feel a need to be the same as or similar to others, he realizes that he must also be at least a little different. But differentiation appears to follow rather than accompany belonging. One cannot readily afford to be different until after one belongs. The exception might be the confirmed outsider or rejected person bent on apartness by conspicuous deviation. Most people, however, feel more secure in deriving the essence of their uniqueness or difference through status, respect, or power.

By ranking people in various orders, such as the hierarchy of an organization, status provides a clear system of differentiation. Through status an individual may not only meet his need to have some place in the sun, but also to have some special place. With the exception of people at the very bottom of the status ladder, a person is assured of at least a minimum of deference and, at the upper limits, probably considerable prestige. The problem with the status ladder is that it usually rests on the bulk of humanity, with very few able to mount its rungs and even fewer able to reach the highest rungs.

Respect, another facet of uniqueness, is more difficult to come by and cannot be maintained automatically. It comes in two forms: self-respect and respect from others. The former may be much more difficult to achieve and maintain. Since most people know their own performance better than anyone else does, the individual may be the most difficult to convince about his own value.

The wielding of personal power provides the sharpest form of uniqueness or differentiation. In many organizations, it is frequently difficult to explain the continued striving of certain individuals whose needs for survival and belonging may be well met except in terms of a deeply rooted need for more power. The need for power expresses itself in many forms. In some it may

be a yearning to shape great events; in others it may be a need to help others. Still others may feel a need to dominate people.

In any form, however, the need to be unique or different is closely related to a sense of personal identity. It is generally agreed that thwarting these needs gives rise to feelings of insecurity, weakness, and helplessness. Such thwarting may result in basic discouragement or compensatory or neurotic actions. At the other end of the spectrum, the satisfaction of these needs may result in a feeling of self-confidence, worth, strength, capability, and adequacy, even in some instances where attainment has been at the expense of others.

As the needs to be unique are met, there is usually a feeling of elation—frequently superiority—but this may fade. As the feeling of elation wanes, the individual may strive even harder for more status, more respect, more power. And as he does so, he may reach a point of diminishing returns. He may end up on a treadmill where the faster he runs, the more he loses, with the result that he seeks more and more out of life and gets less and less.

According to Maslow, if a person has gained a sense of self-accomplishment from his efforts and his needs to be unique are being met, the highest need of all, that for self-actualization, begins to come into play.

SELF-ACTUALIZATION

Self-accomplishment is not to be confused with self-actualization. The former refers to the accomplishment or attainment of some goal or objective; the latter refers to self-development or self-fulfillment. Maslow has this to say about it:

Self-actualization refers to a man's desire for self-fulfillment, namely to the tendency for him to become actualized in who he is potentially. The tendency might be phrased as the desire to become more and more what one is, to become everything that one is capable of becoming.

The specific form that these needs will take will of course vary greatly from one person to another. In one individual it may take the form of the desire to be an ideal mother, in another it may be expressed athletically, and in still another it may be expressed in painting pictures or in inventions.[18]

Other authorities prefer to use the term self-development, since the latter term implies action, never completely predetermined, to meet needs that can never be completely fulfilled. In this respect, the person develops within himself to develop outside himself—that is, the person broadens his life by including in it interests broader than himself. Self-development implies vision and creativity, not necessarily the impressionistic creativity of the painter or the sculptor, but the creativity of a person in his chosen occupation. As Maslow puts it:

The creativeness of the self-actualized man seems rather to be kin to the naive and universal creativeness of unspoiled children. It seems to be more a fundamental characteristic of common human nature—a potentiality given to all human beings at birth. Most human beings lose this as they become encultured, but some few individuals seem either to retain this fresh and naive, direct way of looking at life, or if they have lost it, as most people do, they later in life recover it....

If there were no choking-off forces, we might expect that every human being would show this special type of creativeness.[19]

Self-actualization rises above the law of diminishing returns that accompanies the uniqueness described earlier. There seems to be no satiation point, since one can never attain an ideal of creative achievement nor can one ever learn enough. Consequently, self-actualization leads to the most truly satisfying kind of life.

Human Needs at Work

One should not get the idea that each need must be completely satisfied before the next need comes into play. In a sense, it is possible for all needs to operate simultaneously without the 100 percent satisfaction of any. To use arbitrary figures for the sake of illustration: it is as if the average worker is satisfied, say, 80 percent in his physiological and safety needs, 50 percent in his belonging needs, 40 percent in his uniqueness or self-esteem needs, and 10 percent in his self-actualization needs.

In addition, the emergence of the next highest need is not a sudden happening but rather a gradual overlapping. As Maslow puts it, as "need A becomes satisfied 25 percent, need B may emerge 5 percent; as need A becomes satisfied 75 percent, need B may emerge 50 percent, and so on."[20]

Figure 3—2 shows how the foregoing might take place for a municipal employee or work group. The group or individual is shown at the left, and human needs (goals and objectives) are shown at the right. The heavy line from the individual or group to the survival needs indicates that these needs are being fairly well met—for the sake of the example, 80 percent—and are a minor source of motivation or frustration. The line to belonging needs is somewhat lighter and

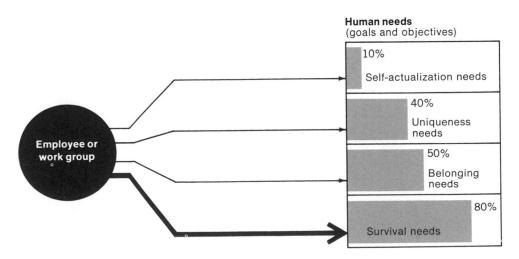

FIGURE 3—2. *Diagram for needs gratification.*

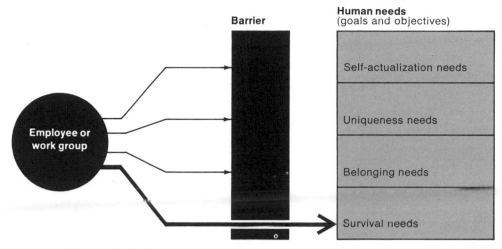

FIGURE 3—3. *Diagram of the barrier factor in meeting human needs.*

represents 50 percent gratification of belonging needs. The next line is even lighter, to show 40 percent gratification of uniqueness needs. The top line, self-actualization, is rather faint, representing only 10 percent gratification of these needs.

BARRIERS TO ATTAINMENT

Looking at Figure 3—2, you might assume that the employee or work group was in a developmental stage and that through a natural process of growth each higher level need would be met in larger measure, eventually resulting in a fully functioning employee or group. This state would be represented by heavy solid lines connecting each level of needs.

But people and organizations are not that simple. Standing between the individual and his needs is usually some sort of barrier. This is shown in Figure 3—3. In meeting survival needs, most municipal employees are able to overcome the barrier to a large degree. This is probably true for most workers in the United States except in emergencies or extreme circumstances, such as economic depression. The most formidable barriers are involved in meeting the higher level needs.

Barriers may take many forms. In some instances they may lie within the individual employee or group, in others within the supervisor or manager, and in still others within the system.

There are many ways in which individuals or groups may react to barriers; for example they may

1. Go through the barrier
2. Negotiate with the barrier
3. Go around the barrier
4. Remove the barrier
5. Change the goal or objective.

Barriers are similar to conflict—indeed, are the source of it; and like conflict, barriers are not necessarily bad. Frequently they provide the spice that makes a situation interesting and challenging. To be useful, however, barriers must be dealt with constructively, and some way must be found to overcome or neutralize them.

Go through the Barrier. When confronted with a barrier, the tendency is to try harder. The individual or group continues doing what it has been doing only with much more vigor. Depending on the persistence and depth of the barrier, this approach frequently works. Extra pressure on the barrier sometimes makes it give.

Negotiate with the Barrier. If pressure tactics fail to overcome the barrier, the usual next step is to attempt to negotiate. The methods in this approach may sometimes be devious, manipulating, and often compromising. Negotiating with barriers, nevertheless, can prove challenging and does not necessarily have to be devious.

Go around the Barrier. Going around the barrier frequently involves elements of negotiation and either legitimate or devious methods. What often happens is that after trying force and negotiation and failing to get results, one looks for more devious routes around the barrier.

Remove the Barrier. Sometimes the barrier itself is illegitimate and shouldn't have been there in the first place. Additionally, the barrier may be psychological, which doesn't make removal any easier. Removal of the barrier may be the most difficult course of action. An awareness that the barrier is removable must be created within the individual and members of the group before a method for removal can be decided upon. Also, one frequently will need help in removing the barrier.

Change the Goal or Objective. Failing to negotiate, go around, go through, or remove the barrier, a person may take another hard look at his goal or objective and its relationship to the barrier. Since needs in the hierarchy may be met by different goals or objectives, one may change the goal, thus removing it from the area of the barrier. A simple example might be the person whose objective is to satisfy his hunger need with a sirloin steak, but who settles for hash when he finds the barrier to steak insurmountable.

The foregoing is by no means a complete list of the ways a person might deal with a barrier, nor is it meant that a person will resort to these ways in the order mentioned. Barriers to goals and objectives exist in almost all situations and, while frequently contributing to conflict, help to make work a great deal more interesting. The important thing is to find constructive ways to deal with barriers and the frustrations they cause.

FRUSTRATION FACTORS

Each of us can stand a certain amount of frustration and, indeed, it can prove to be a motivating force. But every person has his own frustration tolerance level. When this level is reached or surpassed it generally results in some form of dysfunctional behavior.

This process is illustrated in Figure 3—4. As the individual or group interacts with the barrier and is unable to overcome it, frustration builds up. Within the frustration tolerance level this may provide the impetus for finding ways to overcome the barrier. Once it surpasses the frustration tolerance level, however, it is deflected from the barrier to some type of frustration-caused dysfunctional behavior. This is illustrated at the upper left of the diagram. Among the types of dysfunctional behavior caused by frustration are aggression, rationalization, withdrawal, fixation, and regression.

Aggression. We may become very aggressive and hostile, not only toward the barrier but to others around us. We may want to fight to get rid of frustration. The more stubborn the barrier, the more we are deflected into a state of frustration.

Rationalization. To return to a frustration tolerance level, we may begin to rationalize. Rationalization rarely changes the situation or the barrier but is used to explain our way out of a frustrating situation. In a way, it is a form of copout or of burying one's head in the sand.

Withdrawal. In order to get out of the frustrating situation one may simply withdraw, either physically or mentally. In effect, one says, "To hell with it," and removes oneself from the situation, In this process, one may also be involved in some form of rationalization.

Fixation. In this process a person becomes so engrossed in the frustrating experience that he fixes himself on the goal or the barrier and can think of nothing else. In its milder forms, when it is successful in accomplishing the goal, we call this process "stick-to-it-iveness" or persistence.

Regression. When the person resorts to regression to deal with a frustrating situation, he becomes childish. He engages in childish logic and other forms of childish behavior. In the extreme, he may even regress to an infantile stage.

Frustration is a powerful force. If it is not dealt with constructively it can lead to a high level of dysfunctional behavior. In its extremes it can result in mental disorder. In its milder form, a certain amount of frustration may work as a force for accomplishment, but in its extreme forms frustration does neither the individual nor the organization any good.

The manager or supervisor must ask himself, "What is it that I am doing, or what factors in the organization create frustration that keeps people from doing a good job?" When he is

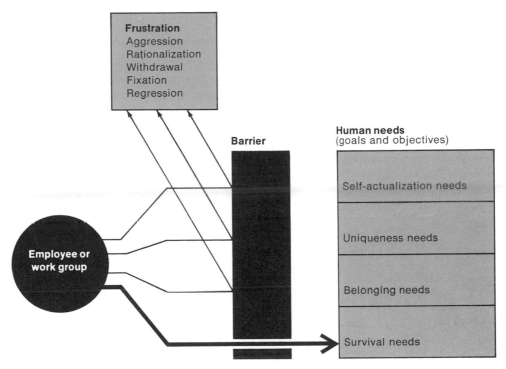

FIGURE 3—4. *Diagram of frustration factors caused by barriers to human needs.*

aware of frustration within the work group he must determine its causes and the effect it is having. By being aware of individual as well as of organizational needs, and by identifying these in terms of goals and objectives, he will be in a better position to locate and surmount barriers.

Conclusion

The classic dilemma in all human relationships is how to reconcile the needs (and rights) of the individual for privacy, uniqueness, and fulfillment with the needs (and rights) of the family, tribe, village, work group, or other organization for group effort to achieve agreed-upon goals and objectives. This dilemma has been a subject for philosophical speculation for centuries. As might be expected, clear-cut answers have not emerged, nor are they likely to. Much of the uncertainty stems from differing interpretations of the inherent nature of man. Is he good? bad? or somewhere in between?

This chapter has been built on the assumption that man's positive (or "good") tendencies are stronger than other forces in his personality and that organization and management should function accordingly. It is our contention that the social climate of the work group can be a positive contribution toward realization of goals and objectives while maintaining the integrity of the individual.

Teamwork and cooperation cannot be commanded by the leaders of work groups; these depend on social relationships and the opportunity for participation. Exactly how closely knit a work group should be for effective performance is not known. It is known that organizations can operate quite effectively without complete understanding of individual problems and personalities provided employees have the opportunity to participate in ways that are meaningful to them.

Lest this sound utopian, it should be pointed out that other major elements enter into the work situation, including systems and procedures, training, coping with organization change, establishment and realization of objectives through systematic management, communications, and management information systems. These and related topics are covered in other chapters of this book.

In this chapter interpersonal relations are stressed, drawing largely on the work of McGregor and Maslow, because they seem to be the most effective way of getting work done in most organizations while meeting basic human needs. They are not, of course, the only way of getting work done.

In the real world of municipal government,

organizations undoubtedly will take on characteristics of all three views of man—good, neutral, and bad—within the same agency on the same mission at the same time. This is not too surprising when you realize that all of us have mixed motives about most of the things we do.

Slogans and short snappy statements are always risky, but this chapter might well be summarized by stating that the effective manager provides opportunities for self-actualization, encourages open working relationships, and respects the dignity and integrity of every employee as a person while never losing sight of organizational goals and objectives.

[1] Frederick Winslow Taylor, THE PRINCIPLES OF SCIENTIFIC MANAGEMENT (New York: Harper & Brothers, Publishers, 1947), p. 59. Originally published by Harper & Brothers, New York, 1913.. Taylor's principles have been outlined in numerous publications over the years. A prolific speaker, Taylor presented many papers and articles concerning his work which has resulted in much duplication and rephrasing of many of his statements.

[2] Frederick Winslow Taylor, "A Piece Rate System: Being a Step toward Partial Solution of the Labor Problem," reprinted in SCIENTIFIC MANAGEMENT: A COLLECTION OF THE MORE SIGNIFICANT ARTICLES DESCRIBING THE TAYLOR SYSTEM, OF MANAGEMENT, ed. Clarence Bertrand Thompson (Cambridge, Mass.: Harvard University Press, 1914). Reprinted from American Society of Mechanical Engineers, TRANSACTIONS OF THE AMERICAN SOCIETY OF MECHANICAL ENGINEERS, vol. 16 (New York: American Society of Mechanical Engineers, 1895).

[3] Frederick Winslow Taylor, SHOP MANAGEMENT, reprinted in Frederick Winslow Taylor, SCIENTIFIC MANAGEMENT [a compilation of Taylor's works] (Westport, Conn.: Greenwood Press, Publishers, 1972), p. 40. This edition originally published by Harper & Brothers, Publishers, New York, 1947.

[4] Ibid., p. 53.

[5] Robert Franklin Hoxie, SCIENTIFIC MANAGEMENT AND LABOR (New York: Augustus M. Kelley, Publishers, 1966), p. 67. Originally published New York: D. Appleton, 1915.

[6] Hugh G. J. Aitken, TAYLORISM AT WATERTOWN ARSENAL: SCIENTIFIC MANAGEMENT, IN ACTION (Cambridge, Mass.: Harvard University Press, 1960)., p. 225.

[7] Frank Barkley Copley, FREDERICK W. TAYLOR: FATHER OF

SCIENTIFIC MANAGEMENT, 2 vols. (New York: Harper & Brothers, Publishers, 1923), vol. 1: pp. 188—89.

[8] Ibid., p. 140.

[9] Ibid.

[10] Elton Mayo, THE HUMAN PROBLEMS OF AN INDUSTRIAL CIVILIZATION (New York: The Macmillan Company, 1933), p. 65.

[11] Ibid., p. 67.

[12] F. J. Roethlisberger, MANAGEMENT AND MORALE (Cambridge, Mass.: Harvard University Press, 1941), pp. 15—16.

[13] Mayo, HUMAN PROBLEMS OF INDUSTRIAL CIVILIZATION, p. 116.

[14] Paraphrased from Theodore Caplow, PRINCIPLES OF ORGANIZATION (New York: Harcourt Brace and World, 1964), pp. 239—40.

[15] Douglas McGregor, THE HUMAN SIDE OF ENTERPRISE (New York: McGraw-Hill Book Company, 1960), pp. 33—34.

[16] Ibid. pp. 47—48.

[17] Abraham H. Maslow, MOTIVATION AND PERSONALITY, 2nd. ed. (New York: Harper & Row, Publishers, 1970). Maslow lists the hierarchy of needs as: (1) physiological needs, (2) safety needs, (3) belonging and love needs, (4) esteem needs, and (5) self-actualization needs.

[18] Ibid., p. 46.

[19] Ibid., pp. 170—71.

[20] Ibid., p. 54.

[21] The following discussion of barriers is based in part on research and on-the-job training conducted, in the past decade, by the staff of the Industrial Relations Center, University of Chicago.

4

The Municipal Organization
as a System

In THIS BOOK WE HAVE TRIED to look at the municipal organization as a system. System is a very chic word of late, and it means many different things to different people. It might be worthwhile to say just what we mean when we speak of the municipal government organization as a system. A system is a bounded set of elements that are more closely related to each other than to elements outside the boundary. The elements in the system act together to achieve something in the surrounding environment. To achieve this the system produces something, technically called an output. To produce the output the system needs resources, technically called inputs, and information about how it is doing, technically called feedback. The basic idea of this kind of system can be illustrated with a simple diagram, Figure 4—1.

Take this idea—an idea familiar to engineers and to political scientists, an idea that was used to understand how to control guided missiles—and apply it to a local government organization. We need to add more detail to better illustrate how the system works, but the basic structure of the system is the same as in Figure 4—1. There are inputs, which are transformed through the bounded system (the organization itself) to produce outputs (services) aimed at achieving goals, and there is feedback on how well the services meet the goals, thus providing the information and new policies so that the organization can correct itself to do a better job. The more detailed system model of the municipal organization is shown in Figure 4—2.

The technical phrase is sociotechnical system. But let's set that aside and look at what a city or county government organization or a council of governments is all about in everyday language.

Starting at the right-hand side of the diagram (Figure 4—2), we find GOALS.

Goals: Where Local
Government Is Going

Local governments exist for a purpose. They are not historical accidents, nor do they exist for the gratification of the people who work for them, as some popular myths would have us believe. Local governments exist to provide public services. These services may be as definite and visible as building and maintaining an acceptable street system—or as elusive as providing just treatment to minority group members or, that favorite of political scientists, the management of political conflict.

These services affect the physical and social city in publicly desired ways. Some services are more measurable than others, but all are real. In other words, local government organizations are concerned with public services which achieve public goals. They are here to do the public's work.

This is a basic precept for the local government supervisor—that the purpose of local government is to do the public's work. The precept is simply stated, but its implications are profound. It says at least three things.

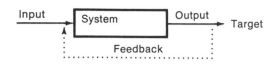

FIGURE 4—1. *The municipal organization as a basic system.*

First, it says that the principal measure of success of the organization lies in its output: the biggest (or smallest) budget, the most employees or the most professional employees, very good or very bad morale, moving X tons of gravel, hearing Y cases, and issuing Y traffic tickets.

A second meaning is that you are in fact a public servant. The goals of the organization are set by a public political process, typically centered around the city council, county commissioners, council of governments, or similar public policy body selected directly or indirectly by citizens under our democratic form of government. Citizens are both your boss and your client in a much more direct sense than in any business organization.

Third, your work is done in the context of a public organization. This is true both in the larger sense that the public helps determine what departments the organization will have—whether there will be a water department, or a department of human relations, or a project team responsible for getting an airport built—and in the smaller sense that the public strongly influences what activities will be undertaken and what the priorities are.

To say that the purpose of your work is to achieve some more or less well-spelled-out public goals puts the emphasis properly on where you are going, rather than on where you have been, on how they do it somewhere else, or on somebody's whim. This orientation is spelled out in more detail in Chapter 12.

Moving across the upper part of Figure 4—2, we come to CITIZEN CONTRIBUTIONS TO GOALS.

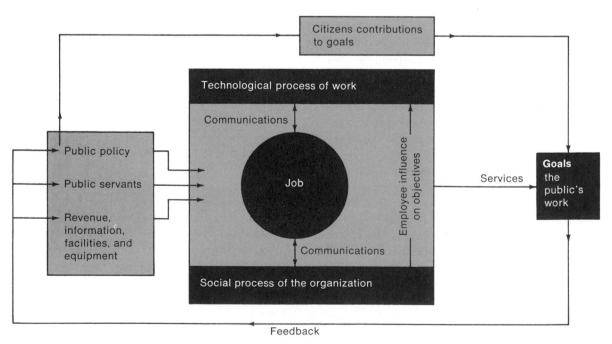

FIGURE 4—2. *A detailed system model of the municipal organization.*

Citizen Contributions to the Goals of Local Government

Where the organization is going depends to a large degree on where the people want it to go, including, as anyone who has suffered through a bond referendum defeat at the polls knows only too well, where the people want it *not* to go. The influence of citizens on the direction of the organization is most easily seen and understood through the city council or other policy body. Every local government has some legally constituted governing body which has formal responsibility for setting policy. In some cities the responsibility is also formally shared with an elected strong executive—the mayor. Under a democratic system this policy body—the council or mayor and council, or county commissioners, or council of governments—is a representative body. Its members are either elected by citizens or appointed by citizen-elected officials.

Citizens can hold the members of the policy body accountable at election time. Elected public officials tend to be quite sensitive to this, and therefore they are usually responsive to individual citizens and groups of citizens who can make the difference in their reelection.

It is important to be clear at this point that we are talking about the ways in which citizens influence the goals of the local government organization. We will argue shortly that the employees of the organization, especially supervisors and administrators, also influence the goals and that this is a good thing.

The discussion of goals to this point has been pure democratic theory of the textbook variety. It describes the legal structure and an important set of realities. Any local government supervisor who ignores the political process of the policy body or who undermines this process does so at his peril. But anyone who assumes that the only way citizens shape the working goals of the local government organization is through this neat textbook process is dangerously naive.

Public organizations in the United States are highly permeable. Citizens feed into the formulation of goals at many places. Setting the working goals—specifically, what the organization is going to produce—is hardly limited to the city council chamber. Some cities are undertaking community goals processes, sponsored either by the city council or by a private group, in which many citizens are involved in intensive discussions of where the community should be going. They come up with recommendations which may be very persuasive because they have a lot of citizen backing.

More frequently, citizens are involved in advisory boards and commissions as appointed experts. Citizens also appear before these boards and commissions and before the city council or other policy body to express their grievances and to attempt to influence the working goals. Some agencies of local government, especially Community Action Programs and Model Cities agencies, have formal representation of citizens from designated neighborhoods on policy advisory boards. In larger jurisdictions the pressures are strong for decentralization and greater citizen and neighborhood control of what the local government does. The city of Dayton, Ohio, for example, has experimented with general fund allocations to neighborhood priorities boards. These boards decide beyond the basic service level what services or improvements will be provided in their neighborhood with available general fund revenue.

All line departments develop special relationships with a select group of citizens within the community that can be considered the clientele of that department. Although the aim of local government agencies is to serve all the people, it is inevitable that clientele groups develop around departmental functions. Developers, realtors, and bankers are particularly interested in the activities of the public works, water and sewer, and planning departments. Commuters and mothers whose children must cross busy streets are particularly interested in the traffic department. Recreation departments usually have support from people interested in community betterment and the use of leisure. Articulate poor people are the clientele of housing authorities, Community Action Programs, Model Cities agencies, etc.

The clientele groups of the line departments are those citizens who feel themselves to be most strongly affected, for better or for worse, by the product of the department, i.e., by the public service it performs. It is in their interest to help shape the working goals of the department and therefore of the total organization. In return for this influence over goals, department clientele groups frequently become supporters of the department in its battles for resources within the organization and of the organization in its attempts to seek support from the total citizenry, as in the passage of bond or tax measures.

Finally, citizens who vote in local elections exercise a veto/approval power over the goals of the local government organization when issues come up for a vote. Citizen behavior as voters is shaped by many things, including the state of the economy, the national mood, and what the school district has done lately; but one of the factors that strongly affects how they vote is how responsive they feel the local government organization has been to their needs.

Positively or negatively, generally or in detail, in a myriad of different ways, citizens of the local community have an influence in determining what the goals of the local government organization will be. Administrators and supervisors may cope with citizen influence attempts in different ways. You may defend the purity and professionalism of your organization by fighting off all attempts by citizens to influence organizational goals except those filtered through the policy body. Alternatively, you may find open and aboveboard methods of entering into partnership with citizens in a variety of ways to determine working goals. There is some evidence that the latter approach is more productive, both in final work output (because fewer projects get turned down after months of work have gone into preparing them) and in citizen support.

Our purpose here is not to recommend any one means of citizen participation, but to indicate that the direct participation of ordinary, nonoffice-holding citizens in formulating and changing the goals of local government organizations is here to stay and will increase.

Now let us take a look at one of the elements within the system:

How Do We Get There? The Technology of Production

The technological process of work is the direct, operating part of the sociotechnical system. It is shown graphically in Figure 4—2. This is the first of two interrelated processes in our system; the other is the social process described in the next section of this chapter. Remember that the focus here is on the local government organization, what it does, and your part in that organization as a supervisor or administrator—not on the physical, economic, or social community out there of which the organization is a part and which it is affecting. The technological process discussed in this section and the social process discussed in the following section are the ways in which the organization achieves output. These two processes are not independent. They interact strongly at all times, but they have distinctive characteristics, and somewhat different techniques are needed to deal effectively with each. The core of your job as a supervisor or administrator is to be on top of both of these processes so that they are directed toward the output goals of the organization. Both processes have a lot of flexibility and can be adjusted to the goals in a variety of ways. Several of these ways are taken up in other chapters.

The technological process is probably the more familiar. This is especially true for supervisors and administrators, who, we know from research, tend to have a high achievement motivation, or a strong desire to focus on "getting out the work." At the risk of sounding simplistic, let us take a look at the idea of the technological process so that we can distinguish it from the social process.

The technological process is doing work as most of us traditionally learned to do it. We look at each of the steps and activities that go in a direct, almost physical, sense into producing the desired product. For example, there is a technology of pavement cuts and replacement which is covered in some detail in ICMA's book *Urban Public Works Administration,* in the Municipal Management Series. The chuckhole repair technology involves all the steps in physically moving gravel from the river bed, or rocks crushed into gravel, to the site of the hole in appropriate quantities. It involves moving tar from its original location, processing it in various ways, and putting the tar and gravel together and into the hole. It involves cleaning and preparing the hole in a prescribed manner and filling and tamping the hole properly so that the patch will last, will not collect water, and will not give an unnecessary jolt to passing traffic.

Every output goal or product, every public service or improvement, and every internal service has a technology or set of alternative technologies for producing that output. The city clerk puts together backup materials for the council agenda and gets these out to council members before each meeting; then he or she publishes the official minutes of the council meeting. There is an information system technology for doing this. The paper and other supplies are received from outside the organization. They are moved from a storage place to the clerk's office. The correct number of sheets are broken out to reproduce the materials that the city manager, department head, councilman, or someone else has given to the office for distribution. Masters are cut or photographed, and copies are reproduced in the correct numbers. They are sorted, stapled, packaged, addressed, and distributed to the councilmen. At the council meeting the deliberations of the council are recorded. These recorded minutes are then transferred by a number of mechanical steps interlaced with legal clearance points into a bound volume of approved minutes. This is a familiar but complicated technology for producing a desired output.

Two important points should be apparent from this example. First, there are a number of alternative technologies available for producing the same output. The minutes may be taken down in longhand or in shorthand, or on a stenocorder, a tape recorder, or another machine, within legal limits, of course. The minutes may be reproduced by longhand, as still required in some jurisdictions, by manual typewriter, by automatic typewriter, by copying machine, or by one of many available printing processes. These different methods usually have advantages and disadvantages in terms of such factors as availability, speed, flexibility, and cost.

The second point grows out of the first. Technologies are studyable and improvable. They are subject to rational analysis to determine the "best" way of doing the thing at a given time and against a given set of constraints and performance criteria. Chapters 13 and 15 are concerned with this kind of rationalization of work technology.

The illustrations of work-technology to this point have dealt pretty clearly with the movement of things from one place to another and with putting them together in different ways to achieve the desired goals. Although often complex, these are the simpler technologies to deal with. The work technology may have social dimensions as well.

Studies show that the typical policeman spends about 80 percent of his time doing something that can be called arbitrating social conflict—cooling arguments and settling family quarrels, for example. Social peace is an important output goal of police departments. There are different sets of actions that the policeman can take when trying to settle a family argument—different technologies for dealing with this work problem. He can arrest one or both of the parties; he can inform them of the law and order them to stop; he can try to reason with them; he can take the side of one party against the other; he can turn his back and let the onlookers handle the situation; or he can rush breathlessly into the room, plop himself in a chair, and pant, "My God, there are a hell of a lot of steps to get up here on a hot day. You have no idea how much work it is to run up them. My feet are killing me. Would somebody please untie my shoe?" Then, when the attention has shifted, he can say, "Now, what was going on in here when I came in?" The point is that except in the unlikely event that he chooses to shoot or club somebody this part of the policeman's work technology is social rather than physical.

Similarly, when the public health officer is attempting to control venereal disease or tuberculosis some parts of his technology are physical or chemical, but others are social and behavioral. They have to do with such activites as finding out what contacts a carrier has had with other individuals and controlling or limiting future contagious contacts. Even in so physical an area as solid waste disposal there are significant behavioral elements in the technology. Engineering approaches are simply unable to deal with such problems as getting the refuse properly wrapped and placed in the proper container in the proper ways—out by the street on

Tuesday morning in plastic bags rather than in the backyard in old oil drums.

The work technology, then, is the process that encompasses that necessary sequence of activities that must occur, that movement and putting together of things and communications that must take place, to produce any given public service.

How Do We Get There?
Social Process of the Organization

The technological process of production is fairly easy to grasp once it has been illustrated in terms of familiar work. That is not so true of the social process of the organization (see Figure 4—2). There is a popular belief that since the production technology is the process that leads to the desired output, that is what work is all about. This belief has been only slightly modified by the trickle into management and supervisory circles of some of the findings of social scientists, especially findings of the famous Hawthorne study.[1] To the extent that administrators and supervisors are aware of these findings they have tended to interpret them as saying simply that good morale leads to high production—the so-called pat-on-the-back school of management. Social science findings that are available to us now are much more highly refined, and their implications are more basic and far-reaching.

The technological process depends totally on a parallel social process. Things don't move by themselves, and they don't get put together by themselves. This is even more true of communications and ideas. It is people who make them move. Even in the most automated process the work is initiated, directed, and controlled by people.

The social process of the organization leads to the same output as the technological process and occurs around the same set of tasks. In traditional management thought the social process of the organization has been seen as secondary to the technological process and completely dependent on it. In actuality, the technology of work is only one of the factors influencing the social process of the organization, and improvement in work technology is probably not the best way to improve the social process of the organization. There is quite a bit of evidence that if the social process is not dealt with separately and in its own way, improvements in work technology will bring about resistances in the social process that can be very costly. Several cities have learned this the hard way by attempting to substitute computerized records for manually prepared ones without dealing with the needs of the people who prepared the records.

What is the social process of the organization? Stated most simply, it is people working together. It is people who are members of a local government organization relating with other people who are members of the organization, or who are not members of the same organization but who share a commitment to the shared task, and some ability necessary to that task, cooperating with each other to produce the desired public service or improvement.

The social process is involved whenever work is done, even for the building inspector who visits houses by himself and makes the necessary judgments by himself and files his reports. He belongs to a work group; he has a position classification that defines the outlines of his job; and he reports to a supervisor with whom he must relate effectively. He has or he does not have ongoing relationships with the electrical inspector, the plumbing inspector, and the housing demolition officer, who may be in the same department or in a different department. He shares office space with people who pass work to him and with others who must pick up where he leaves off. The building inspector may also relate to property owners and landlords to give them assistance or secure code compliance. This is also a social process, but it is part of his work technology. It is not part of the social process of the organization as we are using the term here, because interaction with the owners takes place at an output boundary of the organization rather than within the organization.

Suppose the director of public works, a civil engineer with a great deal of knowledge of the technology of construction, is given responsibility for the design of a civil emergency command center. The task is beyond his capabilities as a single person, both in terms of the time that would be required, given all his other responsibilities, and in terms of his knowledge of complex design elements such as potential usage of the facility and telecommunications technologies. He puts together a design team, of which he may be a member, which will come up with the design by a specified time. The quality of that design team in terms of capabilities and ability to work together effectively will determine the quality of the final design to a significant degree.

The director at this point is working primarily with a part of the social process of the organization, and his success depends on how well he works with that process rather than on what he knows about construction technology. He needs to know the resources that are available in the individuals in his department and in other parts of the organization. He may even need to go outside the organization. He needs to secure the agreement of these people to work on the project; put them together into a working group; provide necessary budget, space, time, and staff, which he may or may not control directly himself; and get the involvement of the users in the design process so that the facility will not only meet their needs but will be seen as meeting their needs. He must see that the resources represented in the design group are shared effectively, so that the best quality product can be produced.

Suppose the sewer crew comes to the city hall dirty and exhausted after being called out at 2:00 A.M. to repair a messy break? They find a note from the city manager on the bulletin board saying, "Sanitary Crew No. 3 are to be congratulated for an excellent job of repairing the break at Third and Main under circumstances beyond the call of duty. Take the morning off to clean up and rest up. [Signed Joe Jones, City Manager.]" Joe Jones here is managing the social process of the organization.

Suppose there is a 30 percent turnover of laborers, most of whom are poor minority group members? Suppose there is also a 50 percent turnover of keypunch operators, most of whom are high school graduates, some with college work, and suppose they are privileged to work with the most advanced computer system around? The technological process of work cannot explain this differential.

All of these situations are realistic, and all can be effectively dealt with, but the supervisor or administrator must understand and respond in terms of the social process of the organization. This is the "socio" part of the sociotechnical system.

Jobs: The Static Tie between the Two Processes

The technological process of work and the social process of the organization come together, obviously, around what people do. The first place to look to see if the two processes are meshing well is around work itself. The building blocks of work in the technological process are tasks, specific activities that have to be done in order to get the work out. These may be highly specific and highly determined by the technology, as in the purification of water, where certain amounts of chlorine gas must be added to a certain volume of water of a certain quality in a set manner. Or the tasks may be quite general and within a technology that allows many alternatives, as, for example, with our policeman attempting to maintain social peace.

The technology of work does not determine who does which tasks or how many tasks of similar or different nature a given person should perform; that is a function of the social process of the organization. In other words, decisions about what has to be done in order to accomplish the objectives are technological and have technological answers; decisions about how to do those things that have to be done and about who will do them are part of the social process and have social rather than technological answers.

The building blocks of work of the social process of the organization are jobs, positions, or roles, which we will take as meaning essentially the same thing at this point. A job, position, or role is a collection of tasks that by some form of agreement has been assigned to a single person.

The tasks are determined, loosely or tightly, by the technology of work, but the division and grouping of tasks are determined by other factors, including tradition, higher authority, either legal or administrative, the way people learned the job, either on the job or in school, and even the insistence of professional associations:

The Municipal Finance Officer's Association says that the job of the finance officer should include the following responsibilities vis-à-vis the city budget. . . .

The International City Management Association says that the city manager should have the following relationship with the council vis-à-vis the development and public defense of policy issues. . . .

The grouping of tasks into jobs is often formalized and may be influenced by a position classification study conducted by the personnel office or by an outside consulting firm such as Public Administration Service. Although good job descriptions are a valuable tool, there is always a danger, when positions are formalized, that jobs will be viewed as simply a part of the technology of work rather than a part of the social process of the organization. The result is often rigidities and false economies that spring from seeking a mechanically efficient division of labor rather than a division of labor that seeks organizational effectiveness by designing jobs for the maximum possible motivational content·as well as technological efficiency.

Finally, the task content of jobs is determined to an important extent by the people who hold the jobs. This is true if people participate directly and formally in deciding what they will do or if they simply go about doing what they want to do and leave the remaining tasks to others. To an extent seldom appreciated, people make their own jobs.

Jobs do not exist in isolation but rather in relation to other jobs, so that between them all of the tasks required by the technology are done, even highly undesirable tasks like cleaning sewer pipes. The technology determines those tasks that absolutely must be performed in order that the service may be produced, and often the technology determines the sequence of tasks as well. It may also determine whether the task is best performed alone, as with a biochemist at a microscope determining the purity of milk, or in a group, as with the forestry crew trimming, felling, chipping, and removing a diseased elm.

Jobs differ in the degree to which the tasks that compose them are routine, simple, repetitive operations that are relatively easy to learn and require a minimum of judgment (running a Xerox machine, for example) and the degree to which the tasks are novel and require thinking and coming up with new solutions or new applications of old methods. Again, the technology may require both types of tasks, but it does not determine how they are divided up. On the one extreme everyone could get an equal proportion of the exciting tasks and of the routine ones, while on the other all the routine tasks could be assigned only to certain jobs (for which we typically pay less and which we give to women) and the exciting tasks given to certain other jobs (which usually have higher pay and go to "comers" in the organization). All of this must be put together with the practical recognition that different people do in fact have different interests, competencies, and potentials for growth on the job. The factor of personal growth is an important one to be aware of, because individuals do grow and change. The set of tasks that was interesting and that stretched one's capabilities six months ago may now be routine. The tasks must still be performed, but perhaps they can be divided differently.

The social process changes at a different rate from the technological process. In some ways, as in the changing task content of jobs, it can be much faster; in other ways, as in resistance to the implementation of a Municipal Information System, it can be much slower. The point is that the social process does have to change with changing technology. If you buy a new type of fire engine, or put the tax billing on a service bureau computer, the tasks change, and so the jobs must change as well. As a supervisor or administrator, you must be aware of the need to adjust the work to the people as well as to help the people recognize, learn, and perform the tasks that need to be done.

Communications: The Dynamic Tie between the Two Processes

In the center of Figure 4—2 is the job, linked by the element that connects the technological and social elements. This vital link is that much talked about but little understood area of communications.

When something goes wrong it is a temptation to say, "It is a communications problem." Before taking that easy way out, however, it may be helpful to indicate three ways in which communications is built into your organization.

First, work in the modern world increasingly *is* communications. The moving of things by brute muscular force is a very small and decreasing part of the total set of tasks that must be performed in local government. Increasingly, the tasks consist of some form of communication. A very large part of the supervisor's job is communication. Of course, thinking and judgment and knowledge of the tasks and of the social process are there, but for these to be used they must be communicated to others in ways that will be understood and acted on. Most of what you know about the organization and the job and about what is going on has come to you in some form of communication. A time study of your work as a supervisor or administrator would probably indicate that 60 to 80 percent of your time is spent in talking to people face to face, in meetings or on the telephone, and in writing or reading memos, letters, and reports.

The second point is a corollary of the first. If work is very largely communication, then the accuracy, appropriateness, and timeliness of communication give a key measure of the effectiveness of the organization. Whenever people are the agents of communication, accuracy, appropriateness, and timeliness are factors to be worked toward and occasionally achieved.

The third point is that most of the communications in a local government organization are between people. Communications are either interpersonal, between two or more individuals, or intergroup, as between two departments, between a department and the manager's office, between a department and a contractor, or between a department and a citizens' group. They are rarely "untouched by human hands."

There are exceptions, however, to people-to-people communications. The city of Wichita Falls, Texas, for example, has a computer-controlled traffic control system which picks up signals by radio from sensors buried in the streets, makes a number of calculations, and turns the lights red, yellow, and green in such a way as to get the best traffic flow. The communications involved are accurate, appropriate, and timely once the program is set. No human agent enters unless there is an electronic failure.

Communication has many meanings, forms, and uses, but effective organizational communication depends on a climate of trust, openness, commitment, collaboration, and problem solving. These subjects are covered in Chapters 5, 9, and 10.

The central element of communication flows in four different ways: technological, public reporting, social process, and personal.

Technological communication is the exchange of data needed to produce a service. The Wichita Falls traffic control system is a pure example of technological communications flow. Technological communications are concerned only with those bits of information that need to go together with other bits of information to get the tasks accomplished—the location of that lot overgrown with weeds, so that it can be put together with the name and address of the owner, so that he can be sent a warning letter about his responsibilities under the weed control ordinance; the name and address of the citizen who complained, so that he can be informed of the action taken, etc. These communication flows are often highly developed in local government.

A second flow of communications that has been fairly highly developed in local government is public reporting. Much information is gathered and fed to the policy body to assist them in making policy decisions and in telling the story of the organization to the citizens. Many governmental reports are of that nature. They may incidentally provide some information useful in other communication flows, but their principal purpose is to report to the public. This is an important flow of communications as long as it is recognized for what it is—a direct service in itself.

The social process is the third flow of communications. These communications have in the past rarely been formalized. They deal, for example, with who relates to whom in what way, with power and control of resources, with the climate of the organization, with the beliefs, expectations, and attitudes that the members of the organization have about their jobs and their place in the organization, and with the ways decisions are made in groups.

Some common documents that play an important part in this flow of communication, for example, budgets, position classification plans, performance evaluations, and tables of organization, have been traditionally seen as controlling the technology of work rather than providing data and knowledge about the social process. In most local government organizations, however, you can still probably learn more in the rest rooms and the cafeteria about the social process. This flow of communication is vital, but it goes on largely under cover.

A final flow is personal communications—data about how you are feeling, what you like to do on your vacation, how things are going with the wife and kids, and information about your hopes and aspirations or about your feelings of warmth or anger toward other people. Personal communications serve to recognize and affirm people as people; they help explain certain things that happen at work that may seem to be out of gear with what is going on.

Personal communication flows have important consequences for work. At a minimum they should be allowed. In some highly effective organizations personal communications are actively solicited. However, it is important to state that they are not the property of the organization. Privacy is a basic American ethic. The use of personal data to hurt and control, especially if the data are covertly collected, is an extremely damaging thing not only to the person but to the total organization. Personal data belong to the person. It is for him to communicate them freely without undue coercion.

In more effective organizations, people do communicate quite a bit about themselves and relate to each other as persons rather than simply as fellow employees. High levels of personal communications may be seen as taking big risks with one's status and future. When fears are confirmed and personal knowledge is used against one, the level of trust and of communications of all kinds goes down. When personal risk taking is rewarded with greater respect, problem solving in the organization often improves.

With the addition of communications we now have the glue to hold our model of a sociotech-nical local government organization together. There is only one more element needed—the people who work there.

The Centrality of Employees and Their Impact on Objectives

All organizations, and local government organizations are no exception, are what they are because of the people who belong to them. There are different degrees of membership in a local government organization. Every citizen in the community has some kind of formal membership as a voter or, as with minors and criminals, as a client for the services of government. Officials on policy boards have a different kind of membership. Elected administrators have yet a third type of membership that is very close, in some ways, to that of the policy board members.

But the people who ultimately determine the quality and character of the organization, the people who *are* the organization in that they have the fullest form of membership, are the employees, whether elected, politically appointed, or part of the classified service under the merit system. These are the people who spend a good portion of their lives in the organization. Most of their personal rewards and satisfactions, successes, failures, and disappointments take place in the organization and around the work they do. For better or worse, this is *their* organization. Anything that takes place in the organization affects their personal world and their lives.

As a supervisor or an administrator you should get to know these people, their beliefs about the organization, and their work. The organization and the work are to a large extent what the employees believe them to be rather than what the charter, administrative code, ordinances, regulations, and work orders say. If the employees in your organization are like the employees of cities and counties that have been studied, they are bureaucrats who typically are more interested in security than in personal achievement.[2] They are somewhat dependent and are comfortable with being told what to do (although this is less true of the younger employees), and they have a strong service motivation, much stronger than that of comparable employees in the private sector or even in such quasi-public organizations as hospitals.

This profile may not match your organization. It is not true of all employees, and it is very likely that you, as a supervisor, will differ from the profile at a number of points, although probably not on the service motivation. You must not take this profile as necessarily describing your employees, but it is important to recognize that your employees probably have certain general characteristics and attitudes which differ from those of employees in other organizations and which differ from your own. Find out what these characteristics are, and try to relate to your employees in terms of their beliefs and aspirations.

We respond pretty much in terms of what other people expect of us. If you expect me to be lazy, the chances are that for you I may well be. This is a very important point. A number of supervisors and administrators still expect employees to behave like those peasants uprooted from their land and thrown into a strange city culture who made up the labor force for factories at the time of the Industrial Revolution.

These expectations have been brilliantly discussed by Douglas McGregor as Theory X: people are basically lazy, incompetent, and stupid, and they resist work.[3] There is an alternative set of assumptions, which McGregor calls Theory Y, that are generally borne out as being true of most people today. Following the assumptions of Theory Y you would expect people to like to work, provided they felt a sense of ownership (ownership here refers to a feeling about things, spaces, or responsibilities), to have quite a bit of capability to bring to the job, and to enjoy responsibility. As a supervisor or administrator you have a great deal of influence on which set of expectations will prevail in your organization and therefore on how employees will probably act.

All of us like to be able to influence our own personal world, including our world at work. Ownership is clearly related to influence. If I feel that my assigned office is my office, that, even though as a piece of property it belongs to somebody else, for all intents and purposes it is mine to arrange, decorate, work in, and invite people into or keep them out of, then I will feel a sense of ownership in my office. I will feel that I am able to exercise a reasonable amount of influence over this space that is part of my personal world, and I will feel pretty good about this and will probably use it respectfully. If I feel that the office really belongs to the Space Control Committee and is held in trust by the Budget and Systems Division, which is looking over my shoulder at everything I do, I will feel that I am in hostile territory. Not having any sense of ownership, I either won't care about the office and will treat it casually or with disrespect, or I will spend a lot of energy fighting for control of that space that could have been better spent elsewhere. I might feel a lot of resentment about not being able to "fight city hall" on this issue and I would take that resentment out elsewhere, probably within the organization.

People similarly feel a sense of ownership, or lack of ownership, in the tasks that compose their jobs and in the position that they have within the hierarchy. Where they have some involvement in determining these and where they have some clarity from their own perspective of why things are as they are, they have a greater sense of ownership. Where sense of ownership is high you can expect a lot of good work. Where it is low you have warm bodies. This is one reason why it is desirable for employees to have influence on the objectives of the organization, within the framework of policy goals and in relation to their own jobs. Chapter 12 goes into detail on how to achieve this.

With the addition of employee influence on the objectives, the model can come to life. Looking back at Figure 4—2, we see that the completed model shows that employees communicating with each other and influencing the objectives of work are the vital link that ties together the social process of the organization and the technological process of work which are directed toward the goals and objectives of the organization as determined by citizens of the community.

Form and Structure: The Framework for Both Processes

We have talked about the public's work and how it is decided upon. We have talked about the technological process for doing this work and the tasks that make it up. We have talked about the social process of the organization and how this supports and underlies the technological process. We have talked about the jobs and communications that hold the two processes together and about the people who are the embodiment of the whole system. Now we look briefly at the context in which the system operates. This is covered in greater detail in Chapters 2 and 3.

Cities, counties, and councils of governments are legal entities. They are limited in what they can do, how they can do it, and how they can be organized. Some of these constraints have been examined in Chapter 1. These constraints set limits not only on organization goals but also on technological and social processes.

The form of government, as set forth in state statutes and the city charter, establishes the limits of what the organization may do. It may rule out some technological choices, especially where size and scope of jurisdiction are important. There may be a better unit cost obtainable by providing water service on an area-wide basis or by providing trash disposal in sanitary landfills serving several jurisdictions.

Financially, the tax base may be shrinking while the higher incomes earned in the community are spent in other jurisidictions. Such a limit on financial resources clearly limits the inputs and then limits the choices of how goals will be accomplished—and ultimately determines whether some goals can be pursued at all.

Jurisdictional boundaries may limit what a local government can do. There is little that Chicago can do about air pollution from the steel mills in East Chicago and in Gary, Indiana. All of these are realities that must in the short run be accepted. Next best work processes have to be developed around them, even if in the long run they can be changed.

The limits that form puts on the social process of the organization are more pronounced. In a county with elected department heads, the climate of the organization may be dominated by political expediency and frequent elections. Interdepartmental conflict is not only present, as it is wherever there are two departments, it is guaranteed by the separate kingdoms that are built into the form of government. In a local government organization that does not have a manager or chief administrator or other individual with responsibilities primarily for the total organizaton, the care and feeding of the organization can become very haphazard.

Some of the implications of organization structure have been described in Chapters 1 and 2. Structure is one step more detailed than form. Structure is the formal organizational hierarchy we all know from the organization chart. It has its formal expression in the ordinances that create departments and assign responsibilities. It is also found in merit systems, position classification and pay plans, administrative memoranda, and similar documents. These are the instruments that shape the social system that is the local government organization. It is your lot to live within these, to use them to help shape the social process.

THE REALITY OF CONTINUITY AND CHANGE

There is some truth to the aphorism that government never changes. At least the changes in local governments often come slowly. Every new goal, any new task, every new practice, is fully tested to see if it agrees with agency tradition. Because of the legal nature of local government, new practices are often tested against the law to see if they are allowable. There has been little dramatic change in many of the technological processes characteristic of cities in the past half century. Fires are put out in essentially the same way, water is purified and piped essentially as it was, city and county streets are maintained much as they were, garbage and trash are still collected much as they were fifty years ago. However, at least traffic technology has changed drastically, and there have been changes in paperwork and telephone communications systems. So perhaps the best way of doing municipal work has not yet been achieved and progress is still possible.

Local government organizations have changed and are continually changing. Except for the many changes of form of government arising out of the local government reform movement, most of the change in organization has been the result of undirected growth and decay. Goals have changed, new services have been added, some very few old services have been dropped, tax resources have expanded and contracted or have been eroded away by inflation, new people have joined the organization as employees, others have retired. Federally funded programs have spawned municipal counterparts. Departmental empires have flourished and languished.

The social process has accommodated itself to all of this. Many people in local government will say, "It has always been like it is now (more or less)," and, "We like it the way it is (more or less)." These kinds of statements reflect their belief that while it is always possible to improve work technology (it would be un-American to think otherwise) it really isn't possible to improve the social process very much because you can't change people. In fact, it is probably possible to improve the social process considerably, and you don't have to change people much to do it, but you do have to approach social system improvement differently from the way you change technology.

Changes in both the work technology and the social process involve problem solving. Improving either process begins with deciding what wants changing and defining the right problem (much more easily said than done). From that point on, the way you deal with a technological process and the way you deal with a social process are very different.

CHANGE BY LOGIC: SYSTEMS ANALYSIS AND OPERATIONS RESEARCH

Technological processes can usually be well understood and worked with as if they were mechanical processes. Engineering systems and engineers' modes of thought can be brought to bear on a technology to improve it. Systems analysis and operations research, which are considered in Part Four of this book, are the prescribed methods of treatment for a faltering or rusty technology. What these do is look at all parts of a technology together and help one to develop alternative possibilities.

DYNAMIC AND ORGANIC CHANGE: ORGANIZATION DEVELOPMENT

The best analogy for change in the social process is biological rather than mechanical. The change that you are seeking is not swift and total but is a growth-like development. The process can be un-

derstood, but there are few formulas to model and predict the effects of different alternatives on different people—even if we knew in advance what was in their heads and what they would do. Organization development, discussed in Chapter 10, deals with the total organization and certain high payoff points in the social process of the organization where improvements can often be made. Using the techniques of organization development it is possible to intervene in the social process, as one might intervene in the course of a river by building a dike or levee, to improve the climate of the organization, to reduce destructive competition between departments, to improve the social and technological problem-solving capabilities of the organization, and to help the structure work for the goals of and the people in the organization.

The Roles of Administrators and Supervisors

In terms of the system sketched in this chapter, the task of supervisors and administrators in a local government organization is to keep the technological process and the social process of the organization functioning well with each other and directed toward the citizen-set and employee-influenced goals and objectives.

The supervisor needs to know enough about the technologies his people are using to know when work is going well and when it is not. He needs to be able to focus on the technology, to help his employees understand the tasks involved in their jobs and how to perform them. He should know which tasks are considered undesirable and which are considered plums, and should have an equitable way of distributing each! He needs to be able to recognize bottlenecks and problems in the process of producing the service and to know something about how to solve the problems or how to seek help in solving them.

The supervisor needs to know enough about the social process of the organization to know what is going on in the organization, between working units and within his own unit. He needs to know when it is important to focus on the social process, and he must know how to do this:

this includes knowing when and how to intervene to improve the process, and when to call in a third party to help things along. He needs to know the skills and knowledge resources of his own people and others and how to put these together. He needs to know his own people well and he needs to be able to work effectively with strangers or organizational enemies to get jobs done. This means that he needs communications, problem-solving skills, and leadership skills for relating with other individuals, for working in a group, for working between groups, and for dealing with the public.

The supervisor must know how goals are set in the organization, including what scope citizens may have in influencing and changing them. He needs to interpret the limits of these goals to his employees in specific terms, and help them see the relationship between their tasks and the goals. He needs to be able to work with employees in setting their own working objectives relative to the goals.

¹See F. J. Roethlisberger and William J. Dickson, MANAGEMENT AND THE WORKER (Cambridge, Mass.: Harvard University Press, 1939).

²F. G. Brown and Richard Heimovics, "What Municipal Employees Want from Work," pilot study in five suburban city governments; paper presented at the national conference of the American Society for Public Administration, Los Angeles, California, April 1–4, 1973.

³See Douglas McGregor, THE HUMAN SIDE OF ENTERPRISE (New York: McGraw-Hill Book Company, 1960).

Part Two

People in the Organization

Introduction

As a matter of intelligent policy, bureaucracies distrust originality, which is always expensive and usually wasteful. They would much rather fertilize their gardens with their own mulch, so long as everything grows properly.

MARTIN MAYER

THE ABOVE QUOTATION represents an attitude about organization that is prevalent among many highly articulate people outside the field of public administration, including journalists, playwrights, novelists, and poets. This particular quote appeared in a book on advertising, *Madison Avenue, U.S.A.*, which was dealing with bureaucracies in the world of business, but the comment characterizes those often directed at governmental organizations.

Whether "bureaucracies distrust originality" is a truth, half-truth, or nontruth is something the reader will have to decide for himself. It is our contention, however, that there is nothing foreordained in the operation of any organization that closes off innovation and creativity. It is the purpose of the chapters in Part Two to show how different kinds of management patterns and situations can encourage meaningful employee participation that will bring good ideas to the surface where they will get an intelligent and respectful hearing with a good chance of being acted on and built into management decisions. In other words, these chapters assume that employees have much to contribute to organizational effectiveness.

All of the chapters in Part Two are based on an impressive amount of research in the be-havioral sciences that has taken place over the past generation. Much of this work, expressed formally in theories, hypotheses, and assumptions, has now been tested sufficiently to be operational. Thus, while some of the discussion in these chapters may seem abstract and even discursive, there is a real point in bringing these findings into the world of management so that you can better understand yourself, the people you work with, and how all of you work together.

Now, a word of caution. The concepts, styles, methods, and processes described in these chapters are not panaceas. They have been tested by experience and are workable given time for planning and development, application and testing, and continual modification on the job. Especially important, and it is the implied theme of this entire book, is that we do not do things to people. We don't manipulate roles, or play games with expectations. One example will illustrate the point: A person does not want to feel important; he wants to be important.

One of the ways to bring out the best in employee creativity is to better understand yourself as a supervisor. Chapter 5 helps in this effort by describing major kinds of management styles that apply to most people and most kinds of working situations. Obviously no one of us is going to be completely one style—say, the good shepherd—to the exclusion of all other styles. The objective is to bring the best of each, depending on the person and the situation, into the all-together manager.

Chapter 6 provides carefully written descriptions of motivation and behavior and the way they interact. Two points in this chapter should be noted because they may not be familiar.

First, self-actualization is the goal of work. When we think about this a little, it makes a great deal of sense. Once we have met basic needs for living and supporting our family and developing psychological security, we seek self-actualization which means fulfilling our potential. The importance of self-actualization is often underestimated by those who place undue emphasis on salaries, working conditions, and other aspects of the job. Given the conditions set forth in Chapter 6, self-actualization is the ideal. As the author states, "In this state, the person is as close to being healthy, wealthy, and wise as he is ever going to be."

Second, the author says that motivation is built on rewards but not on punishment. To put it mildly, this is a point of view many do not share. Read carefully the arguments on rewards and punishment. They are different from conventional thinking and well worth examining.

Decision making is a management area where concepts and definitions abound. David S. Brown of George Washington University has compiled a long list of quotations on decision making that is remarkably varied.

One is quite practical: "In the political process, a good decision may be any one which can be reached." Charles Schultze.

Another is cynical: "If past experience with government is any guide, nothing useless will ever be abandoned." Robert F. Steadman.

A third is humorous: "What with the tendency of one thing to lead to another, I predict a bright future for complexity." E. B. White.

Chapter 7 wisely steers clear of this word game by setting forth clear guidelines on kinds of decisions, the factors that affect decision making, and ways to improve decisions. The straightforward suggestions should be an excellent investment in work planning and follow through.

All of us go to meetings, conferences, and assemblies. Meetings as an integral part of work are dealt with in Chapter 8. Probably no other subject in management has been satirized so often. Meetings have been characterized as ways of avoiding problems, of avoiding work, of avoiding decisions, and even of taking unwanted decisions and recycling them so that they come out in different form.

But of course they don't have to be that way. When planned and conducted within a knowledgeable framework, meetings are an indispensable part of management. In Chapter 8 you will find useful suggestions on how to make the most out of meetings, including selecting participants and planning, scheduling, and conducting meetings.

Communication is a very broad subject, and only one aspect of it is dealt with in Chapter 9. This is administrative communication in the sense of the flow of information throughout the organization. The earlier parts of the chapter explain communication theories that underlie what we actually do on the job when we receive and transmit information in all directions.

Read carefully to see how people can mess up communications; it is not at all like a telephone line transmitting the inputs to a data processing center. With some understanding of the processes of communication you can then benefit from the discussion of communication skills, including listening and questioning techniques. The last section of this chapter, as a matter of fact, shows how an apparently routine assignment can get out of control when communication is not working well.

5

Management Styles
and Working with People

YOU ARE THE MOST POWERFUL INSTRUMENT of supervision that you have available in the total organization. The way you use that instrument, yourself, on the job shapes the work and that small society surrounding the work. The impact that you have on the people you supervise is perhaps largest of all, because they depend on you the most. But a little reflection will reveal that your colleagues and the people who supervise you, whether they are the city council, the city manager, or a department head, also depend on you. The way you use yourself will have something to do with how well they are able to sleep at night. The effects that you have are real. They may be positive in that they help others to work effectively together. Alternatively, some of the effects you have on others may be negative, causing others to be defensive, destructively competitive, unclear about the work and their responsibilities, or even angry, resentful, and uncooperative. Whether you intend it or not, just by being a member of the organization and doing your job, especially as a manager or supervisor, you have an impact.

To be an effective manager or supervisor you should be increasingly aware of the impact you have. We are not suggesting that you change your basic personality to fit the organization, or that the organization be changed to fit your personality. What we are suggesting is that you develop greater awareness of the effects that you have and greater skills in using yourself in working with people.

If we are going to use an instrument well we have to be familiar with the instrument and how it operates. A forester would be appalled at a Planner II using the forester's chain saw to make a wood sculpture unless the planner had a lot more familiarity and experience with chain saws than most of us have. A computer is a positive menace unless used by someone who knows what it can do and the kinds of problems that will develop if he doesn't watch out. It follows that if you are going to use yourself effectively as an instrument in the organization, to turn to the colloquial, "You gotta know where you're at and where you're coming from." In other words, self-knowledge is the starting point.

It may seem surprising to suggest that people with administrative and supervisory experience are not aware of how they affect others. Of course they are aware of this at some level, and of how the behavior of others affects them. Many of these behaviors and attitudinal responses were learned long ago, however, as part of growing up, and are now relegated to automatic response. It is really not surprising that much of the interpersonal behavior of adult managers and supervisors is unconscious and not thought out. As long as one's actions toward others are not intolerably unsuccessful one lets the automatic response serve and pays attention to other matters. Thus, without the "irritation of doubt" that Bernard James speaks of as a prelude to change, behavior toward others in the work setting rarely gets examined. One goes on "doing what comes naturally," and opportunities for more effective use of oneself are lost.

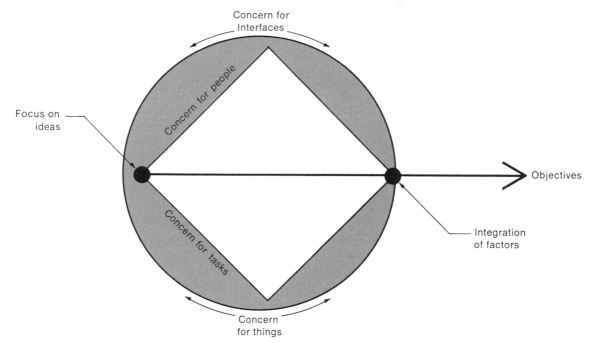

FIGURE 5—1. *The managerial field of vision.*

Management Styles

Every work situation is a little bit different from every other: the task mix is different, the urgency is different, the people are different, the state of the organization at that time is different. What you do as a supervisor or administrator is based on the uniqueness of each situation. We know from hundreds of studies that have been made in this century that one thing about leadership can be said with certainty: leadership is situational. Each situation is a little different, and the kind of supervisory action that works best in one situation may not be as effective in another. The best way to supervise firemen at the scene of a fire is not the best way to supervise firemen testing fire hydrants, and neither of these is the best way to supervise lawyers.

It would be impractical, however, to approach every situation as if it were totally unique and as if there had never been anything remotely like it before. If we did this we would be like perpetual children, always learning our way around and never able to deal with complex situations. What we do in practice is to recognize that many of the situations that a particular person has to deal with are similar (not identical), and each of us develops his own way of dealing with most work situations. This individualized way of dealing with work situations can be called management style.

Your management style is a result of what you have learned about the social process of the organization. It consists of the beliefs you have about what makes things go and how work comes about. It also includes your preferred ways of acting when you are supervising people.

While each person's management style is individual, there are some similarities between styles. Management styles can be characterized by how much active involvement one typically chooses to have with four basic factors involved in achieving work objectives.

Two of these factors are characteristic of the

manager's or supervisor's behavior in the work group itself: initiation of or concern for tasks, and consideration or concern for people. These two universal dimensions of human behavior in working groups have come up over and over again in studies of a great variety of working groups from baseball clubs to production lines.

Surrounding these are two factors derived from the fact that working groups are embedded in organizations and require supporting relationships and resources: concern for interfaces, and concern for things.

All four factors are graphically portrayed in Figure 5—1. It is possible to characterize six "pure" management styles (shown in Figure 5—1) by looking at what a manager or supervisor would be like if he focused the bulk of his attention on any one of the concerns shown here.

Figure 5—1 is an attempt to describe graphically the management styles discussed in the sections immediately following.

The point at the left of the tilted square is the focus on ideas. The downward-sloping line at the left of the square is concern for tasks. The upward-sloping line at the left of the square is concern for people.

Within the square is the work group—the area in which concern for tasks and concern for people mix in different proportions for different managers and supervisors. Some go more in the direction of tasks; others go more in the direction of people; but all are concerned to some degree with both. For example, a supervisor who is strong on concern for tasks and weak on concern for people would be located near the bottom corner of the square. At the other extreme, a supervisor who is strong on concern for people and weak on concern for tasks would be located toward the top corner of the square. A supervisor who is strong on both would be at the right corner of the square.

The lower portion of the circle is the concern for things. It relates to both the concern for tasks in the square and to the outside environment.

The upper portion of the circle is the concern for interfaces. It relates both to the concern for people in the square and to the outside world.

The circle represents the management styles that work in one direction toward the work group (the square) and in another direction

toward the resources and people in the outside world.

The point at the right of the square touching the circle is the integration of factors that leads to achievement of the objectives.

FOCUS ON IDEAS: THE STRATEGIC PLANNER

This point on Figure 5—1 is characterized by a low direct concern for tasks and a low active concern for people. In the pure theoretical form the "strategic planner" neither *initiates* tasks nor *shows* consideration for people, though he may *think* about tasks and *feel* concern for people. The strategic planner is, in the colloquial, "in the head" rather than mixing it up in the real world.

The strategic planner strategy says that you, as a supervisor, shouldn't be too involved in or terribly concerned with current work or the relationships in the work group. That is for others. Delegation is highly desirable. Managers and supervisors should be concerned about the current or ongoing task only when something out of the ordinary occurs. Out of the ordinary events can be flagged and brought to one's attention by management by exception, basically a form of reporting that highlights occurrences that are different from the usual expected events. The manager or supervisor should not be loaded down with a lot of detail about work that is within normal expectations.

Individuals who use this management style focus on planning and on thinking about the objectives and how better to reach them. They are concerned with innovations in the work process; with the way in which the work of their unit is affecting citizens and with how relationships might be improved; with the future of the unit within the organization; with different patterns of organization and training that might be more effective; with long-range planning; and with the policy issues that seem to be shaping up in the community.

The square in the center of Figure 5—1 represents the possible mixes of the two dimensions of human behavior in working groups. The upward-sloping side of the square on the left represents increasing concern for people and the downward-sloping side on the left represents increasing concern for tasks. Every manager or supervisor has a management style somewhere on this square that represents his typical way of dealing with the work group, even if he also has an ideas, interface, or things style. The lower corner of this square represents a primary, or even an exclusive, concern for tasks. Since management and supervision have been seen as primarily task-oriented ever since the Industrial Revolution, and certainly since the advent of scientific management with Fredrick Winslow Taylor in the early part of this century, it seems appropriate to look next at the task-oriented style.[1]

CONCERN FOR TASKS: THE TASKMASTER

There are many variations of the task-oriented management style. In all of them current production is seen as foremost and all else must take a back seat. Two major subvarieties can be distinguished.

The Master Craftsman. If the supervisor sees his job as basically similar to those of others in the work group the resulting substyle can be called the "master craftsman" style. It is not unusual for lawyers, engineers, accountants, and other professionals to be attracted to this style when they join the ranks of management in their own functional departments. This style allows many interactions with the work group at a quasi-peer level. The master craftsman keeps up in his field and serves as a professional model for his employees. He sets high standards for himself and expects others to do the same.

The Boss. The other major task-oriented substyle is more like the coach than the quarterback. The supervisor is concerned with the work itself and sees his job as that of dividing it up and getting it out. This person does a lot of work planning on a short- and a medium-term basis. He is very good at making work assignments and setting production expectations. Schedules are important to him, as are performance standards. He is seen by his men as a hard-driving taskmaster. He gives task-related orders with practiced ease and does not hesitate to use available controls if performance is not up to snuff.

CONCERN FOR PEOPLE: THE GOOD SHEPHERD

We now come to the other basic dimension of human relations in working groups. This is the concern for people. The importance of people in management is periodically rediscovered. The management theorists Mary Parker Follett and Chester I. Barnard sowed the seeds for the consideration of people in the work process.[2] This orientation then flourished after the famous Hawthorne studies (see Chapter 3), in which a scientific management study of the effect of illumination levels in a wiring room demonstrated that the important variables affecting production were social and interpersonal rather than technological.[3] The extreme human relations style manager is part of that honored tradition.

The human relations style of management emphasizes good relationships with employees and recognizes that people are important. The supervisor using this style knows his people and knows how they feel about different things at any given time. He takes this into account when giving them work. He puts a great deal of time and energy into building a solid relationship with employees. He supervises generally rather than closely and gives a lot of responsibility and recognition. He knows that people who respect you and who know that they are fairly treated and that they are well liked will work their hearts out for you.

The remaining corner of the square, to the right, stands for the point at which both task-orientation and people-orientation are strong and are seen as inextricably linked rather than in potential conflict. The associated integrated style of management will be described after considering the surrounding factors.

The circle surrounding the working group square represents the factors which relate the group to the rest of the organization, to their sources of supply, and to citizens. Styles emphasizing these factors are basically different from the supervisory styles mentioned so far in that they deal with the kinds of support the manager or supervisor gives to the working group rather than with how he behaves within the group. The basic arc underneath the managerial field of vision represents an emphasis on the things that are needed to do the job, i.e., materials, machines, and services that the working group requires as input in order to assemble its particular output.

CONCERN FOR THINGS: THE SUPPLY SERGEANT

This style assumes that the employee knows pretty well what has to be done and that relationships will pretty much take care of themselves as long as the working group has what it needs to get the job done.

The "supply sergeant" provides some structure for the tasks, but the supervisor or administrator practicing this style sees himself as being most effective in providing the best setting possible in which the tasks are done. For example, he provides quiet and privacy for precision operations and think jobs, carpeted and countered areas for meeting the public, good lighting and dry floors in the garage. He likes conference rooms and offices that are appointed so as to set people at their ease, the right equipment on hand, easily accessible and in good working order. He also sees to it that supplies, budgets, and other resources are there when needed.

Shifting to the other arc of the circle we come to the management style that emphasizes the interface between the working group and other parts of the organization or the community.

CONCERN FOR INTERFACES: THE AMBASSADOR

This manager is oriented somewhat more to groups and individuals outside the working group. He strives for good relationships with other departments, individual citizens, and policy boards. He maintains two-way communication between the work group and these outside groups. He fights battles for the work group in the outside environment. At the same time he comes back to the work group with the "Sorry, that's the way it is," messages. He seeks to resolve conflicts between the work group and other groups so that satisfactory progress toward objectives can be maintained.

Now let us return to the remaining extreme point in the managerial field of vision—the spot where everything comes together.

INTEGRATION OF FACTORS:
THE ALL-TOGETHER MANAGER

This composite style might be called an objectives-centered style. The "all-together manager" has learned to shift his focus between thinking and doing and between the technological process and the social system. He assesses the objectives and what needs to be done at any given time to meet them, and places his energies there. He works to build a responsible social system with high competence levels and high trust levels, so that he can also stay confidently involved in the tasks—sometimes doing them, sometimes structuring them, and sometimes influencing task performance from further back. He is sensitive to interface boundaries with other groups and maintains effective ongoing relationships.

Similarly, he keeps in touch with the lay of the land in terms of the supply of goods and services to his working group and sees that these flow as smoothly as possible. In his relationships with the working group he assumes that personal objectives and work objectives can and should be very close together, that any conflicts between task requirements and people requirements can and should be creatively resolved. In general, he believes and demonstrates in his actions that objectives are best achieved by competent and respected people working together with a high degree of joint responsibility for, and "ownership" of, the task.

You may recognize yourself in one or more of these styles. You may also have some opinions about which of these approaches is most realistic and which is best for a particular situation.

There is something of each of these styles in each of us. In some situations we might respond in a taskmaster mode, with very close and detailed supervision of tasks—as, for example, when a new set of budget forms is introduced. In another situation we might respond as a strategic planner, with reflective thought about the tasks, perhaps in anticipation of a visit from the city hall reporter.

Each style has its place and is a good response in its own kind of situation. The strategic planner is a good response when the tasks are fairly well under control. The master craftsman approach is good when the work group is a collection of highly skilled persons, like lawyers or professional engineers, and respect, and therefore the ability to lead, is based in significant measure on demonstrated ability to understand and do the tasks. The working supervisor approach also holds promise in skilled craft task groupings where the master craftsman is accepted as the coach who both teaches and calls the plays. The boss style is often productive where the employees are older, the tasks are routine or highly unstructured, or the need for contact between the supervisor and his employees is slight. The ambassador will produce good results where the task structure is fairly clear and the employees are competent and well motivated. The good shepherd approach is good where communications are critical to the tasks, where employees are reasonably competent, and where the task is neither a highly structured one nor a highly unstructured one.

Selection of a Management Style

Each of us probably has some skill in each of these approaches and will use a particular one when the situation seems to call for it. The point about management style, however, is that for most of us one of these styles has become easier than the others and is the one we use in most work situations regardless of whether it is the "best" style. For us, this may prove more successful than the "best" style, unless we take the sometimes considerable time and effort to become skillful in another approach.

Thus, it is a good idea to know what your management style is, both in general terms and in the way it works in specific situations. You can develop that style, use it more effectively, and seek out situations in which your particular way of doing things will be most successful.

How can you discover what your management style is and begin to work on it? You can, of course, try to evaluate yourself carefully in the light of the categories described above. This is probably the least helpful approach: it is too general, and the temptation to make yourself look good in terms of the style you would like to have is too strong. Also, while this method tells you something about where you are, it gives no indication of where you might want to go. In the absence of anything else, however, it is a good starting point.

A more powerful way of getting at your style is to fill out one of the many available supervisory style, leadership style, or management style inventory questionnaires. The questions can be self-scored. In some cases you can compare your profile with that of a control group of public and business managers and with a theoretical ideal. The questionnaires all ask specific, realistic questions about how you behave in the work situation. You can then decide whether you like what they tell you about yourself, and what you would like to do about it—if anything. Some of these questionnaires are available to anyone who wishes to order them; others can only be used as part of a management training session, where you have the benefit of the interpretation, advice, and counsel of a trainer and of other supervisors or administrators.

The most effective way of dealing with your management style concerns is probably in a training setting, where your own perceptions can be sharpened and checked with peer feedback.

Since each of the instrumented and training approaches to management style is a little bit different, and since none is exactly the same as the six "pure" styles in the managerial field of vision, it is useful to review the major alternatives.

THE MANAGERIAL GRID

Perhaps the best-known alternative approach is that of Robert R. Blake and Jane Mouton.[4] Their Managerial Grid®* divides the working group square into eighty-one potential styles. The grid is built on the same two universal dimensions of human behavior in working groups used in the managerial field of vision. The grid's horizontal axis is concern for production, the vertical, concern for people. Each axis is divided into nine degrees of intensity, thus yielding eighty-one different areas representing different mixes of intensity of concern for production and concern for people.

The grid (Figure 5—2) shows five major management styles. Each grid style is referred to by the identifying set of two numbers, seen on the grid. The five major styles are:

9,1 Produce-or-perish. Results may be achieved through this style for a short time. It motivates people to beat the system and cuts down their contribution to the organization.

1,9 Kid-glove permissiveness. This style produces warmth and good fellowship at the expense of results.

1,1 Neutrality. This style is a "see-no-evil" approach that leads to abdication of responsibility, supervisory bankruptcy, and alienation.

*This term is used with permission of Scientific Methods, Inc.

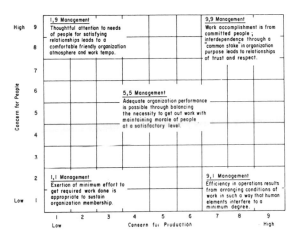

FIGURE 5–2. *The Managerial Grid.*

5,5/Accommodation and compromise. Small gradual progress may be made by this go-along-to-get-along approach, but it is slow and far less than it could be.

9,9/Solution-seeking. High standards are used to achieve rigorous organization goals through involvement, commitment, and the readiness to confront issues needing resolution.[5]

The grid implies a strong preference for the 9,9 style, which in an earlier version was called team management. Correspondingly 1,1 management is seen as bad, and a reading of the descriptions will show that the other three styles are also considered less than perfect. The grid therefore prescribes a clear-cut direction for change independent of the situation in which the manager or supervisor works.[6]

THE TRI-DIMENSIONAL GRID

W. J. Reddin developed a typology of styles which he calls the "Tri-Dimensional Grid." This has the familiar dimensions of concern for people and concern for production along with an additional dimension labeled "effectiveness."

From this framework he comes up with eight styles.[7] These styles are described as follows:

Deserter (Ineffective Deserter): One who often displays his lack of interest in both task and relationships. He is ineffective not only because of his lack of interest but also because of his effect on morale. He may not only desert but may also hinder the performance of others through intervention or by withholding information.

Missionary (Ineffective Relationships) [ineffective concern for people]: One who puts harmony and relationships above other considerations. He is ineffective because his desire to see himself and be seen as a "good person" prevents him from risking a disruption of relationships in order to get production.

Autocrat (Ineffective Task) [ineffective concern for tasks]: One who puts the immediate task before all other considerations. He is ineffective in that he makes it obvious that he has no concern for relationships and has little confidence in others. While many may fear him they also dislike him and are thus only motivated to work when he applies direct pressure.

Compromiser (Ineffective Task and Relationships) [ineffective integration of factors]: One who recognizes the advantages of being oriented to both task and relationships but who is incapable or unwilling to make sound decisions. Ambivalence and compromise are his stock-in-trade. The strongest influence in his decision making is the most recent or heaviest pressure. He tries to minimize immediate problems rather than maximize long term production. He attempts to keep those people who can influence his career as happy as possible.

Bureaucrat (Effective though a Deserter): One who is not really interested in either task or relationships but who by simply following the rules does not make this too obvious and thus does not let it affect morale. He is effective in that he follows procedures and maintains a mask of interest.

Developer (Effective Relationships) [effective concern for people]: One who places implicit trust in people. He sees his job as primarily concerned with developing the talents of others and providing a good atmosphere conducive to maximizing individual satisfaction and motivation. He is effective in that the work environment he creates is conducive to his subordinates' developing commitment to both himself and the job. While successful in obtaining high production, his high "relationships" value orientation would on occasions lead him to put the personal development of others before short or long run production even though this personal development may be unrelated to the job and the development of successors to his position.

Benevolent Autocrat (Effective Task) [effective concern for tasks]: One who places implicit trust in himself and is concerned with both the immediate and long run task. He is effective in that he has a skill in forcing others to do what he wants them to do without creating enough resentment so that production might drop. He creates with some skill an environment which minimizes aggression toward him and which maximizes obedience to his commands.

Executive (Effective Task and Relationships) [effective integration of factors]: One who sees his job as effectively maximizing the effort of others in relationship to the short and long run task. He sets high standards for production and performance and recognizes that because of individual differences and expectations he will have to treat everyone differently. He is effective in that his commitment to both task and relationships is evident to all and this acts as a powerful motivator. His effectiveness in obtaining results with both of these dimensions also leads naturally to optimum production.[8]

In Figure 5—3, the Tri-Grid makes a cube of the working group square. It does not assert that one style is universally more desirable than others but rather contends that the appropriate style depends on the situation and that each point on the square can be used well or poorly, thus the third dimension. Reddin finds that in fact styles of the same manager change in different jobs and that organizations with particular kinds of missions have discernible characteristic style profiles.[9]

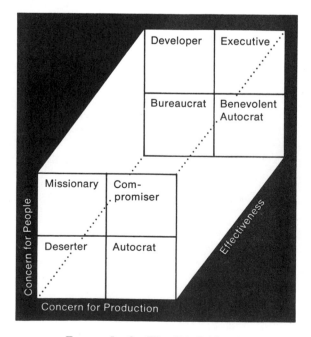

FIGURE 5—3. *The Tri-Grid cube.*

EMOTIONAL STYLES OF MANAGEMENT

Richard Wallen developed one of the earlier and still useful typologies of managerial style.[10] He based his classification on how people deal with emotions rather than on categorical relationships of people to tasks. Wallen followed Karen Horney's theory that emotions may be accepted freely and be fully expressed, or they may be rejected, denied, or disguised. When emotions are separated into the "tender" emotions of love, affection, sympathy, comforting, assisting, etc., and the "tough" emotions of aggression, self-assertion, controlling, pushing, fighting, etc., three emotional styles of management emerge. These can be characterized by the "tough battler," the "friendly helper," and the "objective thinker." The characteristics and some of the consequences of these styles are shown in Figure 5—4.

While they are not exact matches, these emotional styles are frequently associated with three extreme points on the managerial field of vision. The "strategic planner" may well be an "objective thinker," the "taskmaster" may well be a "tough battler," and the "good shepherd" is often a "friendly helper."

THE NELSON LEADERSHIP SCALE

The leadership scale developed by Charles W. Nelson of the University of Chicago Industrial Relations Center is slightly different from the approaches to management style we have discussed up to this point. It is concerned, in effect, with four different techniques of supervisory behavior rather than with one's orientation along the two classic dimensions of human behavior in working groups. It is clear both conceptually and on the basis of the scores that many city officials have produced on the Industrial Relations Center questionnaire that an individual's management style is a mix of two or more of these "leadership approaches" rather than an exclusive use or heavily predominant use of one. The Nelson leadership patterns and approaches are:

1. *A Style—Rule Centered.* This style assumes that the guts of the organization are rules and procedures and the way to influence and control work, workers, and therefore output is through making and applying appropriate

Emotions and characteristics	Tough battler	Friendly helper	Objective thinker
Emotions	Accepts aggression, rejects affection	Accepts affection, rejects aggression	Rejects affection and aggression
Goal	Dominance	Acceptance	Correctness
Judges others by	Strength, power Who is winning? Who is losing?	Warmth Who likes others? Who hurts?	Cognitive ability Who is correct? Who is incorrect?
Influences others by	Direction, intimidation, control of rewards	Offering understanding, praise, favors, friendship	Factual data, logical arguments
Value in organization	Initiates, demands, disciplines	Supports, harmonizes, relieves tension	Defines, clarifies, gets information, criticizes, tests
Fears	Being "soft" or dependent	Desertion, conflict	Emotions, irrational acts
Needs to gain	Warmth, consideration, objectivity, humility	Strength, integrity, firmness, self-assertion	Awareness of feelings, ability to love and to fight
May bring about these characteristics of organization climate	High structure, suspicion, functional dependence on manager, aggressiveness	Low structure, laxness, emotional dependence on manager, sociability	Low organizational involvement, feelings bottled up, efficiency

FIGURE 5—4. *Emotional styles of management.*

rules and procedures. The person using this style believes he should primarily depend upon top management for guidance and support. His contact with employees tends to be somewhat formal and impersonal. Communication is frequently routine and regulative in character, often by memo. He tends to avoid personal relationships with employees that may weaken his official status or make him less objective and impartial.

2. *B Style—Technology Centered.* This style assumes that what counts is the technology of work and that everything else will fall into place around that. The way to control output is to have the best technological process going. The B Style manager or supervisor believes he should depend primarily upon his own technical knowledge and personal capacity for getting the work done. He sees his job as one to modify, improve and reinterpret top management programs to fit his own and departmental needs. He is more concerned with personal status than with official status and he tries to make himself felt and respected by the work group through his technical

knowledge and ability to give specific directions. His contact with employees is usually directive and work centered; his emphasis is primarily on technical controls and procedures; his communication tends to be of a one-way bossman relationship.

3. *C Style—Individual Centered.* This style asserts that it is individuals who do the work and therefore you should be spending your time working with individuals to get each to produce his maximum in his own way. The supervisor works in the social process of the organization and he controls output by knowing everybody well and keeping them motivated as individuals. The C Style manager or supervisor believes he should depend primarily upon his understanding and handling of the individual to get the work done. He sees his job as one of administering the organization's policy and regulations in a flexible manner, adapting them to the needs of each individual employee and stimulating him to carry out the programs to the best of his ability. He emphasizes human relations skills and seeks to understand individual interests,

needs, and abilities, and to motivate and develop the individual. His contact relationships are informal and may be somewhat manipulative. Communication has the tendency to be two-way within the individual man-boss relationship.

4. *D Style—Group Centered.* This style focuses on group processes. It assumes that work is the product of cooperating work groups. If you know how to handle what is going on in the group and can direct the forces of the work group onto the objectives, then you have the handle on control of output. The D Style leader tries to weld employees into a cooperative team whose goals, standards of work, and codes of behavior serve to guide individual employees. He maintains close and informal relationships with employees separately or in groups and tries to create a democratic work atmosphere. In communicating with individuals, he tends to have a three-way relationship: not only between man and boss, but also between employee and employee for sharing ideas, information, and group responsibilities.[11]

Like the emotional styles of management, the Nelson scale does not exactly correspond with the "pure" styles in the managerial field of vision, but a force fit is possible. The A Style corresponds more or less to the Tri-Grid bureaucrat, which in turn corresponds to the Managerial Grid 1/1, which fits into the figure at the same point as the "strategic planner." A strategic planner and an A Style leader are clearly not necessarily the same thing. What they have in common is a low involvement in the ongoing tasks of the organization and a low involvement with people in the work group.

In the Nelson scale, the B Style of leadership corresponds relatively well to the taskmaster style. The C Style and the D Style could both be located at the good shepherd extreme point, or possibly a little way along the axis toward the integrated style.[12]

The characterizations in each of the foregoing groupings of management styles are not exhaustive, they are simply suggestive of possible patterns. If on a questionnaire or in a training session you find your style located at a particular place on the figure, it is up to you to assess, hopefully with the help of your colleagues' perceptions, whether it means you are like the characterization or not and what that means in your particular organization.

To sum up the discussion of management style, the ways in which you typically behave in the organization and in the work group have discoverable effects on others in the work group and on their and your efficiency and effectiveness. It is wise to be aware of what it is that you typically do and what impact that has in your situation. Considerations of management style and management style training can give you increased skill in the use of yourself to achieve the outcomes you want.

Listening and the Helping Relationship

Forty percent or more of the time of most managers and supervisors is spent in listening to other people. As the level of responsibility increases, the proportion of time spent in listening also increases. This is true because the job of supervision and management involves collecting and using accurate information about the work and about the social process through which the work is being done (or not being done). Thus, listening is a universal and important skill of management and supervision.

Listening is much more than simply hearing words. Listening is a learned skill. As such, one's listening ability can be improved by paying attention to some basic characteristics of the listening process and through practice, evaluation, and more practice. In school much time is spent in teaching the presentation side of the communications process. We have all spent hours struggling through English classes learning how to write so that we can be understood. Public speaking, debate, and other forms of oral communication are offered to the interested student.

Most of us were not fortunate enough, however, to have formal training in listening. It has simply been up to us to get the message in whatever way we could. We have learned to listen primarily by imitation and through untutored experience. This suggests that the listening skill is for many people a high payoff area for self-improvement.

Listening is a high-speed activity. According to the research of Ralph Nichols, most Americans speak at approximately 140 words per minute, but they are able to hear and comprehend words at a rate of from 400 to 500 words per minute.[13] This difference between speaking and hearing is both a great advantage and a great disadvantage. Much of the quality and effectiveness of listening depends on the use that is made of the "free time" left over after hearing the spoken words. If that free time is used to drift, to daydream, to consider other pressing matters, there is a great danger that we will drift away from the thread of the discussion and lose our opportunity to gather useful information from what is being said. A particularly unfortunate habit is letting these other matters actually encroach on the "speaking time" of the other person (as well as on the "free time"). We then attempt to monitor the speaker, tuning in from time to time to see what he is saying. Soon the thread is lost entirely. We cover our indiscretion by making some assumptions about what was said and move out of the realm of information into the realm of fantasy. In face-to-face conversations, when one is drifting or monitoring this usually becomes clear to the speaker. It often leaves the speaker with the feeling that the listener does not care about him or does not believe that what he has to say is of any importance.

There are productive ways of using the free time which will improve the listening process. You can listen for key words and for patterns in the thought of the speaker. You can think about the implications and consequences of what the speaker is saying, and in this way be able to anticipate the issues and concerns that are being brought to you. Finally, free time in listening may be used to look for meanings that are conveyed in things other than words. This is what Theodor Reik has called "listening with the third ear." The context in which things are said is often important. Who is speaking? At what time? What is his relationship to you? What has occurred just before or what is expected to occur in the near future? Ideas and feelings may be communicated through the eyes and the posture of the other person.

If either party to a conversation is "turned off" before the communication has accomplished its purpose, then the interchange must be rated a failure. As a party to any communication you have the responsibility to keep the channel of communication open. For a manager this is a special responsibility.

INTERVIEWING

Frequently, supervisors use the more formal communication process of an interview. The interview is generally understood to be a two-person communication with fairly specific and limited communication goals. Whether they are selection interviews, job performance evaluations, or interviews seeking information related to some aspect of the job itself, most interviews have a number of elements in common. The time for an interview is limited, and a certain specified communication must take place within this time. The goals of an interview are limited to specific purposes which are more or less well understood by both parties. Rapport, or the feeling of legitimacy, trust, and good intentions, must be established between the interviewer and the interviewee for accurate communication to take place.

An interview is a planned conversation in which the interviewer must give thought in advance to what he wants to know and what questions he needs to ask. At the very least there should be a checklist of key areas to be covered in the interview. In scientific interviewing it is not unusual to have each question very carefully worded and pretested to guarantee that each person responding will be responding to the same thing and that the question measures precisely what the interviewer wants it to measure. In management it is rarely necessary to go to such lengths of refinement. However, one should be aware of the danger of bias from the wording of questions. For example, in a well-known study of turnover in city manager positions the interviewers asked if the manager had left his last city because of conflict with the city council, conflict with the department heads, conflict with community groups, or some other reason. Not unsurprisingly they concluded that most city managers had left their last positions because of conflict!

It is very easy in interviewing to fall into the trap of the "When did you stop beating your wife?" type of question. This is especially true if the interviewer thinks he already knows the cause or the solution being sought. In this case, the interview moves from truth-seeking to pressing for a confession.

The interview is a tool to help determine facts about work and work behavior which can be used by the manager or supervisor and by the employees or citizens or councilmen to do the job a little bit better. A fact is a descriptive statement about a situation which can be publicly verified. It can be checked with other observers using similar and different means of observing. Facts need to be separated from unchecked assumptions. Experienced managers or supervisors need to be especially sensitive to the danger of acting on unchecked assumptions. When the pressure to do the job is high, it is easy to assume that you really know what the problem is and to act on assumptions. Because of the authority you carry in the organization, and because of your apparent confidence in what you say, others in the organization are not likely to volunteer any corrections or different perceptions of what the facts are—even if they know them to be different. Developing the skills of interviewing will help you to base your actions on facts.

PROBLEM SOLVING WITH PEOPLE

Whenever an interview or other conversation goes beyond the exchange of information and moves into problem solving it becomes a helping relationship. Helping relationships occur when two or more people tackle a problem (technical or social) that one person (or all of them) cannot solve alone. In the typical helping relationship one person has responsibility for something and has resources to bring to bear, but has not yet been able to figure out just what the situation is and what is the best thing to do; the other person has some knowledge or experience about the situation, some reason for being concerned, and some problem-solving skill.

You can be effective in the helping relationship by listening, clarifying the objectives, searching for the criteria which will determine whether the objectives are met, and sharing your experience. This also helps test your understanding of the situation—and the other party's. Later, you can advise on directions that might be followed.

The order in which these processes are followed is important. In an effective relationship the manager's or supervisor's verbal behavior should begin with encouraging statements interspersed with a lot of listening time. It should then move to attempts to restate the problem as presented by the other person, then to attempts to clarify the nature of the problem; then it should proceed to statements about the manager's or supervisor's own experience in similar situations. Only after these kinds of interactions have taken place should recommendations be made.

Effective problem solving takes place where there is a climate of trust, in the sense of respect both for each other's competence and ability to handle the problem and for each other's honesty and good faith. A high degree of openness in communication is also important, so that the problem will not be distorted and will be presented in all its important dimensions, including emotional overtones. Trust and openness of communication make possible a relatively high degree of risk taking on the part of both parties, as well as a high degree of responsibility for one's own ideas, feelings, and actions.

It is not easy to give this kind of help to another person. Similarly, it is not easy to receive it. The National Training Laboratories Institute of Applied Behavioral Sciences identifies some of the difficulties in receiving and giving help. Difficulties in *receiving* help are listed as follows:

1. It is hard to really admit our difficulties even to ourselves. It may be even harder to admit them to someone else. There are concerns sometimes whether we can really trust the other person, particularly if it is in a work or other situation which might affect our standing. We may also be afraid of what the other person thinks of us.
2. We may have struggled so hard to make ourselves independent persons that the thought of depending on another individual seems to violate something within us. Or we may all our lives have looked for someone on whom to be dependent and we try to repeat this pattern in our relationship with the helping person.
3. We may be looking for sympathy and support rather

than for help in seeing our difficulty more clearly. We ourselves may have to change as well as others in the situation. When the helper tries to point out some of the ways we are contributing to the problem, we may stop listening. Solving a problem may mean uncovering some of the sides of ourselves which we have avoided or wished to avoid thinking about.

4. We may feel our problem is so unique no one could ever understand it and certainly not an outsider.

Difficulties in *giving* help are enumerated as follows:

1. Most of us like to give advice. Doing so suggests to us that we are competent and important. We easily get caught in a telling role without testing whether our advice is appropriate to the abilities, the fears, or the powers of the person we are trying to help.
2. If the person we are trying to help becomes defensive we may try to argue or pressure him—meet resistance with more pressure and increase resistance. This is typical in argument.
3. We may confuse the relationship by only responding to one aspect of what we see in the other's problem, by over-praising, avoiding recognition that the person being counseled must see his own role and his own limitations as well.[14]

One of a manager's or supervisor's tasks is teaching people how to ask for and to receive help. A climate of supportiveness and trust coupled with a hard-nosed, problem-solving orientation is part of the answer. A place with many problems constantly being solved should be valued more than a place where all is smooth to the boss and outsiders because problems are not admitted. Another part of the answer lies in the model that you set as the manager or supervisor. If you are able to ask others for constructive help in problem solving, they may well see and learn from you.

In helping other people honesty is still the best policy. People don't fool very easily, especially in a situation of some sensitivity. In the words of Carl Rogers, we should strive for congruence between our feelings and our actions, between our thoughts and our words.

As with listening, the helping relationship is a skill which can be learned only through practice and which can be improved through conscious effort. An exercise that is frequently used is one in which three persons take turns helping to solve each other's problems. In each round one person presents a problem. A second person attempts to provide help and advice, and the third person observes this process and offers a critique after about fifteen minutes of problem-solving time. Learning about helping skills can be further enhanced by the use of video and audio tape.

Certain types of statements are particularly useful in listening, interviewing, and helping others. Some of these are illustrated in the tables on listening and questioning techniques in Chapter 9.

The Use of Time

A final way of checking how you use yourself is to look at your scarcest and most valuable resource—your time. Your personal time is nonrenewable but always available at a constant rate.

Many unavoidable demands are made on your work time, and even on your personal time. According to Leo B. Moore, managers asked to list the impediments to effective use of time will invariably include the telephone, reports, visitors, dealing with subordinates on delegated responsibilities, procrastination, fire fighting, special requests from bosses or clients, delays caused by others, and required reading. The items will not necessarily come up in this order, but they appear to be universal pressures.[15]

One way to deal with these pressures is to give up, to declare the situation hopeless, to say that since you don't control these pressures completely you have no responsibility except to react. The usual consequence of this approach is that creative and developmental work and the maintenance of relationships get driven out by fire fighting and routine work.

A second alternative is to strike out at the load, disown and don't do the things you find distasteful whenever you can get away with it, and protect yourself from intrusion by cutting down the interactions you have with others by erecting a wall of formality and distance around your job. In this way a little bit more of the creative, nonprogrammed work gets done at the expense of disengagement from the work and the people doing it.

Is there a way out? Perhaps you have a creative third alternative, which meets legitimate demands on your time, gives you a measure of control over your time, and avoids most of the unhappy consequences of the other time-control methods. This alternative is essentially to take a problem-solving approach to the use of time.

First, find out what you enjoy and do best. Find out what conditions you do it under. Where, when, and how do you think best? Do you do your thinking alone in your office, in the library, walking in the halls, outside, driving around the city, or interacting with another individual or group? How do you best interact with the public—on the phone, individually, in groups? When are you most productive and satisfied in communicating with the people you work with—face-to-face, in meetings, on the intercom, by memo, in your territory, or in theirs? What are the conditions under which you are most effective in work planning, writing reports, etc.?

Second, find out what you do with your time. You cannot rely on assumptions and memory. There is probably no area in which we lie to ourselves more convincingly. To find out what you do with your time, keep a record for a week or so. Record what you do in half-hour units, or have someone do this for you. Do it in real time rather than from memory at the end of the day.

Third, review the list. Identify the clearly nonessential things and make a mental note to avoid them in the future. Look over the things you *have* to do and see if there are any that can be regrouped for efficiency or are a prime target for a little problem solving to simplify. Then, do so.

Fourth, plan your time. That is the only way to economize on a scarce resource. Detailed planning of time is not rational for managers or supervisors. A fifteen-minute by fifteen-minute schedule is impossible to follow—and would have unfortunate effects on the work. Do your planning in hour to two-hour or even half-day blocks. Instead of detailing what you will do in the blocks of time, make a back-of-the-envelope priority listing of a few things to do each day and revise your list at the end of the day. Two kinds of time blocks should be protected especially strongly: do-not-disturb times for non-programmed problem solving and work planning, and "maintenance" time for working on the norms, relationships, and informal operating procedures of the work groups. Also, if there are decisions on personnel coming up be sure to block reflective time for these, for these are decisions that no successful executive makes quickly.

Finally, after three or four months do a periodic check on how your time is being used. Compare this with your plan, and go through the cycle again.

---

[1]Fredrick Winslow Taylor, THE PRINCIPLES OF SCIENTIFIC MANAGEMENT (New York: Harper & Brothers, Publishers, 1915).

[2]Henry C. Metcalf and Lyndall Urwick, DYNAMIC ADMINISTRATION: THE COLLECTED PAPERS OF MARY PARKER FOLLETT (New York: Harper & Brothers, Publishers, 1942); Elliot M. Fox, "Mary Parker Follett: The Enduring Contribution," PUBLIC ADMINISTRATION REVIEW 34 (November—December 1968): 520—29; Chester I. Barnard, THE FUNCTIONS OF THE EXECUTIVE, 30th anniversary ed. (Cambridge, Mass.: Harvard University Press, 1968).

[3]F. J. Roethlisberger and William J. Dickson, MANAGEMENT AND THE WORKER (Cambridge, Mass.: Harvard University Press, 1939).

[4]Robert R. Blake and Jane Srygley Mouton, THE MANAGERIAL GRID® (Houston, Tex.: Gulf Publishing Company, 1964).

[5]Courtesy of Scientific Methods, Inc., Austin, Texas. From their GRID brochure.

[6]Grid Seminars are offered by Scientific Methods, Inc., P.O. Box 195, Austin, Texas 78767. A well-tested questionnaire based on the Managerial Grid, the Styles of Management Inventory, is also available through Telemetrics, Inc., 2210 North Frazier, Conroe, Texas 77301.

[7]See: W. J. Reddin, "The Tri-Dimensional Grid," CANADIAN PERSONNEL AND INDUSTRIAL RELATIONS JOURNAL 13 (January 1966); and W. J. Reddin, "The Tri-Dimensional Grid—For Integration of Management Style Theories," TRAINING DIRECTORS JOURNAL 18 (July 1964).

[8]Reddin, "The Tri-Dimensional Grid," TRAINING DIRECTORS JOURNAL: 9—18.

[9]W. J. Reddin, TEST INTERPRETATION MANUAL: MANAGEMENT STYLE DIAGNOSIS TEST (Fredericton, N.B., Canada: Managerial Effectiveness Ltd., 1965). A Management Style Diagnosis Test based on the Tri-Grid is available from Managerial Effectiveness Ltd., Box 1012, Fredericton, N.B., Canada.

[10]Richard W. Wallen, "The Three Types of Executive Personality," DUN'S REVIEW, February 1963 [Dun and Bradstreet Publications]. Reprinted in William B. Eddy, W. Warner Burke, Vladimir A. Dupre, and Oron South, BEHAVIORAL SCIENCE AND THE MANAGER'S ROLE (Washington, D.C.: National Training Laboratories Institute for Applied Behavioral

Science, 1969), pp. 78—84. Other versions also appear in uncredited mimeographed training materials.

[11]Charles W. Nelson, THE LEADERSHIP INVENTORY ANALYZER (Chicago: Industrial Relations Center, University of Chicago, 1956; rev. ed. 1965), pp. 6—7.

[12]The Leadership Inventory that scores A, B, C, and D Styles is available from the Industrial Relations Center, University of Chicago, 1225 East 60th Street, Chicago, Illinois 60637.

[13]Ralph G. Nichols and Leonard A. Stevens, ARE YOU LISTENING? (New York: McGraw-Hill Book Company, 1957).

[14]The two quotations are from pages 45 and 46 in the article "Feedback and the Helping Relationship," taken from the 1968 SUMMER READING BOOK of the National Training Laboratories Institute of Applied Behavioral Science, associated with the National Education Association (Washington, D.C.: National Training Laboratories, 1968). The papers were originally prepared for theory sessions at the institute's laboratories.

[15]Leo B. Moore, "Managerial Time," INDUSTRIAL MANAGEMENT REVIEW 9 (Spring 1968): 77—86.

6

Influencing Employee Behavior

Iₙ ᴍᴏsᴛ ʙᴏᴏᴋs this chapter would be titled "Motivation." When we speak of motivation, it is usually done in the following manner: "How do I motivate Betty to come to work on time?" "How do I motivate that (blankety-blank) Bill to work harder?" These and similar questions represent one of the most significant problems a manager has to face.

Why people act (or don't act) in a certain manner has been a source of investigation by behavioral scientists for many years. Freud's pioneering work on human motivation resulted in a splurge of research in the area. Before that it had been a fruitful subject for philosophers to ponder.

The Elements of Motivation

Part of the difficulty in dealing with the topic of motivation arises from a lack of common agreement as to what the term means. For this reason, some distinctions need to be made. Motivation refers to an internal state of a person. What we observe in an individual's behavior are external manifestations of this internal condition. A person *feels* hungry: we don't see hunger, but we do see the person seeking and eating food and *infer* from this activity that the hunger motive is responsible for his actions.

Behavioral scientists do not really know what comprises motivation. We know that there is both biology and psychology involved, but we cannot dig into the human brain and point to a physical locus of motivation. The heart pumps blood and the stomach digests food. We can

locate these organs and understand how they function. But we have not reached the same level of sophistication with the concept of motivation.

At this stage in our knowledge, we must call motivation a *hypothetical construct.* This is a label we attach to a process which we cannot really see but assume exists and can be used to explain something else. We thus use motivation as a means for explaining the behavior we observe.

Tнᴇ Bɪᴏʟᴏɢɪᴄᴀʟ Bᴀsɪs ᴏғ Mᴏᴛɪᴠᴀᴛɪᴏɴ

Although we face some unique problems in that we cannot refer to motivation as a "thing" in the same sense that we can call a heart an entity, motivation research has provided insights which treat the question, "Is motivation biologically based, psychologically based, or both?" It is strongly suspected that much human motivation is derived from man's biology and then tremendously complicated by his mind. Certain drives—hunger, thirst, the need for sleep and rest, seem to be obviously biological. Yet psychology has a powerful influence on even these apparently simple states. Why does one person prefer steak while another selects chicken? Surely our hunger drive is not responsible for this choice, even though it may produce the need for some sort of food.

The complexity increases as we leave the level of biological drives and move toward the more "human" qualities, such as the desire to learn, the need to achieve, the desire to maintain ethical standards, and the like. We are inclined to attribute these states and the consequent behaviors which they produce more to psychology than to biology, even though there is probably less truth to this notion than we commonly assume.

Every species of animal has some unique specialization which enables it to exist in its own particular world. Birds fly, fish ·swim, and giraffes can reach tall leaves. What is man's specialization? His uniqueness is that he is specialized in the unspecialized. His outstanding attribute is not something as simple as wings, gills, or a long neck; rather, it is the complex quality of his mind. Man is a thinking machine. He can do few of the things other animals do on a natural basis, but his mind enables him to do all they can do and much more, because he is capable of thinking up substitutes. Men fly in aircraft, swim in diving gear, and reach tall leaves with ladders.

The mind of man, that is, the brain of man, is biological matter. Whatever is produced by this organ by definition has a biological basis. Man is built to think; that is his only special skill. He cannot help but think. And from thought spring the behaviors which we label distinctly human. It may be alluring to relegate biologically based urges to lower animals and reserve psychology for people, but it is both inaccurate and unnecessary to do so. That man is a biological organism at heart does not lessen his value or complexity.

NOBODY IS "NOT MOTIVATED"

Let's examine the statement "Bill isn't motivated." This assertion is incorrect because the only unmotivated person is a dead one. Everyone behaves, and everyone has a reason for behaving. Translate the statement to a question: "What is Bill motivated to do? He obviously isn't inclined to do what I want him to do, so what is on his mind?" Reconsider our original question "How do I motivate Betty to come to work on time?" These are two questions which represent the same basic problem. The motivation and consequent behavior of Bill and Betty are different from what we, as managers, want or expect. It is not that they lack motivation. It is not that they are not behaving. What bothers us is that they are not behaving as we wish them to behave. They are behaving as *they* wish to behave, and they are motivated to do so. Bill and Betty are motivated to act in a way which is contrary to the desires of their boss.

INFLUENCING INSTEAD OF MOTIVATING

Can we influence how Bill and Betty act? Unfortunately, since motivation is an internal state of a person, we as outsiders cannot supply it. We cannot give an injection of achievement or a pound of punctuality. This motivation, this desire, must come from within the person. If you have just eaten and are full, food can be waved in your face and you will feel no desire to eat. So it is with other motives. If it does not exist within, it will not manifest itself without.

We cannot motivate Bill and Betty—that is, we cannot create a biological or psychological desire within them; but we can influence their behavior by working on existing desires, whether they be overt and expressed or hidden and subtle. This is a very critical point. A manager cannot supply motivation but he can structure the situation—he can manage the environment in such a way as to draw forth or elicit the type of motivated behavior he wishes to see in his subordinates. Seen from this point of view, people who "motivate" others are not magicians: they are sophisticated technicians. This skill should not be demeaned by this label. The art of influencing people is very complicated. What you say or do, the way you say it or do it, the gestures which accompany your words or actions, what led up to it, what may result from it, and a host of other variables influence the total outcome. The manager who is effective at influencing his subordinates is a very acute, sensitive individual.

THE STATE OF THE ART

As was mentioned earlier, the research into human motivation has been considerable. Investigation of human motivation in organizations, a subpart of the field, has been vast.

Motivation research can be divided into two components: (1) the gathering of empirical (factual) data about motivational phenomena; and (2) the development of theories or explanatory systems which can be used to relate and interpret the empirical data.

In general, attempts at theory construction have resulted in the production of applied techniques which have been offered to organizations in an attempt to aid them in influencing the behavior of their employees. One of the purposes of this chapter is to present and discuss some of these efforts. More importantly, this chapter attempts to clarify the relationship between these supposedly diverse approaches, in order to provide the manager with an understanding of the basic ingredients for influencing behavior.

By way of accomplishing this, you should ask yourself, "Am I as a manager more interested in why people do things (motivation), or in what they do or don't do (behavior)?" When you get down to the nitty-gritty, the only reasons you care about motivation are that you are curious or that you feel an understanding of motivation may provide you with a means for affecting behavior.

WARNINGS

There are several pitfalls that you should be aware of. One is that managements are fad-conscious. They like to jump on bandwagons. Over the years many different schemes have been initiated with enthusiasm; in some instances they have proven successful, but in many cases they have failed. If one reviews the history of management practices it is clear that the "hula-hoop" comes and goes. Is there no panacea? Not yet. When evaluating ways and means it is not wise to look for grand schemes that save the world. It takes a lot of little details to compose a successful management program, and no one plan covers everything.

A second warning must be directed toward the application of management practices. Often an idea is theoretically sound and can be executed successfully, but management ruins its application because it undertakes the program with superficial understanding or limited dedication. Management should take a tip from the aircraft industry, which insists on constant awareness and refuses to depend on habit when it comes to flying. No matter how many times a pilot has flown, he reviews a checklist upon taking off and landing. These are the most critical points in flight and are not left to chance. If managers would exercise just half this amount of concern, if they would accept what they do with a questioning attitude and an eye toward improvement, many failures would be turned into successes. While it is simple for the manager to blame a failure on the program or the consultant who started it, he should always ask himself if the fault was inherent in the idea or if it lay in his lack of understanding or of persistence in bringing the plan to fruition. Dealing with people demands insight and hard work: the quality of an approach will not substitute for these ingredients.

A third admonition is in order. In the world of management, one often hears or reads formalized statements of institutional insincerity dealing with the treatment of employees. Some samples are: "Make the employee *feel* that he is important," and, "Make your subordinate *feel* that he is participating."

This is no good. People want to *be* important and they want to *actually* participate. No matter what management strategy you employ, if you enter it with the idea that you are directing a play instead of dealing in real life with actual people, it is bound to fail.

Finally, many managements suffer from an incredible lack of insight, foresight, and long-range planning. They pride themselves in being competent with regard to product knowledge, but even here they fail many times. Often product or service research and development is ten years behind the times when it should be five years ahead of them.

When it comes to the treatment of employees, the situation is a thousand times worse. Can you answer the following questions?

1. Remember that last training seminar you sent a subordinate to? How much did he learn that was useful to his current job? How much "profit" will he now contribute to the organization?
2. How much, in dollars, do each of the following cost your organization per month: turnover, absenteeism, tardiness, illness, accidents, and work restrictions?
3. When an employee is not doing what he "should" be doing, can you quickly pinpoint whether it is owing to his performance, to his lack of knowledge, or to some personal problem?
4. What are the numbers and types of employees you will need on your work force five years from today?

If you cannot answer these questions correctly and in some detail, there is something wrong. But take heart, you have some of the largest organizations in the world to keep you company.

Influencing Employees: Theories and Applications

In this section six major approaches to influencing employees are presented. While the list is by no means exhaustive, hopefully it is representative of the types or categories of effort which have been directed at accomplishing this end.

Each category will involve a description of the approach and its method of application. Only minimal attention will be paid to evaluating the ideas in terms of logic or research findings. In part, this is because the data for most of the programs reflect a fifty-fifty proposition. Half the time an approach works, half the time it does not.

The second reason is that each approach has strong points, weak points, and areas of similarity. In the third section of this chapter, an attempt has been made to cut across all of the schemes and point out their common elements in order to present a method which encompasses the strengths of each.

The systems are not presented in order of chronological development or importance. Some of the approaches, or very close approximations, are discussed in greater detail in other chapters of this book.

ACTUALIZATION OR GROWTH THEORIES

Several major theories in psychology encompass, in whole or in part, elements of the self-actualization concept. The theory to be considered under this heading, Maslow's need hierarchy,[1] is one of the best known (see Chapter 3). Two other popular theories, White's competence motive[2] and McClelland's achievement motive,[3] could also be included in this category but will not be discussed.

Theory. It is very difficult to find a management seminar or text dealing with the topic of motivation in which Maslow's need hierarchy is not presented. Figure 6—1 illustrates the manner in which Maslow envisions the relationship between various levels of human needs.

Maslow maintains that human needs can be classified and ranked in a hierarchy. The most basic needs are *physiological* (hunger, thirst, sleep), next comes *safety* (protection from assault, security needs such as life and health insurance), then *belongingness and love* needs (desiring to give and receive love, to have friends), *esteem* needs (prestige, status, feelings of personal worth), and, finally, the highest level, the need for *self-actualization* (fulfilling whatever inherent potential a person possesses, extreme self-development).

One must satisfy the lower level needs before progressing upward. If an individual were in a constant state of semistarvation, he would have neither the resources nor the desire to be concerned with life insurance, having a home in a secure neighborhood, or other safety level factors.

After someone has satisfied a particular level and progressed to the next higher level, there may be a temporary return to a lower level on occasion. For example, you may be at the esteem level. You have an argument with your best friend (belongingness and love needs), you revert

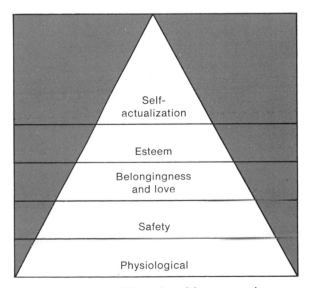

FIGURE 6—1. *Hierarchy of human needs.*

to that level and work on the difficulty until it is remedied and then you return to the esteem level. You are not trapped and functioning at the lower level. You have gone beyond it, and the higher order need is characteristic of your current life-style.

Application. Having presented this framework, the instructor of the typical management development seminar is very quickly asked by one of the participants, "Great, but how do I apply it?" The answer is often unsatisfactory.

Self-actualization is the highest level of need attainment. In this state, the person is as close to being healthy, wealthy, and wise as he is ever going to be. Productivity and creativity are greatest at this stage, and every manager will be so effective that he will have to kick his subordinates in the face (instead of the butt) just to slow them down. Don't worry too much about this frightening state of affairs. Maslow and other self-actualization theorists are not very optimistic. Very few people ever reach this level. Most of us barely make it to the esteem level and at best are just knocking at the door of the highest level.

But your management seminar instructor does let you in on one secret. Your organization, he says, must begin at the lowest level and successfully fulfill each class of needs for your employees. First give them plenty of compensation. This will enable them to have food, housing, insurance, and the like. So much for the two lowest levels.

Next, make sure that the human relations situation is top notch (love and belonging). Do things to make them feel important and worthwhile (esteem). After that, they will be free to self-actualize. At this point, all that you as a manager need to do is to encourage their forward progress and pave the way.

If this sounds like everyone must have everything before they can attain the highest state, your understanding is accurate. You have a good head start on the problem. After many years of union activity and some management enlightenment, the status of wages, working conditions, benefits and other safety and physiological level factors is actually quite good. Remember that your grandfather may have put in sixteen-hour days six days a week working in a coal mine with no safety devices for a few cents a day when he was ten years old. While we are prone to say things are bad today, they were truly much worse then.

Modern employees, then, are fairly well off at the two lowest levels. We, as managers, can draw on extensive experience to help provide belongingness and love, and manage the organization to facilitate employee esteem and self-respect. Then we are ready to contend with self-actualization.

Even if you find that satisfying lower level needs is relatively easy, you will find that an attack on self-actualization in terms of application appears to be difficult. What does one do to help someone else actualize? Does this mean encouraging the subordinate to pursue his own interests? What if these interests conflict with organizational goals and practices? Does it mean letting him go off on his own, unsupervised, to fight his way to freedom? What if he requests help? What does one do if it is felt that the employee is making an error?

In its most practical conception it means providing a person with challenges and an opportunity to exercise independence and individuality. If you don't hold a subordinate down he has a better chance to actualize.

SOCIAL INTERACTION APPROACHES

There are a number of variations on this theme. The human relations movement will be discussed here, but certain aspects of employee participation schemes—the affiliation motive as presented by Schachter,[4] and spinoffs and extensions of the original human relations movement (sensitivity training, transactional analysis)—all have major ingredients which fit into this category.

The Western Electric Company studies conducted by Elton Mayo at the Hawthorne Works,[5] discussed earlier in Chapter 3, gave birth to the human relations movement. For this reason, and because the movement is one of the two major historic forces in management theory and practice, considerable background is presented here.

Theory. Mayo did not make a startling discovery. Other men in the discipline of what is now called social psychology were isolating findings which preceded or were concurrent with his; but Mayo put forth his ideas with considerable force and created an impressive impact.

The Hawthorne Works of the Western Electric Company, near Chicago, had been experiencing employee problems. The incidence of the wrong kinds of behavior was high, and the occurrence of the right kinds was low. Management called in industrial engineers (Taylor's scientific management with its emphasis on work measurement and control was still very popular) to manipulate the environment to discover if it was too hot or too cold, too light or too dark, too roomy or too crowded. Their researches were to no avail. They found no sensible relationships between the environmental changes and employee behavior.

Mayo became involved in this research and began looking at the behavior of the employees rather than just the physical environment in which they were contained. He noted many signs of their unhappiness and inefficiency.

He entered this situation with a preconceived idea—namely that the most important thing to people is other people (Maslow's third level). He began to change the working arrangements among employees and between labor and management and found that attitudes and productivity improved when the interaction and communication among people was quantitatively or qualitatively enhanced. Modern research data support his findings. If people treat each other badly or unskillfully, attitudes and performance suffer. There is also evidence which reinforces another result that Mayo reported. Employees often band together against management, the common enemy, if they perceive that they are receiving unsatisfactory treatment.

Application. Mayo, however, fell into a trap which many people encounter. He entered his studies with the preconception that the social element of human behavior is *the* major determinant of feelings and actions. He gathered evidence which he used to support this hypothesis, declared that he had found *the* answer, and failed to search for or dismissed findings to the contrary. He believed he had found what is referred to as a "simple and sovereign" explanation of human behavior, and he overestimated its significance.

Regardless of the accuracy of his conclusions, he did promote the human relations movement. Part of the human relations philosophy involves the establishment of systems which facilitate the creation of a more human environment in the organizational setting. For example, at the Hawthorne Works he instituted work group activities (as opposed to isolated individual operations), employee counseling, and increased communication between management and labor.

The most significant thrust in human relations, however, has been in training. The fundamental philosophy underlying any type of human relations training is that people treat each other inappropriately and that this treatment affects attitudes and performance in a negative manner. People do not necessarily do this because they are evil or unwilling to treat people well, but because they lack the proper skills for interacting effectively with others. An equally important premise is that people can learn to improve their social (human relations) skills and that this will resolve many problems which currently exist.

The most typical form of early human relations training was the lecture method in one of its various forms. It might be a course on the psychology of human relations (and we'll let you, the participant, deduce how to apply it), or it might be a cookbook approach (here are the ten ways to achieve effective human relationships), or it might consist of a speech on personality change (how to be the ideal person); in some instances, it was the Golden Rule format (here is how to be nice to others).

In the last two decades the lecture as a human relations training method has fallen into disfavor. Modern techniques take the form of sensitivity training or a more structured variation such as transactional analysis. Although the basic intent and assumptions have remained the same, the training methods have evolved and changed because the lecture appeared to be ineffective in teaching people how to improve their human relations skills and insights.

The labels applied to these more recent forms of training are unnecessarily confusing since they are quite similar. T (for training) group, L (for learning) group, sensitivity group, human awareness group, human growth group, interaction group—all refer to the same process or method. While groups may differ somewhat, depending on the leader's philosophy and knowledge, by and large they are similar.

One name which has caused some problems has been that of "encounter group." This reinforces the popular idea that a group involves conflict, struggle, and unpleasant feelings. Actually the word means the same as all the rest.

In sensitivity training people *encounter* each other—that is they come together and deal with each other in a controlled setting. There is no evidence which demonstrates that negative encounters involving conflict are more beneficial than positive encounters marked by warmth and support. On the contrary, such documentation as exists so far suggests that negative encounters run the risk of creating detrimental consequences if they are not resolved properly by the leader.

From the guided interaction which occurs in a sensitivity training group springs a better understanding of oneself and how one relates to others. A group should also provide an opportunity to develop and practice more effective skills should a deficiency be revealed.

Advocates of this method of training over the lecture method argue that the lecture provides *cognitive* elements (what is right and what is wrong with human interactions) but fails to furnish the *emotional* impact which is necessary to bring about a change in attitude or behavior.

Think of the following contrast. If a speaker stands before an audience and says that people often don't attend to what others say, it is easy for you as a member of that audience to think, "Some people, but not me." On the other hand, when the man sitting beside you says, "Hey, buddy, why didn't you pay attention when I spoke to you?" you are much more apt to respond in a very personal manner.

MATERIAL INCENTIVE PLANS

Piece rates, profit sharing, bonuses, commissions, contests with prizes, the name on the door, and carpeting on the floor are all versions of material incentive plans.

Most of the material incentive plans are not open to municipal governments because of unavailability (bonuses and commissions are rarely offered), lack of a valid measure (most municipal government services do not show either a profit or a loss), and legal restrictions (piece rates, for example, are seldom allowed). Under carefully circumscribed conditions, however, a few of these plans may be available for utilities that operate more like private sector counterparts and for incentives that are primarily in the form of status (preferred office locations, name on the door, certificates and awards, and other forms of visible recognition).

Even with all of these restrictions, it is useful to have at least a brief introduction to material incentive plans, because their principles illustrate some of the points relative to employee relations that are discussed in other chapters.

These plans can be evaluated in many ways, but two critical factors with regard to their effectiveness are the proximity in time between performance and reward (receiving a commission upon closing a sale versus getting a bonus at the end of the year), and the correlation between performance and reward (a monthly paycheck is a reward for both the good and bad performance which occurred during the month, whereas a commission is the direct result of successful action). In general, the more quickly a reward comes and the more closely it is related to desired performance the more effective it will be.

The number of variations of incentive plans is as infinite as one's imagination. Since it is impossible to even begin to enumerate them, the Scanlon Plan is described because it is an interesting combination of a suggestion and an incentive scheme; thus it is a bit more complex than a simple incentive program.[6]

Theory. The Scanlon Plan is more of a philosophy than a plan with extensive rules and regulations. Its flavor is very similar to the ideas presented in the discussion of participative management in this chapter.

The major tenets are: (1) employees have profitable ideas, and should be provided with a mechanism for communicating these thoughts and participating in their evaluation and enactment; (2) employees will improve production in exchange for a monetary reward, recognition for suggestions, and an opportunity to participate in establishing work procedures and policies; and

(3) productivity will be greatest when the financial rewards deriving from a useful thought are distributed to a group rather than just to the individual (this also enhances cooperative behavior).

The components of the Scanlon Plan are: (1) the sharing among the employees of any savings or earnings above normal operating costs and income amounts which can be attributed to their efforts; and (2) the mechanism for processing suggestions which will result in increased profit. Any net profit which can be linked to an employee suggestion is distributed, at least in part, among all employees.

Application. The most difficult element in establishing the Scanlon Plan is the development of a good cost and income accounting method which measures the current state of affairs and calculates the monetary payoff of a suggestion. Management must be scrupulously honest with this cost accounting part of the plan. If it cheats in some manner, it will not only defeat the scheme but will also create new problems.

A unique element of the plan, in contrast to traditional "suggestion box" approaches, is that both employee and management representatives evaluate ideas and become involved in the initiation of the usable ones. If the profit sharing and participative elements of the Scanlon Plan are present, there is evidence that it produces measurably positive results.

SUPERVISORY AND LEADERSHIP BEHAVIOR

One of the most intriguing topics in management is leadership and supervision. Are leaders made or born? What are the qualities of an effective supervisor? Is leadership a function of the person or the situation in which he finds himself?

Leadership and supervision are typically treated as a separate chapter in most books, and this is the case here (see Chapter 5). They are discussed in this chapter because it is impossible to ignore the fact that supervisory behavior has a definite impact on subordinate behavior.

As a small test, think of the best and the worst supervisors for whom you have worked. Then think of how you felt and acted. The chances are that when you worked for a good boss you were happier and more productive than when you

worked for a bad one. To return a moment to the word discarded early in this chapter, the effective supervisor "motivates" or influences his subordinates to behave in a positive manner, whereas the ineffective superior does just the opposite.

In the early part of this century and up until World War II, much of the research on supervision was directed at identifying the characteristics of effective and ineffective leaders and supervisors. To make a long story short, little was accomplished. Good supervisors did not seem to be any taller, smarter, or thinner than poor ones.

In the late thirties attention turned to styles of leadership. The amount of data collected on this topic is huge and points in the same basic direction. Just as with the labels used for sensitivity training, many designations have been applied to results in the area of leadership styles. Democratic—autocratic style, Theory X—Theory Y style, employee-centered versus task-centered style, initiating versus consideration style—all indicate the dichotomous nature of leadership.

Theory. While the work of many men could be presented as excellent models to illustrate the nature of leadership research, the findings of Edwin Fleishman and his associates at Ohio State University have been selected because they graphically demonstrate the major results.[7]

After making the decision to take a new and intensive approach to the study of leadership and supervision, the Ohio State people began investigating both the attitudes and actual on-the-job behavior of supervisors, and the responses which their subordinates made to them. Following much effort, they isolated two major dimensions of supervision: *consideration* and *initiating structure.*

They then developed two sets of scales, one to measure supervisory attitudes on both dimensions and another to measure actual supervisory behavior on the dimensions. These inventories could then be given to supervisors and their subordinates, and a picture would emerge regarding a supervisor's attitudes and behavior as seen by himself and his employees.

The consideration dimension reflects a supervisor's attitudes and behavior toward the people who work for him. Does he attempt to help them get their jobs done? Does he care about them? Does he support them? Is he fair?

Initiating structure represents a supervisor's orientation to the job, the task at hand. Do his attitudes and on-the-job behaviors indicate a concern for accomplishing his defined objectives?

The ideal supervisor measures high on both dimensions. He wants and tries to get his job done through the proper and effective management of his subordinates. The worst supervisor is low on both dimensions. He cares about neither his job nor his subordinates. The most typical supervisor is one who is high in initiating structure and low in consideration. He is the autocratic boss who forces his people to produce regardless of the long-range cost to the organization or the personal cost to subordinates. He gets the job done not because of, but rather in spite of, his employees.

Application. Training is the method most frequently used in modifying supervisory behavior. There is a close relationship between developments in supervision and the human relations movement. Emphases in both areas began at about the same time, and both are directed at improving employee performance through the development of human relations skills in people.

One of the most extensively used training programs is that of Blake and Mouton, who created the Managerial Grid which is summarized in Chapter 5. At the beginning of training, each participant is measured and his style with respect to the consideration and initiating structure dimensions is plotted on a graph (see Figure 5—2). When the participant's standing has been diagnosed, he is submitted to a training program designed to remedy his deficiencies. If he is high on initiating structure and low on consideration, the latter is emphasized during training. Hopefully, on completion of the course he has moved closer to the ideal manager who is high on both dimensions.

JOB MODIFICATION

Job modification consists of taking an existing job and changing it in some manner so as to improve performance. One can make a job easier, more difficult, more interesting, more complex, more simple: the range of variation is great.

An employee's tasks as reflected in his job description are probably not as rational as the description attempts to make them. Most jobs seem to be created in the following manner. Two partners begin a business and the volume of work increases. Mac says to Art, "Art, I need some help. I can't handle this alone." They hire a man and he asks Mac, "What do you want me to do?" Mac thinks a minute ("Let's see, what are the tasks I dislike the most?") and assembles a list of unrelated duties and says, "There's your job." The moral of the story is that the work an employee ends up doing is frequently the result of a haphazard combination of tasks.

Job development and modification has a fascinating history, not only because it has seen several major changes in direction but also because it reflects the state of American organizations at a given point in time. At the turn of the century, Frederick Taylor and the Gilbreths were doing their pioneering work in motion and time study. Concurrently, Henry Ford's assembly line was tooling up and the blessings of mass production were upon us. When these two movements came together they produced the following situation.

In order to make an assembly line efficient, work had to be simplified by breaking it down into its smallest component parts. Men and machines had to be arranged so that they got along well together. Enter the time and motion study man, the human engineer, the efficiency expert, to work out a combination of men and machines which separately are useless but when added together produce a car, a dishwasher, or a radio. The technical term for their work is *job simplification* or *job rationalization*.

Although some engineering efforts are aimed at making machines more comfortable for men, a surprising number of engineers make machines, such as the assembly line, which are efficient from a mechanical perspective but are dehumanizing and inefficient from a human psychological vantage point. These engineers expect men to adapt themselves to this unsuitable state of affairs. Actually, this is not unnatural. Men can adapt to many conditions, and it is sometimes inconvenient to make a machine that fits man.

If hindsight and current thought are at all accurate, the attitude that a man should be satisfied with being part of a machine has led us in some very unfortunate directions. Elton Mayo interpreted many of the symptoms of industrial unrest (strikes, turnover, absenteeism, work slowdowns, tardiness, complaints, sabotage, etc.) as signs of the failure to satisfy the social needs of man. He accepted the production line philosophy and believed that the negative consequences must be combatted by getting people more sincerely involved with one another. While this did not change the nature of the job, it did provide an outlet for the frustration which dehumanizing work created.

Others, interested in the elements of work itself, saw these symptoms as inseparably connected to the nature of the job which men were required to perform, and they began to attack the task. The first manifestation of this movement was a trend toward *job enlargement,* which consists of taking several simple jobs and adding them together to create a more extensive task. It is the opposite of job simplification. However, the basic nature of the work is not changed by this technique. The quality remains the same in that an employee ends up doing five simple tasks instead of one. The psychological impact on a worker may be more negative than positive.

Suppose you had a job which consisted of bolting on the left front wheel of a car. Your boss came along and asked you to bolt on the steering wheel and the door in addition to what you are already doing. The variety and change of pace might relieve your boredom for a few days, but this would soon pale as the work again became routine. Wouldn't you tend to have the attitude that you were doing essentially the same thing—bolting on parts—but that you'd been required to do three times as much? To add insult to injury, your boss told you that you *should be happy* because you have a more responsible, interesting job.

In the last ten years job enlargement has been replaced by the concept of *job enrichment.* This change has been due largely to the research of Frederick Herzberg.[8] Since this is where most current efforts are directed, it deserves particular attention.

Job enrichment represents a return to the craft or guild concept of work, wherein a craftsman had extensive control of his job and his labor resulted in a product for which he could assume most of the credit. The silversmith, the carpenter, and the armorer of old had involvement and pride in their work. A primary motive behind the efforts of each was that he was creating a total product with high quality. This gave him a feeling of satisfaction. Often the skill which he brought to his craft was highly distinctive, and his products were as identifiable to the expert as are the styles of artists. Again, compare the past with the present. A Revere hallmark on a piece of silver represented something very different to Paul Revere from what a brand name on a TV set represents to the worker who solders one transistor onto one subunit.

Theory. Herzberg became interested in the interaction between a man and his work through some early research which he and his associates did on the relationship between job attitudes and performance.[9] After reviewing thousands of job attitude studies, they found that no firm conclusion could be reached concerning the relationship between worker attitude and productivity. In some instances satisfied workers were high producers, but in many cases they were not. Similarly, dissatisfied employees were good producers under certain circumstances and poor producers under others.

One relationship which was discovered was that employees with poor attitudes or low job satisfaction tended to exhibit a lot of negative behavior, such as absenteeism, turnover, and tardiness. Poor attitudes seemed to involve an employee's attempt to getting away from his required work but did not necessarily mean that performance was poor when the person was actually on the job.

Leaving the literature, Herzberg took to the field to study men at work. His first investigation, in which he interviewed two hundred employees using two questions ("Tell me about a time you felt especially happy at your work," and "Tell me about a time you felt especially unhappy at your work"), led him to conclude that the traditional method of portraying job attitudes as they relate to satisfaction and productivity was inaccurate.[10]

Up until then it had been believed (and still is by many investigators) that feelings about work

Single factor theory
Dissatisfaction . . . . Satisfaction

Two factor theory
No satisfaction . . . . Satisfaction
Dissatisfaction . . . . No dissatisfaction

FIGURE 6—2. *Single versus two factor theory.*

could be placed on a single continuum running from dissatisfaction to satisfaction. Herzberg maintained that his findings demonstrated that there were two continua and that the presence or absence of certain elements of work accounted for feelings of satisfaction or of no satisfaction, while the presence or absence of other ingredients was responsible for feelings of dissatisfaction or of no dissatisfaction. Hence, he called his theory the "two factor" theory (Figure 6—2).

Herzberg found that the following elements were mentioned in his interviews as being associated with happy or satisfying times on the job: interesting work, opportunities to advance and to achieve, recognition for achievement, and opportunities to learn and to gain additional responsibility. These ingredients were inherent in the work itself. Unless the job permits it, you cannot learn and use new skills, feel a sense of achievement, etc. Herzberg saw these elements as content or intrinsic components of the job and called them *motivator factors,* because their presence led to high productivity as well as high levels of job satisfaction.

The other set of factors, those mentioned in connection with unhappy or dissatisfying times, was composed of pay, status, working conditions, interpersonal relations, company policy and administration, and security. He envisioned them as context or extrinsic elements and named them *hygiene factors.* He derived this term from the public health field. Garbage collection or innoculation programs do not make people healthy; they prevent disease from occurring. By the same token the presence of the hygiene fac-

tors does not create satisfaction, it merely prevents dissatisfaction from arising.

The availability of hygiene factors does not motivate exceptional behavior. At best, hygiene factors prevent destructive behaviors from developing. The negative behaviors mentioned before (strikes, sabotage, absenteeism, etc.) result when hygiene factors are missing in large numbers. The employee who has good hygiene, on the other hand, does not produce exceptionally, but he usually does not cause trouble because he does not want to be fired and lose his hygiene benefits. Therefore, he works hard enough and keeps his nose clean enough to prevent any drastic action on the part of management.

Several clarifications should be made. Unlike Maslow, Herzberg does not maintain that these two sets of needs are in a hierarchical arrangement. An employee can be satisfied (and motivated to perform well) and dissatisfied at the same time. Such is the case of the starving artist who has few hygiene elements in his life and feels dissatisfied but also has many of the motivator factors and feels satisfaction concurrently.

A second point is that the best of all possible worlds is found when large numbers of both factors are present. Then an employee feels both satisfaction and no dissatisfaction, his production is high, and he displays no negative behaviors.

Substitutions cannot be made between the two sets of factors. Giving a person additional pay will not compensate for his boredom with his work. An employee's interest in a job cannot be purchased. The only way to eliminate the feeling of boredom and meaninglessness on the job (that is, no satisfaction) is to change the nature of the work.

A situation frequently found in organizations is that people become trapped in jobs which they dislike intensely. Perhaps you feel this way. Certainly you know others who do. Think about what happens. A person takes a job which he comes to hate, but his wages are high, he is involved in nontransferable insurance and retirement programs, and he has constructed a comfortable niche for himself in his relations with his boss and fellow employees. He is trapped. He is in a situation in which he is literally tolerating the intolerable, and he berates himself for falling into the trap but he cannot afford to break out. This is another demonstration of man's adaptability. People are the only animals who deliberately remain in conditions which give them pain. It is behavior such as this which makes one inquire as to whether man's brain is so wonderful after all.

A final qualification relates to the idea of rewarding behavior. If a manager wishes to encourage productive behavior, he should offer motivator rewards. If a subordinate performs in an outstanding manner, one of the most meaningful rewards he can be given is the opportunity to undertake another task in which he can feel a sense of achievement. The manager who gives the employee a financial bonus alone is missing the boat. Everyone wants money, but we place too much emphasis on it. The employee sees the bonus as something he deserves for his excellent work; this is a question of fairness not motivation. What he wants and what he will respond to is an opportunity to engage in additional meaningful work. If he does a good job, he needs the chance to do other good jobs. This is what gives him a feeling of satisfaction.

Application. Job enrichment is a form of job modification which consists of loading a job vertically in order to make it more psychologically meaningful. Contrast this with job simplification, where a job may be made psychologically meaningless.

In operational terms, enrichment requires that the job be changed in such a manner that the number and types of motivator factors are increased. Theoretically, by taking a simple job and adding job duties which enable the employee to gain recognition, feel interest, experience a sense of achievement, feel that he is learning, take on added responsibility, and do work which logically leads and relates to the next position in the hierarchy will lead to an increase in satisfaction and in quality and quantity of performance. This is really a commonsense notion. If you love what you do, you work hard. If you don't, you try to get away with as little work as possible.

The hygiene factors should also be attended to. If they are ignored, even though motivators are present on the job employees will quit or complain because they don't feel they are getting what they deserve for their efforts. And as people do better and better, they feel they deserve more

and more. One thing which can be definitely said about human beings is that they are never satisfied! So stop fighting it and learn to live with this fact.

Initiating a job enrichment program requires the analysis of jobs, to identify the type and extent of motivator factors which currently exist. An additional analysis should be conducted to ascertain how these jobs fit with others in the organization. Although jobs are often carelessly developed, there is enough of a relationship among positions so that a change in one often requires some modification of another.

Next, the job duties should be modified so as to incorporate as many of the motivator factors as possible. The most direct method is to analyze an existing job or a proposed change by asking, "Is the opportunity for learning, achievement, and interest present?"

To recapitulate, the intent of job enrichment is to make work psychologically meaningful. If the job is significant to him, the employee will work hard to gain the personal satisfaction which comes from doing meaningful work well, just as did the craftsman of old.

While job enrichment can be applied to a wide range of work, a lower level may be reached in which you cannot change the job much without upsetting the whole organization. What is the answer to this? You have three choices: (1) automate this hopelessly meaningless work out of existence; (2) hire intellectually limited people who will find even the most simple work challenging; or (3) keep things as they are and learn to live with problems created by a paucity of motivators.

PARTICIPATIVE MANAGEMENT AND
THE ACCOUNTABILITY CONCEPT

Participative management and accountability could be incorporated under the headings of both supervision and human relations, because they are closely connected with supervisory behavior and the philosophy which an organization directs toward its employees.

Management by Objective employee suggestion plans, brainstorming, teamwork, and autonomous or unsupervised work groups are manifestations of participative management. Detailed attention has been devoted to several of these procedures in other chapters of this book.

Certain organization theorists, among them Argyris[11] and McGregor,[12] approach the concept of the meaning of participation from a broad point of view. They say it somewhat differently, but both maintain that the typical employee is an adult who has problems and ambitions which are similar to those experienced by his boss. Like his superior, he will assume responsibility and act in a responsible manner if given half a chance. But the management of organizations, so the argument goes, is unduly pessimistic regarding the worker's potential. This may be due in part to the manager's ignorance: he truly thinks that his subordinate is a different breed of cat.

In addition, it may be due to the manager's ego. Often a boss feels that he wins more by holding people down than by helping them to forge ahead. How many times have the thoughts, "If my subordinate looks good, I may look bad," or, "If I let John show his stuff, he may take my job," passed through a manager's mind? Why not think, instead, "If my subordinates are powerful and effective, I as their boss will be powerful, too"?

Whatever the reasons, the effect tends to be a repression rather than an encouragement of individual progress. This begins a vicious circle. For example, a boss feels that a subordinate is a poor performer; he exerts more control, which has the effect of holding the employee down; he then points to the deteriorated performance as proof of his opinion and communicates this to the subordinate in one way or another; the subordinate then stops trying altogether; then the boss chews him out for not working harder.

If you tell someone he is crazy convincingly enough and often enough, he may begin to believe it and start acting that way. This is called a *self-confirming hypothesis*. A person gets an idea that something may be happening and then arranges the situation so that it cannot help happening and uses the results, which he has determined, as proof that his judgment was correct. This is both wrong and unfair, but it happens every day.

One of the more formalized and popular participation schemes is that of Management by Objective (MBO), as presented by Charles Hughes.[13] There are factors other than par-

ticipation involved in MBO, but one of the ideas underlying most accountability systems is that the subordinte has an important hand in making the system operative. Chapter 12 presents a more detailed discussion of an MBO approach.

Theory. The assumptions which provide a foundation for MBO are as follows: (1) an individual works more effectively when he has a clear, understandable, and well-defined conception of where he must head (a goal or objective); (2) people feel more comfortable and cooperative when striving toward goals which they have helped to establish; and (3) an individual enjoys being allowed to choose the means by which he attains his goals (some MBO writers would not agree very strongly with this third assumption).

MBO is another variation on the theme that people tend to work better when the tasks in which they are involved are personalized and meaningful. They don't enjoy their work and don't work well when they are told what to do, how to do it, and when to do it. This is not only an insult to their intelligence; it also robs them of their autonomy and makes them feel completely dependent. Most people do not like to be locked into a situation where they have little control over their own destiny.

Application. MBO is a theoretically sound system which has a lot of practical difficulties. The steps in enacting the procedure are as follows.

1. Perform an organizational needs assessment. An analysis must be conducted to determine the broad long- and short-term needs of the organization. Basically, this consists of the question, "Where are we now and where do we want to go?" Any discrepancy between the two is a need.
2. Establish specific organizational objectives based on this need analysis. In this step the needs or deficiencies are translated into measurable goals which furnish the direction for all organizational processes and provide a basis for organizational decision making. It should be emphasized that the objectives are directed toward *end results,* not activities which lead to them.
3. After establishing organizational goals, super-

visors meet with their subordinates from the top to the bottom of the organization and draw up specific result-oriented goals for each person which, when added together, lead to the attainment of the organizational goals.

There are two principles which must be adhered to if MBO is expected to work. One is that all goals must be measurable. This is not to say quantifiable. In some instances numbers can be attached, but not always. For example, "To increase production by 10 percent by December 31 while holding costs constant" is a quantified goal.

"To complete the municipality's section of the new highway by July 1" is a measurable but unquantified goal. The measure is either yes or no—you either did or did not meet the requirement.

The purpose behind making goals measurable is that they then become understood and more or less indisputable. To tell the fire chief and the city planner to locate fire stations so that the city has good coverage is a nebulous directive subject to a number of interpretations. On the other hand, to say that they must submit a map by May 15 of this year indicating the location of all fire stations and proposed fire stations, which must be located in such a manner that any building may be reached in not less than two minutes after an alarm is received, produces a specific result directed at solving a specific problem.

After the goals are jointly developed, the subordinate must be given the authority which goes along with his accountability. This is the second important aspect of the MBO system. He must be given the freedom to act as he sees fit in accomplishing his goals. If the means are dictated, it not only thwarts the positive effects of participation but also destroys the accountability aspect of the plan. If the boss determines the means to the subordinate's goals then he, not the subordinate, should assume the accountability for their attainment. If a subordinate's hands are tied, he is going to do the correct and natural thing—blame the boss in the event of failure and hesitate to feel that he deserves any credit in case of success.

Among the difficulties one might expect to en-

counter there is, first and foremost, the fact that, when a manager attempts to apply MBO in an existing structure, there is a lot of mistrust and anxiety. Will the boss really be willing to delegate? Will the subordinate accept responsibility? How can we possibly reach agreement on goals? How do you get the top men to draw up organizational goals on which to base individual job goals?

Another major problem involves technical matters. Who is going to train all the employees to write goals in the proper format? How can we handle all this new record keeping? How can people break free for a few hours a month to assess progress and formulate new goals or revise existing ones?

A repeated word of caution: the technical aspects of MBO are a necessary but not a sufficient condition for the operation of the system. Without the proper spirit and philosophy behind it, the manager will find that he is little better off than he was before the system was introduced. If both the technical and attitudinal factors in the system are operating, the benefits can be very rewarding.

Conclusions

You have read about six categories of methods which have been developed and applied to influence the behavior of people at work. It is now time to interrelate these systems and draw some conclusions.

A superficial reflection on the material presented will reveal that the overlap between the approaches is extensive. In order to point this out more intensively, let's quickly analyze each system and see if it contains, *when properly applied,* ingredients which have been shown to have an impact on human behavior. This can be accomplished by means of the following questions.

1. Is the focus placed on the individual's personal needs and directions?
2. Is the individual encouraged to grow, learn, and do more?
3. Is the employee stimulated to act independently?

4. Does the employee receive both material and psychological benefits from his good performance?
5. Does the system encourage cooperation rather than destructive competition between employees?

The answer is yes to each of these questions for all six systems. Again, it must be stressed that the spirit behind most of these methods is basically the same even though the particulars vary. And, as we have mentioned, unless the proper attitude is present on the part of the manager, he will probably be unsuccessful in applying any of the approaches.

THE CONCEPT OF REWARD

Moving to a lower level of analysis, we can ask if there is one quality which is a common denominator among these systems. We may ask the question: What is the one similarity in the following situations?

1. A salesman gets a commission upon making a sale.

2. A manager is delegated a challenging task in which he sees an opportunity to achieve.
3. The boss compliments a subordinate for his good work.
4. The subordinate is asked to develop his yearly goals.

There is a single and vitally important thread which connects these events: the concept of *reward*, as presented by B. F. Skinner.[14] In each instance the employee receives a reward for his performance. The salesman makes a sale and gets money; the manager achieves a goal and receives satisfaction; the subordinate performs well and gets a pat on the back; and the employee is trusted and given the freedom to plot his direction. In each case the employee can obtain a material or psychological benefit for his efforts.

THE NATURE OF REWARD

A reward can be defined as any action or material thing which gives a person pleasure or a positive feeling. There is a simple question you can ask to discover if something will be reward-

Situation	Reward
The subordinate is given	*The subordinate feels*
1. Authority and accountability	Trusted, competent, pleased that his boss will have a firm idea of the quality of his performance
2. An opportunity to learn something new	Pleasure from learning, adding to skills
3. Interesting work	Excitement, enjoyment
4. A Promotion	Pleasure at being judged competent, worthy of undertaking more important work
5. A compliment by his boss	Flattered at having someone pay attention to his performance, important in the eyes of the man who counts, happy because he has received an idea of where he stands in terms of his performance
6. Financial remuneration for good performance	Pleasure in getting something he feels he deserves, pleasure in having someone care enough about him to give him a material reward, happy to receive money which enables him to purchase the items he desires, relieved because his financial insecurity is lessened
7. An award or status symbol	Delight at this public sign of his worth

FIGURE 6—3. *Rewards associated with common management actions.*

ing to someone: "Would you (the person to whom you are speaking) like such and such?" If you wish to accomplish the same purpose non-verbally, watch people. What they seek is rewarding, what they avoid is punishing. People flock to a coffee break. It must have a positive attraction. Employees avoid the boss. He must be punishing and aversive. Some common rewarding situations, along with the rewards which accompany them, are shown in Figure 6—3.

CONTROL OF REWARD

The most important point in this chapter is that *the manager is the major controller of rewards.* By employing rewards properly, the manager can produce the behavior which he desires in his employees. As a matter of fact, this is what managers currently do. Unfortunately, they usually control rewards very badly.

There are three components in a reward system: (1) the situation which produces behavior; (2) the behavior which occurs in a situation; and (3) the consequences (rewards or punishments) which accrue to the employee as a result of his behavior. If the behavior is followed by a reward, it will tend to be repeated. If it is followed by no action or by punishment, it will tend to cease.

Take the following example. A department of public works truck driver arrives on the job (situation), climbs into his truck, and starts to drive out of the garage (response or behavior). His boss catches him at the door with the comment, "Did you check your oil? How many times have I told you to check that damn oil before you burn up an engine (consequence)?" In this case, undesirable behavior (starting the truck without checking the oil) is being punished.

The next day the driver comes in and checks his oil before heading out. Does his boss reward him? No. His boss ignores the good behavior or he punishes it ("Well, you fool, I see you finally got the message!"). Maybe the correct behavior will cease, but let's say the driver continues to check the oil for a while. Is there any reward which is influencing his behavior? Certainly, but it's not a very pleasant one. He comes to work (situation), checks his oil (response), and keeps that so-and-so off his back (positive consequence or reward).

Let's look at the ideal situation. The employee checks the oil, adds a necessary quart, and receives a good word from his boss. This has the advantages of (1) giving the employee constant feedback on what is *right* in his behavior, rather than what is wrong; (2) developing a positive rather than a negative relationship between boss and subordinate. Rewards and punishments are inevitably tied to the person who gives them. A bad boss, from a subordinate's point of view, is one who gives many punishments. A good boss gives many rewards.

Rewards can be and usually are given in combinations. You may promote a subordinate and praise him at the same time, or you may give him an important task and the authority to do it.

In addition, the way a subordinate interprets a manager's act may make the reward of even greater value. If you send a subordinate to a training course he wants to attend, you have rewarded him by giving him the opportunity to learn, indicating that you are concerned with his progress and welfare and showing him that you have faith in his ability.

The significant point to keep in mind is the primary principle of rewarding desired behavior and *ignoring* undesired behavior.

Do not punish undesired behavior. If a situation threatens to go out of control, thus directly affecting the desired behavior of other employees, it may be necessary to step in. Violations of safety rules or abusive treatment of citizens in the performance of work are examples. These are last resort measures that are not taken primarily for punishment but to protect the rights of others.

We are, unfortunately, accustomed to think in terms of punishment. We have learned since childhood to criticize and prevent the further occurrence of bad behavior by punishing it the first instant we see it emerging. We are literally conditioned in this way, and we have created a very negative world because of it.

Since we are not used to thinking in terms of desired behavior, we have difficulty in identifying it. Remember back at the beginning of the chapter, when Bill and Betty weren't behaving as their bosses wanted them to behave? Rather than punishing the undesired behavior the manager should wait until the desired behavior occurs—Betty shows up on time, or Bill produces more than he normally does—and then he should reward it.

Also, it is important always to reward more than just the desired behavior in its completed form. You reward any progress toward that end. If Betty comes in only five minutes late instead of her usual ten minutes, you say, "Betty, I'm glad to see you here this early." And you do this every time she comes closer to the standard—always remembering to ignore any backsliding.

Never lose track of desired behaviors. It is all too simple to lose the forest for the trees. Behavior is very complex, and you, as a manager, have to encourage many positive behaviors in subordinates, not just one or two. Returning to Betty, suppose you ask her if she was late yesterday and she answers affirmatively. You proceed to give her hell. What are you doing? You think you are punishing her tardiness. What else are you punishing? You are punishing her for being honest. Don't you want honest subordinates? Shouldn't you rather have said, "Betty, I'm glad you are aware of it, and it's very honest of you to admit it."

A WORD ABOUT PUNISHMENT

Since we are so inclined to use punishment in our relations with others, some attention should be devoted to it. The only time punishment is really necessary is in an emergency situation or as a last resort. Rather than making punishment or the threat of it the first thing you try, do everything else and resort to it only if other methods don't work.

But always be aware of the consequences you reap with punishment. First, it has specific effects in that, when the punisher is absent, the behavior tends to recur. Second, the punisher comes off as a bad guy—that is, the punishment generalizes to all aspects of the relationship. Finally, punishment creates many negative by-products. When you scolded Betty for being late, she may have been on time for a while, but did you keep track of this? Did she badmouth you to other employees? Did she extend her coffee break? Did she make errors which inconvenienced you? One way or another, Betty got back at you. If you didn't see it, it was because you weren't paying attention.

PRINCIPLES OF REWARDING

It is impossible to capture all the nuances of rewarding on paper. At best, some guidelines can be produced, but you will have to do some trial-and-error learning in order to make them work effectively.

1. Rewards are individual in nature. What is one man's meat is another man's poison. The extent of rewards is tremendous. A compliment, the opportunity to assume responsibility, and money demonstrate the quality of rewards available. Don't forget the quantity. A lot of money has a different effect from a little money.

   You must, when working with rewards, have a feel for what has an impact on each subordinate. For one employee, five dollars may be more rewarding than a challenging task. Although many things appeal to most people, sooner or later you will have to make some individual determinations.

2. Give rewards as quickly as possible after the desired behavior occurs. A year-end bonus, a compliment at the time of the six-month performance review is too long. People not only lose the power of the reward because of the delay, but they are also rewarded for any undesirable behavior which occurred during that period. Immediate and specific reward is important.

3. Get the subordinate to keep records of his own behavior. People tend to lose track of what they do. The chances are if you asked Betty how often she was late, she would say, "A few times in the last month," and she wouldn't be lying. She has an impression of her tardiness: it is just that it is wrong.

   In allowing employees to keep records of their behavior you give them the opportunity to obtain feedback on their performance. Without this feedback no improvement is possible, since employees won't know where they are coming from or going. Also, by allowing subordinates to keep their own records you have delegated a responsibility and indicated your belief that they can be trusted—two rewarding events.

4. Borrowing from Management by Objective,

set standards which are measurable. Unless the employee has a very clear idea of where he is going, he cannot head there.

5. Give rewards as the employee moves toward the standard. This should be done consistently. This may create the impression that all a boss should do is hand out rewards. This is not true for several reasons.

   First, there are only a few behaviors among your subordinates that you will want to work on at any given time. Start with your largest problems and let the minor ones wait until a later date.

   Secondly, people become less dependent on actions from the boss over time. You may begin by giving a lot of rewards, but soon the employee begins to create internal rewards for himself by maintaining or meeting standards. While this does not eliminate the need for rewards from the boss, it does reduce the amount of work on his part.

6. Give rewards only when they are deserved. The employee knows when he deserves or does not deserve a reward. If you reward someone when they know they don't deserve it, you come across as a fool or a hypocrite.

7. When you reward, mention the standard or objective. Be specific, not general. Don't say to Betty, "I see that you are getting to work on time these days." Instead, say, "Very good, Betty, you have been on time for the last three days."

FINALE

Let's return to the big picture again. What about the employee attitude and behavior problem, the idea of motivating people? What should you worry about? If you think of rewarding behavior, it has the advantages of (1) producing the kind of behavior you desire, and (2) improving attitudes.

What is the manager's job in relation to his subordinates? It is to arrange the work situation so that a wide variety of rewards are available and to see that these rewards are properly applied to productive behavior. The good manager is a superior technician.

What do the management approaches discussed in this chapter represent? They are merely different formats for delivering rewards. By not adopting any one scheme but by taking points from all of them and using the concept of reward as a guide, the manager will actually be utilizing all of the programs to their fullest advantage.

[1] Abraham H. Maslow, MOTIVATION AND PERSONALITY (New York: Harper & Row, Publishers, 1954).

[2] Robert W. White, "Motivation Reconsidered: The Concept of Competence," PSYCHOLOGICAL REVIEW 66 (September—October 1959): pp. 297—333.

[3] David C. McClelland, J. W. Atkinson, R. A. Clark, and E. L. Lowell, THE ACHIEVEMENT MOTIVE (New York: Appleton-Century-Crofts, 1953).

[4] Stanley Schachter, THE PSYCHOLOGY OF AFFILIATION (Stanford, Calif.: Stanford University Press, 1959).

[5] Elton Mayo, THE HUMAN PROBLEMS OF AN INDUSTRIAL CIVILIZATION (New York: The Macmillan Company, 1933). Twelve years later Mayo added to his earlier contributions considerable thinking about the industrial scene around World War II. This appears in his book THE SOCIAL PROBLEMS OF AN INDUSTRIAL CIVILIZATION (Boston: Harvard Business School, 1945).

[6] F. G. Lesieur, ed., THE SCANLON PLAN (Cambridge, Mass.: The M.I.T. Press, 1958).

[7] Edwin A. Fleishman, E. F. Harris, and H. E. Burtt, "Leadership and Supervision in Industry," in BUSINESS EDUCATION RESEARCH (Columbus, Ohio: Ohio State University Press, 1955).

[8] Frederick Herzberg, WORK AND THE NATURE OF MAN (Cleveland: World Publishing Company, 1966).

[9] Frederick Herzberg, Bernard Mausner, Richard O. Peterson, and Dora F. Capwell, JOB ATTITUDES: REVIEW OF RESEARCH AND OPINION (Pittsburgh: Psychological Service of Pittsburgh, 1957).

[10] Frederick Herzberg, Bernard Mausner, and B. Snyderman, THE MOTIVATION TO WORK (New York: John Wiley & Sons, Inc., 1959).

[11] Chris Argyris, PERSONALITY AND ORGANIZATION (New York: Harper & Row, Publishers, 1957).

[12] Douglas McGregor, THE HUMAN SIDE OF ENTERPRISE (New York: McGraw-Hill Book Company, 1960).

[13] Charles L. Hughes, GOAL SETTING (New York: American Management Association, 1965).

[14] B. F. Skinner, SCIENCE AND HUMAN BEHAVIOR (New York: The Free Press, 1953).

7

Making Decisions

SOME YEARS AGO the writer was wandering around the gift shop at one of our major airports while waiting to board a plane. In the humorous card section he was attracted to a card which pictured three bright-red fire plugs with a perplexed dog leaning against one of them. The caption on the card read, "Decisions, Decisions, Decisions." That picture was not only funny: it said more about the perplexities of decision making than a million words. Anyone who has had to choose between almost identical alternatives can appreciate that poor dog's predicament. The best that can be said is that some decisions turn out better than others.

Basically, decision making is problem solving, and problem solving occurs when one chooses from among alternatives. Sometimes the alternatives are very simple. If one owns only two pairs of shoes—one brown and one black—and they are both equally comfortable, the problem of deciding which pair to wear will be solved by determining which pair will look better with the clothes one will wear that day. Unfortunately, the supervisor in local government rarely if ever has the opportunity to make decisions that involve so few complications. Fundamental, then, to the decision-making process is recognition of a problem. (And if no problem is recognized, one has consciously or unconsciously decided for the moment that one has nothing to decide.)

The decision-making process consists of the steps which groups or individuals go through in choosing among or between alternatives. In recent years a great deal of research has been undertaken on this subject; perhaps the most important result has been the discovery that the process cannot be reduced to a formula. No for-

mula for decision making has been discovered, or, perhaps, can be developed, that will permit decision makers to quantify their data and apply a formula to the alternatives, and thus guarantee that the best alternative will be selected in all situations. The research has led to the development of interesting theories of decision making, but the theories may be of more interest to the theoritician than to Jim Jones, the street superintendent, Sam Smith, in charge of the operation of the water purification plant, or Frank Smith, the police sergeant investigating a wreck. They are probably not even of major interest or of passing interest to the harried mayor or city manager.[1] John McDonald, writing in *Fortune* some years ago, quoted high-ranking businessmen as saying that they themselves do not know how they make decisions. The article quotes company presidents as saying:

"If a vice president asks me how I was able to choose the right course, I have to say, 'I'm damned if I know.' "...

"I can tell when I make a good decision. I sleep well at night."...

"You don't know how you do it; you just do it."[2]

The same type of survey conducted among all levels of public management personnel today would without much doubt yield the same result. The man on the firing line whose "cream is curdled" by problems requiring decisions a few minutes after he arrives at work may have little use for exotic theories about the decision-making process. He is basically concerned with choosing between alternatives that will resolve the present problem and hopefully cause him the fewest problems in the future.

Kinds of Decisions

In every municipal government three basic types of decisions are made: (1) policy decisions, (2) administrative decisions, and (3) management decisions.

POLICY DECISIONS

Policy decisions are normally made by the city council. As pointed out in Chapter 4 of this book, the decision as to "where the organization is going depends to a large degree on where the people want it to go, including ... where the people want it not to go." Within these and other constraints, the council is going to make its policy decisions. This is not to say that administrators are not going to have considerable input into the policy process. As a matter of fact, an administrator in many instances may use interest or clientele groups to further his goals by seeking to have these groups front for decisions he has already made and wants to see become public policy. The administrator may know or feel that if he proposes the idea to the council it will probably be rejected.

To illustrate this, let us suppose that the director of the parks and recreation department in the city of X, as a matter of public policy, would like to operate public swimming pools as part of his department. Only private club pools presently operate in his city. His instincts tell him, for one reason or another, that if he proposes such a policy the council will reject it. Very quietly he implants the idea—to some child-centered person or interest group, for example. This might include the heads of the local PTA, the Boy Scouts, or the local ministerial alliance. These persons carry the idea to their groups and one or more of the groups consider the idea meritorious. Within a short time a ground swell of public opinion for public pools confronts the council. The council decides to put the matter to the electorate, and a bond issue is proposed and passed, and the pools built and put into operation.

Who, then, really decided that public pools should be built in the city of X? The extent to which this kind of activity to influence policy decision making in a city goes on is unknown—but it is common knowledge that it occurs.

Administrators also vitally affect policy-making decisions when the council recognizes a problem and asks the administration to recommend a policy. Suppose your community has difficulty with dogs running loose. Councilmen are deluged by complaints from citizens. No policy dealing with this problem exists, and the city council asks the administration to make recommendations.

After lengthy study the administration decides to recommend an ordinance providing that: (1) dogs must be on leash, but licensing is not required; (2) annual rabies vaccinations are required, and a copy of the immunization record with the dog owner's name and address must be forwarded to the county health department by the veterinarian; (3) dogs picked up in violation of the leash law and wearing a collar with the vaccination tag attached will be held seven days and the owner will be notified by phone or mail: upon claiming the dog the owner will pay an impounding fee of $10; (4) any dogs, whether ownership is identifiable or not, will be disposed of after seven days by methods approved by the Humane Society.

The recommendation is formally presented to the city council, and the council orders that an ordinance incorporating the proposed policy be prepared and introduced. After debate, and after public reaction has been received (with a dog ordinance this can be lively!), the ordinance implementing the recommendation is passed. Who really made the policy decision? Obviously the council did—but as a matter of fact it was given only one recommendation, and the council's alternatives, unless it rejected the report and asked for alternatives, were: no policy or the administration proposal. The administration's proposed policy was obviously more desirable to the council than no policy at all. In effect, the council decided between no policy or the administration's proposed policy. Therefore, the argument could be advanced that the administration made the policy and the council merely ratified it.

Another way in which administrators vitally affect the policy decision-making process is when the council recognizes a problem and asks that the administration prepare a report on possible solutions so that the council can then decide on a policy. The administration may find that it must go down to the lowest level of supervision for recommendations necessary to develop alternatives. The lowest level of supervision then factors out those bits of information not considered relevant and passes its decision, in the form of acceptable alternatives, on to the next highest level of supervision, where it is reviewed and further factoring takes place. These decisions are forwarded up the ladder until, at the top, several alternatives emerge.

Who has made the decisions on alternatives that will eventually be considered and decided by the council? To illustrate, suppose the council must decide on whether to build a sewage disposal plant. This decision may be relatively simple. In fact, there may be no decision to make, since the federal government may have said build a plant or face either one or all of the following: (1) probability of a damage suit; (2)

loss or withholding of federal grants; (3) an order to permit no further connections to the existing sewerage system. The alternatives facing the council are two: build, or don't build. In this case, the problem and the facts are predetermined by outside forces. The council has only to weigh the consequences.

The decision-making process in this situation is analogous to a shotgun wedding. As a result, the council votes to construct a plant and instructs the administration to recommend what kind of plant should be built. The problem now becomes more complex. The council eventually must make this policy decision, but the administration must gather the facts and make the recommendations. To fulfill its obligation, it begins at the lowest level of supervision. Figure 7—1 illustrates the process.

In deciding what kind of plant to build, there

Policy decision by:	Possibilities	Adopts
Council	A	J
	J	
Input by:	**Possibilities**	**Recommends**
Chief administrator	A	A (equally
	H	J acceptable)
	J	
Department head	A	A (equally
	G	H acceptable)
	H	J
	J	
Next level supervisor	A	A (equally
	C	G acceptable)
	G	H
	H	J
	I	
	J	
First-line foremen	A	A (equally
	B	C acceptable)
	C	G
	D	H
	E	I
	F	J
	G	
	H	
	I	
	J	

FIGURE 7—1. *Process of factoring out for policy decision made by city council.*

were ten possibilities that the first-line foremen considered. They found six of them acceptable. Their decision was probably based on many factors, including, but not limited to, familiarity with operating processes, and their personal likes and dislikes (based on experience). The next level reduced the acceptable alternatives to four, the department head to three, and the chief administrator to two, which he presented to the council. The process of factoring eliminated four possibilities that were never considered beyond the lowest level. These four plus the two factored out by the next level of supervision and the one factored out by the department head might have been acceptable to the chief administrator. Of the ten possibilities only two alternatives were presented to the council. The others might have been equally acceptable and satisfactory solutions as far as the council was concerned but it never had the opportunity to consider them.

Who really made the decision? This process of factoring goes on constantly. It is probably most commonly observed in decision making in the budgetary process. A well-prepared budget leaves the council with very few budget alternatives; the real decision making occurs at lower levels. For the reasons mentioned above, supervisors must be acquainted with the decision-making process and make every effort to improve their decision-making ability. Far too often, supervisors may not realize their importance in the process. By underestimating this, they may underestimate the seriousness of their decisions and may deny to superiors and council alternatives in making policy.

ADMINISTRATIVE DECISIONS

Administrative decisions are those that must be made to implement a policy. It is popular in many quarters to assume that such decisions are less important than policy decisions. Carried to the extreme, this concept can lead to disaster. A sound and popular council policy may be totally discredited by poor administrative decisions made in the process of implementation.

For purposes of illustration, suppose the council of city Y decided that it would be the public policy of the city to operate its own garbage and trash collection service rather than to continue contracting it to private haulers. Although there

had been no basic criticism of the contract system, the council anticipated reduction in the costs of collection. The overwhelming majority of the citizens were willing to support any change that might reduce costs. The council acted with considerable enthusiasm and began to discuss services that could be improved by the anticipated savings. In the process of implementing the policy, however, administrative decisions were made which resulted in the selection of packer trucks that were inadequate for the job in size and durability. In a few weeks trucks were out of service, pickups were missed, and a public outcry arose. The crisis was intensified by hot weather. The public outcry became so great that the council was forced to pass an emergency ordinance rescinding the policy and ordering a return to the contract system.

In this case the crisis brought about by the administrative decisions was important enough to force the council to reexamine its alternatives and change its policy. Had the administrative decisions been more carefully thought out, the policy decision would have been implemented successfully and a great public hassle with the resultant loss of face by the council could have been avoided. Administrative decisions created not only chaos but injected the probability that any suggestion to place the city in the garbage and trash business in the future would be prejudiced.

Administrative decision making is a day-by-day occurrence in every department. It takes place in the enforcement of building codes, the issuing of the building permits, the scheduling of inspections, and the approval of completed work. Ordinances providing for these activities could not be implemented without administrative decisions. In the public works department supervisors are continually making administrative decisions with regard to such seemingly mundane problems as the best time to sweep streets or to start work crews with heavy equipment on the streets in order to avoid heavy traffic hours.

MANAGEMENT DECISIONS

Management decisions are those internal decisions that are made at the actual work scene. The decision to promote or not promote a worker or to grant or withhold a pay raise to a worker are examples. These types of decisions may not be considered by some to be as important as the policy or administrative decisions, but experience shows that this is not necessarily true. The dismissal of a worker for failure to obey work rules may have far-reaching consequences, especially if workers are unionized. If other workers feel threatened or abused by such an action, work may slow down or come to a stop. At worst, a strike completely disrupting the whole municipal operation may result. A "bad" management decision may force the council to change public policy dealing with employees.

The supervisor who has been through this sort of ordeal will not be impressed by the thought that management decisions are not of equal importance with administrative or policy decisions. The fact that management decisions sometimes result in a whole new set of policy and administrative decisions is often overlooked by those who try to assign degrees of importance to the three types of decisions made in municipal government.

For purposes of illustration a decision-making scale may be set up, with policy decisions on the left, administrative decisions in the middle, and management decisions on the right. It can be seen that policy decisions will require administrative decisions, which in turn will probably require management decisions. Management decisions may require administrative and policy decisions, and administrative decisions may require policy or management decisions, or both.

Figure 7—2 illustrates this process and demon-strates that it is impossible to assign primary importance, except in specific instances, to any of the three basic kinds of decisions.

Individual and Organizational Decisions

Within the three parameters of decision making discussed above, individual and organizational decisions are made. A council decision on policy is a collective one and normally is the product of compromise. Every member voting yes on a proposed policy is probably dissatisfied in some way. However, each has made the decision that the proposal is probably the best he or she can hope to get at the time and that something must be done. This is the heart of the process that we call compromise. Those who feel that their dissatisfaction outweighs their satisfaction vote no. Those who cannot compromise are in effect saying that no loaf is better than half a loaf.

In the realm of administrative decision making, individual decision making has become more and more important with the growth of the decentralization and delegation movement in modern organizations. Lower level decision makers can make city government look efficient or inefficient depending on the time and the circumstances surrounding their actions. The clerk who decides to reject an application for a building permit with a curt, "It isn't complete," rather than with an apology and an offer to help complete the form may permanently prejudice the citizen against his government.

As a supervisor or administrator it is imperative that you impress upon subordinates the importance of the decisions they make when deal-

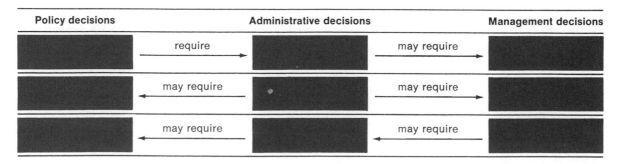

Policy decisions		Administrative decisions		Management decisions
	require →		may require →	
	← may require		may require →	
	← may require		← may require	

Figure 7—2. *The flow of decision making.*

ing with the public. A pleasant smile and time taken for a courteous explanation of why a decision was made or not made may not suffice to overcome ire, but it will not give the citizen cause to complain about the rude, and therefore obviously incompetent, person who made the decision. How a decision is announced may, indeed, make an angry or disgruntled citizen accept a decision he does not approve of with a minimum of complaint.

Much the same can be said about management decisions. The supervisor who explains in a calm, dispassionate manner why the decision to discipline an employee has been made may make the difference between the decision being accepted (although not necessarily liked) or the decision resulting in insecurity or other morale problems in the organization.

The Role of Policy Analysis[3]

Policy analysis is a process that uses the scientific method to solve problems. In contrast to most decision making, it is a more formalized or systematic process to help city managers, mayors, city councilmen, department heads, and others choose a course of action.

It does this by investigating decision problems, searching out objectives and alternatives, and comparing objectives and alternatives in the light of their consequences—using a constructed framework (a model) to bring the decision makers' judgment and intuition to bear on the problems. The aim is to develop guidelines, so that the public and private actions necessary to solve problems can and will be initiated, and will ultimately result in improvements in the lives of citizens.[4]

Loosely defined, policy analysis has always been with us as the application of the scientific method to the precise definition of problems, the development and testing of alternative solutions, and the selection of appropriate courses of action. In the sense used here, however, it is a precise analytic process, often based on mathematical analysis, computer technology, and quantification of data.

Policy analysis has developed from two main streams of activity over the past generation: the defense and space exploration programs of the federal government, and the continuous efforts of local governments to improve management through efforts extending back to the early part of the twentieth century; these efforts have drawn on political science, business and public administration, industrial engineering, urban planning, and urban economics.

The term policy analysis is often used synonymously with such terms as systems analysis, operations research, cost-benefit analysis, economic analysis, and management science. Increasingly, however, policy analysis is the preferred term because it implies broader coverage.

Although policy analysis often depends on quantitative data, mathematical models, and computer technology, its distinctive features are the application of the scientific method to the precise definition of the problem and the development and selection of alternatives for action. It is a logical process—the essence of the scientific method. This is its great strength, because it forces analysts—planners, budget officers, assistants to city managers, city managers, and department heads—to delineate problem boundaries, develop and catagorize information, and take other systematic steps. Policy analysis helps in asking the right kinds of questions. It can broaden the range of possibilities and stimulate the kinds of questions that generate creative approaches to traditional problems. So much of policy analysis has been publicized through development of elaborate mathematical models that it is not nearly so well known that nonquantitative techniques can also be used and are equally appropriate depending on the nature of the problem.

Policy analysis is not a substitute for expert judgment; nor does it assume anyone's responsibility for making a decision. It does, hopefully, help in making better decisions.

Policy analysis can be a powerful tool for those who invest the time and effort to gain understanding of the process and the way it works. It also has severe limitations, particularly because it is in early developmental stages and is more of an art than a science. Policy analysis has shown, however, given carefully defined and delimited problems, that it can provide an impressive payoff for governmental action.

Factors Affecting Decision Making

How do individuals make decisions? Early in this chapter it was suggested that people really just don't know. However, there are influences, conscious or unconscious, which affect the way problems are faced and solved. How else can we explain why two or more human beings recognizing the same problem and having the same set of facts and alternatives before them make different choices? What goes on within the human brain when it is confronted with a problem that makes mandatory a choice between alternatives is not capable of explanation by our present state of knowledge. It is known that some or all of the following factors in differing degrees and under different circumstances influence the decision maker: (1) form of the question to be answered; (2) time in which the decision must be made; (3) views of others; (4) habits, custom, and practices; (5) emotions; (6) personal needs; and (7) skills that the individual possesses.[5]

FORM OF THE QUESTION

The form of the question put to the decision maker may vitally affect the answer. The supervisor who is asked, "Should we patch the streets today?" may give quite a different answer than if asked, "Should we patch the streets today or clear the winter collection of gravel from the catch basins?" In making a decision on the first question the supervisor must supply his own alternatives. In the second question he is given two alternatives and may choose between them or add additional ones himself.

TIME OF DECISION

There are "crisis decisions" and decisions which permit more careful consideration of alternatives. The fire chief who finds that several major fires have broken out at the same time may have to make a crisis decision on the deployment of his equipment. All he can hope for is the best, and that the result will be the maximum use of equipment with no further need to redeploy the trucks. The police chief and his captains may have to make many crisis decisions in the event that a riot breaks out in their city. The best they can hope for is that they "guessed right," and that their decisions are such that the riot will be

quashed rather than accelerated. On the other hand, the people in the planning department rarely find themselves involved in this kind of decision making. Generally, these supervisors have ample time to weigh their alternatives. Ample time alone, however, does not guarantee that the decision will be better or worse in the long run than one made in a crisis.

Decision makers sometimes find themselves trapped as a result of thinking out loud or of off-the-cuff comments. The budget analyst may be asked by a department head about the possibility of securing funds to expand a particular function. He may casually answer, "Good." The department head assumes (rightly or wrongly) that a commitment has been made and proceeds to include such a request with justifications in his proposed budget. Some time later he discovers his request has been rejected further up the chain of command. The department head then prepares to fight for his request because he believes he has been misled. The reaction would probably have been quite different had the analyst said, "I don't know, but you might try putting it in and we can see how it is received on up the ladder."

VIEWS OF OTHERS

Under some circumstances the views of others have great influence on the decision maker. A supervisor might like to try something new with respect to employee working conditions, but in discussing his plan he may find that his peers in other departments frown on the idea. He decides not to try the experiment for fear of alienating his fellow supervisors. If he tries his idea and it works the others may be put in the position of having to follow. If the experiment fails he will be subject to the "I-told-you-so" syndrome. Peer group pressure may be so important to some supervisors that they will never do anything, no matter what the merits of a proposal, if they feel that it might discredit them in the eyes of their equals.

HABITS AND CUSTOM

Habits and custom also condition a decision maker's options. "We've always done it this way" is perhaps one of the most common excuses for not trying something new. Thus, without the examination of any other facts a decision has been made that assumes that what is being done is being accomplished in the best way. "We've always done it this way" may be so firmly established that to try it another way could cause turmoil. To change such a behavior pattern in the organization may require so much effort that the decision maker decides that for the time being it is not worth it, even though the alternatives may be much better.

By way of illustration let us suppose that a council member suggests that city offices might be kept open with skeleton staffs on Saturday and perhaps Sunday for the convenience of the citizens. No matter what the merits of the idea, employees in departments with a Monday-through-Friday schedule who would be affected by the change might raise so much opposition that the administrators and council would decide to abandon the idea. The fact that other departments (police and fire are obvious examples) have been on the seven-day work week for years would probably be ignored in the heat of argument.

EMOTIONS

Emotions control decision-making processes more than most of us like to admit. The supervisor who decides not to hire a long-haired young man because long hair offends him is acting on an emotion. He is not likely to admit this openly. He will find some other excuse to justify his decision. To openly admit his reason for rejecting the applicant might discredit him in the eyes of others in his organization. This kind of decision is based on prejudice. Prejudice can be defined as an opinion or bias against someone without just grounds. It may surface on a wide variety of fronts: race, sex, age, national origin, regionalism, dress, section of the city, etc.

Every individual is prejudiced in one way or another. Decisions based on prejudice are perhaps among the most difficult to deal with. It is rarely possible to get individuals to admit that prejudice has entered into their decision process because they do not realize that they are prejudiced. Some individuals will discard an alternative to solving a problem solely because it was advanced by someone they dislike. It is not unusual for some council members to reject the

proposals of managers or mayors purely because of the source. Their prejudice in these cases may be because of personal dislike or because other suggestions they have accepted from the mayor or manager have turned out badly. Sometimes council prejudice against an administrator becomes so widespread that the only alternative is for the administrator to resign or be fired. This kind of prejudice can also be found between a supervisor and his subordinate.

The individual who recognizes his prejudice may be able to cope with it and balance it by weighing his alternatives with other considerations. Supervisors in municipal government must constantly be aware of the threat prejudice poses to rational decision making.

PERSONAL NEEDS

Every individual has personal needs that affect his decision-making process. Some individuals are "drivers" and may be classified as "success seeking." They may be so interested in succeeding and moving up the promotional ladder that they weigh all decisions on the basis of what the result will do for them rather than what it will do for the good of the organization or the city. This may lead to "chance taking" if the odds seem to favor the decision being considered sound. On the other hand, these individuals may refuse to be daring in their choice of alternatives because they fear failure.

Family needs may also influence the decision maker. Illness, the fear of moving and upsetting the wife or children, or debt and other financial problems may lead to overcautiousness on the part of the supervisor when weighing alternatives. He may decide to do what is safe rather than sound for fear that the wrong decision might cost him his job.

INDIVIDUAL SKILLS

Some individuals are more skillfull at making decisions than others. This can be a result of their ability to absorb and digest more information. They may be able to see pitfalls in certain courses of action that others are not aware of. An administrator once told the author that he was rarely sure of what he should do but he was damn well aware of what he should not do. This kind of skill automatically eliminated for this administrator many alternatives that another person might have spent considerable time pondering.

Such skills may be the result of experience or may be almost "instinctive." In any event the decision maker who has them is blessed but is not guaranteed immunity against making bad decisions.

Judging or Evaluating Decisions

Whether we discuss individual decisions or collective decisions we know that decisions are constantly evaluated by others. The citizen as well as the city employee reacts to decisions by a judgment: "That was a good decision," or "That was a bad decision." This implies that there are ways to evaluate a decision. People generally judge the worth of a decision, whether it be a group or an individual one, in terms of their own social and economic well-being. If a decision makes our work easier it is a good one; if it makes it more difficult it is a bad one. If a decision improves our economic well-being it is a good one; if it hurts our well-being, it is a bad one.

No decision ever makes everyone happy, and some seem to make everyone angry. The only absolute that stands out is that once a decision has been made someone loses and someone gains. The administrator as well as a city council soon learn that losers tend to be more vocal than winners. Administrators and councilmen react to criticism and praise in different ways. Some assume that if there is a great deal of screaming it must have been a good decision. Others react to the same situation with great fear and assume that they must have made the wrong decision. Some practitioners argue that survivial is the key to judging decisions. If one survives over a long period of time his decisions, on the whole, must have been good.

In reality, it is extremely difficult, if not impossible, to judge the worth of some decisions. Whether they were good may not be known for months or years. Other decisions may be judged in relatively short time. Even then, one cannot truly be sure. It is possible that a decision that has been judged good might have been better if

another alternative had been picked, and one that has been judged bad might have been worse if another alternative had been chosen. The supervisor can expect to find himself damned if he does and damned if he doesn't.

One might question the whole process of evaluating decisions on the basis of what good it does. Perhaps the whole evaluation process is of academic interest only. The practitioner on the firing line will know soon enough whether the decision has been satisfactory or unsatisfactory. Why should he worry about evaluation? The best argument that can be advanced is that by evaluation one can learn to improve one's decision-making ability. Evaluating may give us group decision insights that will provide a basis for improving the group decision-making process. David S. Brown sets down four useful criteria for evaluating decisions.

1. Furtherance of organizational goals
   —Increase in the quantity of production
   —Improvement of quality of product
   —Enhancement of efficiency of operations
   —Profit or other return to decision makers
   —Prestige
   —Development of new opportunities
2. Improve relations with clients or publics
3. Cost
   —Money
   —Technical difficulty
   —Time
   —Interpersonal problems within the organization
   —Opposition from outside the organization
4. Methods used in making the decision.[6]

Brown maintains that by examining a decision and reducing these criteria to the scale in Figure 7—3 a rating can be assigned.

An average of the numerical ratings of the components will produce an overall average, assuming that each has an equal weight.

Those scoring in the upper percentiles (65 [%] or above) qualify as "better than average." Those scoring in the lower percentiles (40 [%] and below) are not really adequate.

The ratings can be made by a single person or there can be a shared judgment. The value of a rating system similar to the above is that it provides an opportunity for discussion and self-analysis—something that most executives should welcome.

There are, of course, a number of caveats to be observed. The decision should be a recognizable one, preferably one in which pros and cons have developed. Also, it should be one in which the decision maker has had authority to act. Raters should bear in mind also that the ultimate test of decision making is *what happens* as a consequence of it. This may not be immediately apparent; sometimes months or even years must pass before the results are clear. On the other hand, indicators are often available at an early period. Much of the time the perceptive executive can quickly begin to spot the results of the action taken.[7]

The supervisor must be cautioned about the reliability of such devices in evaluating decisions. In order to evaluate, the rater has to *make decisions*. In making his ratings he is going to be affected by the factors affecting decision making in general. The time of the rating, his own views, habits, custom, practices, emotions, and skills are all going to influence his decision as to what numercial value to assign to each of the criteria. Five different evaluators may give you five widely varying ratings. Averaging these doesn't tell you a thing except that you have added five numbers and divided by five. Only if there is a high degree of correlation among the raters can you assume the decision on the *decision* has any degree of reliability. Even then you cannot be sure that five different raters might not come to a different decision. These observations are not meant to discourage the supervisor from trying to evaluate his decisions. They merely point out that to decide the worth of a decision you have to average in the decision-making process with all of its fallibilities.

Improving Supervisory Decisions

Collective decision making is the product of individual decision making. If collective decision making in city government or any organization is to be improved, the decision-making ability of supervisors at all levels of the organization must be improved.

In order to make improvements one must identify the various elements that must be considered in problem solving. Once these are identified it is possible to develop a checklist, which might include such things as: (1) defining the problem; (2) gathering the facts (including opinions) about the problem; (3) discovering the alternatives for solution of the problem; (4) in-

vestigating the feasibility of the alternatives in terms of cost, implications for the future, and objectives; (5) evaluating which alternative best suits the needs of the organization; and (6) analyzing the problems involved in implementation of the proposals. The elements included in the above checklist have been identified and stated by others in different words. David S. Brown has developed an excellent checklist that

1. Furtherance of Organizational Goals

0	25	50	75	100
Failure	Poor	Average	Good	Success

2. Improvement of Relations with Clients and/or Publics

0	25	50	75	100
Failure	Poor	Average	Good	Success

3. Cost

0	25	50	75	100
Very low	Low	Average	High	Very High

4. Methods Used in Making the Decision

0	25	50	75	100
Very poor	Poor	Average	Good	Very Good

5. Other

0	25	50	75	100

6. Summary

0	25	50	75	100

FIGURE 7—3. *Suggested system for evaluating decisions (Directions: First, identify the decision to be rated. Then on the basis of available information, rate it according to the four criteria indicated below. A fifth possibility is provided in case additional standards are pertinent. Once the rating has been made, the sixth continuum provides an opportunity for indicating the average of the other four or five. Note: A greater weight on certain elements can be expressed by doubling or tripling the value attached to any one rating element. Further individual criteria can have subsidiary scales for which they serve as the summary: e.g., the organizational goals criterion can have a subordinate scale for each of several different goals.)*

consists of twelve elements to be analyzed in problem solving:

1. What is the problem?
2. What are the pertinent facts?
3. Who should be involved in the decision?
4. What are the objectives?
5. What are the alternatives?
6. What do they cost?
7. Which course of action best serves the objectives?
8. What does the decision imply for the future?
9. What are the procedures for making it work?
10. How are the results to be tested?
11. What arrangements are there for its modification or change?
12. Is the decision maker prepared to live with the result?[8]

One could hardly devise a more comprehensive list. If the above is conscientiously followed, decision making ought to be improved on any level of management. Regardless of the list that might be developed and used, good information is needed. It is probably impossible to get all of the facts, but you must always be prepared to ask the "last question." In order to ask the last question, you must develop an inquiring mind—and a suspicious nature! Too often the information you get may be tailored to what the fact-gatherer thinks you want. History is replete with examples of decisions which turned out badly because the facts given to the decision maker were those which subordinates thought he wanted to hear rather than the true ones. It is important to constantly remind your staff to tell it like it is.

The ability to ask the last question is critical in the decision-making process. The writer once had the privilege of spending some time with the late Louis Brownlow, who had little formal education but became one of the early city managers and, later, an adviser to several Presidents. In discussing decision making, he had a favorite story about an event that occurred when he was a city manager.

It seems that a well-known dowager who lived just over the city limits was hounding him to extend the city water line to her house. It was not legally possible to do it under the laws of the state. Nevertheless, she kept the pressure on. One day, when Brownlow was returning to the city he noticed the city water department laying a water line to the lady's house. He proceeded to his office, called in his assistant, and asked why they were laying this water main in violation of the law.

The explanation was quick and to the point. It seemed that someone had called the health department to complain about a dead mule on a vacant lot. A crew was sent out to investigate. There was the dead mule. A few feet away was what appeared to be an abandoned well. The mule was in a sad state of disrepair; to expedite matters the mule was dumped into the well and the hole filled in. As fate would have it, the well was the dowager's only source of water.

Brownlow used this as an example of a bad decision that was made because someone failed to ask the last question—who owned the well?

Supervisors, take heed. Many questions need to be asked in the decision-making process. Just be sure you ask the last question before deciding.

---

[1]Some excellent books and articles have been written on decision-making theory. See: William J. Gore, ADMINISTRATIVE DECISION-MAKING: A HEURISTIC MODEL (New York: John Wiley & Sons, Inc., 1964); Charles E. Lindblom, "The Scence of Muddling Through," PUBLIC ADMINISTRATION REVIEW 19 (Spring 1959): 79—88; Amitai Etzioni, "Mixed Scanning: A 'Third' Approach to Decision Making," PUBLIC ADMINISTRATION REVIEW 27 (December 1967): 385—92; Ernest Dale, MANAGEMENT: THEORY AND PRACTICE (New York: McGraw-Hill Book Company, 1969). Chapter 23 of this last work is a thoughtful and interesting discussion of the theories of decision making in the business world. While much of the discussion might not be particularly useful to the decision maker in municipal governmental agencies financed out of general revenue, some of it would interest those administrators operating utilities or other services that are self-sustaining.

[2]John McDonald, "How Businessmen Make Decisions," FORTUNE, August 1955, p. 85.

[3]This section is based in part on Kenneth L. Kraemer, POLICY ANALYSIS IN LOCAL GOVERNMENT: A SYSTEMS APPROACH TO DECISION MAKING (Washington, D.C.: International City Management Association, 1973). See especially Chapters 2 and 3.

[4]Ibid., p. 21.

[5]David S. Brown, "Making Decisions," in MANAGING THE MODERN CITY, ed. James M. Banovetz (Washington, D.C.: International City Management Association, 1971), p. 135—36.

[6]Ibid., p. 140.

[7]Ibid., p. 139.

[8]Ibid., p. 143.

8

Groups and Meetings

ONE OF THE MAJOR METHODS of communication used by management is the conference or meeting intended to formulate plans, solve problems, give information or instructions, and seek acceptance of policies and procedures. The degree to which meetings are successful depends in large part on the knowledge, skills, and attitudes of the people who lead them. Thus, any member of management who leads meetings is facing a task which calls for a specific body of knowledge, appropriate attitudes, and a set of special skills. The leader must know what to do and how to do it if he wishes to maximize the communication potential of a meeting. In this chapter we will explore three types of meetings from the point of view of their purposes, memberships and leadership. We will also be concerned with group methods in communication and how these influence the outcome of meetings.

Kinds of Meetings

The terms "meeting" and "conference" are used synonymously here to denote a purposeful activity of a group of people who seek, cooperatively, to reach a common goal. This definition includes three essential factors:

1. Purpose: there must be a reason for calling the meeting. It may be to give information, to discuss a subject, or to consider a problem.
2. Membership: two or more people must be present to form a group, and at least some of them must feel that there are benefits to be derived from working together which cannot be attained working alone.

3. Leadership: direction in the activity must be maintained by the leader or by one or more of the group members.

These three factors are interrelated. The purpose of the meeting is basic to the other two and determines: (1) the kind of meeting to be held, (2) who should attend the meeting and the responsibilities these people should assume, and (3) the leadership methods and techniques that should be used in the meeting.

Meetings may be called with many different objectives. In this chapter three basic purposes will be considered: (1) to give information, (2) to get information, and (3) to solve a problem. These three types of meetings are called the *informational* meeting, the *advisory* meeting, and the *problem-solving* meeting. Briefly outlined below are the distinguishing characteristics of each of these meetings.

THE INFORMATIONAL MEETING

The primary objective of the informational meeting is to communicate information to the group. The information which is to be presented is decided on before the meeting begins and becomes the content of the meeting.

There are three aspects of the information-giving process: (1) communicating the information, (2) helping the group members to understand it thoroughly, and (3) increasing individual acceptance of the information. The leader controls the meeting and makes all important decisions. He is primarily concerned with the dissemination of information and with getting group members to understand and accept it. The leader is not so concerned here with the attitudes and feelings of group members as he is in other types of meetings, but good rapport and understanding are important here as elsewhere.

The informational meeting is most successful for communicating facts, with a minimum of emphasis on changing attitudes. It is most effective in situations where the information is fairly straightforward and the attitude of the group members cannot change it. Thus, facts about the organizational structure of a company, a profit-sharing plan, a pension plan, or a labor contract are all suitable for informational meetings. The purpose of this type of meeting is to bring information to employees and to help them understand it and use it effectively.

For example, in considering the provisions of a labor contract in an informational meeting it is important to understand what the provisions are, why the contract exists, and how it came into being. The purpose of the meeting is not to discuss what the labor contract should be. The content of the meeting is further limited to a specific labor contract. The aim of the meeting is not to study labor contracts in general. Likewise, a meeting set up to give information about pension plan provisions is limited to how the benefits affect employees. Such questions as whether the plan is good or bad or whether the provisions should be changed or administered differently have no place in this particular meeting.

An informational meeting cannot be considered a success merely because the leader has presented a certain volume of information to the group. There must be some feedback to see how well the content of the meeting has been understood. Some of the most frequently used methods for checking understanding are questions (both from the leader and from the group), asking group members to comment on the subject matter, and, occasionally, check sheets or short quizzes.

The informational meeting does not have to be used in its pure form. It may be used as an overlapping part of an advisory or a problem-solving meeting. In such cases, giving information serves the following purposes:

1. It can supply the *background information* the group needs before it is ready to act in an advisory or problem-solving capacity.

2. It can be *motivational.* At job planning meetings, for example, information can be given in such a fashion that group members are motivated to try for new goals.

3. It can *facilitate understanding* beyond the specific material presented. For example, members may come away from a meeting on the interpretation of a specific labor agreement with a better understanding of the philosophy behind such contracts and how they contribute to better functioning in the organization.

On the other hand, the leader should not call an informational meeting with the expectation that, after imparting a few facts, he can change attitudes or uncover the true feelings of the group. To accomplish these purposes greater involvement of the participants is necessary.

THE ADVISORY MEETING

An advisory meeting is called when information or advice from group members is needed to solve a problem or initiate a course of action. The members are not expected to reach a solution to the problem but merely to contribute information or ideas which can be used by the leader or someone else in reaching a decision. In this type of meeting the flow of information is from the group members to the leader, who guides the discussion so that he can get the information he needs.

It is important that group members know why the meeting is being held, why they are asked to participate, and how they can best make a contribution. If this is clearly spelled out at the beginning, members will be in a position to supply the needed facts, ideas, or opinions.

The leader, in most advisory meetings, takes the most active role in defining the task. In preparing for the meeting, he should consider what background information the group will need in order to give advice intelligently on the problem and how he can best convey this information. Only after the group members have been briefed on the problem and understand the role they are to play in the meeting can they supply the needed information and suggestions.

Notice that there is a distinction between information and advice. When a leader relates how things work at present—what the present schedule is, how closely it is met, what difficulties are encountered in trying to meet it—he is giving information. When he opens the meeting for ideas on how to eliminate bottlenecks or improve service, he is asking for advice. Group members participating in an advisory meeting should understand that they will not make the final decision on the problem. They will, however, be kept up-to-date on developments and be told about the final decision and how it was reached. In this way the advisory meeting becomes one of the most effective ways for building confidence in management and encouraging continuing cooperation.

Although the advisory meeting is used primarily to get advice from qualified people, it has certain by-products. When an employee is asked to give advice on a problem, he gets a sense of belongingness, of being on the team. Where supervisors have been asked to give advice, they will be much more concerned with the problems on which they have been consulted. The advisory meeting also widens understanding of the many problems faced by all levels of management. When people have been involved in the decision-making process they understand its many ramifications. Even though they may not be in complete agreement with the decision, they will probably realize that it was the best that could be reached at the time and under the circumstances. With this knowledge they can accept the decision and put it into effect as the first step toward improvement.

The advisory meeting will be most effective if it is thought of as a continuing supervisory responsibility. When the advisory meeting is a part of management operation, individual members of management have an opportunity to develop skill in giving advice on company problems, to learn which kinds of problems can be most effectively handled in advisory meetings, and to improve their skills in communicating with other members of management. Advisory meetings set up on an interdepartmental basis help people achieve a wider perspective on city-wide problems. The values of such meetings can become lost, however, if the goals are not clear and straightforward.

To be effective, an advisory meeting should be used only where there is a real purpose. For example, such a meeting would not be appropriate at the foreman's level when the problem is one that only top management can handle. The advisory meeting is not effective when members are not in a position, for whatever reason, to give meaningful advice.

THE PROBLEM-SOLVING MEETING

The goal of the problem-solving meeting is to get a group of people to work together on a common problem and to reach a workable solution. Authority and responsibility for making the decision are delegated to the group, which in most cases is also responsible for putting the solution into effect. This type of meeting provides a medium through which those who are responsible for carrying out policy can participate in its development.

The problem-solving meeting is organized so that the leader and group members work on a problem together. The decision or recommendation is made through joint efforts. Everyone is involved; everyone has a stake in the solution. Communication and interaction are free among all group members, with the leader participating as a group member. In a good problem-solving meeting it is often difficult to tell who is the official leader. Various group members may take the most active part at those points in the discussion where they have the greatest contributions to make in terms of ideas, knowledge, experience, and leadership skills.

Responsibilities may be divided in a number of ways. The leader may be the man or woman who first recognizes the problem and decides to call the meeting. Or he may be appointed by someone else to conduct the meeting. Here the group responsibility may be to reach a recommendation which will be used by higher management. The leader may be responsible for clearly defining the problem and planning the meeting. Or the whole group may be asked to determine both the problem and the method of approach. The responsibilities for presenting the problem, clarifying it, suggesting and testing solutions, and reaching a decision are all taken by members and leader together.

The leader's major responsibility in a problem-solving meeting is to see that all the functions are performed which are necessary to reach a decision. He must keep the meeting moving toward its objectives (as he does in other types of meetings); but here he should not try to perform all, or even most, of the duties himself. His job is to see that someone performs them—preferably as many group members as possible, since they generally are involved in carrying out the final decision. In a problem-solving meeting the leader sometimes must purposely take a back seat to avoid swaying the decision one way or the other. Control is in the group; the leader is more concerned with providing an unrestrained atmosphere so that a wide range of alternative choices can be proposed and evaluated.

The problem-solving meeting is limited to those situations in which authority and responsibility for reaching a decision or making a recommendation can be vested in the group. In cases where the group can act solely in an advisory capacity—to supply information or suggest courses of action to be taken—the advisory meeting should be used. The location of the decision-making authority is the primary factor which distinguishes the advisory meeting from the problem-solving meeting. In the advisory meeting the decision is made by an agency outside the group. In the problem-solving meeting the decision is reached in the group.

Roles in a Meeting

In meetings we usually work with fairly complex problems, and we need all the help we can get. We could talk about this help in terms of the people who can offer different skills and knowledge, but it is better to talk about the jobs, roles, or techniques that are needed in a meeting, rather than about who does what.

ESSENTIAL ROLES

When a group of people get together to work on a problem, the number of roles they can play is almost unlimited. Let us consider, however, just those which are *essential* to a good meeting.

1. *Initiating* new ideas, problems, and activities for the group to work on. This does not mean disrupting current activities; it does mean suggesting new things to think about and do when the group is ready for them.
2. *Orienting* the group to make sure that members know exactly where they are going and why. Such points as the relationship between what the group is doing and the subject of the conference should be brought up for group consideration.
3. *Clarifying* the task to make sure that everything that is said and done is understood by all members of the group. Statements and actions may have to be restated or rephrased before they are clear enough for everyone.
4. *Informing* the group by bringing out the facts with which to work.
5. *Integrating* the facts that are brought out and the thinking of the group so as to come up with answers that make sense to everyone. The job is to get the group to consider all sides of a question and to try to arrive at an answer that combines the best points made.
6. *Summarizing* the meeting by pulling together all the ideas that the group has been talking about and showing their relationship to each other and to the whole problem.

WHO PERFORMS THESE ROLES?

Most of us at one time or another have sat in a meeting and assumed these various roles, but we have also sat in meetings where we did not do anything. The time when all members of a meeting are expected to pitch in and do all the jobs necessary for solving a problem is usually after group members are used to meeting together and have a problem no one can solve.

During the first meeting the leader is expected to play many of these roles. He continues with them until he gets across all the information the group will need and until group members understand what is going on well enough to take over some of the roles. Certainly, when presenting information the leader would not want group members to interrupt with comments that would distract the group's attention. He wants to do most of the initiating, orienting, and summarizing himself, and the group will probably expect him to. He may want group members to help in giving information and, at times, in clarifying and integrating; but mainly he wants group members just to be good listeners.

GROUPS AND MEETINGS 117

But we all know how boring listening can become. Increasing participation through using group members for gathering information is of some help. But to really pep things up, the leader should remember that there are many sides to most questions and that different points of view should be encouraged. If the leader can present these ideas himself or better still, get group members to come out with them, the clarifying and the integrating of these points of view can be done out loud. This can turn a dull lecture into an interesting session.

The leader must realize that he is not the only one who is able to play the needed roles. As rapidly as possible, the good meeting should move from a one-man show to one in which all members get into the act. In this way all the group's abilities are put to work.

Encouraging Participation

Only when a group has brought its maximum resources to bear on the problem can it be sure that the solution it has reached is the best possible solution.

How does the leader encourage members' participation? First, he must make his desire for this clear. Second, he must state the problem and tell the group that they have the resources for solving it. Third, the leader should let the group know he means what he says, by refusing to solve the problem himself or lead the group to a prearranged solution. Finally, the leader must listen and try to understand what the group members are really saying. Success in using these pointers depends on an honest desire to have group members participate in the meeting. If sincerity is lacking, the technique will be ineffective.

In using member contributions, make certain you and other members of the group understand the contributions. Try hard to understand the essence of what is said. If the points are not clear, ask for a restatement of what is meant. It is helpful to tie contributions into the ongoing discussion when they do not fit in automatically. When a statement seems vague, try to get at the essential element that is related to the ongoing topic. Ask if people are all discussing the same thing when comments seem to be irrelevant. Let

the group, as well as yourself, decide how to use or not use the contributions of other members. Many times the group may see important points in the contributions which you have missed. Finally, accept all contributions as being of possible value until the group decides by words or actions that the contribution does not fit into the discussion. Different questions will help the group move through various difficulties they will experience at each stage of the meeting.

Progress may not be as steady and well ordered as many would like. It may be necessary to stop so as to reconcile contributions based on different experiences. This process is often slow and frustrating. It is often difficult for the group and for you to tell whether a contribution is really relevant or not. Relevancy can usually be established by requesting the contributor to expand on his idea or to explain it a little further.

A group member often feels that his idea has not been understood by the leader or by other members of the group. The member must be satisfied that he has made his point clear. However the difficulty may be that everyone does understand the point, but no one has conveyed this understanding to the individual.

You may become impatient when the group fails to make the progress you think could be made if the group would just listen to you. The group, on the other hand, may feel very successful. This may leave you feeling frustrated and perhaps even angry. When both the leader and the group can share their feelings about progress and problems, they are likely to be able to handle their impatience.

Some may feel that no learning is taking place because no "expert" is telling them what is happening. Most of the learning which results from the discussion method is not quickly recognized. In fact, one gains in many intangible ways, for example, through an added feeling of confidence, increased comfort in a social situation, or a feeling of accomplishment when a difficult problem is worked out. Learning of this type cannot be measured as readily as the accumulation of a body of facts. Hence, it may take the group much longer to understand what is being learned and how it is helping them function more effectively and efficiently, both in the group and in the organization.

Planning and Conducting the Meeting

As discussion leader you are responsible for planning and preparing for the meeting as well as for conducting it. You will be concerned with the objectives of the meeting, the introduction of the subject, and the progress of the discussion.

Careful planning can eliminate many unnecessary difficulties during the session. Adequate preparation will give you confidence and enable you to concentrate on the ongoing discussion. Planning is the best way to ensure that the meeting time is put to the best possible use. Here are a few suggestions which will help you in your planning.

OBJECTIVES

Although group meetings have found increasing acceptance in industry, community organizations, and government, the mere holding of a meeting is no assurance that anything worthwhile will be accomplished. Before any meeting is called, there should be a clear understanding of its purpose and an assurance that a meeting is the best method to use in solving the problem or presenting the information.

Your objectives should be clearly outlined in your own mind. You should understand what you expect of the group. Are you asking them to give you information or advice? Or are you asking them to help solve a problem? In some meetings you will be giving information to the group; in others you will be leading a group which has formulated a problem on which it wants to work. After you have thought through what you expect of the group you will have a clearer idea of how you can use the knowledge, experience, and abilities which the individual members possess.

Here are some questions you might ask yourself to help crystallize objectives:

What is the primary objective I hope to achieve during the meeting?

What other objectives (development of people, teamwork, improvement of morale, etc.) may be furthered at the same time?

How can these objectives best be achieved? Through an informational meeting? Through an advisory meeting? Through a problem-solving meeting?

PEOPLE

When the purpose of the meeting has been decided on, consider next those who will be asked to participate. Some of the questions which may be helpful in thinking about this problem are:

What people are involved? Who is most concerned with this problem? Who will have to carry out the decision?

What resources are needed? Who has information to contribute to the solution? How many people are needed to solve the problem? What levels of supervision should be included?

Will these people be able to work together? What will be the problems involved in obtaining cooperation among those participating in the meeting? Will some people be reluctant to give their ideas if there are too many supervisors present? Is it necessary to have different levels of supervision present to solve the problem or give the proper advice?

You may have knowledge about individual members which will help you understand them better. For example, John Smith is an older foreman who resents the young college men in the organization. Bill Jones has some excellent ideas, but he gets tongue-tied when he tries to express them in a group. Henry Brown thinks that people getting together in groups takes up a lot of time when one person could just as well make the decision. These are only a few examples of the kinds of information you may have about your group, or will soon learn, which will help you to better understand how the group will operate as a whole.

ADVANCE INFORMATION

After you make up the list of people who are to take part, you should let them know when the meeting is to be held, the subject to be discussed, and why they are included. The conditions of each meeting will determine how much advance information is needed. The members should know in advance what is expected of them.

Other meetings may be called to increase communication or discuss common problems. All that would be necessary in the advance notice for such meetings would be a clear statement of the purpose of the meeting, the time, and the place.

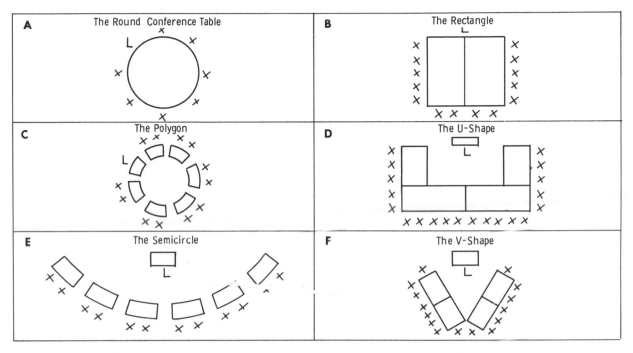

FIGURE 8—1. *Suggested seating arrangements for conferences and meetings.*

PHYSICAL SETTING AND MATERIALS

None of us is completely oblivious to the surroundings in which he lives and works. The meeting room need not be elaborate, but it should be conducive to the purposes of the meeting. Seating arrangements for group members are limited by the room size, the kind and quantity of equipment available, and the purpose of the meeting. Some possible seating plans are shown in Figure 8—1.

The following questions may help you in preparing the physical setting that you will need for the meeting:

Does everyone know the location of the meeting room, or would a sign on the door be helpful? Is a place to hang hats and coats necessary? Are there plenty of comfortable chairs? What is the best seating plan for this meeting? Can everyone see the leader and the materials he is using? Does everyone have a place to write? Is the room well ventilated and lighted? Is the room quiet and free from distractions? Are there plenty of ashtrays? Has drinking water been provided?

Prepared materials will not be necessary at all meetings. If, however, you are using prepared materials such as visual aids or printed booklets, everything should be arranged for in advance. You should be able to find whatever you want to use at any time during the meeting. In this way you will be able to change the plan of presentation if that seems to be the most helpful thing to do.

You will want to make your own checklist of materials. Here are some suggestions: paper and pencils for note taking, sufficient copies of handout materials for everyone, name cards if the members do not know each other, and visual aids. Since visual aids requirements vary from meeting to meeting, it is well to make your own checklist. If sound or projection equipment is to be used, be sure to check the location of outlets and to test the equipment beforehand. If slides or motion pictures are to be shown, make certain that the room can be darkened sufficiently and that chairs can be turned easily so that the screen is visible to all. If sound equipment or the tape recorder is to be used, be sure there will be no disturbing echoes.

PREPARATION OF SUBJECT MATTER

Make certain that you know what the meeting is to accomplish. What subjects will be taken up and what decisions will be reached? How will the topic be introduced and by whom? Will you need an outline of the material to be covered? Do you want to prepare questions in advance? What examples will you need to emphasize special points? Where will you want to ask the group to give examples?

The object of your preparation is to enable you to be most helpful to the group. There are wide individual differences in how leaders prepare for and handle their meetings. Some leaders like to "dry run" the meeting—i.e., to visualize beforehand what is apt to happen in the meeting. Whatever preparation you make should enable you to give undivided attention and understanding to your group during the meeting itself.

STARTING THE MEETING

Get your work done in advance of the meeting so that you can greet the group members as they arrive. This will help the members feel at ease, and you will begin to create the kind of atmosphere which will make your group most effective.

If you are working with persons who know each other well but haven't seen each other for some time, a few minutes of friendly conversation may be more important to the success of the meeting than starting on time. If several members of a group have not arrived, you will probably want to delay starting for a few minutes to give them a chance to come in before the meeting begins. On the other hand, if all the members of the group but one or two are ready to start, you should begin without waiting for those who are late.

In a first meeting with a group of people who don't know each other, introduce yourself and ask the group members to introduce themselves. When making introductions be as natural as you can. Many group leaders like to request that the group members call them by their first names (or perhaps a nickname) at the first meeting. The way you introduce yourself will set the tone for the introductions for the rest of the group. It may be helpful to have each person write his name on a card and place it on the table in front of him.

You will want to give the group some background on why the meeting is being held. This will bring everyone up-to-date. You will want to help the group understand the topic or problem. You may get some cues from the group as you introduce the topic. Do they seem to understand it? Do they seem interested? If there is any doubt about the group's interest or understanding, check with them about what is not clear so that they can further explore it.

As the discussion progresses, does the group indicate an interest in a somewhat different aspect of the problem than was originally stated? Do their questions indicate that they are not clear about the purposes of the discussion? Watch for these and for other cues which will help you take into account the wishes and needs of the group and fit them into the purposes of the meeting.

HANDLING THE MEETING

As the meeting progresses, try to be as relaxed as you can. Don't feel that you have to be perfect or that the meeting will fail if you make some mistakes. Mistakes can help you to improve your meetings if you learn from them rather than worry about them.

There are no hard and fast rules for accomplishing the purposes of a meeting. You may have read somewhere, or heard someone say, that the discussion must be kept on the subject. Sometimes, however, it is more important for the group to talk about something completely unrelated to the subject before considering the topic announced for discussion. When there are strong feelings which demand examination; when something has occurred which overshadows the meeting; or when the group members are very tired, you may find these matters have to be talked out first. In these instances, you may want to let the discussion progress freely until you think the group members have talked about whatever is bothering them enough to move on. You can try bringing them back to the subject of the meeting by asking a question or simply asking if they are ready to start the discussion. You can judge from their reactions whether they are ready to go ahead.

Everyone has a need to feel important and accepted by others. You can help your group members to feel accepted by (1) refraining from giving the impression that you think some contributions are good and others are not, (2) not showing impatience with the person who talks too much or has difficulty expressing his ideas, and (3) letting every group member know that you are honestly trying to understand what he has to say.

You may wonder how you can accept group members' ideas which are not on the subject or are factually incorrect. Remember that in the discussion you should encourage the group members to *express* their ideas. It is more important that the group members feel free to express themselves than that they should always come up with the "right" ideas. It should be pointed out, however, that the leader has a real part in helping the group organize individual contributions and reach a creative solution to a problem. By asking pertinent questions, pointing out areas of agreement, or diplomatically resolving differences, the leader helps to mold the individual contributions into a group accomplishment.

CLOSING THE MEETING

Some meetings have no definite time limit. The discussion may go on until the problem is solved. If the problem proves too complicated to be resolved in one session, the group may decide to meet again to work on it. In meetings of this kind the decision to close the meeting is made by the group.

Many meetings, however, must be conducted within definite time limits because of work requirements or shift hours. In these meetings, when the discussion is going along well and the group has a lively interest, you may be tempted to let the meeting run past the closing time. One of the most important reasons for closing the meeting on time under these circumstances, however, is that the group members may have other commitments and will resent being held overtime. If you have time and wish to do so, you may want to stay on informally with some of the group members who want to continue the discussion after the close of the meeting.

Even though time limits must sometimes be dealt with, you will not want to stop the discussion too abruptly. The group understands that there is a time limit. When it is nearly time to close, announce this fact and summarize what has happened to that point or ask a member to summarize for the group. If the meeting is one of a series, be sure to announce the time and place of the next meeting. If the discussion comes to a logical end before the announced closing time, don't hesitate to close a few minutes early.

Groups at Work

So far, we have discussed meetings and how to make the most of them in terms of leadership, purpose, and process. It is just as important to understand the nature of groups and how they function in order to conduct effective meetings. We are not concerned with the more complex issues of social psychology but rather with working concepts of group effectiveness.

How does a collection of individuals become a group? In general, by developing a number of interests in common and by developing effective interaction. Both of these are are accomplished by open, face-to-face communication. People share enough about themselves, their problems, and their needs to identify what they have in common and to develop a sense of common purpose. From the sense of purpose they develop insight about what they can expect from each other in the way of help, support, and conflict. Leaders can tell that this is happening by the way the group behaves. Do people express their real feelings? Do they disagree openly with each other? Do they speak up without being asked? Do the ideas flow from all members, not just one or two? Also, do they show self-discipline? Do they handle problem members? Can they handle conflict and disagreements when they arise?

Answering yes to most of these questions indicates group maturity and ability to get work done.

At times it is more important for the group to consider how its members feel about things than to discuss the topic. When people are angry, tired, playful, or bored, they will not concentrate on the problem. Until they settle disputes, relax, work off excess energy, speak their piece, or talk out something which interests them, they will not be productive. In situations such as these, feelings have priority over the topic for discussion.

A good group atmosphere allows for emotional needs as well as productivity. Such an atmosphere alleviates certain difficulties—for example, being afraid to talk, or needing to talk too much. This, in turn, enables the individual to be more helpful and satisfied in the group. The less an individual is concerned with his personal difficulties, the more he can concentrate on the group's topics or problems. A good atmosphere, then, after it has helped members work through their personal difficulties, makes the group as a whole more efficient.

What Group Atmosphere Is

Group atmosphere is the sum of the attitudes which exist in the group and of the feelings that group members have toward their personal affairs, toward the leader, toward one another, toward the meeting agenda, toward the people or the job which got them into the meeting, and toward their supervisor. A good group atmosphere exists when: (1) bonds between people are strong enough so that the group members can act naturally with each other; (2) people really try to understand what other members of the group say and feel, so that a member making a contribution realizes that there is a sincere attempt to understand him; (3) individuals feel free to participate as fully as they desire when they desire; (4) the major responsibility for what happens remains in the hands of the group and the leader (instead of solely in the hands of the leader or a few members), and the group carries out that responsibility with consideration for the feelings and ideas of all members; and (5) the members have a desire to be together which is strong enough so that it can withstand expressions of anger, fear, and conflict. When such feelings are expressed and the group is able to handle them, people tend to clear up their own differences and see where the others stand. This, in turn, allows them to take up other matters more effectively.

A group is becoming effective when people can tolerate the tension, anxiety, and frustration which are necessary to progress in solving a problem. People can understand and accept the

ups and downs in the group. In every group there are cycles of relaxation and hard work, of agreement and disagreement, of humor and seriousness, of doing things and thinking, of frustration and accomplishment, and of conflict and unity. All these cycles are necessary if the needs of the members are to be met and the group is to be productive.

The group members sense when *tension* is beginning to be too disturbing. They are then able to switch over into a more relaxed atmosphere. They know when they can no longer work to resolve conflict and are able to change from the conflict situation to an activity which makes them aware of the essential unity and agreement within the group.

The group recognizes the need for individual members to think things through when they want to. Many times, the most significant ideas come out after people have been *thinking quietly and hard*, rather than when a lot of words and motions have been going through the air.

Good group atmosphere develops when the members are given and accept the major responsibility for working on their own problems and determining the direction in which they will go. When this is not possible, group members should have confidence that their feelings and desires count in determining what the group does.

The Leader's Role in Setting the Atmosphere

At first the group tends to be only as comfortable, purposeful, and free as the leader is. As time goes on, the members themselves will tend to create a comfortable atmosphere.

The leader should try to understand each individual contribution and help the group members understand it. If the meaning of a contribution seems uncertain, the leader should try to clear up the confusion before the discussion continues. If at all possible, the leader should weave every contribution into the context of the discussion. He can do this by fitting at least a part of each one into the present discussion, relating it to an earlier discussion, or checking to see if the group would like to consider the idea at a later time. He should check with the group when he thinks they are ready to, or should, move on to something else.

When a good group atmosphere exists, people are natural and spontaneous. They try to understand what fellow members are saying, and they feel free to participate in the discussion. When such an atmosphere exists, group members find it easier to work together and are thus more productive.

The leader has much influence, especially at first, in determining the atmosphere of the group. If he accepts all contributions as worthy of consideration, tries to understand and relate each contribution to the discussion, makes sure everyone has a chance to express himself, and helps group members to work through individual differences, he will be doing his part toward building a good atmosphere.

Getting Work Done in Groups

Leaders play a key role in getting the group building process started and in helping the group to keep going as a self-directed entity whose purpose is to help the organization achieve its goals.

There are many signs of this task-oriented behavior to look for in working groups. For example, are the members suggesting new ideas or methods of attacking the problem? Are they defining the problem clearly and proposing solutions? Do their contributions reflect personal experiences or opinions? Are they investing themselves in the job at hand? Are they helping others clarify contributions? Do they seek additional information or opinions in order to redefine the problem or goal? Are things pulled together to show group consensus or agreement on alternative solutions or choices? Finally, do they evaluate their performance, measure their accomplishments, check for agreement, and examine how a proposal might work out in action?

They key difference between a grouping and a group is the way the work gets done. It is the difference between coaction and interaction. Coaction is summing up the individual's work in a group setting. Interaction is a face-to-face situation in which the team collectively develops the solution and accepts the result. Effective interaction requires within-group or team communication and clear roles and relationships for results that satisfy both group members and organization goals.

Reaching a Decision

So far we have talked about meetings and groups and how leaders must put the skills and techniques involved in making the most of meetings together with an understanding of how groups develop and work to accomplish goals. Implied throughout this discussion has been an end point, where a decision is reached, a goal set, or a vote taken.

Reaching common agreement involves making many decisions. It involves deciding where to start and what procedures to use. Often, the question is not whose ideas are better, but what solution can best solve the problem. It is possible to combine thinking or ideas to form a third and sometimes better alternative. It is not as easy as it sounds, because it involves discussing basic disagreements and trying to predict the ways contrasting ideas would work out in practice. Very often, a group is able to break the disagreements down into subpoints and recombine them to get more realistic solutions. In reaching agreement, more information from resource people may be needed or further analysis of the problem may be necessary. All of the preceding steps may be followed and still result in a compromise. In this last step, therefore, it is important that the group try to avoid, if possible, making a decision by just combining old ideas in a new way.

Reaching consensus is not always possible, and generally it is a long and hard process. But when a group has done it, then it has arrived at a solution that is better than one which any single individual could work out.

Most meetings can reach a workable plan for their operation if the group wants to, and if the leader is helpful.

Voting may be necessary when a group is too large to sit around a table and talk things out. Many formal decision-making processes require that a vote be taken—for example, city council adoption of an ordinance. Some type of voting can be helpful at stages in group development, to show the thinking of the group at any particular time, but it should not be used when a small group is trying to reach a common decision.

Leaders should remember a number of points about decision making. First, the purpose of problem solving is to reach a solution for the benefit of all, not to make certain individuals feel that they have won or lost. Second, everyone's contributions become the property of the whole group and can be accepted, rejected, combined, or changed as the group sees it. Third, views of the minority should be carefully considered; the minority may be disagreeing because it has ideas or knowledge the others do not have or have overlooked. Finally, the best solution usually contains the thinking of many people.

A final decision can be changed by the group at any time if new information comes up or if the decision does not work out in practice. However, a group solution can be changed only by the group, and to do this the group must again go through the steps ordinarily taken in reaching a solution.

Conclusion

In this chapter we have been concerned with groups functioning effectively to get work done in meetings. We have looked at the kinds of meetings and their purposes, described ways of planning and conducting meetings, and reviewed the nature of groups at work: group atmosphere, leadership roles, how work gets done.

Managers and supervisors need leadership and communication skills to operate effectively with groups, and many of these skills have been identified and discussed. It is through the application of these management skills in real-life meetings that the validity of the group process can be tested. Most management development takes place on the job, face-to-face with real problems. Considered this way, it is self-directed self-development.

Understanding small groups, working as teams, committees, or crews, is essential in our management system. Groups conduct the overwhelming proportion of the nation's governmental and industrial business. Thus the effectiveness with which these groups work is of the most practical concern. Management is, in the final analysis, a function of society and must be a useful enabling agent in the improvement of society. It is in face-to-face groups working on problems that society comes together. It is here that society is changed and adapted to its times.

9

Administrative Communication

EFFECTIVE COMMUNICATION POLICIES at the top encourage better communication throughout the organization. Communication in the sense we are considering here is the flow of information throughout the organization, the processes involved, and the use of information.[1] Studies of communication and information flow themselves are comparatively new, beginning in the forties with Claude Shannon's schematic outline of a communication process (discussed later in this chapter).

The Nature of Communication

Studies of administrative communication today are somewhat more sophisticated and are built around three theories: (1) an uncertainty or quantitative theory; (2) a connotative or content theory; and (3) a hybrid theory or a combination of the first two.[2]

Uncertainty theory includes those approaches which attempt to reduce uncertainty in communication by quantifying information and analyzing it through mathematical formulas of chance. While this approach has been used extensively in the behavioral and social sciences, it also provides the basis for management information systems, especially those that are computer based.

The many forms used for communication in the municipal organization may also be included under the uncertainty theory. Forms which ask precise questions and in some instances provide a checkoff list of precise answers are examples. The utility meter reader's form is an example of a simple uncertainty reducing device in the com-

munication process. It contains spaces for recording precise meter readings and communicating these to the billing department without cluttering up the communication process with extraneous information.

Job descriptions, written personnel and other rules, inspection forms of all types, budget request forms, and a number of similar forms are all attempts to reduce uncertainty in administrative communication by limiting the alternatives open to the communicator. This can be a disadvantage where other information might bear on the situation but no provision has been made in the form for communicating it.

Another disadvantage is that forms are depersonalizing. A form listing a person's name, age, employee number, sex, marital status, etc., tells very little of a personal nature about the person. Humorists have had a field day with the depersonalizing aspects of communication forms. Some readers may recall the cartoon of a college student who is refused a class admission card because he cannot remember his student number. His reply: I don't exist as a person because I can't recall my student number. Some information must of necessity be depersonalizing in order to reduce clutter and provide speed and accuracy. The difficulty comes in deciding which communications should and should not be personalized.

Connotative or content theories of communication are more broadly based, and provide infinite possibilities for uncertainty. It is this type of communication that we will be talking about here, both written and oral/aural (speaking and listening). The principal difference between uncertainty theory and content theory is that the former tries to eliminate uncertainty by limiting alternatives and constructing a closed or limited system in which communication takes place. Understanding may or may not be a factor. Content-oriented theory, on the other hand, may also reduce uncertainty, but it does this by generating understanding of a wide number of alternatives dealing with many' meanings and definitions. While it provides opportunities for rich personal interaction, this very fact produces a high risk factor for misunderstanding.

John Parry points this up when he writes:

The dictionary, for example, describes a goat as a "hardy lively wanton strong-smelling usually horned and bearded ruminant quadruped." ... If a man points to an animal and says, "That is a goat" ... the person to whom he is addressing this remark is not automatically made aware of all the creature's qualities. It follows that in using the expression goat-like one speaker may have in mind a smell, another a beard, and a third licentious behavior.[3]

Thus, a term with a rich connotation will give rise to many interpretations based on each person's frame of reference. Studies measuring the level of agreement between managers and their subordinates point up this fact succinctly. Managers and employees, when they are discussing some plan or decision affecting the organization and its work, usually assume that they are in agreement about the nature of the problem and the work involved. Suppose the manager says to a department head: "You know what the council is looking for and the effect this will have in your department." The reply generally is, "Yes, I've been expecting they'd take that action and we're ready for it over here." On the surface it appears each understands the council's action and that each also understands and is in agreement about what has to be done. The assumption is probably wrong.

Goals, persons, problems, and a myriad of other things in management and administration are subject to individual interpretation. According to an American Management Association study, chances are better than even that the manager and the department head, as well as those at other levels, will have different understandings of the council's action and the action to be taken by the department. The study centers on four principal areas, which are: the employee's concept of his specific job, the requirements he must fulfill in order to do his work well, his anticipation of future changes in his work, and the obstacles which prevent him from doing as good a job as possible. In almost every area, managers and subordinates either did not agree or differed more than they agreed. In addition, there was little agreement on the priorities involved.[4]

Hybrid approaches to examining the communication process include those theories with both an uncertainty and a content factor. While these will be touched on here, few specific references will be made. Hopefully, the reader will notice when elements of the two theories are present to form a hybrid theory.

The admonition in organizations to "put it in writing" might constitute a sort of hybrid theory. The assumption that putting it in writing will always reduce uncertainty, however, is somewhat of a fallacy. Words, written or spoken, are still open to interpretation and thus to misunderstanding. Additionally, putting it in writing tends to depersonalize relationships, or at least makes rich interpersonal experiences less likely. The many memo fights, usually between operating and staff departments, are an example. Such misinterpretations and misunderstandings might better be dealt with over a cup of coffee.

The Communication Process

Something in human nature compels a person to make sense out of that which he chooses to become involved in. One of the major functions of the communication process is to help us make sense of these things. Learning to make sense out of things, to communicate, begins very early in life. Not too long after birth the child begins to establish a communication system with his mother. Each experience puts him further along in the process. He soon learns to offer a smile for a smile; though he may sometimes giggle at a frown, once he experiences the consequences he learns to respond in an appropriate manner. He finds that such signals are a means for making his feelings and desires known to others. At the start he is learning body language. Later he will learn speech and ways to put both together.

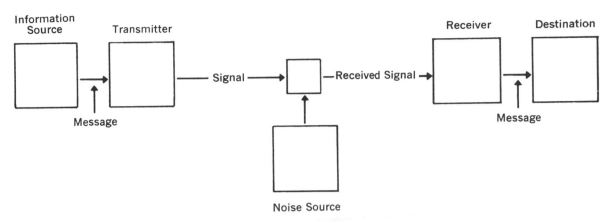

FIGURE 9—1. *Basic communication model.*

Long before he reaches adulthood he will have had many experiences with the complexities of the communication process. To some degree he will have been conditioned to respond to certain stimuli in certain ways. As he moves through the educational system, he is further conditioned in the communication process.

Alvin Toffler in *Future Shock* has argued that our education system appears to be designed largely to condition us for assembly-line factory work.[5] Others have argued that the system is designed more to stifle creativity than to encourage it. Students are rewarded for passive behavior, leading some critics to say that the "scholar" is the one who absorbs the most and asks the least.

Certainly the educational system generally constitutes the person's first experience as a part of a formal organization. What he experiences and learns of the communication process there will have a profound effect on how he communicates in the formal organizations he becomes involved with in later life. It is argued that he is encouraged to be a passive recipient in the classroom, relying largely on written words and multiple-choice examinations to demonstrate his learning ability, thus failing to develop face-to-face communication skills in formal organizational relationships.

Thus conditioned, the argument goes, the person early develops a lack of motivation for face-to-face communication in the formal organization. Dysfunction in face-to-face communicating among adults in organizations is quite common. Dysfunctions are equally evident, however, when using complex nonface-to-face communication channels.

While the educational system is definitely a factor in the development of communication skills, neither the degree nor the direction of this development is precisely known. This raises the question of why some administrators are much more skillful in all types of communication than are others. The answer lies in a complex and interrelated web of physical and psychological factors, family and neighborhood environment, peer group standards, parental expectations, and educational, vocational, and leisure interests. It is beyond the scope of this chapter to explore this question (which could easily be a book by itself).

Because of the newness of the study of the communication process, and because of its many complexities, there is much that we still do not know. Nevertheless, enough is known to provide the guidelines shown in the balance of this chapter.

A BASIC COMMUNICATION MODEL

One basic model of the communication process, developed by Claude E. Shannon at the Bell Telephone Laboratories, appears in schematic form in Figure 9—1.[6]

Originally developed for physicists and mathematicians to illustrate a telephone communication system, it consists essentially of five parts: (1) an information source, (2) a transmitter, (3) a channel, (4) a receiver, and (5) a destination.

The information source could be a person, a radio or television studio, a stock exchange, or the news room of a press service. Information is selected by the source to be transmitted through the transmitter, which could be a microphone, a television camera, or a teletypewriter. The transmitter encodes the message into a form suitable for transmission over the channel. In a telephone system this consists of changing sound pressure into a proportional electric current. The channel may be a pair of wires, as in a telephone system, or a coaxial cable, as in a television network. As the message passes along the channel it may have to overcome a noise source—possibly static—and in the process can suffer some distortion. The receiver decodes the message into a form understandable by the destination, which is the person or the thing for which the message is intended.

An Expanded Communication Model

Communication in the interacting organization, however, is much more complex than Shannon's model is able to illustrate. The latter's elements are mostly mechanical or electronic; subject only to "noise" distortions, they can be expected to transmit and reproduce messages quite accurately. When humans serve as transmitters, channels, and receivers, such faithful reproduction is much less certain.

One way in which human factors can affect the communication process became apparent in studies of employee morale during the fifties. An initial research hupothesis centered on the notion that effective communication could raise the level of morale among the work force. It soon

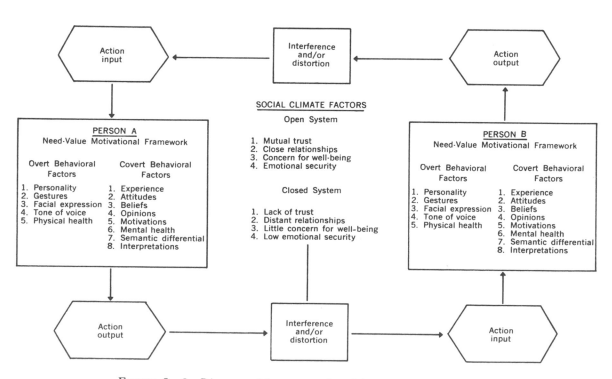

FIGURE 9—2. *Diagram of intrapersonal and interpersonal communication.*

became evident, however, that the reverse was true: morale levels affect the quality and quantity of communication. In order to give more meaning to Shannon's basic communication model, it is necessary to consider some of these human factors involved in an organization's communication process.

While learning communication skills, the individual also acquires likes and dislikes which provide a framework for evaluating experiences and situations. Certain values are developed within this framework, and these influence one's perception of what is communicated. For our purposes, this framework is referred to as a person's need-value motivational framework and is illustrated in Figure 9—2.

The diagram may be described as follows: Communication starts with an action input (hexagon in upper left-hand corner) to Person A (left-hand rectangle) within a situational setting and social climate (depicted by the frame around the diagram). This action input is decoded through the need-value motivational framework of Person A. Once the message is decoded, Person A may choose not to respond, and this will be communicated by no action output. If, however, he chooses to respond, the action output will be influenced by the same factors used in decoding the action input, plus Person A's interpretation of the action input.

This action output will be passed along the channel (arrows at the bottom of Figure 9—2), where it may be subject to interference and/or distortion before becoming an action input to Person B. As an input to Person B, the message is decoded within his need-value motivational framework and his perception of the social climate and situation. The communication process may be terminated at this point if Person B chooses not to respond, but a no-response output may trigger another action output from Person A indicating either that he agrees or that he feels further communication is necessary.

Either way, the action output from Person B will travel along the channel (the arrows at the top of the diagram), again being subject to interference and/or distortion. The process continues in this circular way until terminated by the persons involved, by interruption from a third person, or by a change in the situation.

Take a few minutes now to trace a message through the diagram in Figure 9—2. Consider the many factors in the need-value motivational framework that will influence how the message or action input will be interpreted. Think how these will influence the action output or response. The several key elements in the expanded diagram involve overt and covert behavioral factors as well as the social climate in which the communication takes place. Each element interacts with the others to determine the interpretation of the action input and the response that will be generated in the form of an action output. The "ideal" communication combination might consist of favorable covert behavioral factors in each person coupled with an "open system" involving mutual trust, close relationships, concern for well-being, and high emotional security. Under such circumstances it is likely that communication would be open and effective.

Where unfavorable covert behavioral factors are coupled with a "closed system" involving a lack of trust, distant relationships, little concern for well-being, and low emotional security, communication will generally be dysfunctional and very possibly nonexistent.

BEHAVIORAL FACTORS

Experience. All experience has some influence on behavior, and repeated experiences have a reinforcing element. The most immediate influence on communication, however, centers on Person A's experience in dealing with Person B, and vice versa. If it has been favorable, it may have a great deal of influence on the effectiveness of the communication. If it has been unfavorable, the opposite will generally be true.

Attitudes, Opinions, and Beliefs. Significantly involved in communication are attitudes, opinions, and beliefs, listed under covert behavioral factors. These exert a direct influence on the behavior of the communicator and on his decoding processes, thus affecting not only the content of the message but also the intent attributed to the message. Where individuals in the communication hold different attitudes, opinions, and beliefs (AOBs), there will be a tendency for each selectively to perceive those parts of the message which reinforce his own attitudes, opinions, and beliefs. By the same process he will tend to reject those AOBs that are not in harmony with his own.

Motivations. Motivations may be categorized as (1) self-oriented, (2) receiver-oriented, or (3) jointly-oriented. Messages falling in the self-oriented category may be sent merely to influence the receiver to accept the kind of information that the transmitter wants him to have. Self-orientation may also lead to the use of false or deceptive messages. When the transmitter assumes it to be rewarding to have the receiver believe that information between them has been equalized, he may send deceptive messages. In competitive situations, or when one wants to avoid blame, messages may be sent deliberately to unequalize information. Since this may take place in receiver-oriented messages as well, the category is often termed "individually-oriented communication." Jointly-oriented messages are useful in promoting teamwork and are more akin to group-oriented communication.

Semantic Differential. Words or other stimuli serve as signs or symbols in the communication process. If one person has access to more signs or symbols than the other, this may constitute a semantic differential. More frequently, however, semantic differential will exist when signs or symbols mean one thing to one person and another thing to the other person. In speaking of signs and symbols, some sociologists label as "signs" those words or other stimuli that aim at evoking overt behavior, and as "symbols" those that encourage concept formation. In rule- or technology-oriented situations, signs are best used to communicate, and in individual- or group-oriented situations, symbols are best.

Semantic differentials may exist also in non-linguistic communication. The most common form of semantic differential, of course, is body motion or gesture. Some gestures used as symbols have more or less agreed-upon meanings, such as the meanings involved in a handshake, nod, frown, wink, and many others. Still other gestures must be considered within the context in which they take place. As they interact, Person A and Person B encode into signs or symbols some aspect of their own psychological state, although this may not be readily apparent.

Interpretations. As information passes between Person A and Person B, many interpretations are available to either or both persons. Through each action input and action output, the number of alternative interpretations may be reduced and a level of understanding reached. If the action inputs and action outputs increase the number of interpretations available, there is great danger of the exchange ending in dysfunctional communication. There will be instances, however, during the course of the interplay between A and B, where the number of alternative interpretations may initially be small, rise to a large number, and taper off or abruptly center on one or a few. Effective communication, in short, reduces the number of available interpretations.

Perception also plays a large part in interpretations. In the interplay between Person A and Person B, each plays a dual role as the perceived and the perceiver. While Person A is playing the role of the perceiver, he is also playing the role of the perceived as Person B perceives certain qualities or lack of qualities in him. Each has motives and attitudes as well as many other attributes. During the interplay, as they become more aware of each other, each will look for cues about the other. These cues are organized within the person's own need-value motivational framework.

Situation, Person, Self. Effective communication, therefore, depends in many ways on the ability of the communicators to judge people. Perception of others represents a complex set of learned skills that comes into play in relation to conditions in the person being judged, conditions in the observer himself, as well as conditions in the situation and the social or organizational climate.

During the interplay, each person searches for constancies in the other, as well as for discrepancies. If a communicator is confronted with enough discrepancies, he may reevaluate his impression and come up with a new or modified view of the person.

In any interaction, the perceiver will be influenced also by situational cues, and these may enter into his judgment. Thus, knowledge of the situation, of the person involved, and of the communicator himself will influence the degree of effective communication: the more knowledge the communicator has of the situation, the person, himself, and his attunement to the social climate, the better results he will have with the communication process.

EGO PROTECTION AS A COMMUNICATION FACTOR

One of the most formidable barriers arising out of the need-value motiviational framework is ego protection. Most people have a need for others to see them in a favorable view—usually the view they hold of themselves, or one which compliments it. Psychologists refer to this self-view as the ego and the need as an ego need. This self-view or ego is important to the individual. When it is threatened, especially if it bears little resemblance to reality, it can produce defensive behavior. The situation is complicated by the fact that the ego is not readily apparent to others.

Using Person A and Person B again, we can demonstrate how ego protection enters into communication by abstracting Person A and Person B as circles and further abstracting "reality" as another circle, as shown in Figure 9—3. The first circle (1) represents Person A as he sees himself—in other words, his ego. Circle 2 represents Person's B's view of Person A. Circle 3 represents "reality."

In Figure 9—3 there is no interaction depicted, neither with reality nor between the two persons. In Figure 9—4 we find Person A (circle 1 relating to reality, but not completely, which is generally the case for most of us, though we may not readily admit it. While part of the view he holds of himself is consistent with reality, a portion is not.

As Persons A and B begin to interact, to communicate, B's circle (circle 2) moves into the situation. The diagram then looks as it is shown in Figure 9—5. The point at which the three circles overlap represents the effective area of communication. In this area Persons A and B have a true view of each other and of reality. A fairly large part is hidden from both of them and another large part is evident to one but not the other. Additionally, each sees a part of the other which is not consistent with reality.

Over time, as Persons A and B interact, there is circular movement within the diagram.

Through interaction and communication each begins to share with the other things that are not readily apparent. In effect the circles begin to rotate (Figure 9—6). It is this process which contributes to growth and the healthy development of individuals. As persons share their ideas, thoughts, and behaviors, the circles are drawn tightly together.

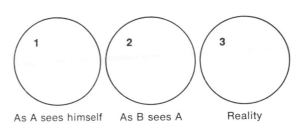

As A sees himself   As B sees A   Reality

FIGURE 9—3. *The three "selfs."*

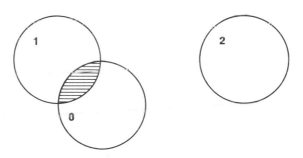

FIGURE 9—4. *Interaction with reality.*

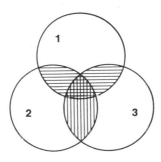

FIGURE 9—5. *Interaction of the three "selfs."*

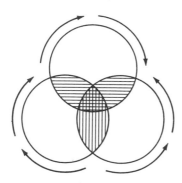

FIGURE 9—6. *Interaction for communication.*

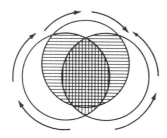

FIGURE 9—7. *Communication learning and growth.*

An effective communication situation between two self-actualized individuals (see Chapter 3) would be depicted by Figure 9—7. Through interaction and exposure, a learning and growth factor has been introduced. Circular motion still exists, and has helped to tighten the diagram, making the overlap nearly complete so that both parties are interacting with a maximum amount of awareness of reality and each other. It is doubtful that the circles would ever completely overlap, and it is probably not desirable anyway. Each of us, as well as the situations we find ourselves in, needs a certain amount of mystery or unknowing to add a little spice.

According to the diagrams, the communication appears quite simple. Each person, then, is actually three persons. He is the person he really is (circle **3** or "reality"); he is the person he thinks he is (circle **1** or self-view or ego); and he is the person others see him to be (circle **2** or what he projects). As persons interact they expose various parts of these three "selfs," and through this exposure it is possible to expand the area where the three "selfs" are consistent. This

is represented by the cross-hatched area in the diagrams and represents the effective communication area.

Attacks on the ego and efforts to defend against such attacks are what keep the process from working effectively, resulting in less effective communication. This is the classical win-lose situation where both parties usually end up losing. Ego protection is almost always a win-lose situation. The parties to the communication, sometimes unknowingly, begin to attack each other's egos instead of focusing on the real problem.

By subordinating his ego, by adopting a sense of humility, an administrator is better able to understand his own ego and to feel more secure in it, thus being able to react more constructively. In this manner he increases his understanding not only of himself but also of the other person and of the problem at hand.

None of the foregoing should be interpreted as meaning that persons must be identical or similar in nature and values to communicate effectively. The most effective communication takes place when persons understand and accept their dissimilarities and can use these in the solution of the problem.

INFORMAL CHANNELS OF COMMUNICATION

Those factors in the need-value motivational framework which can distort formal communication "through channels" can also produce informal channels of communication—and distort the information which passes through them as well!

It is doubtful if an organization ever existed that did not have such informal channels of communication as "grapevines." The municipal organization is no different in this respect. Because of the widespread interest of citizens and the press in the activities of the municipal organization, there are probably even greater opportunities for a grapevine to flourish here than in organizations of other types.

Grapevines come into existence when normal communication channels fail to provide enough information, are used to misinform, or simply convey information too slowly. Their existence illustrates an important rule: every person wants the information coming to him to "make sense."

When it does not, he generally tries to make sense out of it. In this search for meaning he may invent additional information or place unjustifiable interpretations upon fragmentary data. The whole of his thought—actual information plus personal speculations—is normally passed on to others.

Of course, it is true that sometimes the information an employee receives does really make sense, but not to him. It is also true that sometimes he has only a part of the information, and that this part—out of context—does not make sense. However such grapevine data are generated, the end product is quite similar.

Administrators typically discuss the grapevine solely as a network for rumor and malicious gossip. Grapevines, however, are not necessarily without administrative utility. They can serve a useful purpose through helping to create and reinforce an interest in the workings of the organization.

A healthy grapevine can exist, however, only if employees receive enough information so that the messages they receive make sense to them. If the information being fed into the system *does* seem sufficient, yet an unhealthy grapevine flourishes, the cause may be a blockage at some point in the chain of command: information is filtered out, and employees are receiving too little. A similar filtering process may work in reverse and filter out too much upward communication.

In municipalities where the city council frequently holds executive sessions or informal sessions "off the record," a grapevine will generally flourish. It will be the result of both internal pressures and external pressures from the press and citizens. In such cases, information traveling the grapevine is usually far more harmful than the real facts would be.

Erroneous reporting by the news media also feeds the grapevine. Any planned change incorrectly reported will travel very rapidly—sometimes constructively but frequently with undesirable ramifications.

In summing up the grapevine, a few words must be said about hoarding information. There is no question that information is power. It is also true that some persons try to hoard information so as to increase their power and that

these persons may exist at any level in the organization. There are many instances of managers giving out just enough information to handle one step of a task at a time. When that step is completed the worker must return to his boss for additional information, and so on, until the completion of the task. Ironically, after forcing this kind of dependency, it is not uncommon for this type of boss to complain because his workers "just won't take any initiative." In using the communication process as a device for control, the manager is relinquishing his responsibility for facilitating and coordinating work. In effect, he is creating barriers which prevent workers from doing the best job possible. The worker must then resort to the grapevine if he is to function effectively. And if the grapevine fails, it is not unnatural for the worker to say: "To hell with it! If the boss wants to goof up on information, then he'll have to live with the consequences."

COMMUNICATION AND CHANGE

Communication, then, provides the circuitry in the interacting organization by which work groups deal with change and reduce uncertainty.

"Change" is a word that is often used today to cover a variety of personal and institutional reactions to technological, sociological, and intellectual developments that are occurring at a much faster rate than ever before in the history of man. In this sense, change is "situational," to use a currently fashionable term—i.e., change depends on who is involved, the kind of problem, the product or service affected, the decision to be made, etc.

The management of change within the organization is the subject of Chapter 10, and the coverage includes resistance to change, strategies for change, the manager as a change agent, and change within the framework of organization development.

For purposes of this chapter, the discussion of change is limited to how it works with communication. We know that ineffective communication is a major cause of trouble (but not the only cause, as is explained in Chapter 10) when an organizational change has to be made. All of us will fight off change that is sudden, unexpected, unexplained, and vague or unknown. It is the communications job to anticipate such reactions so that the worst of these effects can be foreseen and prevented.

One way to gain some understanding of the interaction between communication and change is to look at the terms "reactive" and "proactive." Reactive behavior is the fact that something happens and we react to it. Proactive behavior may be defined as deciding what we want to happen and then making it happen. Most cause-and-effect theorists would have us believe that man is basically a reactive being. He is constantly reacting to what is happening in his environment.

When we then take up the theory of man as a proactive being, making things happen, the arguments become confused. Does man become proactive because he is reactive or does he become reactive because he is proactive? The argument here is that man is both reactive and proactive and that he can best be described as *interactive*. In other words, reactive and proactive elements are so intertwined in his environment that every reaction is a proactive move in an attempt to change the situation or circumstances. In this effort he reacts to the new situation, thus triggering another round of the proactive cycle.

Looking broadly at management history (see Chapter 3), it can be seen that the Taylor efficiency movement was a proactive reaction to the sloppy use of the emerging technology. The aim was to increase efficiency by reducing uncertainty in the production process. This was done by attempting to control the communication process and by structuring each job and the instructions that went with it. The human relations movement in turn was a proactive reaction to Taylorism. Modern management theory is a proactive reaction to the human relations movement, attempting to take the best from each school of thought and meld this with a concept of man as a developing, problem-solving individual.

Each movement has depended on a communication process for the accomplishment of its goals. Taylorism designed communication to reduce or eliminate uncertainty in work processes. The human relations movement attempted to humanize the communication process through a paternalistic and counseling

approach. Neither is necessarily incompatible with the other. In any organization there are elements that demand a reduction in uncertainty just as there are elements that demand a more creative approach.

Emerging management practice calls for creative communication skills that encourage and focus the best thinking on organizational problems. These skills must allow for input from relevant functions at all levels. Faced with adapting a largely authoritative or benevolent authoritative structure to a complex participative structure under a new set of circumstances, management must be able to use the communication process to the best interests of all concerned.

Communication Skills

Along with developing a reasonable understanding of communication processes, the administrator must also master communication skills himself and at the same time develop subordinates' skills.

THE ART OF LISTENING

The ability to listen is one of the basic communication skills. Listening, however, is not only a skill but also an art and a discipline. As with other skills, it requires control—intellectual, emotional, and behavioral. Hearing is not necessarily listening. It becomes listening only when one pays attention to what is said, follows it closely, and understands it correctly.

To listen, the administrator must subordinate his ego and actively encourage the other person to speak. Too frequently, a manager is so intent on letting the other person know about his own knowledge of the situation or problem that he does all the talking himself. In the extreme, he asks questions and then answers them—almost as if talking to himself.

In listening, the administrator has certain objectives which relate to the communication process. Basically, these include five goals:

1. He wants the person to talk freely and frankly.
2. He wants the person to cover matters and problems that are important to both of them.

3. He wants the person to furnish as much information as he can.
4. He wants both the person and himself to get greater insight into and understanding of the problem as they talk it out.
5. He wants the person to try to see the causes and reasons for the problem and to figure out what can be done about it.[7]

There is an old Arabic proverb that says, 'Listen to what men say, but find out how they feel." The administrator must remember that everyone listens to people through a baffle screen made up of his own attitudes, values, beliefs, and preconceived notions and judgments (the need-value motivational framework). Thus, in listening to others, the administrator will tend to add something to what is actually said in terms of what he already thinks, feels, and believes. He must try to minimize this. Some listening Dos and Don'ts are given in Figure 9—8.

Figure 9—9 is a table developed by Robert K. Burns of the Industrial Relations Center of the University of Chicago. It sets forth some of the key listening techniques, the purpose of each, and examples of how these can be used.[8]

DO

1. Show interest.
2. Be understanding of the other person.
3. Express empathy.
4. Single out the problem if there is one.
5. Listen for causes of the problem.
6. Help the person to associate the problem with the cause.
7. Encourage the person to develop the competence and motiviation to solve his own problems.
8. Cultivate the ability to be silent when silence is needed.

DON'T

1. Don't argue.
2. Don't interrupt.
3. Don't pass judgments too quickly or in advance.
4. Don't give advice unless it's requested.
5. Don't jump to conclusions.
6. Don't let the person's sentiments react too directly on your own.

FIGURE 9—8. *Listening dos and don'ts.*

Study these over carefully and become familiar with the purposes of each. Learn to identify the different kinds of listening situations and the appropriate types of questions. Recast the examples into your own vocabulary and use as much variety as possible. Avoid constant repetition.

QUESTIONING TECHNIQUES

In addition to listening, the administrator must be able to ask questions. Asking the right questions in terms of the needs of the individual and the needs of the job is a basic part of development and an important administrative skill. The power of the question is that it requires an answer. If the right question is asked in the right way (in terms of information, experience, reactions, or other data sought), it follows that one will get a useful answer. If the wrong question is asked, even the "right" answer may be of little use.

Frequently the administrator feels that, since his job is to manage, he must tell people what to do and how to do it, and must make all the decisions. No better example of dysfunctional communication exists. An administrator's decisions are only as good as his information. He cannot know as much about certain problems as his subordinates. If he cuts off communication with them he will be without adequate information. He will make poor decisions, and he will lose his subordinates' respect and cooperation.

Asking. By asking questions, the administrator increases his stock of information and discovers the feelings and sentiments of subordinates; these invariably affect what the administrator will do, what he will say, and how he will act. When he asks the subordinate about his work, the subordinate is able to indicate his needs, interests, problems, and concerns. The administrator is then in a better position to give him information, extend help, pass on advice, or issue orders or instructions.

Telling and ordering lead to dysfunctional communication. They tend to weaken the self-respect, independence, and initiative of the subordinate. They increase his dependence on the administrator and consequently retard his own development as a self-directed, fully func-

TYPES OF LISTENING	PURPOSE	EXAMPLES
1. **CLARIFYING**	1. To get at additional facts 2. To help him explore all sides of a problem	1. "Can you clarify this?" 2. "Do you mean this . . .?" 3. "Is this the problem as you see it now?"
2. **RESTATEMENT**	1. To check your meaning and interpretation with his 2. To show you are listening and that you understand what he is saying. 3. To encourage him to analyze other aspects of the matter being considered and to discuss them with you.	1. "As I understand it then your plan is . . ." 2. "This is what you have decided to do and the reasons are . . ."
3. **NEUTRAL**	1. To convey that you are interested and listening. 2. To encourage the person to continue talking.	1. "I see" 2. "Uh-huh" 3. "That's very interesting" 4. "I understand"
4. **REFLECTIVE**	1. To show that you understand how he feels about what he is saying. 2. To help the person to evaluate and temper his own feelings as expressed by someone else.	1. "You feel that . . ." 2. "It was a shocking thing as you saw it." 3. "You felt you didn't get a fair shake."
5. **SUMMARIZING**	1. To bring all the discussion into focus in terms of a summary. 2. To serve as a spring board for further discussion on a new aspect or problem.	1. "These are the key ideas you have expressed . . ." 2. "If I understand how you feel about the situation . ."

FIGURE 9—9. *Listening techniques.*

tioning person. Asking, questioning, and listening tend to stimulate the subordinate, to motivate him, and to encourage him to take initiative and responsibility. The proper use of questioning methods can have an important effect in building a man-boss relationship that is stable, satisfying, and productive. Such a relationship depends on and supports effective communication.

Positive Attitude. The administrator must, then, have a positive attitude toward the importance of asking rather than telling. Once he has this basic attitude, he must supplement it with the attitude that people are important and that through communication he can draw on their unique experiences, background, and training. In this way, he is helping them to make a personal contribution to the management process. With these attitudes, he must: (1) understand the different types of questions—their nature, purpose, and use; (2) understand the direction of questions—how to channel and handle them; and (3) develop skill in using questioning techniques in appropriate situations.

Seven types of questions and four directions which questions may take are listed in Figures 9—10, and 9—11, along with purposes and examples of each.[9] As with the listening techniques, study them carefully until they become a part of your own management style.

LEADERSHIP STYLES AND COMMUNICATION

Related to listening and questioning is the administrator's own leadership style. His leadership style will have a great deal of influence on the climate of the organization, which in turn affects the degree of openness of the system and the kinds of responses elicited through listening and questioning techniques. Using the Nelson Leadership Scale, the Industrial Relations Center at the University of Chicago has identified four basic styles of leadership found in governmental and other organizations. These include: (1) rule-oriented leadership, (2) technology-oriented leadership, (3) individual-oriented leadership, and (4) group-oriented leadership.[10] Rule- and technology-oriented leadership tend toward authoritarianism and place human values below the values of the organization; individual- and group-oriented leadership tend toward participation and attempt to reconcile human values with the values of the organization. Definitions of the four styles are set forth below.

Rule-Oriented Leadership. The administrator focusing on this style of leadership relies primarily on the rules and policies of the organization to communicate with and control employees. When a problem arises, he cites provisions in the charter or the employee manual to reinforce communication. His communication is usually one-way—downward—and he tends to operate in an authoritative manner. His relationships with subordinates will generally be rather distant.

Technology-Oriented Leadership. This leader is the expert. Most of his leadership and communication will be in terms of the technology and this will play a large part in his decision-making system. His communication will tend to be one-way, downward. He, too, will tend to operate in an authoritative manner.

Individual-Oriented Leadership. In this style of leadership the administrator focuses on the individual. His relationships with subordinates are generally warm and close. His communication is two-way—both upward and downward. He depends heavily on his friendship with his subordinates in the communication system and makes decisions in terms of how these will affect individuals on his staff. The style's disadvantages are that it tends to be manipulative and this sometimes backfires. Many employees do not care to be manipulated, and when they discover that they have been they react unfavorably, to put it mildly. Additionally, the style tends to encourage currying favor with the boss and sometimes gives rise to petty jealousies.

Group-Oriented Leadership. The administrator practicing this style of leadership engages in three-way communication—upward, downward, and horizontal. He involves the group in problem solving and setting objectives, and most decisions are based on consensus. His relationships are generally warm and close, and people in his work groups not only feel a sense of participation but actually participate in the decision-making process.

Other styles of leadership are identified in Chapter 5 and may also be related to communi-

TYPE	PURPOSE	EXAMPLES
1. FACTUAL	1. To get information 2. To open discussion	1. All the "W" questions: what, where, why, when, who and how?
2. EXPLANATORY	1. To get reasons and explanations 2. To broaden discussion 3. To develop additional information	1. "In what way would this help solve the problem? 2. "What other aspects of this should be considered?" 3. "Just how would this be done?"
3. JUSTIFYING	1. To challenge old ideas 2. To develop new ideas 3. To get reasoning and proof	1. "Why do you think so?" 2. "How do you know?" 3. "What evidence do you have?"
4. LEADING	1. To introduce a new idea 2. To advance a suggestion of your own or others	1. "Should we consider this —as a possible solution?" 2. "Would this—be a feasible alternative?"
5. HYPOTHETICAL	1. To develop new ideas 2. To suggest another, possibly unpopular, opinion 3. To change the course of the discussion	1. "Suppose we did it this way . . . What would happen?" 2. "Another city does this . . . is this feasible here?"
6. ALTERNATIVE	1. To make a decision between alternatives 2. To get agreement	1. "Which of these solutions is best, A or B?" 2. "Does this represent our choice in preference to—?"
7. COORDINATING	1. To develop consensus 2. To get agreement 3. To take action	1. "Can we conclude that this is the next step?" 2. "Is there general agreement then on this plan?"

FIGURE 9—10. *Questioning techniques by types of questions.*

TYPE	PURPOSE	EXAMPLES
A. **OVERHEAD:** Directed to group	1. To open discussion 2. To introduce a new phase 3. To give everyone a chance	1. "How shall we begin?" 2. "What should we consider next, anyone?" 3. "What else might be important?"
B. **DIRECT:** Addressed to a specific person	1. To call on a person for special information 2. To involve someone who has not been active	1. "Al, what would be your suggestions?" 2. "Fred, have you had any experience with this?"
C. **RELAY:** Referred back to another person or to the group	1. To help the leader avoid giving his own opinion 2. To get others involved in the discussion 3. To call on someone who knows the answer	1. "Would someone like to comment on Bill's question?" 2. "John, how would you answer Bill's question?"
D. **REVERSE:** Referred back to person who asks question	1. To help the leader avoid giving his own opinion 2. To encourage the questioner to think for himself 3. To bring out opinions	1. "Well, Dick, how about giving us **your** opinion first?" 2. "Bob, tell us first what your own experience has been"

FIGURE 9—11. *Questioning techniques by direction of questions.*

cation style. It is doubtful, however, that any administrator practices only one style of leadership, although the tendency is to focus primarily on one style. None of the styles is absolutely wrong. The most successful administrators usually practice a balanced style of leadership, determining from the situation and the person involved which style is appropriate. Nevertheless, even with a balanced style of leadership, the tendency is to lean more heavily on one style than on the others.

Dealing with Communication Problems

To illustrate communication under rule- and technology-oriented, as well as under individual- and group-oriented leadership, the following role play has been used in training numerous municipal management and supervisory personnel. The role play is based on a modification of the "Snow Shovel Case" originally developed by Jay Hall. The two ways of handling the situation outlined below come out of two different training sessions. The italics after each paragraph refer to the type of communication taking place.

To set the scene, the situation involves a conversation during a coffee break, where two employees (B and C) are razzing a third (A) about the preparation of a periodic report that is generally assigned to A. All three know it will be assigned soon—probably that day. A is saying that he does not like to handle the report and that he hopes the department head won't assign it to him. He feels others in the work group should handle the job from time to time. B and C jokingly imply that A really likes to prepare the report and they wouldn't think of depriving him of this; besides, both of them are busy at more important work. They also imply that A is afraid to tell the department head how he really feels about the particular job. (*Informal communication from the grapevine challenging A's need-value motivational framework.*)

From this point on, the role play develops in a spontaneous manner. The person playing the part of the department head knows nothing of the razzing; he has been out of the room during the first part of the role play. He knows only that A usually handles the job, that it has to be done within two days, that B and C and others in the work group are tied up on higher priority jobs and A is not.

The department head mentions the report and in a nice way tells A to handle it. He is somewhat surprised when A resists the order and tells him that someone else should handle the job. A claims that the job he is on now is rather high priority and he shouldn't leave it. (*Individual-oriented communication, with subtle ego protection overtones, resulting in a combination of rule- and technology-oriented response.*)

Deliberately restraining himself, the boss points out that others are working on higher priority jobs than A's and gives A a direct order to handle the job, adding that he'll look into the matter at some later time. (*Rule-oriented communication—ego deflating—with possible individual-oriented overtones.*)

When A continues to tell him he doesn't want to take on the job, hints that he might quit, and then flatly refuses, the boss is really exasperated. He forcefully points to the logic of preparing the

report, adding that A is the only one he can assign it to today. He'll just have to do it and any misunderstanding can be cleared up later. (*Combination of technology- and rule-oriented communication—definite ego deflation.*)

When A refuses again, the boss has just about had it. In no uncertain terms he points out that he is head of the department here, that he has given A a direct order, and that he'd damn well better carry it out. A's reply is to tell him to carry it out himself. The role play ends with A quitting, and the department head having to find someone else to prepare the report or do it himself. In addition, he has to recruit and train a new man for A's job. (*Rule-oriented communication—challenging ego of both communicators and leading to dysfunctional communication.*)

After one use of this role play, the person playing the role of A adamantly defended his position and said that "in real life he certainly would quit his job if he had to work for a boss who put him in a position of being ridiculed by his fellow workers." He admitted that he was trying to save face and that he felt "looking into the matter later" didn't give him any out. (*Need-value motivational factors at work.*)

At this point the person playing the part of the department head entered into the discussion with: "How the hell was I to know you were trying to save face? Nobody told me those guys were razzing you." He added that he had given A a direct order and "when a boss gives a direct order it has to be carried out. If it isn't, he loses all his authority." (*Rule-oriented communication and leadership, ego and need-value motivational factors also at work.*)

After this exchange the two participants, with some help from the group, began to work through the "communication breakdown." But it soon became apparent that in the role play they really were communicating. It was dysfunctional communication, but communication nonetheless. Through their behavior, each was saying: "I'm more concerned about me than I am about you. I don't know what your problem is, but I know what mine is if I lose out in this struggle." In other words, early in the role play encounter each had taken a win-lose position. But when the situation was analyzed, both had lost.

The above role play has been used with many

groups. In another experience, the person playing the boss took a different approach and demonstrated effective communication. The event went very much the same up to the point where A implies that he may quit if he has to prepare the report. At this point the boss calls a halt in the trend of the conversation by telling A that he is much too valuable a man for the boss to let him quit over the assignment of a job. He frankly admits that he didn't know A found the job unpleasant. In a spirit of concern, he helps A to talk about the report. (*Individual-oriented communication, responding to ego and need-value motivational framework.*)

A tells him that it's a rather boring job, that he's not sure the report is even necessary, that nobody in the work group likes to handle it, and that he always seems to get stuck with it. As the department head listens, A becomes a bit more relaxed and hints at the razzing he has received from his coworkers. As this comes out, the boss expresses understanding. As the tension subsides in A the boss is able to explain his position. He asks A how he feels the report should be assigned. The role play ends with A agreeing to draft a recommendation for assigning the job in the future for presentation at the next staff meeting, and to handle the job today to keep the work group from getting into a bind. (*Individual-oriented communication with group-oriented overtones.*)

In the discussion that followed, A pointed out that he knew he was in a difficult position with his coworkers, that he couldn't let the department head push him around. "But the boss didn't try to push me around. He kept trying to help and I couldn't keep clubbing a man who was trying to help me." (*Responding to need-value motivational framework.*)

The person who played the part of the boss said at first he didn't know what was going on. I could see "something was bugging him and I didn't think I could get him to do the job until I found out." He added that once it was out in the open and they could level with each other, "There didn't seem to be much of a problem in working out a solution." (*Encouraging an open communication climate.*)

This was a prime example of a win-win situation brought about through effective communication. Once it became evident that nobody had to lose in the situation, the participants could work out a satisfactory solution. Once the department head realized that A was threatened by his order, he didn't dissipate his energies in defending his authority and resorting to rule-oriented communication. Asserting his authority, as in the first example, could only have widened the communication gap and led to dysfunctional communication.

Conclusion

In the interacting organization, overlapping groups offer the best opportunity to use the communication process effectively. The organization must provide an atmosphere in which persons feel valued and respected—one in which openness and mutual trust exist and in which ego-deflating and threatening communication is minimized.

The open organization, in which interpersonal skills are encouraged and developed, leads to full, candid communication. Persons tend to pass relevant information to others and tend to be interested in and receptive to relevant information themselves. A full flow of useful and relevant information provides accurate data to guide action, calls attention to problems as they arise, and assure sound decisions based on a maximum amount of available facts.

As persons receive an accurate flow of relevant information, they will develop a feeling of having greater influence on what happens in the organization and what happens to themselves. This effect will be noticed at all levels within the organization and will be particularly true in the individual's own unit or department. With a feeling of being able to exercise influence themselves, individuals will tend to respond more favorably and cooperatively to influence which may be exerted upon them. Such a reciprocal influence process will certainly help to weld the organization into a strong, highly effective institution.

¹Much of this chapter has been taken verbatim from Stanley Piazza Powers, "Administrative Communication," in MANAGING THE MODERN CITY, ed. James M. Banovetz (Washington, D.C.: International City Management Association, 1971), pp. 188–204.

²John Parry, THE PSYCHOLOGY OF HUMAN COMMUNICATION (New York: American Elsevier Publishing Co., Inc., 1968), pp. 41–50.

³Ibid., p. 45.

⁴Norman R. F. Maier et al., SUPERIOR—SUBORDINATE COMMUNICATION IN MANAGEMENT (New York: American Management Association, 1961).

⁵Alvin Toffler, FUTURE SHOCK (New York: Random House, Inc., 1970).

⁶Claude E. Shannon and Warren Weaver, THE MATHEMATICAL THEORY OF COMMUNICATION (Urbana, Ill.: University of Illinois Press, 1949), p. 34.

⁷Robert K. Burns, THE LISTENING TECHNIQUES (Chicago: Industrial Relations Center, University of Chicago, 1958), p. 4.

⁸Ibid.

⁹Robert K. Burns, THE QUESTIONING TECHNIQUES (Chicago: Industrial Relations Center, University of Chicago, 1958), p. 4.

¹⁰Charles W. Nelson, THE LEADERSHIP INVENTORY ANALYZER (Chicago: Industrial Relations Center, University of Chicago, 1960), p. 6.

Part Three

Organization Development and Renewal

Introduction

The management of change is the effort to convert certain possibles into probables, in pursuit of agreed on preferables.

ALVIN TOFFLER

ONE OF THE MOST deeply held beliefs about bureaucracies, at least as expressed in popular writing, is their resistance to change. There is an element of truth in the belief because some bureaucracies are notoriously rigid, authoritarian, procedure-ridden, and tradition-bound. Any of us can think of examples in both the public and private sectors. But generalized condemnations overlook the many bureaucracies or organizations, the term we use in this book, that are alert, innovative, receptive to change, and even ahead of their time. One of the implicit purposes of Part three is to help you better understand processes of change not only to avoid unpleasant surprises but also to keep your organization effective, responsive, and accountable—those words that are so fashionable today.

Chapter 10 deals specifically with the management of change by pointing out that change is a continual management process, not Event A, Event B, and Event C. This chapter provides some useful findings about this process.

First, every manager and supervisor is a change agent.

Second, employee resistance to change is to be expected under many circumstances, but it is not necessarily a negative or destructive attitude.

Third, plans and strategies are available for facilitating the change process.

Finally, change agent skills can be learned.

Another way of stating the idea of change is to use the term "organization development and renewal" which is an approach to facilitating planned change in organizations. It works through the people in the organization with an open, problem-solving climate to provide meaningful participation, responsibility, and self-direction. Organization development is built on the premise that people work better with self-control and self-direction.

The process of change, the development of people, the impact of technology, and the changes in municipal government responsibilities are among the major factors that mandate employee training as a built-in part of the organization. Such training, as Chapter 11 outlines, can range from broad considerations of society at large to the specific skills needed by the data processing technician. Training is so much a part of organization development, and of all of the coverage of this book, that it would be a temptation to include a section on training in every chapter.

Three major types of training are covered. The most important for our purposes, and probably the newest for most, is applied behavioral science training which works with the social process of the organization to improve its effectiveness both as a production unit and as a social group. Chapter 11 quite sensibly points out that training is not something "out there," but is a responsibility of all managers and supervisors.

Chapter 12 also is a change oriented chapter, and it deals with the future through a "pro-active" rather than a reactive style, taking the initiative for making changes rather than waiting for changes to occur. Management by objective is a familiar term in industry and the armed forces. It has a great deal of appeal because it emphasizes results.

Management by objective is a disciplined endeavor. It takes hard work to get realistic agreement on goals and objectives that are reasonably measureable and attainable. It is even harder to plan the work so that it proceeds steadily in that direction with continual evaluation of work in progress. Some of us may feel threatened because of the way the objective can cut across traditional organizational lines and because decisions are made at many additional levels within the organization. Management by objective has perhaps its greatest appeal for engineers, planners, and other more professionally oriented people who can look upon specific task achievements as more important than the prerogatives of different boxes on the organization chart. Those who are used to the formalities of authority and supervision will find it harder to adjust to.

Management by objective, however, is not an all-or-nothing choice. A start can be made in setting objectives systematically, a step that every organization should take from time to time anyway.

Management by objective helps pull together the goals that the organization strives for. Then the organization can develop specific plans for attaining those objectives, including the marshaling of people and other resources. It provides a way for people within the organization and people affected by the organization to decide their future.

10

The Management of Change

Don Holliday could see the trouble brewing. It always happened in situations like this. "When is my boss *ever* going to learn?" Don thought, as he reviewed in his mind the events of the past few weeks.

It had all started with a rational decision and the best of intentions. Don's immediate superior was George Brill, director of administration. George prided himself on being a keen analyst of the administrative process and a ready supplier of methods and procedures for solving any problem. He worked hard—sparing neither his own time nor that of others—to make the units under his supervision run like well-oiled machines. A feasibility study of the installation of a new electronic data processing system had been under way for several months. George felt that it was important to keep up with new technologies and to use the latest in equipment design.

The employees, including those in Don's unit, had been told only that the organization was considering purchasing more up-to-date equipment. The fact was, however, that significant changes in the structure of the work units and in employees' jobs might result. It was George's opinion that to say much about the change would only upset employees unnecessarily and cause rumors to fly. "When the study is finished and we've made the decisions about implementation, we'll tell them about the new procedures," he told Don.

When the study was completed George analyzed the results and after considerable study issued a long memorandum outlining the new system, the changes it would require in the operation of the work units, and the procedures required for implementation. After receiving necessary approvals from his own superior, George reviewed the procedures with Don and other staff and ordered the document to be sent to all affected employees for implementation.

The next morning when the memos arrived Don could immediately sense the reaction among the people in his unit. He received some coldly worded requests for clarification, which he provided as best he could. Employees gathered at each other's desks to grumble. And there was much confusion as they tried to work out the details of the new procedure.

Don could only speculate about the longer-term results of the memo. Certainly morale could drop, because people were used to the work relationships within their units. Probably the resentment would spill over into work performance and less work would get done—especially when it pertained to the new system. It was likely that people would devote time and energy to trying to figure out how to get around the new rulings and keep their work relationships from being disrupted. And if past experience indicated anything the new system would be full of bugs. Since the employees resented the new system they would probably be slow to identify and resolve deficiencies and bring performance up to its optimum level. Usually, George forgot about the details of new projects after a few weeks as he became interested in some new issue. And unless he prodded his unit heads, they felt little responsibility for the continuing enforcement of his rulings.

"It's too bad things have to work out this way," Don thought to himself. "Certainly George is right that the EDP system must be improved. But it's the *way* he tries to bring about change that seems to cause trouble. He builds up resistance to what he's trying to accomplish. Wonder why he didn't get my opinion, or the opinions of the other unit heads? We know more about the situation than he does. Come to think of it, I wonder why he didn't get the opinions of the employees themselves?"

Jim Cowan was new director of the planning department. He came to the job with a lot of energy and high hopes that the department could really be an effective and important part of the organization. After spending some time getting to know the people and the operations and talking with other members of management, he realized that he had a difficult problem on his hands. The department was stagnant. It was old and set in its ways. Things were done "the way they always have been done." The personnel, while technically qualified at the time they joined the department, had failed to keep up with the field, and they had not grown in their ability to work as an effective unit. There were few new ideas, and those that emerged were usually rejected. The most serious problem was that the department was decreasing in usefulness to the overall organization. As the organization strove to maintain its effectiveness in a rapidly changing world, the planning department kept working on the same old problems—many of which were no longer very relevant. The city's chief administrator had made repeated requests to the planning department for help with some of the new problems and issues, but he had received very little. The response seemed to be, "That's not our job."

Jim's challenge, very clearly, was to revive a stagnant operation and get it moving in new directions. What was the best way to proceed? One colleague proposed that he replace most of the personnel: "Get rid of the deadwood." A consultant recommended reorganization: "Restructure the department so that subunits are assigned problems and held responsible for them." The personnel director proposed an ambitious training program: "The supervisory personnel need to understand how to get people to be more open to change."

"Just which approach," Jim wondered, "is most likely to help me renew my operation?"

The Change Process in Government

One of the most common and often valid criticisms of urban government is that it has been unable to upgrade its structure and operations quickly enough to solve the problems of change. It has been Model T government in the supersonic age. It has cherished and protected its hard-won civil service and professionalism while neglecting some of the newer approaches to organizational effectiveness. In short, local government has not distinguished itself in the management of change.

THE ADMINISTRATOR'S ROLE

Yet one finds that many managers are not particularly interested in the concept of change. "After all," they say, "my job is to manage—to see that the work gets done—not to fiddle around changing things. Change is best left to policy decisions by legislative bodies."

However, there is growing consensus that the manager in any public institution cannot much longer ignore the need for understanding and carrying out processes of planned change. John Gardner, in his book *Self-Renewal,* speaks of the need for striving to keep our major institutions flexible and adaptable in the face of mounting social and economic change.

No one can fail to see in some segments of our society the dry rot produced by apathy, rigidity and by moral emptiness. Only the blind and complacent could fail to recognize the great tasks of renewal facing us—in government, in education, in race relations, in urban development, in international affairs, and most of all in our own minds and hearts.[1]

What, then, is the role of the municipal manager in the process of change? What should he do to help avoid organizational hardening of the arteries and bring about a more dynamic and viable problem-solving process that assures full utilization of new ideas and approaches?

First, he should recognize that resistance to change is to be expected under many circumstances. This is discussed in the next major section of this chapter. Second, he should watch for constructive elements that may be present in the employee resistance to change: the need for clear and direct reasons for the proposed change;

the employees' desires for stability; and the desirable parts of the present situation that should be retained when the change is made.

In this chapter we will review some of the concepts of organization as they relate to change, and we will then look at several topics in the area of change management, including dealing with imposed changes, overcoming resistance, planned change strategies, and change facilitator roles.

BUREAUCRACY AND CHANGE

The traditional form of organization was designed to assure reliability and responsibility. Today it is sometimes labeled a "command" or "compliance" system. The major assumption is, of course, that the key to getting people to do work is *authority*. Well-defined regulations and procedures rigorously enforced are viewed as the requirements of productivity. In theory, one of the major kinds of change problems should be easy to resolve. That is the problem of getting subordinates to accept and incorporate changes in their work. Since employees work on the basis of command, all that is necessary (presumably) is to change the orders—and behavior change should follow. The fact that behavior doesn't necessarily change when the orders are changed is self-evident to all managers and will be discussed later on in this chapter.

The other major change problem is troublesome at the theoretical as well as the operating level: How do we keep the organization and its subunits from getting outdated and inflexible? How do we keep it adaptive, responsive to new approaches, and able to see and deal realistically with its problems and deficiencies?

Little provision is built into the fiber of most organizations that will help them to be self-renewing. The usual assumption is that once the more or less well-oiled mechanism is set in motion it keeps moving in the same way. And the manager's job is to see that it does this.

To deal with these change problems requires more than simply changing a few procedures or installing a new program. It requires new ways of thinking about organizations, some knowledge of the dynamics of change, and some modifications in the roles and skills of the line and staff administrators.

Timothy Costello, in his analysis of change in municipal government, lists the following categories of change observed to take place in New York City in the late sixties:

1. Planned change. Structural reorganization was undertaken with assistance of outside consultants. Operating units were regrouped and integrated according to a carefully devised plan.
2. Confluence of forces. A variety of interest groups and forces within the community combined to bring situations to a head and move things in the direction of change. An example was the combination of forces which brought about school decentralization.
3. Event-dominated change. Changes which are unplanned and unanticipated occur through a sequence of events. Each event is linked to past and future events in chain-like fashion with the outcome being a result of the various events leading up to it.
4. Accidental innovation. Clearly, a significant amount of innovation and change comes about by accident. Methods developed to deal with one problem are found useful for dealing with others and new ideas arise unexpectedly.
5. External intervention. Outside groups such as legislative bodies or administrative agencies impose change upon the organization from the outside through the use of funds, regulations, etc. In similar fashion interest groups, professional or scientific experts, and others might intervene from the outside with formally or informally imposed change.[2]

Only the first type of change (planned change) comes about largely because of the prior analysis and problem solving of managers. It should be noted that planned change as described by Costello may be reactive to problems or conditions, and it may well be imposed through the use of authority. There may be some elements of planned efforts in the second and third categories (confluence of forces and event-dominated change), but these and the last two (accidental innovation and external intervention) call for significant *reactive* responses on the part of the organization and require adaptation to—rather than development of—change. It is reaction to change which is probably most usual, and it will be discussed first in this chapter.

Responding to Imposed Change

One kind of problem has to do with changes that the manager or his subordinates have not devised but which are imposed by authority from within or without the organization. This type of problem includes policy and legal measures arrived at by legislative bodies, management decisions aimed at solving problems or incorporating new methods (such as technological changes), and structural reorganization.

The classic change dilemma, experienced if not recognized by every manager, is described in the first case study at the beginning of this chapter. In order to improve operations the administrator (in this case, George Brill) devises a solution. Implementation takes place through traditional bureaucratic methods. Employees are informed via written orders of the "new" behavior they are to follow. Having fulfilled his obligations to bring about the change the manager moves on to other problems, leaving the supervisor on the scene to take care of any difficulties.

Frequently, the new program does not work as it should. Efficiency and productivity may fall off, employees grumble, some adhere to the old ways. The manager may have to be called back to modify some of the provisions of the change which don't square with the realities. In the end, the new program, now a shadow of its former self, may survive or it may fade away. And the employees' suspicions that management does not understand and appreciate the real guts of the operation are confirmed. As are management's assumptions that the employees really don't care about the best interests of the organization and will always resist efforts to bring about change.

When changes which affect his operation are imposed on the organization, the manager has several overlapping problems to resolve: (1) how to bring about the necessary changes as quickly and efficiently as possible; (2) how to overcome employee resistance and gain understanding and acceptance of the changes; (3) how to carry out objective observation and evaluation of each change so as to assess its progress and value.

It will be useful, before discussing strategies for managing imposed change, to pause in an attempt to understand some of the causes of employee resistance to change.

Understanding Resistance to Change

The folklore of management holds that employees are naturally negative toward change—any change—and may generally be expected to resist it. Thus the manager, according to the folklore, must use persuasion, coercion, and patience to overcome resistance. But this is not always the case.

Research evidence about employee attitudes toward change indicates that under *some circumstances, some proportion* of the employees in a *given situation* will resist *certain kinds* of change introduced in *certain ways.* Under other circumstances there will be no resistance. In other words, employee response to change depends on a variety of factors, including: (1) the characteristics of the employee; (2) the climate or general feelings in the organization in which the change is taking place; (3) the nature and extent of the change; and (4) the methodology which is used to implement the change. Fortunately, enough is known about resistance factors to provide some assistance to the manager who must grapple with change situations.

Threat to Job, Wages, Security. It is sometimes assumed that the major threat involved in change, especially technological or structural change, is economic. Since workers are often thought of as primarily economic creatures it is natural to assume that economic concerns are the major source of fears of change. Although economic factors may be important in some situations, it would be a mistake to assume that they are always at the bottom of resistance to change.

Coping with New Situations. Fear of being unable to adapt to new situations may account for resistance to change. It has been found that workers who are most competent (as seen by themselves and others) and who have positive past experiences with change are likely to be least resistant. Fear of failing may stem from a variety of real or imagined problems.

Status. Changes may be perceived by employees as threats to their status. They may fear that they will be unable to adapt to the new way of doing things and may be seen by others as inferior. Or the initiation of a change may be taken as a signal that the individual has been performing his job inadequately. Or, as is sometimes the case, changes which bring about switches in job titles, chains of command, or scope of responsibility are resisted because employees experience them as threats to their present levels of influence or standing.

Social Relationships. For many employees the establishment of social relationships is extremely important. Changes which break up cohesive groupings, prevent friends from talking or getting together, isolate individuals, or create new conflicts or competition are likely to be resisted.

Importance of Changed Aspects. Some aspects of work are extremely important and central in one's job and in one's conception of oneself. Other aspects are relatively unimportant and, if changed, are less likely to be resisted. The important aspects may include such factors as freedom to operate as a "professional" in one's chosen field, amount of authority (number of people supervised), latitude in decision making, and access to positions at higher levels in the organization.

Employee Trust and Confidence in the Organization. If, in the employees' views, the organization has a record of demonstrated concern for its workers and has protected them in past changes, there probably will be less resistance. In organizational climates in which the trust level is low and the past history of change has been unpleasant, there is likely to be resistance regardless of programs undertaken to overcome it.

Uncertainty. Most managers are aware that employees react negatively to uncertainty. When upcoming changes are suspected, the rumor mill goes into high gear and the air is filled with talk of dire possibilities. Fear of the unknown is probably greatest in organizations which have a history of unannounced, unpleasant changes.

Reactions against Authority and Manipulation. Some employees resist change because their attitudes cause them to respond negatively to any attempt by persons in higher positions of authority to influence or determine their behavior.

Thus, it is not the change measures themselves that cause the resistance; it is the fact that they are being imposed by management.

Generalized Resistance to Change. It is probably true that some individuals are generally less ready than others for change of any kind. They may be individuals who, because of past experience with a number of the above factors, just do not want to have things changed. It should be noted, however, that this group does not usually constitute a majority of employees, as has been sometimes assumed.[3]

OVERCOMING RESISTANCE TO CHANGE

The approach of many managers to employee resistance to change is to concentrate on making the orders more detailed and more explicit, to watch employees more closely to see that they conform to the new procedures, and to punish nonconformity. These measures may work, but frequently they lead to increased resistance and further problems in implementing change. In order to deal most competently with resistance to change and to plan a strategy for overcoming it, it is important for the manager to understand the possible reasons for the resistance and the various measures for dealing with it. Useful strategies may include those listed below.

Communication. A commonly prescribed approach to preventing resistance is to "tell them the complete story well in advance." The assumption is that if employees could only understand the change fully they would not fear it. This may be only partially true. It should be remembered that reaction against uncertainty is only one of the possible causes of resistance. Probably the best solution is to level with employees as soon as possible about upcoming changes but to recognize that this may not overcome all the resistance.

In communicating about upcoming changes it is important to assure that the communication is two-way. When management gives news of changes, employees must be encouraged to react, ask questions, clarify, etc. Only by opening up the feedback channels can management learn employees' real feelings.

Participation. Much research on overcoming resistance to change has focused on allowing employees to participate in planning and decision making related to change. Evidence is clear that in many change situations the employees respond more positively and constructively when they have been involved and have had some influence in the change process.

A number of approaches have been explored. In some cases committees have been formed to work with managers in analyzing the need for various kinds of changes, proposing alternatives, and dealing with problems of implementation. In other situations employees have been involved more informally, and have simply been invited by managers to sit in on discussions and contribute their ideas toward ways of bringing about change. Participation programs which are not legitimate attempts to develop involvement and shared influence are likely to be perceived by employees as phony and to result in lowered trust of management. It is wisest to let employees know clearly how much influence they will have in dealing with change, and then to act in good faith.

Dealing with Economic Issues and Working Conditions.   When there is a suspicion on the part of employees that their economic or working conditions may be altered because of change, it is often best to face the problem areas directly and deal with them prior to the implementation of the change. For example, employees may fear that their work pace will be speeded up by the change and that this might lead to a decrease in the number of employees needed, to more fatigue, or to less pay. If there is a realistic fear of such consequences, it is probably wisest to bring them out into the open and bargain about them, rather than pretend that they do not exist.

Working Through Feelings.   Frequently, the problems arising from resistance to change are based on feelings rather than "hard" economic issues. When upcoming changes in their work lives threaten employees, they are likely to develop a variety of strong feelings about those changes which they may not be able or willing to express openly. Yet if these concerns go unexpressed they are likely to be causes of future difficulty. Therefore, the manager may wish to create conditions under which it is legitimate to discuss feelings in a nonthreatening climate. This responsibility for the "management of feelings" may not be one which the manager is used

to assuming, but it nevertheless may be a useful strategy for overcoming resistance.

Sensitivity to Human Relationships.   The major organizational problems in change frequently relate less to the mechanical and economic aspects of work than to the impact on human relationships. The wise manager will ask himself, "What will this proposed change do to the social system of the employees in this unit?" That is, what communication patterns, habits, friendships, informal groups, or values is the change likely to disrupt? It then becomes possible to redesign the implementation of the change so that it is less socially disruptive or to take special measures to provide alternative ways of meeting the social needs of employees. It should be stressed, however, that it is the *employee's* view of the social system that is important, not the supervisor's view of how it should operate.

Developing Organizational Trust and Respect.   In spite of all the various strategies for overcoming employee resistance to change, the manager is likely to be less than effective where employees do not trust and respect the organization and its administrative personnel. When there is a low trust level, employees are prone to be suspicious of *any* change. They assume that management will not look out for their interests and is likely to betray them. Resistance to change, then, becomes a mechanism for defending oneself and one's group. There is no short-term answer to the problem of employee trust. It must be built over longer periods of time, based on the actual performance of management rather than on crash programs in employee communications or human relations training.

Voluntary Change

In some situations the employee has a good deal of control over change. The question of whether he wants to change therefore becomes of prime importance. This can occur in situations where the organization or the manager does not have full "command" power, for example, when an employee is expected to act as an effective group member on team project, exert a maximum amount of commitment in an activity, be creative

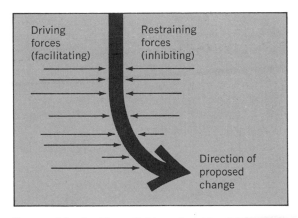

FIGURE 10—1. *Force field analysis by driving and restraining forces.*

2. Professional jealousy among some employees of the two departments
3. Units are physically separated from each other
4. Top management tends to look for one or the other department to blame when something goes wrong, causing buck-passing
5. Few organizational provisions for departmental collaboration, i.e., no joint committees, no personnel to act as links between units, etc.
6. People in organization lack skill in teamwork across units.

By analyzing and documenting a given change problem the manager can look quickly at what seem to be the major forces operating in the situation. It is often useful to check these perceptions against those of others who also have familiarity with the situation. After filling in the forces it may also be useful to attach weights or values to the forces on both sides—that is, to decide which ones are strongest and most important. It is then possible to discuss ways of either increasing the strength or number of the forces for change or decreasing the number or strength of the resisting forces.

In the example above, it may well be that the long history of rivalry and professional jealousy will not be overcome to any extent by the administrative orders of the heads of the units. It may be necessary to take other measures. Alternatives might include a training workshop involving members of both departments, in which the feelings of rivalry and jealousy are addressed directly and explored and, hopefully, overcome—or a process of temporarily exchanging members across the two units so that each can gain understanding of the problems and dilemmas of the other unit.

It may be more effective to reduce the resisting forces than to attempt to increase the driving forces. This strategy, of course, runs counter to the usual approach. That is, we often try to overcome resistance by invoking more rules, administrative orders, and persuasive techniques instead of attempting to understand and deal with the causes. Simply increasing the strength of the driving forces seems sometimes to increase the amount of tension in the system and also to bring about the addition of still further restraining forces.

and spontaneous, or develop new solutions to a problem. In such cases it is difficult if not impossible for the organization to bring about change if the employee has no desire to change.

A model for analyzing such situations has been adapted from the work of the social psychologist Kurt Lewin.[4] In any change situation, the pressures for and against the change may be viewed as a field of opposing forces, as shown in Figure 10—1.

Any change problem can be analyzed according to this model. Take, for example, the problem of getting two departments in the same organization to collaborate more effectively. A careful analysis of the situation might reveal the following forces in action:

Driving Forces
Forces toward More Effective Collaboration

1. Directors of the two departments have expressed desire for better collaboration
2. Projects get slowed down when these departments do not collaborate well
3. Chief executive of organization has requested better collaboration among units
4. Awareness of the problem by both groups.

Restraining Forces
Forces against More Effective Collaboration

1 Long history of rivalry between the two departments

Redeveloping and Renewing Organizations

In the second case at the beginning of this chapter Jim Cowan's task as new director of the planning department was not to implement a specific change in procedures or work, but to find a way to help his department change from a somewhat stale and outmoded system to a more vigorous and effective one. As an experienced administrator, Jim was wise enough to know that he could not bring about the needed changes simply by written orders or pep talks. The characteristics of the old system had developed over a number of years and were probably caused by a variety of factors characteristic of the individual members, the way the unit was operated, and its role in the overall organization. Ways had to be found to modify some of the basic styles, feelings, and roles of the planning staff.

Leavitt, in analyzing approaches to change in organizations, specified the following avenues for change.[5]

Structural approaches involve such methods as reorganization of work units and their relationships, work-flow planning, and staff-line configurations. They seek to change the way work gets done by changing the basic skeletal structure (organization charts, procedures, rules) of the system.

Technological approaches seek change through the use of more advanced systems. Automated machinery, planning-programming-budgeting systems, and computer applications are among the techniques of those who would change and improve the organization by improving its level of technology. The assumption is that technology can help upgrade the quality and increase the quantity of output and improve the validity of such tasks as planning and decision making.

People-oriented approaches focus on training programs, personnel placement, job counseling, and measures to improve the human relationships within the unit. It is assumed that a well-integrated and qualified team, free from major morale and communication problems and able to understand its own functioning, can better come to grips with the necessities for change.

In any real situation, of course, the three areas above interact in their impact on the organization. The approach or approaches which a manager uses will depend on a combination of his own personal background and skills, his perception of the problem, the resources available, and the receptivity of the organization to the various change approaches. There is of course no way of determining, in the abstract, which of these approaches is most useful. All have their advocates and their histories of successes and failures.

The structural approach is probably oldest. Early investigators in the fields of administrative management and public administration were interested in finding ways of devising organizational structures which would enhance the ability of the system to get work done. They proposed a variety of rather elegant organization charts and models and backed them up with elaborate procedures. This approach, has, of course, been carried too far in some instances, and the modern manager is well aware of the wide discrepancy which sometimes exists between the real organization and the organization which is depicted on the official organization chart.

If the issues and conditions which are causing problems are structural in nature or stem from structural conditions (such as too many links in a communication process, unclear lines of responsibility, or unrealistically broad spans of control), the structural approach is useful. When the problems are not structural such changes frequently do not help. Nevertheless, there is great temptation on the part of managers and consultants to reorganize and redefine only the structural elements of the organization whenever things go wrong.

The technological approaches to change are currently among the most popular. They constitute a special area of study and will not be dealt with here. Suffice it to say that in many organizations the adoption of new technologies and new technological systems has contributed enormously to the effectiveness and success of the operation. In other situations, in which the technology was misapplied, incompetently applied, or used as a panacea, the results have been less than positive.

People-oriented approaches to change are now in their second generation. Earlier approaches included elaborate communications programs designed to make the employees like and admire their company, and human relations strategies which were aimed at raising morale and job satisfaction. Newer approaches which are now being perfected are labeled organization development, organization renewal, or action research. Because of their newness and relative unfamiliarity to most managers they will be discussed in greater detail in the following section.

Organization Development

Organization development or OD is a new approach to facilitating planned change in organizations through the human system. It is based on the behaviorally-oriented theories of human behavior and management which emerged in the fifties and sixties and uses a combination of clinical, consulting, research, and small-group skills. It aims at helping members of the organization learn how to diagnose their own problem situations and bring about needed changes.

The objectives of organization development have been stated as follows:

1. To create an open problem-solving climate throughout the organization.
2. To supplement the authority associated with role or status with the authority of knowledge and competence.
3. To locate decision-making and problem-solving responsibilities as close to the information sources as possible.
4. To build trust among individuals and groups throughout the organization.
5. To make competition more relevant to work goals and to maximize collaborative efforts.
6. To develop a reward system which recognizes both the achievement of the organization's mission (profits or service) and organization development (growth of people).
7. To increase the sense of "ownership" of organization objectives throughout the work force.
8. To help managers to manage according to relevant objectives rather than according to "past practices" or according to objectives which do not make sense for one's area of responsibility.
9. To increase self-control and self-direction for people within the organization.[6]

Although there is no single formalized set of procedures for OD, a typical effort has been described as containing the following stages:

1. A problem recognition stage in which the organization recognizes the fact that its productivity is being hampered by ineffective interpersonal relations or other kinds of socially related variables, and calls in outside consultants or addresses its own members to exploring these problems.
2. A data-gathering stage in which interviews, observations, meeting-analysis techniques, or other approaches are utilized to pinpoint difficulties involved in the organization's operation and provide suggestions for reasons for these difficulties.
3. A data analysis and feedback stage in which members of management are brought together and involved in reviewing the findings, diagnosing problem areas, and planning strategies for improvement and change.
4. The intervention programs which are designed to bring about desired changes may include meetings (on-site or at retreats) at which organizational members are helped to participate in developing new programs or new approaches to existing situations.
5. The responsibility for helping the organization come to grips with change problems and to work its way through the difficulties encountered is often assigned to someone in a "change agent role" who is either a member of the organization or an outside consultant. This individual usually does not play the role of the expert advisor, but rather uses his clinical skills as well as his knowledge to help facilitate the problem-solving process of the group.
6. Members of the organization collaboratively develop procedures, policies, and norms which reinforce and implement the new ways of operating developed in the previous change efforts.
7. Training is an important component of OD. Ongoing programs integrated into the change process are made available to employees. Training methods tend to be participatory and experience-based. The laboratory approach of the National Training Laboratories (T-Groups or sensitivity training) is frequently used to help employees develop interpersonal competence and teamwork skills such as group problem-solving and decision-making.[7]

It is important to emphasize that organization development involves more than simply teaching good human relations and going off on weekend retreats for cathartic purposes. OD is a continuing process, not a project. One of the central concepts in the process is confrontation. Emphasis is placed on helping organization members recognize and come to grips at the human interaction level with organizational problems which are often ignored or swept under the rug under the assumption that conflict is to be avoided at all costs. Structural and procedural change, often the beginning points of the more traditional approaches, may be the end result of involvement in OD.

THE ROLE OF THE CHANGE AGENT OR CHANGE FACILITATOR

Organization development programs are most frequently conducted by an external consultant working closely with one or more individuals located within the organization. This new kind of professional is developing to fill a gap in our change-oriented society. In spite of the very rapid rate of social and technological advancement that has taken place in the past generation, little has been known until recently about how to understand and facilitate the process of change in human systems. Now, through the work of a number of applied behavioral scientists, it is possible not only to discuss some of the principles of change but to define a professional role which is useful in the implementation of change—that of the *change agent*. The change agent differs from the traditional consultant or expert-adviser in that his function is not to tell the client or system what it should do to solve its problems or improve its performance, but rather to help it undergo a constructive evaluation and change process which will make it more effective and more receptive to continual growth and development. In a sense, the change agent is a catalyst and a facilitator. His expertise is not in the methods or principles which the organization should be adhering to but in the processes whereby it can undertake change.

The change agent most frequently works with the top management group or with the leadership of a major unit or project. His activities may include data gathering (through interviews, questionnaries, etc.), diagnosis, consulting to teams and work units, training, and individual counseling with managers on skill development and problem solving.

Skills required of the change agent include the following:

1. The ability to separate his value system from the value system of the client. It is not up to the change agent to decide what is good for the client's system or what is the desirable course to follow. His job is to help the client's system face and deal with those issues itself.
2. The effective change agent possesses skills useful in diagnosing difficulties in human systems. He helps the client see itself more accurately and in greater depth and helps it understand its strengths and weaknesses and the reasons for them.
3. The change agent often refrains from giving advice or making prescriptions. He helps the client's system develop its own solutions to its problems and select from alternative ways of proceeding.
4. Sensitivity in human interactions. The effective change agent knows how to listen carefully and look for the real meanings involved in what is being said, how to appreciate and deal with the feelings underlying communications, and how to develop relationships of trust which will sustain a sometimes difficult change effort.
5. Ability to deal effectively with conflict and confrontation. Real organizational problem solving and improvement frequently involves dealing with subject matter and relationships which are uncomfortable. They may have to be faced directly and openly and resolved before the necessary changes can take place.
6. Ability to get involved without being overly controlling. One must be able to restrain one's own impulses to step in and set the situation straight or provide the needed leadership or obvious solution in favor of allowing the client group to proceed at its own pace to resolve the problem or deal with the situation in its own ways.

Organization development is not a set of training exercises or one-shot techniques for triggering change. It is a long-term (two- to three-year minimum) approach which uses a variety of strategies for building change capabilities.

INTERNAL CHANGE AGENTS

Although the original conception of the change agent role was that of the outside consultant, the relevance of the values and skills surrounding the change agent role are being explored for positions within organizations. Individuals, often with graduate education or experience in the behavioral sciences, receive special training in organization development and change agent skills and are given titles such as OD Specialist or Internal Consultant. They may be attached to the personnel or training department, or may report directly to top management. The responsible person in this position is to act as a resource to the overall organization and its subunits in identifying problems and facilitating the change process.

The requirements for the internal change agent are much the same as for his external counterpart, but there are special problems. Since he depends on the organization for his position and his livelihood, the internal change agent finds himself in a riskier spot when it is necessary to ask unpopular but important questions, challenge traditional practices, or confront individuals in positions of authority. The person who fills such a role will not be able to rely on policies and procedures, but must succeed by sensitivity, skill, and courage.[8]

THE STAFF ADMINISTRATOR AS CHANGE AGENT

Traditional staff roles such as personnel director, accounting and control officer, or systems engineer could be redefined as change agent roles. Their responsibilities, at least in part, are to help bring about constructive changes in the way individuals and units in various parts of the organization operate. Frequently, their approach to accomplishing these goals has been through administrative orders. They have used the formal authority of their position within the organization to require that certain procedures and standards are adhered to.

The many difficulties in relationships between line and staff do not have to be documented here. It is frequently the case that members of the line in the organization do not see the efforts of the staff person as helpful, or in the direct service of the goals of the organization, but rather as a hindrance. One of the reasons for this is that the staff person, in fact, rarely sees himself as a helper, or facilitator, or change agent, but rather sees himself as an authority or perhaps as an expert.

THE LINE MANAGER AS CHANGE FACILITATOR

Many managers in modern public organizations are faced with the need to rethink their managerial styles. The traditional authority or command role does not operate effectively any more in most situations. For example, traditional command is not feasible or effective for the following:

1. Situations in which the line manager holds no authority over some or all of the personnel involved: for example, interdepartmental task forces, citizen groups, and interagency commissions
2. Situations in which sophisticated or high-level behavior is required, but cannot be commanded: for example, complex decision making, problem analysis and solving, planning, and various professional activities
3. Situations in which building collaborative problem-solving efforts is required: for example, situations in which people must work together smoothly, listen to and consider each other's ideas, and develop a spirit of teamwork
4. Situations in which attempts are made to overcome resistance to change and renew commitment and sense of mission.

In these and other situations the stance and skills of the previously described change facilitator almost certainly are more effective in bring about desired results than is the usual authority role. The manager is called upon to use his skills to "intervene" in such a way that he influences others to behave in a more positive, valid, or productive direction. Or, put another way, he is called upon to help develop a climate which supports and promotes the desired behaviors. Of prime importance is the need for the manager himself to provide a "model" of effective interaction—that is, his behavior sets an example for others. Some important examples of effective facilitative behavior for the manager include the following:

1. *Self awareness.* Understands his impact on others in affecting their attitudes and behavior.

2. *Commication.* Helps others develop frank and open communication in which relevant information about needs, problems, and feelings is freely shared. Demonstrates his willingness to listen to and deal with such information.

3. *Diagnostic (rather than punitive) approach.* Encourages use of data (reports, measurements, etc.) for objective diagnosis and problem solving, rather than placing blame, punishing, scapegoating, etc.

4. *Conflict management.* Faces up to conflict and helps others deal appropriately with conflict situations involving important differences, issues, or feelings. Does not stir up conflict unnecessarily.

5. *Innovation.* Strives to build a system which encourages and rewards creativity, innovation, and risk taking. Minimizes punishment for failure of sincere efforts or ideas.

6. *Personal growth.* Places value on actively developing and on using new strengths and abilities—for himself and others.

7. *Support.* Works to build a positive climate of support, trust, and empathy.

8. *Group skills.* Functions effectively in group situations (meetings, etc.) to bring about positive participation and contribution of others.[9]

Developing an Organization Climate

Many of the problems of change have come about because organizations as we know them are not flexible and adaptable. Avenues and approaches to change have had to be grafted onto many organizations in order to keep them operating under changing conditions. Many managers are currently addressing the problem of how to reconstruct organizations so that they are more open and receptive to change and adaptation. The requirements of such a system are awesome. Such an organization would require members who have the skill and courage to meet and cope with change and who are able to function without continually falling back on traditional guidelines and structures for security.

One authority believes that an organization that wishes to avoid stagnation by carrying on a continuing process of renewal should ask itself the following questions:

Does the organization have an effective program for the recruitment and development of talented manpower?

Has the organization an environment that encourages individuality and releases individual motivations?

Is there an adequate system of two-way communication in the organization?

Does the organization have a fluid and adaptable internal structure?

Are there ample opportunities and situations where the organization provides a process of self-criticism?

Is the organization able to cope with procedural buildup?

Does the organization have the ability to cope with vested interests?

Has the organization developed effective face-to-face groups for accomplishment of work goals?

Is the organization able to cope with change?

Does a climate of trust exist between individuals and groups in the organization?

How frequently and willingly has the organization evaluated its objectives and purposes, decision-making processes, and goals?[10]

The development of public organizations that are flexible and susceptible to change is not easy, but organizations that are able to accomplish this goal will be the leaders in carrying out the important tasks of the years ahead.

[1]John W. Gardner, SELF-RENEWAL: THE INDIVIDUAL AND THE INNOVATIVE SOCIETY (New York: Harper & Row, Publishers, 1963), p. xi.

[2]Timothy Costello, "The Change Process in Municipal Government," in EMERGING PATTERNS IN URBAN ADMINISTRATION. ed. G. Brown and T. P. Murphy (Lexington, Mass.: D. C. Heath & Company, 1970), pp. 18–22.

[3]For a review of some of the research behind the above generalizations, see: W. A. Faunce, E. Hardin, and E. H. Jacobson, "Automation and the Employee," ANNALS OF THE AMERICAN ACADEMY OF POLITICAL AND SOCIAL SCIENCE 340 (March 1962): 60–68; E. Hardin, W. B. Eddy, and S. E. Deutsch, ECONOMIC AND SOCIAL IMPLICATIONS OF AUTOMATION: AN ANNOTATED BIBLIOGRAPHY (East Lansing, Mich.: Michigan State University Labor and Industrial Center, 1961): E. Hardin, J. M. Shepard, and M. S. Spier, ECONOMIC AND SOCIAL IMPLICATIONS OF AUTOMATION: ABSTRACTS OF RECENT LITERATURE (East Lansing, Mich.: Michigan State University School of Labor and Industrial Relations, 1966).

[4]K. D. Benne and M. Birnbaum, "Change Does Not Have To Be Haphazard," SCHOOL REVIEW 68 (Fall 1961). Reprinted as "Principles of Changing," in THE PLANNING OF CHANGE. ed.

W. G. Bennis et al. (New York: Holt, Rinehart & Winston, Inc., 1969).

[5]H. J. Leavitt, "Applied Organizational Change and Industry: Structural, Technological and Humanistic Approaches," in HANDBOOK OF ORGANIZATIONS, ed. J. G. March (Skokie, Ill.: Rand McNally & Co., 1965), pp. 1144—70.

[6]National Training Laboratories Institute for Applied Behavioral Science, NEWS AND REPORTS, June 1968, p. 1.

[7]W. B. Eddy, "Beyond Behavioralism? Organization Development in Public Management," PUBLIC PERSONNEL REVIEW 31 (July 1970): 171—72.

[8]For an analysis of the differences in role between the OD specialist and the traditional trainer, see W. B. Eddy, "From Training to Development," PERSONNEL ADMINISTRATION 34 (January—February 1971): 37—43.

[9]J. K. Fordyce and R. Weil discuss the role of the internal change agent in MANAGING WITH PEOPLE: A MANAGER'S HANDBOOK OF ORGANIZATION DEVELOPMENT METHODS (Reading, Mass.: Addison-Wesley Publishing Co., Inc., 1971).

[10]Gordon L. Lippitt, ORGANIZATION RENEWAL (New York: Appleton-Century-Crofts, 1969), p. 21. Based in part on John W. Gardner, "How To Prevent Organizational Dry Rot," HARPER'S MAGAZINE, October 1965, pp. 20—26.

11

Training

TRAINING IS OFTEN something that public organizations sponsor out of a sense of duty, but to which they show little commitment. Yet it is not at all unusual for 60 to 80 percent of the municipal budget to be devoted to personnel costs. This is the very nature of a service organization, in which people are the primary resource. Most municipal organizations have treated manpower as a wasting resource—that is, they have left the responsibility for developing and maintaining the quality of their human resources to society at large or to individuals themselves, rather than developing a training policy for the people they employ. They have expected manpower support to come from external sources, and have supported this with only a minimum of job rotation, on-the-job coaching, technical training, and orientation to rules and procedures. Organizations have survived this way, and so they may rationalize the neglect of people resources by pointing to budgets, capital improvements, library book circulation, and other numeric measures of accomplishment.

Many signs suggest that achieved success is less than it ought to be, or, in fact, seems to be from the viewpoint of municipal management. These omens include the low level of prestige accorded to municipal employees, the apparent inability of municipalities to respond effectively to major problems, and the pervasive cynicism of citizens about local government performance. The point is that municipal governments need to invest in their primary resource in order to maintain and develop it. That is what training is: an investment in the human resources of the organization.

This chapter is designed to help you think about and plan the training investment. It seeks to outline training alternatives and to raise questions which must be answered in order to build a beneficial training program. In the past, most discussions of local government training have been organized around either the chronology or the location of training: pre-entry training, post-entry training, on-the-job training, etc. Other discussions of training have centered around techniques, such as the conduct of a group seminar or the use of audiovisual materials.

We prefer to deal primarily with the substance of training, especially of three types.

The first type of training is *big picture training,* sometimes appropriately labeled education rather than training. This is concerned with the context in which municipal activities occur rather than with the activities themselves. It also covers the fundamental skills that society in general provides for and expects of citizens.

The second type is *functional training,* the type most commonly found in municipal organizations. Functional training is concerned with the technology of particular professions or task specializations and with the highly specific information and expectations that an organization must transmit to its members. Management and supervisory training are included in functional training.

The final type is *applied behavioral science training.* It springs from a recognition that in social systems—and every organization is a social system—training can be a means of problem solving and of improving the social process of the organization.

When we speak of training we are referring to

a programmed effort for the individual or the small group which is intended to bring about a change in the competence and orientation of the individual, the working group, or the organization. Training in the applied behavioral science sense may also lead to change in the character, processes, or structures of the organization.

For training to be effective it must be accepted as a legitimate means of using time and money within the organization. When this commitment is lacking, training becomes marginal and the organization muddles through with its current, probably low, level of human resource utilization.

As a manager or supervisor you can make use of three strategies to fill training needs. These are, in order of increasing complexity and effectiveness: (1) a random strategy; (2) an opportunistic strategy; and (3) a programmed strategy.

A random strategy is really no strategy at all. It is the equivalent of substituting television watching for elementary school education. Under a random strategy one assumes that each employee in his own way will acquire, by hit or miss, sufficient understanding of the requirements of his role out of the rich flow of educational and informational opportunities available to all members of American society.

An opportunistic strategy takes selective advantage of the offerings of television, films, periodicals, other forms of mass media and publications, and training programs of educational and professional institutions at the time these offerings occur. This strategy focuses on using an opportunity for a specific purpose. An example would be the "big picture" training use by a municipal organization of a documentary television series on city life or race relations.

A programmed strategy is systematic in both finding and developing training opportunities, as well as in developing training objectives and identifying training needs. The programmed strategy pulls in and pulls together training opportunities and resources that already exist, or else it initiates internal development of training programs. In either case the programmed strategy responds to specifically identified training needs.

Each of these strategies has different consequences for the quality and effectiveness of the training received by employees. Different strategies may be appropriate for different areas of training, depending on the particular needs and levels of commitment to training in the organization. Generally speaking, managers and supervisors should try to use the most comprehensive strategy possible—the programmed strategy—since the resulting benefits are greater.

Big Picture Training

THE BACKGROUND

The majority of training programs in municipal organizations are built solely around functional training opportunities, although more progressive organizations may also offer opportunities for general education, justifying them in terms of the relationship of general education to promotional requirements. This concern with general education is manifested by the fact that just as a high school diploma was once required for certain jobs, many positions now require a junior college certificate or a bachelor's degree.

These requirements reflect a basic societal trend. General education has moved from the realm of luxury to the realm of necessity. Municipal organizations, which seek to provide efficient and responsive services to society, have increased their need for educated manpower in proportion to the increase in the quality and complexity of urban services. Big picture training is any educational opportunity which leads to better understanding of society at large—historical, cultural, political, social—and of how society impinges on the immediate world of the municipal organization.

Increasingly specialized and complexly interrelated technologies give rise to a need for more big picture training. In some ways local government has had a generation of respite in technological change. We have been building streets and processing sewage in about the same way for several years past. Increasing intensity of land use and increasing urbanization of the population, coupled with higher and more rigidly enforced standards of environmental health and safety, are rapidly putting an end to this comfortable situation. The nation's rising level of technological achievement as evidenced by the attainments in the aerospace field are being transferred increasingly to the civil systems market and particularly to the solution of city problems. Examples may be found in the functional fields of public safety, traffic control, public health, and information systems. A higher level of sophistication is required to understand and relate to these changes.

Adaptability to change thus is a highly prized characteristic of any individual member of the organization. While we do not perfectly understand what goes into adaptability to change, we do know that there is a strong positive correlation between level of general education and an individual's ability to adapt to changing circumstances. Therefore, it is in the organization's interest to invest in the general educational development of employees. Some cities and counties already provide for this through released time, purchase of books, and payment of tuition and other expenses for employees seeking high school and college degrees or professional certificates.

Big picture training is also utilized because it is important for employees of municipal organizations to understand the issues involved in, for example, race relations, suburbanization, employment, unemployment and welfare, housing, and education. These issues bear very directly on their work objectives. For example, a policy decision to adopt an equal employment opportunity policy of affirmative action is directly translated into recruitment and hiring practices. A decision to attack the problems of a blighted area will be translated throughout the organization into such specific work requirements as changes in the patterns of trash collection, street sweeping, code enforcement, liquor control, etc. Virtually no city department remains untouched.

On a more philosophical but no less important level governments are not simply technical agencies. They are an integral part of the democratic political process. Decisions of the policy body, however clearly stated, may still be open to administrative interpretation and judgment. These interpretations are not straightforward judg-

ments about how to get the work done, but involve the very intent of the city council. Citizens judge the responsiveness of government by what it does, so employees should know what the citizens want. For example, the decision to provide "equal levels of service in street cleaning throughout the city" may be interpreted by a well-trained public works director to mean sweeping all streets an equal number of times per year. If mandated by a socially conscious city council, however, the intent may actually be that streets be kept "equally clean" throughout the city no matter how many times the sweepers must be sent down the same streets. This distinction is very real to the street cleaning foreman.

Similarly, it is important for municipal employees to understand the intergovernmental environment in which they work. Local governments function in a complex framework of counties, adjoining cities, school districts, special districts, regional planning organizations, and, of course, the state and federal governments. Through professional service contracts and other means of purchase of goods and services, most municipal organizations are also substantially tied to a network of business organizations in the community. It is clear that doing effective work as a public agency requires effective relationships with individuals in numerous other organizations. The quality of those relationships may depend on the amount of understanding gained through formal education that municipal employees have of the purposes and processes of these other organizations.

THE STRATEGY

The training and educational programs which build the big picture are found primarily outside the organization, but the organization has a major role to play in locating the opportunities and mechanisms for this kind of training. For a municipal organization to do a credible job of big picture training a combination of strategies is needed. Some organizations provide released time from work assignments for employees who are pursuing high school or college credits; some provide financial assistance to employees for tuition, books, and other educational expenses; some develop policies which tie promotional opportunity to the achievement of certain educational objectives. In short, the progressive municipal organization will have taken a careful look at its policies for promoting big picture training and will have developed appropriate ordinances and administrative policies to carry it out. Where necessary, policy should be established in ordinance form or through administrative regulation and should be very clearly communicated to all municipal employees.

In addition to policies which leave the responsibility for training to individuals while clearing the way for them to proceed, there should be an assessment of the various opportunities which can be recommended to these individuals. Many good training experiences can be plucked opportunistically from the random stream of events. These can be noted and their availability circulated. An overall programmed strategy could be formulated to supplement these contributions and to provide a well-rounded offering of general education for municipal employees in relevant big picture subjects.

Functional Training

The most familiar area of local government training is functional training. Local governments have long taken pride in the attention they have given to training which increases the specific functional competence of employees and relates visibly and directly to the work process. This training is generally seen as increasing the specific job capability of employees and thereby increasing the return on the taxpayer's dollar. Improvement in individual competencies relating to work flow can result directly in improvement in the outputs of the work flow, i.e., in more and better service.

There are three broad groupings of functional training: orientation training; technical training for functional specialties; and management and supervisory training.

ORIENTATION TRAINING

The Background. Orientation training has been interpreted traditionally as dealing with the communication of basic organizational policies and expectations to new employees. It has also been associated historically with medium- and large-sized cities. Unfortunately, when orientation training is viewed as appropriate for new employees only it quickly becomes something to be disposed of rapidly and then forgotten. This is a limited view. We have chosen instead to use the term to refer primarily to ongoing training needs. Reiterating new policy, specifying operating guidelines, and communicating these along with more general organizational expectations to all employees, old-timers as well as newly hired, is a broader interpretation of orientation training.

While employees should become acquainted with long-standing expectations, policies, and procedures of the municipality as well as with the materials, for example, that might make up a personnel handbook, older employees may need to rethink these topics. Accordingly, orientation training should be a regular part of the training program for all employees.

Orientation training as described here goes beyond a one-time exposure to basic municipal policies. In addition to basic orientation training, there are various temporary needs for orientation training. Examples might be orientation to the following: a bond program or a new revenue source that is being offered for citizen approval; the introduction of a federal grant program; the institution of a new department or of a major new function within a department. Frequently these needs have not been met with regular orientation training programs, and employees have been left to their own sources of information, largely the grapevine, to secure an understanding of program goals and strategies.

When something new to the organization affects large numbers of people, they should be briefed: employee response can have far-reaching effects. Frequently these one-shot orientation needs (when met at all) are met through means which are more appropriate to routine work-related communications, for example through staff meetings, memos, notices posted on bulletin boards, etc. Such efforts should be supplanted by the more thorough technique of orientation training.

A third type of orientation training is of an ongoing nature. Every organization has expectations and policies about the way employees will behave toward other people while doing their work. This is a particularly sensitive area for public organizations. We are talking here about the way in which local government employees deal with citizens when talking to them at the service counter or on the telephone. We are also talking about the way in which they deal with fellow employees who may come from disadvantaged minority groups or the way in which they deal with such representatives of clientele groups as land developers and members of the chamber of commerce. This kind of orientation training is mostly concerned with attitude.

The Strategy.   Training can provide not only orientation to the policies of the organization; it can develop employee skills in carrying out these policies. Municipal organizations have offered "telephone courtesy," "meeting the public," and even "dealing with the disadvantaged employee" courses for many years. Nevertheless, such training is often undertaken with a less than comprehensive outlook toward organizational health and efficiency. The tendency has been to consider individual skill deficits in a segmented way as opposed to focusing on a total package of needs. Often, little problems have been dealt with in a big way and big problems have not had the benefit of training help. The municipal organization which takes a concerted approach to ongoing orientation will quickly recognize that the blending of consistent policies with well-coordinated skill training results in more effective behavior on the part of employees and greater public satisfaction with this behavior at small cost to the organization.

TECHNICAL TRAINING

The Background.   Training in technical specialties meets more specific needs than does orientation training. In the area of technical training, one is presented with an almost overwhelming array of choices. Among these sources are the Institute for Training in Municipal Administration of the International City Management Association, with its Green Book (Municipal Management Series) courses, and the seminars, short courses, and workshops conducted by such professional associations as the Municipal Finance Officers Association, the International Personnel Management Association,

the Labor-Management Relations Service, the National Recreation and Park Association, and the International Association of Chiefs of Police. There are also the National Training and Development Service for State and Local Government and the training programs offered by several of the state municipal leagues. Also helpful are national, state, and regional governmental agencies and many junior colleges and universities offering technical-functional courses pertaining to municipal functions.

The pre-entry training required for specialized jobs typically takes place in universities, high schools, or trade schools. For certain functions the initial skills training must take place at the time of employment, since the desired skills are too specialized for common usage.

While pre-entry training is typically associated with the police and fire departments, the manager and supervisor also need to think of pre-entry training in other departments. Municipal organizations require many different technical and functional skills, and in the case of strictly municipal functions it is a rare instance where the individual presenting himself for employment will possess all the necessary skills. Pre-entry training, then, becomes the responsibility of the municipal organization for functions as widely varied as governmental accounting, street maintenance, sewage plant operation, and zoning inspection.

Technical training can also be a valuable tool in the case of employees who are already on the job and performing well but whose performance and effectiveness could be improved.

Technical training is largely skill training—that is, it is mostly training in how to do something. Knowledge and understanding may be important, but primarily to the extent they improve skills and performance. Contrast this with big picture training, which is concerned primarily with knowledge and attitude. Because of the high skill component involved, it is not surprising to find that many of the methods of training for technical performance rely heavily on the experience factor. On-the-job training, coaching and consulting by supervisors, job rotation, apprenticeship training, internships, and similar formats are quite common. Public organizations are like private firms in this regard. In one study of 112 manufacturing and commercial firms, job instruction training and conference or discussion were consistently ranked as the two most frequently used training techniques. These were followed closely by apprenticeship training, job rotation, and coaching.[1] The central role of the supervisor in the latter three approaches underlines the fact that the manager or supervisor has a heavy training responsibility as a normal part of his job.

The Strategy. Numerous techniques are available for technical training. The choice depends on the style and skill of the trainer, the objectives of the training program, and the specific nature of the technique being communicated. It depends also on the training and the levels of interest and skills that the trainees possess. Included in the available training technology are numerous audiovisual techniques such as films, cassettes, and closed-circuit television. Training texts, correspondence courses, programmed instruction, simulations, programmed group exercises, role playing, laboratory training, and case studies are several other commonly used techniques.

MANAGEMENT AND SUPERVISORY TRAINING

The Background. Management and supervision are specialized organizational functions that will benefit from training. However, some special characteristics of management and supervision deserve mention.

Most supervisors and administrators in local government have come to their role as a second career. The only major exception is the city manager; many city managers have specialized training in the form of a master's degree in public administration and supervised general management experience as an intern or assistant. When management or supervision is a second career achieved by promotion from the first career, for example, by promotion from water engineer to director of public utilities, a major reorientation and relearning process is necessary.

Smaller organizations present a particularly difficult problem in recognizing the need for and providing management and supervisory training, because the individuals with management and supervisory responsibility may still have direct

operational responsibility in the specialty of their first career. For example, a city engineer may still carry out certain types of inspections personally because he is the only person qualified to do so. It is not at all unusual to find local government department heads who see themselves as solely responsible for a technical function—as a police chief, a finance director, a director of community development and planning. These department heads do not think of themselves as managers or supervisors, although the tasks they perform are the tasks of management and supervision. The department head who sees himself as basically a technician deprives the organization of what it most needs—the management function.

Supervision is the hard job of getting work done through others. It requires skills in leadership, communications, planning and scheduling work, the effective use of time, definition and achievement of objectives, and relating the working group to other working groups and to citizens.

Management includes supervision as part of its responsibility. It also includes problem-solving relationships with other managers. The National Academy of Public Administration, in a study of scientists and engineers becoming managers, found several differences in the frequency and qualitative nature of functions performed by the managers as opposed to what they had done in the role of scientists. The most striking change was a shift in focus from task-centered skills to those skills needed to master the organization system.[2] This is probably the key to understanding management. Management is concerned with the whole organization, with its purposes—that is, with the formulation and recommendation of policy—and with translating purposes into achievable objectives and seeing that they are achieved. It follows that training for management includes the development of skills and understandings relevant to the whole organization and to policy matters, including skills in group and intergroup behavior, communications, decision making, and conflict management, as well as understanding of the staff functions of personnel, budgeting, and organizational planning.

The Strategy. In an area as nebulous as employee training and development it may be misleading to categorize training strategies as though each were in a separate compartment. The three strategies described in the following paragraphs have a lot of overlap but are sufficiently distinctive to be identified as traditional management, interaction with people and groups, and information and systems.

Supervision and management have large skill components. Traditionally, training has centered on factual material on planning, organizing, staffing, directing, "co-ordinating," reporting, and budgeting. These elements of the management job were given the acronym POSDCORB by Luther Gulick in 1936.[3] While there is much to be learned about them in traditional ways, their application is basically a matter of learning skills. Thus a strategy for training in management and supervision should also include skill training. Many of these skills are part of interpersonal relations or leadership. Improvement of these skills requires knowledge of how people work as individuals, in groups, and as part of a larger organization or system of groups.

Improvement also requires practice in effective work-related interaction with other people. In other words, it cannot be taken from books alone but must be developed by individuals as they work with other individuals and groups. Experience-based training techniques, such as simulation, role playing, peer interaction analysis, and other varieties of what is called laboratory learning make it possible to speed up the long and painful process of developing leadership skills. Management laboratories, when conducted by competent and experienced trainers, are well worth considering.

With the developments in information, systems and the computer during the fifties and sixties, management training now includes, or should include, appropriate aspects of decision making. Some of this is touched on in Chapter 7 in a brief discussion of policy analysis, and in Chapters 13, 14, and 15 in coverage of systems analysis, management information systems, and work analysis. The field, for such a new one, is large and complex, but the overriding purpose is to help management make better decisions. Specific training can be built around such

methods as cost-benefit analysis, cost-effectiveness analysis, program evaluation and review technique (PERT), and the critical path method (CPM), as well as the broader approaches of systems analysis and information systems.

Applied Behavioral Science Training

THE BACKGROUND

In the last two decades a new type of training known as applied behavioral science training (ABS training) has emerged. During this time it has gained considerable acceptance as a training resource in the public sector, including local government. This type of training, however, is only one aspect of a larger developmental process with which many people are not familiar. This is a process in which behavioral science knowledge and methods are brought to bear on the social process of an organization with the goal of increasing its effectiveness both as a production unit and, importantly, as a social group or system of groups. To make this more specific, the applied behavioral science process includes four steps:

1. Agenda building: a preliminary list of the major issues and concerns of the organization is compiled.
2. Data collection: diagnostic techniques are used to collect valid and useful data about the nature of the organization and its problems and issues.
3. Feedback: data are thoroughly outlined to responsible individuals in the organization to facilitate more specific agenda building.
4. Problem solving: in the course of the problem solving, a new agenda will be built which may in turn lead to another round of data collection, feedback, and problem solving to create a continuous process of applied behavioral science.

Training of individuals and groups may take place at any point in the above sequence. Some of the skill training mentioned as important for management and supervision is also relevant to applied behavioral science. In addition to training as a basic skill development technique, there are several training formats used in applied behavioral science which can be roughly described as forums for focused problem solving; these are: management team building, interdepartmental confrontation meetings, problem-solving task groups, and third party process consultation. Each of these techniques is described later in this chapter.

Starting with the assumption that the organization is made up of the people in it, instead of consisting of the abstract formality of the organization chart or the budget (although the allocation of authority to agencies, positions, budgets, etc., shapes the behavior of the people), applied behavioral science leads to the development of a problem-solving climate. It generates change strategies within the framework of a systematic diagnosis of social and technical processes.

At this point, applied behavioral science may seem strange, abstract, and even unreal. "OK for the encounter group but not for me!" It is different from the material world of money, materials, and equipment and from the formal, abstract world of the organization chart, the budget, and laws and ordinances.

Applied behavioral science is intended to create an "organizational self-consciousness," which will make it possible for the organization to consciously direct its future. The organization develops awareness of actual patterns of authority, actual roles of individuals (in their jobs and as these jobs relate to other people), actual processes of making decisions and actual interrelationships of people.

ABS training takes place within the context of the organization's work and in an important sense is the organization's work. The training agenda will be related to specific organizational issues. These issues may be historic problem areas in which something needs to be put right in the organization; they may be issues of direction and future growth and development; or they may be issues of maintenance of the social system.

Perhaps the identifying characteristic of applied behavioral science training is the presence of training interventions which enhance the organization's ability to handle its regular work

by going directly to the site of work problems. In a sense, training of any kind is an intervention in the work process. Whenever someone is sent outside the organization to add to their knowledge or skills something happens upon their return. Things are not quite the same. In this sense, the organization's capability and climate have been affected. What is different about ABS training interventions is that they are organized around specific and real problems of a particular organization, and they attempt not only to improve individual capabilities but to improve organizational behavior directly.

THE TECHNOLOGY

Let us turn our attention to the characteristic training interventions that might be found in an applied behavioral science training process. A few illustrative techniques are summarized here. These techniques were developed to implement the process of diagnostic data collection, feedback, agenda building, and problem solving discussed above.

Diagnosis. Diagnosis is a process whereby members of an organization identify problems, issues, and concerns of specific importance to the way the organization or its subunits conduct business. Survey feedback techniques are commonly used. A structured list of questions is presented to a large number of people in the organization through a combination of interviews and questionnaires. Although there are some standard lines of inquiry, the survey is typically tailored to the specific organization. Questions may cover such subjects as employee motivation, processes of communication and decision making within the organization, perception of roles, interpersonal conflict, organizational commitment, management styles, evaluations of management individuals, the management climate, leadership, and the quality of life within the organization.

Following the *anonymous* collection of such data, results are processed by the consultant in charge and are prepared for feedback to appropriate members of management. The feedback may be limited to top management or may be extended to the lowest supervisor within the organization, depending on the preliminary design of the survey-feedback mechanism. The target group is usually determined at the same time that survey questions are designed for the organization.

Feedback will generally take place in circumstances conducive to small group discussion, with opportunity for the members of each group to discuss the new data about the organization and to begin to develop some conceptual notions about the organization's problems. Growing out of these small group discussions, an agenda-building exercise is frequently undertaken to develop a strategy for action in the ongoing process of organizational renewal and improvement and ABS training.

Professional assistance from outside the organization is desirable—some would say necessary—for the process of diagnosis. Those who attempt diagnosis should have an understanding of the role of the behavioral science consultant in constructing a design for diagnostic inquiry. His role is that of a facilitator rather than an expert. He helps the organization design the initial process of diagnostic data collection. He knows how to conduct interviews, develop questionnaire schedules, and design training formats. As a third party he is able to assure the confidentiality of information and thus protect individuals who might be taking severe risks by revealing sensitive but crucial insights during the embroyonic first stages of the program. He is, finally, well versed in organization behavior and the characteristics of different organizational systems. By virtue of this knowledge he is able to provide perspectives through which the information may be viewed productively.

It is important to note that the applied behavioral science consultant does not provide answers. Rather, he provides frameworks from within which the members of the organization may seek and develop answers.

As a second form of diagnostic technique, interviews may be used apart from or in conjunction with a full-blown survey feedback sequence. The sample of people interviewed may vary greatly depending on the scope of the proposed program. It may include only top management or it may include individuals throughout the organization. It may include as a unit employees in various work groups as well as key individuals external to the organization who interface with it

and are in a position to affect its work. Typical interview questions may cover subjects similar to those mentioned in relation to the survey feedback technique. Open-ended questions will provide an occasion for employees to talk about organizational issues from their own perspective. One form of interviewing might appropriately be titled "conversations." In this situation the interviewer may meet with groups of people within the organization and conduct a group interview or rap session about life in the organization, or he may talk with individuals around the water cooler, in the halls, riding in the squad car, or perhaps even in the training room of the fire department.

Observation is a final diagnostic technique used by consultants. A third party consultant may simply observe the organization at work. For example, he may attend the weekly staff meeting and take notes concerning the manner in which problems are addressed and solved. He may attend a city or town council meeting or observe a problem-solving group at work in a department. Observation provides additional perspectives through which to view data gathered through a survey feedback technique or through interviews.

In those organizations that have had a great deal of experience with diagnosis with experienced third party help, additional problem-sensing techniques can be used without this outside help. The essential characteristic of these techniques is that the data are collected by particular units of the organization for their use and for the use of the other departments with whom they work. For example, a team of two or three people from a budget and systems division might spend an hour or more within various other departments asking such questions as, "How do you see us?" "What do we do that is helpful to you?" "What do we do that gets in your way?" "What could we do that would be more effective and more helpful to you?"

Such techniques are effectively used only in organizations which have a climate characterized by a high trust level and some experience in explicitly dealing with the social system of the organization. Without this trust and experience, internal data collectors are too likely either to become defensive of their unit when told things they do not like or to find that people are telling them only what they think the inquiring unit wants to hear.

When diagnostic data collection has produced a body of valid and useful data and that data have been looked at by the organization, three directions for action will present themselves.

First, certain problems that can be solved by well-known methods will be identified. For example, it might be clear that there is a less than desirable level of skill in the technical area of street maintenance; as a result, it would be decided to start a training course.

A second type of direction for action will typically be the identification of needs for training in human relations. This includes training in such skills as communications, decision making, management style, and conflict management. These are basic skills that must be present at a fairly high level for an organization to effectively use ABS techniques.

Third, problem-solving needs may be identified which can best be met through the development of training interventions which deal directly with specific problems of the organization. At this point it is appropriate to mention some of the major training formats that are available for direct organizational problem solving.

Team Building. One of the most widely used training interventions is known as team building. Briefly stated, team building refers to a rather intensive problem identification and problem-solving discussion among groups of people whose individual work directly affects the performance of others. Team building attempts to get to the heart of the human relationship problems which frequently stand in the way of getting the job done more effectively. A major axiom of team building is that the human organization relies on effective collaboration among administrators and other individuals. Real collaboration does not come easily or automatically. It is often hindered by communication difficulties, competitive forces, conflict, and an inability to identify, confront, and solve problems. Many organizations have found that teams of management and supervisory people working with a consultant can often deal with problems and plan for more effective collaboration in an open and non-threatening atmosphere.

Team building utilizes a meeting that lasts from a minimum of a half day to several days. Participants work together to evaluate their ability to be open and honest with each other, explore their feelings and attitudes in relation to each other and the organization, identify problems and issues which hamper their collaboration, and suggest approaches to solving these problems. It should be noted that the content of such discussions is considered confidential with the group, that participants are never pressured to say more than they wish to say, and that, to extent possible, there is a commitment to work through and resolve person-to-person differences which may arise during the course of the meeting. In the team building meeting, status differences among the management group are minimized and the group operates as a team of equals. Communication is as open and direct as is possible within the climate that is established.

Confrontation. Another type of training intervention that is frequently used is the confrontation meeting in which two or more organizational units which have had difficulty working together call on a third party consultant to help them arrive at some resolution of their differences. The third party leads them through a series of steps; these steps include a listing by each group of its perception of itself and of the other group, a sharing of these perceptions, and a working out of priority action steps designed to reduce the conflict and increase collaboration. Critical conflict issues are raised. The meeting provides a format in which it is possible to arrive at a positive and effective resolution of some of these conflicts. The confrontation meeting, with its emphasis on specific, mutually agreed-upon action steps, is an effective way of reducing nonproductive conflict and channeling interdepartmental energies into collaboration around organization goals.

Third Party Consultation. In third party consultation, or process consultation, a trained observer looks at a particular process and provides feedback to the individual or group. It is a variation of the process of diagnosis described earlier.

Process consultation may be carried on at the level of one-to-one individual relationships, as, for example, where a third party helps individuals who have trouble working with each other to improve their interpersonal relationships.

Process consultation may also be used at the group level. In this case a trained third party consultant observes the functioning of a staff meeting, a public hearing, or some other typical group process. He then provides confidential feedback to the participants regarding his observations and his judgment of the effectiveness of their behaviors. Then the individuals in the group are in a position to take whatever action, if any, they find appropriate and possible.

Problem-Solving Task Groups. A final example of a training intervention (and one which illustrates the range and variety that these interventions can take) is the use of temporary task teams charged with developing solutions to particular organizational and managerial problems.

Other Interventions. Other problem-solving mechanisms that may be indicated by ABS include: working out new organizational roles based on new understandings and identification of new needs in the organization; establishing new authority relationships, new decision-making patterns, and perhaps even alterations of the formal organizational charts of particular departments or of the organization at large. For example, in at least one city that utilizes applied behavioral science training, the team concept of management has resulted in an ordinance which describes the organization chart in accordance with this concept.

THE STRATEGY

The resources for effective applied behavioral science training are primarily within the organization. To make good use of internal resources, however, a limited number of highly skilled outside consultants are almost certainly necessary.

Not all organizations and individual managers will find applied behavioral science training to their liking. The manager who is contemplating such a training program should take stock of the openness of his organization and examine the willingness of the organization to make constructive changes. In addition, the manager should make a careful analysis of his own com-

mitment to such a process. Some discussion within the management group is advisable. ABS training requires the commitment of top management for its effective application.

One very likely outcome of ABS training is that department heads will begin trying out leadership and decision-making skills which have usually been the preserve of top management. Supervisors will expect to be fully functioning members of the team. Parochial views of the organization and its individual units will no longer be possible or adequate for decision making. The responsibility for managing the resources of the organization will most certainly become a responsibility shared by all persons exercising supervision, most likely as members of a mutually supporting team.

Clearly, then, the changes in the organization that are the objective of applied behavioral science training are achieved by a process spanning an extensive period of time. The payoffs may not be recognized for several months or perhaps even years. This suggests that the organization that is contemplating ABS training should be prepared to make a long-term commitment. Applied behavioral science implies a particular philosophy of management—a creative, problem-solving philosophy that puts great stock in the capabilities of ordinary people.

It is highly improbable that any organization could undertake a program of applied behavioral science without competent outside help.

Planning a Training Program

Training is the responsibility of management and supervision. It may be formally located in the personnel department or in the chief administrator's office, yet the progressive manager and supervisor will also recognize that effective training must be considered an integral part of his job. Let us first look at the major issue that the manager and supervisor must consider in organizational training—a commitment to training. Ask yourself, "Do the policies and the management philosophy bring receptiveness to training? Are people rewarded or punished if they take time away from work for training? What are the attitudes of managers and supervisors toward learning and improving skills? Are the resources of money and released time regularly made available for training?"

If the basic commitment of time and financial resources is there, then you and your organization are ready to develop a training program. Suggested steps in developing the program are disucssed below and include analysis of training needs, review of training policies, functional training, your organization as a social system, training resources, and training methods.

Analysis of Training Needs

General training needs in the organization probably will be readily apparent to many administrative and supervisory personnel, and specific needs often are readily apparent to departmental supervisors. Other needs that are important to the organization are not so apparent. These less visible needs require a more deliberate and systematic approach to the identification and development of the program response. In identifying training needs, there is a significant danger of adopting faddish solutions to complex problems. Some of these are traps for the unwary developer of training programs.

The Training Package. Perhaps the most insidious trap is the temptation to purchase a packaged solution to unknown problems. Training has become a lucrative market, and many individuals and institutions are glad to sell you their package whether you need it or not. Such packages are often set forth in elegant brochures with carefully stylized writing that is a sophisticated hard sell.

Manpower Analysis. The second hazard may be called the manpower analysis trap. It consists of treating the human resources of the organization in the same fashion as the material resources. Traditional manpower analysis assumes that one knows exactly what is needed in the way of competence for the specific jobs of the organization. It then proceeds to inventory the individuals in the organization and to make assumptions about each individual's level of competence. The second inventory is subtracted from the first, and a training and development program is recommended to fill the gaps.

Such an approach is seductively attractive. It makes intuitive sense. In fact, it can provide a good first cut at identifying functional training needs, but it ignores the continually changing nature of the organization and its work. A determination of needs at one point may be obsolete or off target in a period of a few months because of the addition or departure of employees, changes in policy, or changes in the internal issues of the organization. As some problems are solved, new ones are added in their turn, and others get worse.

Finally, manpower analysis may be too generalized to identify some important needs. It tends to look at positions and at formal education rather than at people and their demonstrated skills. To find what the resources really are, it may be necessary to go to the people who have them—the employees.

Economic Analysis. A third pitfall is the economic analysis trap. If you insist that any training event must show specific and measurable production benefits exceeding its costs, you have fallen into this trap. The effects of training, though they may be substantial, generally cannot be measured that directly. Also, many of the benefits of training are long-run rather than immediate. The dollars-and-cents criterion is a double edged sword.

It is equally wrong to assume that a training program is desirable because it is offered to your employees free of charge, perhaps under a grant that some other institution has received. First, the time cost involved when employees are away from their jobs can be substantial. Second, if the training is not meeting a priority for the organization then it may distort other priorities of the organization.

One-Shot Training. The danger of judging each training opportunity on its own merits but stopping there encourages one-shot, project-oriented training. This leads to dissipation of resources, because the effort is not focused and because one training opportunity does not build on another. Too often, training is based on availability rather than program.

The census of training needs must be current, comprehensive, and real. Training which occurs because of a historic need or which attends to a popular area may inhibit any creative response to more fundamental needs.

REVIEW OF TRAINING POLICIES

The next major step is to review organizational policies for training. Are there such policies? Are they formally stated? Do they reflect the needs of the organization? Are training and development policies consistent with personnel practices encouraged by management for promotion and personal development? Do policies support big picture training? Do they provide for the systematic development of individual programs of self-improvement which are related to organizational priorities?

In the absence of formally adopted policies or in the absence of *effective* policies, the manager or supervisor must begin to think about what constitutes an effective set of policies for his organization.

FUNCTIONAL TRAINING

Looking over the functions of the organization or of your unit, it is important to ask yourself the following questions. Have the needs for functional and technical training, including orientation needs, technical training needs, and management and supervisory needs, been systematically surveyed? Are there unmet needs for functional training which have been identified through a survey?

Functional training by definition will vary in type and content from unit to unit and department to department, and only in some instances will it be uniformly applicable to the total organization. Therefore a department-by-department review of such training needs is an ideal way to make a start. Involving the employees who might be eligible for training obviously is a desirable part of this review of training needs.

THE ORGANIZATION AS A SOCIAL SYSTEM

Next, ask questions that relate to the organization as a changing social system which may in part be dealt with in training formats. For example, is communication between departments effective? Do members of management and supervision know their managerial styles and how they affect others? Are groups and meetings effective? Are there opportunities for learning more effective ways of making decisions?

TRAINING RESOURCES

So far, we have talked mostly about needs, but it is also important to consider resources. Some of these are internal, but you should also seek out the many resources available in the community. Is there a local college which has courses that fit your needs? If a local college does not have these courses, would they be willing to develop some tailored educational opportunities for public employees? Are there industries in your vicinity with relevant training programs which might be made available? Are there other municipalities or municipally related organizations with training resources?

Another source of training is the group of programs sponsored by such national trade and professional organizations as the International City Management Association.

TRAINING METHODS

To evaluate external training opportunities and to develop internal training programs it is good to have some ideas about training methods. Two facts about employees are immediately important in thinking about how to train. First, employees are adults, not children. Second, they are workers, not students. As adults we can expect them to control their learning themselves. They are capable of initiating thought and inquiry while recognizing their interdependency with other people. As employed adults, they have a good store of remembered relevant experience.

Employees are likely to appreciate training most when it has a specific payoff for them or their work group. They prefer to have training that is problem centered rather than subject centered. This suggests that the more successful curriculum will be the one that goes through the subject matter as the employee understands the problem rather than following textbook logic.

Conclusions

Learning involves direct experiences (even if they are no more than reading and listening to lectures), critical analysis of these experiences, experimentation and new analysis, testing of options, and practice of newly acquired skills.

There is the kernel of a great truth in the old idea of taking people where they are and letting them learn by experience. It assumes that individuals learn through interactions with their environment rather than through passive subjection to a teacher and a classroom. The experiential approach is a summation of some of the most sophisticated educational theory found today.

Most functional and ABS training involves the development of skills, and skills are developed only by the individuals who are their ultimate possessors. Just as one cannot learn to drive a car by simply studying the driver's manual, so both manual and human relations skills must be learned through some form of experimentation and practice in the skill area. Thus, the development of skills must involve some active experience and experimentation on the part of the learner.

Training can also lead to the development of new information—by the active learner himself, by a third party observer, or by some more impersonal means of observation and feedback. As management is hard work that is concerned with helping work to occur, so training is hard work that is concerned with helping learning to occur—not with simply transmitting wisdom from the wise to the less wise.

It is the responsibility of top management to adopt, and practice, the policy that training is an important part of the development of the human resources of the organization. Additionally, top management needs to provide the mechanisms—staff, money, time—for training programs. In the small city, the manager may perform this function himself. In larger organizations, while it is common for such a function to be delegated, this delegation should not be handled in a fashion which removes training responsibility from top management.

If the organization has a progressive philosophy, the two-fold role of the supervisor should be clear: first, to act continually as a trainer within the organizational unit; and second, to identify the employees who have needs which must be met and see that appropriate training is made available to them. Even when lacking a comprehensive organizational strategy for training, the supervisor is not necessarily blocked from doing something positive. He may initiate elements of the above strategy for his own working unit; he may interpret the needs to his department head; and he may provide personally whatever training he himself feels qualified to give.

In summary, management and supervisory personnel are responsible for getting work done through other people. Not only should they provide their employees with opportunities for training, they should also strive to be trainers themselves.

---

[1]Stuart B. Utgaard and Rene V. Dawis, "The Most Frequently Used Training Techniques," TRAINING AND DEVELOPMENT JOURNAL 26 (February 1970): 41.

[2]National Academy of Public Administration, THE TRANSFORMATION OF SCIENTISTS AND ENGINEERS INTO MANAGERS (Washington, D.C.: Government Printing Office, 1972).

[3]Luther Gulick, "Notes on a Theory of Organization," in PAPERS ON THE SCIENCE OF ADMINISTRATION, ed. Luther Gulick and Lyndall Urwick (New York: Columbia University Press, 1936).

12

Managing by Objective

THOSE WHO MANAGE the affairs of cities know that the future will place new demands on urban government. They cannot escape the problems that are developing. An Associated Press urban affairs writer, for example, starts an article by stating that the nation's cities are "a little older, a little poorer, and a little more desperate," and then presents a familiar list of maladies: poor housing, inadequate public transportation, deteriorating schools, unemployment, increase in crime, bad air and water, racial conflict, poor health facilities, and lack of open space.[1]

To manage by objective is to deal with the future in a way that recognizes existing problems but also recognizes the possibilities for improvement. It is a "proactive" rather than a reactive style; those charged with responsibility for any part of a city's government take the initiative for making certain changes and do not wait for changes to affect them. Managing by objective is a continuing process which develops the capability of an organization to meet its own needs and, in so doing, to develop further capability.

True objectives are statements of future attainments. Priority decisions can be made when possible courses of action are weighed in terms of their contribution to reaching a future goal; skill and talent can be mobilized with a definite end in sight; and people are most willing to work on a project which has a definite payoff. A future goal is the keystone of any process of management by objective.

In practice, "goal" and "objective" are synonymous, but technically goal has a more restricted meaning. The goal is the end point of all the effort exerted by an organization. An objective,

as it is understood in the process of managing by objective, refers to the work planned to reach the goal as well as to the goal itself. The goal is, by analogy, a city at some distance which the manager and his organization have taken as their destination; the objective is a map including that city which sets forth in some detail how the city can be reached. The process of managing by objective is following the map to reach the city. What this analogy lacks is a fourth dimension: managing by objective takes place over time, and schedules are an integral part of this process. And, like any analogy, the map analogy is not as complicated as the real world. In the real world an organization may be traveling along several roads simultaneously, managing by objectives, reaching for several goals.

If several goals are pursued simultaneously, however, there is the possibility of conflict. To have a safe community and to make it a pleasant place to live in are two aspirations which seem compatible. If, however, bright street lights are installed to reduce crime, and those lights bother people who are trying to sleep, it may appear that the pursuit of one goal has interfered with pursuit of the other. The question of hierarchy is raised. Which goal is more important? If safety is more important than pleasure, or, to put it another way, is a condition for living a pleasurable life, it may be that people should put up with the glare. The point is, that people's pursuits and aspirations, no matter how irrational they may be, must be fitted together in a rational framework in order to make choices.

A hierarchy of goals or objectives is, in a sense, a substitution for organizational hierarchy.

Present-day workers are not so willing to obey commands from up the line. They ask for what used to be assumed in commands: good reasons. But the reasons are often vague and remote. Why install bright street lights, for example? What does that have to do with reducing crime? It is a managerial task, therefore, not only to make explicit the high priority goals but to help define subgoals which contribute to the overall goals. A subgoal is a workable unit on which a department or work group can concentrate.

Management by objective frees the leaders of an organization from one of their most severe constraints—the structure of the organization itself. In the normal course of doing business, many of the best ideas and most hopeful plans for action get lost in "channels." People in the organization may know very well what actions are called for, but they cannot proceed because "You just can't do things that way." In management by objective the organization structure, while useful, is secondary, and the objective is primary.

The process of managing by objective starts with an attitude—that the future can be shaped to fit the aspirations of a community. Very quickly, however, practical implications can be seen for the departments of a city government. Before we discuss the practice of management by objective, the importance of an objective-setting process should be noted

Priorities Are Established. When goals and purposes are consciously spelled out, priorities are established for making choices.

Capabilities Are Realized. A governmental work force can exert great strength. Skill and talent are available; when these capabilities are focused on a common objective, they are used most fully.

Commitment Is Gained. Management by objective is a process of involvement. People who are going to take part are enlisted at the beginning, when the objective itself is decided upon.

The Work Force and the Community

Management by objective enables a leader to use a work force which is designed for a specific task. The people who work on an objective are organized *toward the objective* rather than according to office or rank. Thus, an objective in the field of public health—for example, to establish medical facilities for migrant farm worker families—might enlist people from the departments of sanitation, police, finance, and planning, and from nongovernmental bodies—as well as from the department of health. Interdepartmental coordination is often required in local government, but the process of managing by objective means more than coordination. It means organizing work assignments ans responsibilities in terms of *achieving the goal;* the chain (or chains) of command is subordinated to the accomplishment of the objective.

A new relationship between work and the worker is established. The worker joins with others to decide on a common objective; the requirements for meeting that objective determine the relationships among the workers. There is still leadership. A manager is needed to coordinate the project. But the payoff is in completing the project rather than pleasing or answering to the manager. This method for organizing a work force has grown up in recent years, most obviously in contract work done by private industry for the federal government. As the federal government has pushed farther into the development of futuristic hardware for space exploration and military defense, the bureaucratic chain-of-command organization has been unable to get the job done.

A chain of command assumes that the people at the top know everything about the job to be done (or at least they can find out). Communications among the work force, therefore, take the form of directives. The top office plans the work and makes assignments. Division directors, department heads, and unit bosses all down the line make sure that their parts of the organization carry out their parts of the task. It is not necessary for one division, department, or unit to understand what the others are doing. In some cases they may not even know why they are doing their particular work. If top management knows what it wants and how to get it, and if the work force can realize some benefit by following management directives, the chain of command system can function.

If goals are not clearly understood, and if top

management is not equipped to comprehend all the means for reaching the goals, a work force is stymied. In the case of space hardware, for example, neither government leaders nor industrial leaders are in a position to understand what can be achieved beyond the earth's atmosphere, and they certainly don't understand the science and technology required. So they have set up task forces managed by objectives, task forces which cut across old lines of jurisdiction and which decide not only the *means* for reaching space objectives but the *nature* of the objectives.

Modern city government is like space exploration in that the nature of changing urban society, and projections about the near future of cities, are not fully comprehended. It cannot be assumed that police are getting their job done by keeping traffic violations and thefts at a minimum when society's concepts of law are radically changing; or that sewers and sanitation are doing satisfactory work if all the waste is efficiently disposed of outside the city limits; or that children are being educated if school absenteeism is low and a fair percentage of eighteen year olds make it into college. The changes that are occurring in every community not only challenge the operations of city government but call into question the objectives as well.

Objective setting, as a managerial process, requires intraorganizational democratic participation. People all through the organization help establish the objectives. Democratic involvement in setting objectives is not formal, but vital. Without consensus the objective-setting process leads to worse failure than the chain of command. When top management gives directives, at least top management is committed to seeing them through. When people go to work on objectives without reaching real agreement, no one is committed.

The process of reaching real agreement creates a community. Municipal employees are part of a larger community; they are citizens of the government they work for. But when they work together on shared objectives they are members of a community in a double sense. They have decided not only to cast their lot with neighbors who live in the same governmental jurisdiction but also to work together with other city employees for a common purpose.

A Scale of Satisfaction

The possibility of creating a work community makes sense for a manager or department head. From the manager's standpoint, pressures stronger than attachment to the democratic ideal are operating. Managers today work with people, especially younger people, who are professionals and specialists. People with special training have worked for a long time for municipal governments. Today the engineers, librarians, maintenance men, are needed more than ever. The difference now is that each profession or specialty group is more conscious of its special contribution, of the relative demand for what it has to contribute. At the same time, city governments are hiring systems analysts and planning technicians, and other members of a new generation of specialists. All these people are in demand elsewhere, and none of them, it can be assumed, will work indefinitely for an employer who does not actively enlist his special competence. To enlist such talent requires a new development in managerial skill.

To make the job of management even more difficult, the supply of specially skilled people is less in many areas than the demand. When a manager has a chance to hire a finance man or a recreation director he may have to take the man who is available. Subsequently, the manager may find some difficulty in fitting the man in if the manager has some strong personal ideas about how that particular department should be run.

The more complex the technology of his position, the less susceptible is the employee to specific authoritarian supervision. So the higher skilled employee must be capable of directing his own behavior to an increasing extent. The resulting decrease in the utility of authoritarian approaches combined with an intensified interdependence of all roles and units requires a high level of social maturity of all participants.[2]

"Social maturity" is an expression indicating that people may actually enjoy taking responsibility in a group. To perform a task on your own initiative that benefits the community, to create more effective solutions to common problems, and to share your solutions freely are signs of social maturity. Most managers, who by definition hold responsibility for the success of their organizations, are socially mature; at least, they pursue such maturity as an ideal. The fact is, however, that most people at every level of an organization—in every department of a local government—pursue the same ideal. They *want* to take responsibility, given the fact that it is real responsibility and not merely an opportunity to absorb blame. They want to help the work force create better solutions to common problems.

Self-direction, in the sense of sharing responsibility for the achievement of a goal—in the department, in the government, in the community—is at the top of the scale of satisfaction for local government employees. Some must work for less: the satisfaction of pleasing a boss whom they respect, the satisfaction of keeping a budget snug in their department, the satisfaction of pleasant working relationships, the satisfaction of a respected title. There are many genuine satisfactions in government work, but all may be subsumed under goal achievement. Work that is directed toward the accomplishment of a goal calls forth the best motivations and provides the fullest satisfactions.

Survive or Attain?

Management by objective starts with a definition of goals. The manager engages his entire organization in a mutual search for purposes which are of deep concern to the people in the organization, which make sense in light of the nature of the organization, and which have some possibility of accomplishment.

If management by objective is to work at all, however, an important distinction must be made. An organization can be managed by an objective only if its objective is an attainment outside itself; if its objective is merely to survive, the management by objective process will not bring much help. Survival is already an assumption underlying the existence of every government, every agency or enterprise; to elevate survival to the position of an objective may help people think more about it, but is apt to have as much of a disturbing as a motivating effect.

When the manager or department head is selecting possible goals, he often thinks first of survival needs. "My goal is to balance the budget next year." "My goal is to raise $500,000 more." "My goal is to consolidate the sanitary district and keep it operational."

If a manager has not been accustomed to making clear-cut statements about the work of his organization, statements of survival needs are very useful. Such statements focus attention throughout the organization on problem areas. Department heads and supervisors read the statements and gain some understanding of the things they can and can't do. If a city needs a unified accounting procedure, for example, the manager will profitably devote himself to installing it. The result of such effort, however, is only a better likelihood of survival—measured in terms of continued services, facilities remaining open, no staff reductions, or some other survival index—and should not be confused with attainment of an objective.

One of Parkinson's laws is that every bureaucratically managed organization tends to start out with attainment goals, then, once it believes it has achieved these goals, takes survival to be its chief remaining goal. The younger the organization, supposedly, the livelier it is; the older and more established it gets, the more rigid it becomes. Management by objective continually renews an organization by bringing it back to a starting point with the question: What are we going to accomplish?

Managerial Roles

With management by objective, some of the familiar managerial roles are no longer usable: final arbiter, information funnel, lone decision maker, the man who takes the rap when a project fails. Instead, the leader of a governmental organization takes on new roles. Or, more precisely, he is able to direct his energies more profitably in *managerial* rather than *directorial* roles. For some people who have operated comfortably as directors, the changeover can be difficult. Other managers feel that managing by objective is what they like to do and perhaps have been trying to do all along.

The person who takes the leadership in accomplishing a particular objective is, for the duration of that project, a manager. He is not dictating or, in the top-down sense, directing. On the other hand, he is more than a coordinator who brings people together to make decisions about joint purposes. "Project manager" might be an appropriate title, since it implies that the managerial responsibility is related to a specific job rather than to organizational structure.

Roles for the manager in an objective-setting process include: raising issues and alternatives to a point of awareness in the organization so that the appropriate people can tune in; clarifying ideas, attitudes, and responsibilities involved in getting the work done; and coordinating the efforts of those inside and outside the organization who contribute toward achieving the goal.

The Power of Representation

For a city manager, the city council is one group which is intimately related to managing by objective. The council is the official policy-making body for the city government. It expresses the will of the people and has authority, legally, to carry out that will. Whether it has the power is another question. It is a practical question from the standpoint of managing by objective.

Who does have power to shape the future of a community?

The city manager and the city council together can provide some answers to this question. They work at the point where feelings and hopes for the community intersect with knowledge about the community. The manager is important in giving shape to the future of the community because of his tenure, his constant involvement, his professional background, and his capacity to change his stance.

A change is called for if an organization is going to adopt a positive attitude toward the future. The formal kind of organization so familiar in both government and business supposes that the future will be pretty much like the present. It keeps reacting, adjusting, adding a department here and dropping a project there, keeping its head out of the water but staying mainly submerged in the currents of the moment. The philosophy for dealing with change in this familiar situation can be summed

up as problem solving. Problem solving is necessary; but when one problem has been solved, the manager must get ready for the next one, and it seems as though the problems never stop coming. Again, a manager may be a highly successful problem solver, but his essential stance is the same as that of an unsuccessful problem solver; he is static, a counterpuncher, ready to roll away when outweighed or come back strongly if he sees an advantage.

The stance of a manager who manages by objective is to be looking constantly for opportunities, reading the ability and desire of those in the organization (or the community) who can make something of those opportunities, and *moving* the organization to an explicit commitment.

The city council takes part in managing by objective because, despite its difficulties in being truly representative, it is the best available channel for public needs and aspirations. The council can also investigate and criticize. Any organizational or communal objective needs criticism. In order to attain its goal a group must agree on the goal. Agreements reached prematurely will not last. The city council must be convinced of the value of an objective, and be committed to it, with fullest possible knowledge.

In the course of debate the stated objective will almost certainly change. The manager may come in with a proposal that looks good to some of his department heads and then watch the council alter parts of it. He has several alternatives: he may tell the council it is all or nothing; or he may accept the altered proposal as the best he can get, then go back and try to convince the department heads; or he may bring those who feel strongest about the proposal together with those who have the greatest reservations and help them reach a mutually satisfactory conclusion. The last alternative would be part of the process of managing by objective.

The manager who follows an objective-setting process is a catalyst. He is an agent who brings together those who would otherwise be separate, so that they may act together.

The first step in the process is for a group to outline what it wants to accomplish. This group comprises those who will assume leadership in accomplishing the task, regardless of their titles.

The group may include both a corporation counsel and a streets and sanitation foreman, given the nature of the objective. The leadership group for any given objective may include the manager and all council members. And it may not. The manager and council may instead monitor the progress made toward the objective and give support if changes in the leadership group are required. It is important that the goal be attained; it is not important that formalities of structure be observed through every step of the management process. The formalities are not consistently observed during any management process, for that matter.

Individual Objectives

The objective-setting process is primarily a group activity. Before we go on to the steps of that process, however, it should be noted that management by objective may also be applied to individuals. Just as the whole organization decides what goals it would like to pursue, so a manager or department head may meet with individual subordinates and decide what goals each one is going to pursue.

Just as the work group unit takes mutual responsibility for setting objectives in the organization, the manager-subordinate unit takes responsibility for individual objectives.

A process for setting individual job objectives would follow these steps:

1. The manager and subordinate, working separately, spell out in detail their own perceptions of the subordinate's job responsibilities. At the top level of city administration the city manager would write out job responsibilities for the police chief, for example. The police chief would write his own responsibilities.
2. The city manager and the police chief would then meet to compare their perceptions of the police chief's job. They would reach agreement on each responsibility and on its relative importance. Significant disagreement on the manager's role and the nature of the chief's job must be worked out before proceeding.
3. Again, the manager and subordinate work separately on their perceptions of *possible* goals

for the subordinate. Each takes into account the agreed-upon job responsibilities and the organization's goals as they affect the subordinate. Thus, if one of the job responsibilities for a chief of police were personnel development, and if one of the stated goals for the city were to build some integrated housing, it might be suggested that the chief promote and complete a training program in police-community relations for his whole department.

4. Suggested goals can come from either the manager or his subordinate. They discuss the possibilities together. Then they agree on which goals *both* will commit themselves to. If the city manager and the police chief decide that they will start a community relations training program, the manager must support the chief at every step. They should help each other form a realistic picture of what they are getting into. Whatever they decide must be written down for later reference.
5. Every objective has a completion date. The goal must be reached by a certain time. As is usual in scheduling, completion dates for some objectives are more flexible than for others. A training program might be completed in, say, eighteen months, while the preparation of a brief by the corporation counsel might be required on a certain day, say, November 30. The value of definite completion times is that they allow the manager and his subordinate to gauge progress. An objective reached on time provides a plateau for setting a further objective; if the objective is only partially completed by the required time, the next projections will have to be altered.

A city manager can apply the objective-setting process to his own job. Most likely he would confer with the city council, first on his job responsibilities, then on specific goals. Very likely the manager would have to take the lead. The council's attitude is, "He knows the job better than we do; after all, he is a trained professional." And they are right. But knowledge of the manager's job is not at issue. The issue is, can the responsible leaders of a community agree on their best possibilities, and can they identify their possibilities in personal, workable terms? Questions about what we want to do—that is, accomplishment—come down to questions of what we personally want to *be*. A city manager will tie his personal objectives to the objectives of the community if those are based on agreement and are clearly stated.

Some points to observe in setting objectives are apparent. First, they must be clearly spelled out and written down. Written objectives are working papers. Second, objectives provide benchmarks. They provide a means for measuring progress and allow a manager to take a proactive stance toward the future. Third, objectives must be understood in context. They emerge out of a particular social, economic, and political context; they are created by people in a particular organizational context; and the objectives of individuals are decided in the context of objectives for the whole organization.

Criteria for Workable Objectives

The first steps of the objective-setting process are creative and analytical. They help the manager think through his goal statement. The statement may be judged by four well-tested criteria to establish its workability. These criteria are: *significance, attainability, measurability,* and *understandability.*

An example of a goal statement that meets the criteria is, "To build and staff a hundred-bed community hospital within three-years."

Sometimes the objective-setting process never gets started because of confusion about the nature of a goal. Managers commonly confuse goals with problems and operating procedures. This is not surprising, because a manager's notion of his job is often confined to solving problems and keeping the ship afloat. To think about possible destinations for the ship is quite difficult. Preliminary goal statements, therefore, come out something like, "To cut down on traffic accidents by 25 percent," or, "To get cooperation among the neighborhood groups on the West Side." The first statement would make a good problem statement by prefixing the word "How?" The second statement, if it means anything, has to do with improving methods of operation. Neither statement is a statement of purpose. Neither is a goal for action.

Goal statements are usually vague in the beginning. Since they capture deeply felt aspirations, it is only natural for them to be imprecise. "We would like to develop a community in which law and order are respected, a city with healthy personal relationships among its citizens." "It is necessary now to guarantee a pure water supply for the future generations who will live here."

The job of using goals to manage work activity, however, requires that statements be more specific. Writing them down and then rewriting helps make them specific. Preferably, several people should rewrite and compare their versions of the goal, but it is the manager's task to evaluate the goal according to the four criteria.

Is the Goal Significant?

If a goal passes the test of significance, it passes because enough people want it. If it is significant, to whom is it significant? The people who are going to work on achieving the goal must feel that it is significant enough for them to invest their time and effort. The work force may be wholly inside the formal organization. On the other hand, some potential workers may not draw any pay from the organization. All workers are going to have to be united in achieving the objective, and that unity will come from the objective itself.

The manager can assess the significance of a goal by listing all the departments, individual persons, and groups who may be called on to work for the objective. Then he lists, beside each name, those benefits that that person or group might expect to gain. If the objective is successfully completed, is it probable that they will get what they are seeking? The manager can consult with representatives of the various groups to find out their expectations, if they have not already contacted him.

Is the Goal Attainable?

Here the question is one of capability. By whom is the goal attainable? Some people who express early interest in a project will drop out when the work starts or when the demands for money start. Among those who remain, necessary skills may be lacking. A city manager is particularly vulnerable in making this kind of assessment because his objectives must be tax-supported, and the most significant objectives, i.e., those that stand to benefit the widest spectrum of the community, are those which would involve the greatest amount of volunteer support.

The manager who is charged with overall responsibility for an organization must also ask himself, "Is my agency the appropriate one for doing this work?" There may well be widespread community support for an objective, but that is no assurance that the city government should handle the job. Isn't it obvious that the recreation department should handle the proposed new arts center? Well, perhaps not. And how about the health department? Shouldn't they be taking a lead in plans for an elderly care facility? That will have to be discussed with the regional office of the U.S. Department of Health, Education, and Welfare.

The city manager is conscious of jurisdictional lines. Similarly, he has to be aware of managerial lines of responsibility.

The manager's own responsibilities are tied to his job functions. There are certain functions which he properly performs. While these functions are broad, they are not all inclusive. They do not give him carte blanche. Some goals, while proper for the community, may not fall within the city manager's leadership functions. Furthermore, while the manager may "properly" pursue many goals, it may be that certain of these goals are not well matched with his capabilities or his managerial priorities.

It is helpful for a manager to use a checklist of job functions when assessing the appropriateness of a goal for his organization. A list of typical job functions for city administrators includes:

1. Scheduling work
2. Setting work standards
3. Developing and training people
4. Coordinating programs
5. Self-development
6. Professional association activities
7. Communicating
8. Government relations: city council
9. Government relations: other government units
10. Citizen group relations: boards, committees, associations
11. Public relations
12. Formulating objectives and priorities
13. Use of equipment and facilities
14. Budgeting and cost control
15. Interpreting policies and ordinances
16. Encouraging morale and participation.

Each administrator, at his own organizational level, will emphasize different job functions. He will operate more capably in some areas than in others. The manager needs to understand which of his own functions are more important for him, given his situation, and which of the important functions he can perform well. His understanding should be shared with his superior. For the city manager, this means an agreement on job priorities that has been worked out with the city council.

The same process of agreement is essential for the city manager and *his* subordinates. Each department head should work through his managerial priorities with the city manager. Department heads work through their subordinates' job priorities with the subordinates. On the basis of these understandings, the city manager can make a judgment about the ability of his organization to pursue a proposed objective.

"Can we manage all the activities and relationships that this project calls for?" This is the question about capability a manager must answer. Enough funds, equipment, and skills may not be on hand, but if the managerial skills are adequate, then it is likely that the organization can tackle the objective and attain it.

IS THE GOAL MEASURABLE?

This criterion can be misleading. It might better be termed "knowability," since the criterion requires, simply, that you know what you have accomplished when you have accomplished it. But numbers are such an easy way to measure accomplishment, or at least to give the appearance of measuring accomplishment, that there is a temptation to rely on numbers to the exclusion of other measurements. When the goal is reached, how many cases will have been handled, units produced, beds furnished, acres renewed, gutters cleaned? Such numbers may tell us exactly what we need to know. Or they may tell us nothing. If the goal means creating a more satisfying living situation for people in a city, numbers will be secondary. If reaching the objective will enable some people to help other people in a way they never experienced before, numbers won't get at it. Yet there can be measurements. Systematic methods for recording feelings and attitudes in the community can be set up and made part of the evaluation.

If a city government sets the goal of establishing effective rehabilitation for criminal offenders it might draw on several skills: social workers, doctors, policemen, teachers, lawyers, judges, and personnel people. These professionals might keep statistics on the number of "cases" they handle. But to actually measure the effectiveness of the program, the feelings, of its staff and, even more important, the feelings of those rehabilitated would have to be taken into account. Whoever managed the project—from the time the first support contacts were made until the time people with jail records were back in the community, with their families and holding jobs—would have to measure progress in terms of satisfaction and worthwhileness for all concerned. The criterion of measurability recognizes that measurements appropriate to the goal should be within reach of the manager. Only those who are involved in reaching the goal, however, can tell the manager exactly what to measure and how to measure it. They are the people by whom the accomplishment is judged.

IS THE GOAL UNDERSTANDABLE?

A secondary group of people is involved in considering for whom the goal is understandable. The primary group, as always, is made up of the people who are going to do the work—staff people in various municipal departments, elected officials, perhaps community volunteers, and outside fee-for-service people. These people must understand what they are going to accomplish, because the goal itself is going to be the chief guide for their actions. The secondary group consists of those people who are not going to work on the objective but who must be sold on it: the voters, people in a particular neighborhood, one of those "publics" that the city council members worry about.

Management by objective is a democratic process. A characteristic of democratic processes is their circularity. An idea starts somewhere in the social system, catches on, comes to the attention of people who can act on it, is reformulated, is put into effect, and eventually affects that part of the system in which it originated. Workable ideas become public acts. These ideas require myriad translations, however. It is the manager's job to translate an idea, perhaps a constellation of ideas, into a goal which some will find a satisfactory pretext for personal effort and others will find an acceptable statement of what they want their community to do and be.

A city manager cannot do all this by any amount of personal concentration. He does it by making himself a catalyst, a broker of aspirations. He brings individuals together in groups and brings groups together into a work force.

To manage by objective is to carry out the manager's task of educating the community. That education is not so much a knowledge education: no man can tell a community what it needs. It is rather a behavioral education. The manager can show the community how to go about making its own future.

How It Might Start

No one can realistically propose that a city government sit down and plan a whole new future. It can only be suggested that a new approach be used in working through the decisions involving community interest that are constantly facing every city government.

Let us look at a city, built up before the turn of the century and now containing about 30,000 people, which serves as a suburban dormitory for a great American metropolis. This city offers an example of a situation in which an objective-setting process might be used. The commuter railroad line has been vital to this city since it began its growth many decades ago. The railroad maintains two stations in the town, one in the main business district and another at a smaller business district about a mile away. A third station is located at the edge of the city, really in a neighboring village, but there is not much commercial activity there. The railroad is proposing that the three stations be consolidated into one. All three present stations would be abandoned, and the new station would be placed in a residential area between the main station and the station in the nearby village. The railroad expects to save a considerable amount of money by doing this.

Reactions vary. Downtown businessmen think they might benefit by a move, since they might use the railroad parking facilities and turn Main Street into a mall. Residents in the area of the proposed station are horrified, since it would create huge parking areas, generate heavy auto traffic, destroy a park, and perhaps bring in a new highway. People in the subdivisions are concerned about convenience. The new location would be slightly harder to reach than the old, but building a new highway would solve that problem.

If the city government merely reacts, it can either block the new station or watch the railroad have its way. But it can take a different approach. It can set its own objective and work with the railroad on that basis. The city manager and city council would begin exploring possible objectives, and then city departments and spokesmen for community interest groups would be involved.

One idea might be to create a bus system which would be a feeder for the railroad, thus reducing traffic and parking problems wherever the station was located. Another approach might be to extend light industry zoning along the tracks, giving the railroad more profit and keeping street traffic in the residential areas at a minimum. A third, more ambitious, plan might be to depress the rail right-of-way all through town and put parking above it. Such a plan might be stated thus as an objective: "To reduce the space requirements, pollution, and hazards of transportation, while maintaining an attractive downtown shopping area and convenient access to the railroad." Such a goal would have to be reworked, with all affected groups, including the railroad, represented in drafting the working statement.

Most important from the city manager's point of view, relevant city departments would help create the goal. Whatever happened, they would be involved; but if the city management merely reacts, the departments will be limited to react-

ing, each in its individual way. If the railroad was moved to a new station as was originally intended, the department of streets would be affected by changed parking; police would be affected by traffic shifts and a new source of complaints; the zoning agency would have to reconsider land use; the legal department would have a load of work to do with the railroad. But all separately. The difference between reacting to new situations and creating the kind of new situation you want is that the organization working creatively is working together.

City government functions are often, by their very nature, reactive: police chase the criminal after the crime; firemen race to the scene after the blaze is going. Thinking in terms of management by objective may present some alternatives that, while they may at first seem far-fetched, will ultimately bring results.

A problem faced in cities with deteriorated housing is apartment house fires. The buildings that burn usually have a history of building code offenses. The inhabitants are poor but pay high rents. If renewal is going on in the area, buildings may burn "mysteriously" soon after the occupants are evacuated, with insurance benefits for the owner. Firemen try to stop the fires; inspectors cite violations of the code; and police may look for arsonists. Meanwhile, editorials in the daily newspapers talk about "social forces."

What is the objective of city government in this situation? Usually it is unclear. But if there is a strong governmental commitment to public safety as opposed to private advantage, it is possible for city departments to act in a way that will help keep people out of danger. Firemen, policemen, and building code inspectors can work together to develop responsibility for unsafe housing. There may be governmental agreement not to support evictions for failure to pay rents in unsafe housing; the only evictions would be total evacuations when the dwelling had passed a certain point of deterioration.

In cases like the above, the manager's task would be to bring units of municipal government together and ask: "Does our goal meet the criteria? Is it significant? Attainable? Measurable?" And, we might also ask, "Is our goal understandable?"

Goal statement:

Plan		Program				
Steps	Completion date	Facilities, resources	People	Leadership training	Agreements, decisions	Results

FIGURE 12—1. *Objective set forth as plan—program grid.*

Writing a Plan and Program

When a manager has evaluated the goal by the above criteria, he has what amounts to a statement of agreement and intent. The goal does not belong to him alone but to all who have helped develop it. Now they must go to work. There must be a plan and program. A *plan* is a step-by-step schedule of activities, including completion times. A *program* is a description of the resources and behaviors called for to complete each step of the plan. Figure 12—1 shows the relationship between a plan and a program.

The goal statement at the top of the grid controls everything on the grid. If the grid were intended to picture the dynamics of the managing by objective process, the goal statement would be at the lower right-hand corner, since completion of the last step means that the goal has been reached.

The whole content of the grid, including goal statement, plan, and program, is a statement of an objective. When an organization works on an objective it is working inside such a grid, understanding where it started, what it is doing, and how what it is doing is related to what it wants to accomplish.

A written objective is a prediction, and it suffers from the limitations of a prediction. Things can happen that will slow down progress toward the goal; or there may be a breakthrough. Perhaps some steps can be skipped. Writing out

a complete plan and program is a valuable discipline, however, and the writing itself is a sign that a process of interaction is going on among responsible people in the local government.

A PLAN IS A SEQUENCE

The movement in planning is from general to specific. The manager translates the general objective into specific tasks. The group he has brought together to define the goal begins to assume responsibility for reaching the goal.

A plan can be written several ways. It is important only that the plan when completed include all the activities necessary to achieve the goal.

One planning method calls on each department, or work unit, to search the objective for any responsibilities that may lie within its jurisdiction. Thus, if the goal were concerned with elimination of pollution in a community, the sanitation department might study and install new methods of sewage treatment where feasible; the health department might embark on a program of public education regarding pollution sources and hazards; the police department might set up a special unit for enforcing antipollution laws. Each of the specific tasks must be related to the overall objective. These tasks may be thought of as "subobjectives" or "implementing objectives."

The difficulty encountered originally in confusing statements of goals with statements of problems or operating procedures occurs again at this point in the objective-setting process. Subobjectives may easily be confused with the overall objective. One department or work unit may identify its particular activity with the overall goal. The confusion arises when the final goal is not adequately clarified and emphasized.

It is helpful to view the activities leading to accomplishment of the goal as a means-ends continuum—that is, every activity is a means to an end, but it may also be an end in itself if no further work is done. The goal of eliminating pollution in a community may not be reached, but it would nevertheless be possible for the sanitation department to install the most up-to-date equipment for sewage treatment and thus achieve its own "end." In fact, the various divisions of government commonly operate by seeking their separate goals. A process of managing by objective is intended to bring the capabilities of separate divisions to bear on unified objectives. It is necessary to break down common objectives into workable parts, but it is necessary at the same time to keep the interrelationships clear and the final end in sight.

Another planning method calls for the identification of "key result areas." Representatives from all departments involved decide jointly on major tasks that must be performed in order to reach the objective. Departmental lines are not important. If, for example, the installation of smokestack filters is a key aspect of local pollution control, members of the work force, including the city manager and department heads, would decide which of the total government resources would be required to legislate and enforce the installation. Once again, the achievement of a key result is only a means to the final end of pollution elimination.

Yet a third method for approaching the plan is to have each managerial member of the work force relate his own job functions to the goal. By this method it is possible to arrive at very specific task definitions. Each man thinks of reaching the objective through his own best capabilities. A building inspector, for example, takes responsibility for training people to check on furnace violations; an equipment supervisor whose vehicles are on public display makes them exam-

ples of efficient, nonwasteful operation. All these activities are consciously tied to the explicit goal of pollution elimination.

A plan is more than a set of activities, however. A plan is a sequence. Each activity must be assigned a definite beginning and ending time. Some activities will overlap, but all must be put into a sequence because all are leading toward one date when the goal will be accomplished. Only the time sequence of the necessary activities should be decided, however. Coordination issues must be decided *after* the sequence is established.

Thus far in the process of managing by objective a work force has been formed around the statement of a common goal, and that work force has developed a schedule of activities that will lead to achieving the goal. While much of the work done to this point has a preliminary feeling, an awareness—of the issues that must be faced, of interpersonal help and support that is available—has been gained by those in the work group and by the manager who bears chief responsibility. Such an awareness is absolutely essential before a group effort of this kind can succeed. The manager, meanwhile, has been absorbed in developing the awareness. He has also helped clarify some responsibilities toward the task at hand. Now his attention will be devoted largely to coordination, as the phase of programming begins.

WHO, WHAT, AND HOW

While the goal-stating and planning phases of the objective-setting process are creative and analytical, the programming phase is practical and judgmental. Whereas the initial issue was dealing with the *why* and *when* of an objective, it is now necessary to deal with the *who, what,* and *how.*

In practice, an organization should begin the process by working through a single objective. In time, members of the organization may be involved in several objectives simultaneously. At the same time, however, operating procedures must be maintained and problems must be solved. Managing by objective is not a panacea that does away with the need for present government operations. It is a process for dealing with the future before the future presents more problems than can be solved and robs government services of their meaning.

The written program for an objective predicts what facilities and resources will be used; who will be working on each step of the plan; who will be called on for leadership and training; how agreements and decisions will be reached at each step; and, finally, how results will be judged. Since a program is a prediction, it is subject to change. In fact, one advantage of a written program is that is allows the persons responsible to make changes in time to avert real trouble. It gives them clear indications of how well the plan is progressing. It shows them exactly *where* changes, if any, need to be made. An administrator will not have to hire extra and unnecessary people, for example, if he knows that a computer requires a certain lead time, or that a training program started three months beforehand will adequately prepare staff people already available.

A written program calls all forces into account: who will be free to work on the objective, and when; how much money, or which statistics will be needed, and when. These data are called for in the program. They will help the persons responsible make sound decisions. More important than data, however, are the results called for by the program. The key to making decisions is a go/no-go criterion. This is what is meant by results. Part of the program is a statement of results anticipated for each step of the plan. If the results are accomplished by the scheduled date, the criterion has been met and the plan can continue. If the results have not been accomplished, adjustments or revisions will have to be made in the plan.

Decisions are made at every step in keeping with the results outlined. And every result, of course, is in keeping with the final goal.

Statements of results written down in the programming phase are predictions; at the time scheduled for accomplishment, these statements become the basis for evaluations, and the manager makes decisions accordingly.

The objective grid suggested earlier (Figure 12–1) shows the relationship between planning steps and elements of the program. A program is spelled out as outlined below.

Facilities and Resources. The manager writes down what will be needed to complete each step in the plan. He includes such things as physical properties, equipment, money, statistics, rules and instructions, and background information. What should members of the work force have on hand when they go to work? Some of these things may already be available; others may not. Write them *all* down. "Set of architect's drawings, $5,000." "Radio-TV coverage for kickoff dinner speaker." "Snow removal truck for new parking areas." "Office space for director, assistant, and three secretaries." "Three hundred copies of federal study on effluent treatment."

Members of the work force which has been formed in the process of stating the objective will have ideas on what facilities and resources will be needed. The list written by the manager should reflect their suggestions. As in every other step of managing by objective, it is assumed that the people doing the work are in the best position to know what they need.

People. If the manager has played his role effectively in developing awareness throughout the organization and has carefully considered attainability, he will have little trouble deciding which people will be required to carry out the steps of the plan. Most of these people will already have tuned themselves in. It may be that people outside the organization will be called for: a design consultant, a social work administrator, or others who can bring skills not immediately available. People in the local administration can identify outsiders who can help.

Leadership and Training. One person typically is given the responsibility of helping things to happen. This person may be the city manager, the city administrator, a department head, or someone else with management responsibilities. He is the coordinator for the objective. As coordinator, he has leadership responsibility. He is not the only leader: he enables other leaders—members of the city council, department heads, spokesmen for civic groups—to mesh their efforts. The city manager and the department head have always been regarded as professionals, but too often professionalism has been equated with expertise: "Let him tell us what *he* thinks."

The professional leadership role emerging in

many kinds of organizations is not that of the expert but that of the enabler, or catalyst. The manager works on an assumption of interdependence rather than authority. He is the convener of the work force. He still interprets policies when necessary, he still makes assessments in light of the budget, he still knows how to persuade a swing voter. But these leader skills are subordinated to the objectives of the work force. In other words, the manager who uses objectives effectively labors to help a group of people discover what they really want to accomplish, then he helps them stick by their resolution. In programming for leadership, the manager anticipates what skills he will have to employ—listening to groups, persuading individuals, laying down the law, hammering out compromises—to bring about action at each step.

Training required to meet the objective may be highly organized or casual. Supposedly, people in the work force already have basic job skills: stenographers know how to type, engineers know how to draw plans, men in the water department crews know how to lay pipe. But in a group work project some of the knowledge held by certain people will have to be shared. The manager can provide means for that sharing. Further, some people will need coaching for particular tasks. If a civil engineer is going to make a major presentation to the city council, he may need guidance and encouragement; a director of finance, meanwhile, may need the manager's assistance if he is going to explain costs to the engineer. People from outside government coming in to work on the objective probably need information on relevant laws to be observed; they should know who the right contacts are to get jobs done. The city manager cannot expect to train everybody, but he can anticipate training needs and provide for them.

Agreements and Decisions. As with leadership and training, the manager here is concerned with relationships. How are people going to come together during the course of working on the objective? The manager can plan the kinds of meetings which will be held; who will attend; what style of meeting to hold. One sure way to destroy group morale and commitment is to invite people into a decision only after the decision has been made and then *tell* them what they are going to do. "It seems apparent that our only course of action at this time ..." is a tested phrase for introducing rebellion. At the same time, though, people may be lacking information and may want to be filled in. "Telling" them, in that case, is appropriate.

Generally speaking information giving and getting dominate the early part of an objective-setting process and also may dominate the early part of any particular meeting. Information shared includes personal feelings and opinions. If the feelings are suppressed at the start, they will be expressed at the end, often in obstructive fashion. The latter phases of the process, if the beginning has been frank and accepting, are characterized by suggested courses of action, tentative agreements, and, finally, resolutions to try it and see if it works.

In the objective-setting process, agreements *are* decisions. It is always difficult to reach agreement, since genuine agreement depends on the expression of genuine disagreement. The manager cannot assure agreement; but he can bring people together, over time, in a series of meetings in which the work of the group is accepted in good faith and acted on. That is how people learn to agree. When the goal is significant and clearly understood, people will make up their minds.

The work of writing an objective is by this stage becoming cumulative. A series of tasks has been set forth in the plan; then the program has indicated who is involved, what they will be working with, and the kinds of leadership required. Now the question is: What action should be taken? Suppose the overall goal is to create a centralized data processing system for all the cities in a geographical area. The manager, or managers, writing the program have reached a step in their plan which calls for a survey of capital equipment needs in the participating cities. The resources listed for that step will include inventories, estimates of the present condition of the equipment, department requests, user projections, and costs. The people listed will include directors of purchasing and finance. The leadership and training methods will include personal reassurances from city managers to purchasing people and a study by an outside firm which can make comparisons with purchasing practice in an industrial conglomerate. Now the finance and purchasing people must be brought together to reach an agreement as to which capital equipment needs can best be handled by a centralized group and how they will constitute that group.

Or, again, the goal might be to create a pleasing physical appearance in an area at the edge of a business district where buildings have been torn down and parking lots put in. As one part of the objective, the street department is charged with landscaping the area. Resources the department would need might include botanical information on the kinds of trees and shrubs that flourish in the area, along with information on blight susceptibility, nursery and landfill suppliers, and plans for future changes in the area. People might include landscape architects, additional summertime workers, and someone from the city finance office. The street department could expect to be concerned with leadership and training in public relations, especially dealing with owners of nearby real estate. And agreements would have to be reached with the city planning department, with the financial officer, and with police during the course of the work.

Results. The payoff for managing by objective is steady accomplishment. Working stepwise toward a goal permits the organization to see its own progress. Results rest on the work of an organization and prepare the organization for further work.

The Possibilities

Effective municipal administrators and department heads have always had objectives. The process of managing by objective is perhaps more comprehensive than traditional management methods, but the real difference is one of emphasis. While the traditional methods may stress the manager's leadership skills, or the desires of interest groups in the community, both important elements in managing by objective, they do not focus the efforts of the local government organization on the objective itself. The formulating of commitment to a common objective is so dominant in the process of managing by objective that the actual performance of required work is simply fulfillment of an obligation already established. That makes managing by objective sound easy, but of course managing is never easy. A city manager or local government administrator needs all the skills and intuition at his disposal if he is going to use this process.

The very process of managing by objective is a precentation of the future in today's organizations. It is interactive to a degree that seems dangerous for many managers. Decisions are made on every level of the organization for every other level. It doesn't matter where the decision is made as long as the decision is a product of the whole, but in practice decisions will be made at the lowest possible level, closest to the action. The sanction for this practice is an agreed-upon objective. What suits the objective suits the organization.

Management by objective is not a particular formula, nor a convenient grid. Yet it may be helpful when beginning the process to use a scheme of some sort, such as the one that has been described here. The elements to remember are: open exploration of desired goals in a community, with people given the option to shape a common purpose; testing the goal statement by the criteria of significance, attainability, measurability, and understanding; helping people assign tasks they can handle; setting up a definite schedule of activites, with specific responsibilities written out; constant face-to-face meeting and checking out progress; and taking results seriously.

Underlying the steps in this process is an attitude. A manager is willing to manage by objective because he believes the people of a community can decide their own future and he can help them help themselves.

[1] Ken Hartnett, "Our Cities Are Sicker Than Ever," CHICAGO SUN-TIMES, 21 June 1970.

[2] Edgar L. Sherbenou, "Major Issues in Personnel Administration," in THE MUNICIPAL YEAR BOOK, 1968, ed. International City Managers' Association (Washington, D.C.: International City Managers' Association, 1968), p. 180.

Part Four

Management Systems, Information, and Analysis

Introduction

Much of the technology of the postwar period is the technology of organization.

RICHARD N. GOODWIN

THE MORE CLEARLY DESIGNATED logical-rational side of organization is covered in three chapters on information in terms of data and other specific kinds of facts that are fed into analytical processes.

The quotation above appeared in an article in the *New Yorker* where it was referring critically to interweaving of bureaucracy and technology in large national and multinational corporations that control natural resources, but the statement has much relevance for this discussion because systems analysis, Management Information Systems (MIS), and work analysis are a continuation in some ways of the traditions and concepts of scientific management.

At least two principal differences should be pointed out, however. First, the new technologies are considerably more scientific and mathematical. The computer is indispensable for solving some of the problems of large scale. It is not just a difference in magnitude but in concept involving careful problem definition, data selection and analysis, classifications of information by use rather than by organizational or jurisdictional boundaries, and a feedback to monitor the operation.

Second, these approaches are not as remote from people and the social process of the organization as were the earlier approaches to scientific management. Much has been learned about people through the human relations school and through recent developments in behavioral psychology, and many who work with information, in the rather specialized sense of these chapters, are well aware of the constraints placed on any system by the hopes, fears, reactions, and expectations of the people involved.

Chapter 13 introduces the subject of systems analysis which is a useful way of organizing your thinking. In some respects systems analysis is nothing more than the common sense application of the scientific method. In practice it can go considerably beyond that in the application of data and computers in quite complex operations. The point is, however, that systems analysis is an aid to making decisions. It will show you how to look at your city as a system and at various components within the city as subsystems. When you begin to think like this, you will be able to plan better.

A Management Information System, as described in Chapter 14, is one part of problem solving that helps identify, program, and schedule information for better reporting and management control. It is a particularly useful method when it is defined, limited, and controlled for information on day-to-day operations. It can be considered as part of the larger framework of an Urban Information System (UIS) which deals with the physical and social municipality, often on a regional basis. The UIS can be a fascinating excursion into the big picture of developments affecting a municipality and its environs, but it is better suited to the work of regional planning agencies to provide the framework within which the municipality can set up the Management Information System.

Chapter 14 is helpful in distinguishing the two kinds of systems which often are confused in discussing information needs for physical and social planning, economic development, and health and welfare needs, on the one hand, and more limited physical development and service-oriented objectives of the municipal government on the other.

The ongoing review of work to keep it moving smoothly and efficiently is the primary concern of Chapter 15 which describes some management tools for work simplification, including forms, procedures, and layout, and ways of planning, surveying, and improving procedures. The chapter also gives attention to the work environment, including physical space, furniture, office machines, and special equipment.

13

Systems Analysis and Urban Information

THE PURPOSE OF THIS CHAPTER is to provide an instructive summary of information systems concepts and design techniques. The chapter looks at how data are collected and processed in an urban environment. After conceptual approaches to information systems have been presented, systems project management and operating techniques are described.

Many cities either are engaged in or are considering computerizing their basic procedures. The degree of automation can vary all the way from a fairly straightforward tax billing system to an extremely complex Management Information System (MIS) which automates major government processes. The extent of a city's automation will depend on the city's needs, resources, and understanding of the problems and advantages associated with automation. A city of less than 50,000 population may wish to cooperate with other jurisdictions in buying computer time for basic operations such as utility billing. A larger city with some experience in elementary data processing applications may want to develop a total MIS to provide planning and evaluation data in addition to performing routine procedures.

With the widespread acceptance of computers in both industry and government, basic concepts and procedures for analyzing these operations have been developed. Whether a city is interested in automating fundamental procedures or in forecasting and evaluation, these basic tools are applicable.

This chapter should acquaint the urban ad-

ministrator with the essentials of information systems analysis, design, implementation, and project evaluation. The chapter has been organized into six major sections, as follows:

1. The Systems Approach: looking at a local government's processes as an interdependent system, as opposed to a collection of independent activities
2. Systems Project Organization: describing patterns for organizing internal and outside resources to integrate effectively the technical systems efforts into the planning and operating needs of the city
3. Project Planning, Scheduling, and Control: outlining the PERT, CPM, and Gantt techniques for developing project objectives and keeping the project on course
4. Description and Analysis: describing practical techniques for analyzing and documenting the information requirements of the city's decisions and procedures
5. Design: designing a system to satisfy information requirements
6. Evaluation: outlining major considerations in determining project feasibility and success.

The Systems Approach

Webster's New Collegiate Dictionary (Merriam-Webster, 1973) defines a system as "a regularly interacting or interdependent group of items forming a unified whole." In the past decade,

FIGURE 13—1. *Basic steps in a system.*

looking at a city as a system of interacting functional objectives as opposed to a collection of independent activities has become fashionable. The new systems approach to urban organizations has been in large part inspired by the adaptation of computer technology to urban processes. The array of systems-related terminology—systems analysis, computer systems, information systems, data management systems, etc.—has grown out of the trial-and-error approach required in building a computer system. In building a system, all components within the scope must be carefully identified and any interrelationships between them described. Within the context of a system each element will have some direct or indirect effect on the functioning of all the other elements and hence on the functioning of the entire system.

The basic depiction of a system can be seen in Figure 13—1, which shows three basic steps: input, processing, and output. Since no system oriented to people and organizational needs can function independently of people, the computer system needs to be integrated into operating personnel procedures.

The objective of systems development is to effectively integrate an electronic machine into the daily operations and decisions of the organization. A technically perfect system without effective integration would result in two competing and expensive systems—the computer system and the people system.

It is essential that the administrator recognize the organizational and operating implications of the systems approach. Only when these implications are understood is the administrator in a position to guide technical personnel into building a system that is effectively integrated into the clerical and managerial functions of the

city. Returning to the basic system depicted in Figure 13—1, effective system integration adds the additional key dimension to this incomplete technical process. Figure 13—2 shows the user as the key link in system functioning, preparing input and interpreting output.

The systems approach to information systems design requires the administrator to be aware of the total system, including the realization that, by definition, any one part of the system will have both obvious as well as subtle impacts on other parts. Although no administrator is in a position to fully understand all the obvious and subtle interrelationships, he can consider areas of primary importance. From a managerial standpoint, technical sophistication is subordinate to the total operating system of the organization.

A well-designed and successfully implemented system goes far beyond the technical system depicted in Fig. 13—1. As depicted in Fig. 13—2, the integrated system comprises two separate subsystems: the computer ("processing") and the user. The user subsystem is in turn broken down into existing manual forms and procedures, organization objectives, organization structure, and decisions.

The following questions should be considered when evaluating whether a proposed system will adequately "integrate" the user and automated data processing: (1) Have major decision areas been realistically addressed in the proposal? (2) Does the proposal reflect a thorough understanding of and reasonable respect for existing

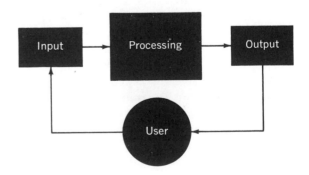

FIGURE 13—2. *Integrated system.*

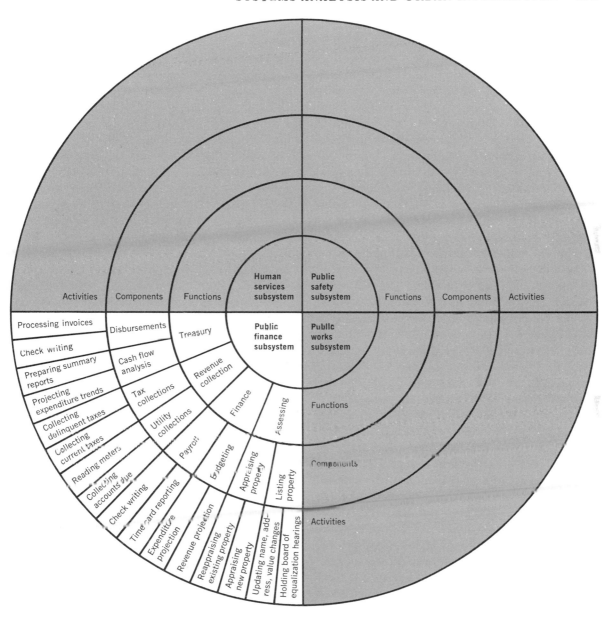

FIGURE 13—3. *The city viewed as a system.*

forms and procedures? (3) Does the proposed organization structure place the user, and not the systems people, in the primary position of intelligently defining and revising system objectives?

Although the need for a strong user orientation may appear self-evident, in many urban computer systems the user has taken a back seat to technical expediency. The fault lies with both the user and the systems people—with the user for not aggressively and persistently defining his objectives, and with the systems people for not continuing to force users to become actively involved in establishing system objectives and procedures.

A common way of systematizing the examination of a city is to establish a hierarchy of functions. Figure 13—3 shows a typical approach to developing a system structure. Three of the quadrants show the basic hierarchical framework comprising a subsystem: functions, components, and activities. This framework is essentially a way of classifying activities according to their objectives. In the fourth quadrant the final subsystem-related activities have been grouped by components and functions. Normally, activities within components are performed by a single department. Contemporary systems theory assumes that the interaction between the activities within a subsystem is more frequent and pronounced than the interaction between activities in different subsystems.

The advantage of viewing the city as a system is that it helps determine the sequence for systems development. It is unlikely that any city can develop a total MIS all at once. A more realistic step is to determine which functions should be developed first. In determining a logical development sequence it is essential to know which activities share the same data. For example, a city may rank police complaint processing as the first priority for implementation, and automated assessment assistance as the second priority. Once activity data relationships have been isolated, however, it may become clear that other activities have more data in common with police complaint processing than does the assessment application. Therefore, based on data relationships, the city may readjust its priorities for automation.

Another aspect of interaction between departmental activities is that of horizontal and vertical data flows. The data flow in two directions. One direction is vertical within a department, from point of data collection to final point of statistical analysis. An example is the collection of building inspection data by the inspectors during an on-site inspection. The raw data flow vertically, are aggregated, and eventually are used by the inspection department head to forecast the following year's work load.

The horizonal flow is between departments or components. An example would be the flow of the building inspection data mentioned above to the assessment department, where it would trigger a property assessment.

The systems approach is a method of ensuring that a computer system will be integrated into the existing organization. A computer system designed to automate appraisal inspection which did not address the horizontal flow of data from the building inspection department would not be an integrated system.

Although the systems approach seems like nothing more than applied common sense, quite an opposite approach has characterized the majority of urban systems development projects. For a number of reasons, the traditional approach to viewing cities as a collection of independent functions rather than as a system has been reflected in the development of single-purpose information systems to prepare tax bills, payroll checks, and other such activities. Normally, the sound reason of expediency has prompted the decision to develop single-purpose applications to perform high volume, high priority tasks. Regardless of scale, the systems approach would argue that an initial attempt be made to look at the city as an interacting, interdependent system.[1] Even if a city wishes to do no more than automate utility bill preparation, this activity should be placed in the context of the total system. Vertical flows within the utility collections department and horizontal flows between utility bill preparation and other activities should be identified. This will help ensure that the resulting application will not be designed in a vacuum.

Systems Project Organization

Depending on circumstances, municipalities may use internal staff, outside consultants, or service bureaus to develop their systems. However, technical data processing personnel, systems consultants, and service bureau representatives, no matter how skilled, cannot integrate the system into the organization without internal management guidance and user participation. Supervisory personnel and top local officials must establish system priorities and approve system development schedules. Local government professional and clerical personnel should be involved in developing user procedures that will affect the total integration of the system.

The project organization structure is a useful tool to ensure that the computer is integrated into the user system, not the other way around.

The user-oriented project structure is characterized by the following organizational attributes:

1. Participation of top city officials
2. Advisory assistance of key executive users
3. A systems project manager with a functional specialty in addition to systems expertise
4. Full-time assignment of key representative users to the systems project. These representatives should be selected from those clerical and supervisory line personnel who actually perform the work in the organization.

These elements should be included in the basic systems project organization to ensure that the user, not the system, dictates direction.

The top municipal project representative should take an active role in project planning, scheduling, and control. Although the techniques and forms will be developed by the project managers, they must be clearly understood by the top city project representative.

From the beginning of a project, formal provision should be made for steering committee and user participation and training. The frequency of meetings and reports, as well as report formats, should be specified initially and revised as necessary. Too many projects have failed to involve users effectively because no formal provision for user participation was specified.

Once the systems project has been integrated into the city's organizational structure there remains the question of internal project organization. The municipal project manager takes direct responsibility for ensuring that system plans and schedules are followed. He deals on a day-to-day basis with the consulting project manager. He should have a technical background as well as a good understanding of the municipality's operations. Leadership qualities are particularly helpful, since he will be responsible for ensuring cooperation between analysts and users as well as sustaining project morale throughout tedious design and implementation phases.

The primary qualification for systems analysts is a thorough familiarity with the functions to be automated. In addition, an understanding of the potentials and limitations of computer systems and some programming experience are essential. The key role of the analyst is to translate user decisions and operating procedures into computer system specifications that meet user requirements. For this reason, the analyst is user-oriented. He is in the best position to find out what the user needs and to orient the user to procedures associated with the new system.

The programmer's responsibility will be to prepare and test system and application programs, based on specifications prepared by the analysts.

User committee members should be those departmental employees who are open to change and influential in their departments. In addition, they should understand all of a department's activities.

In summary, the project organization should integrate all organization levels into the management and design tasks by involving top municipal representatives, middle management, and operating personnel.

Project Planning, Scheduling, and Control

The management of a systems project can itself be viewed as a system. The principal system elements are planning, scheduling, and control. Just as each element of a system affects every other element, so do the elements of project management affect each other. The scope of the objectives will affect the schedule established, and successful implementation of the schedule and accomplishment of the planned objectives will depend on the control exercised. The evaluation associated with the control function will, in turn, feed back into a revision of the plan and the schedule. This section outlines the key aspects of planning, scheduling, and control and concludes with a discussion of tools for accomplishing management objectives.

PLANNING

Planning begins with identifying tasks and subtasks. As planning progresses, each subtask will be broken down into activities. The task-subtask activity relationship for project planning is an

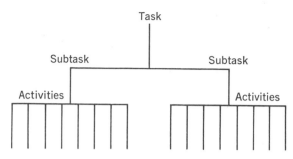

FIGURE 13—4. *Systems approach to project planning.*

adaptation of the subsystem-function-component activity approach to analyzing the municipal government processes. The advantage of this form of project planning is that it institutes a mechanism for scheduling and controlling subsequent project efforts at any desired level of detail. Project managers will operate at the subtask and activity level in scheduling and controlling progress, whereas upper management will be concerned only with total tasks. The basic systems planning structure is depicted in Figure 13—4.

Once task and subtask objectives have been established, timing and manpower considerations must be addressed. Figure 13—5 shows a form for documenting the results of initial planning. In addition to task identification, provision should be made for specifying criteria for evaluating task performance. Note that space is provided for pertinent task timing and manpower characteristics. As with the subtasks in this example, many tasks in a systems project will be performed repeatedly throughout the project. In the planning stage it is necessary to establish the general date for beginning a task and the task frequency. The third column provides for establishing the frequency for reviewing and evaluating each task.

SCHEDULING

Once tasks have been identified and manpower requirements estimated for system tasks, a coordinated schedule must be developed to take into account project personnel and finances. Consequently, manpower and timing estimates may well need to be revised during the scheduling phase. The scheduling task is obviously very complex. It requires that many independent and

		Begin period	Frequency	Review intervals	Project manpower
Task name:	User participation	2nd week	Weekly	Biweekly	700 man-hours
Objective:	To involve users in all phases of systems development				
Subtasks:	1. General user orientation	3rd week			40 man-hours
	2. User committee selection	5th week			40 man-hours
	3. Set up time reporting system	6th week			40 man-hours
	4. User visual aid preparation	2nd week			40 man-hours
	5. User committee seminars	8th week	2 weeks		320 man-hours
	6. User committee special system training classes	13th week			320 man-hours
Evaluation criteria:	Positive user feedback				
	Understanding of project objectives demonstrated by response to written and oral questions				
	Amount of user time contributed to project				
Estimated total cost:	$17,000	Prepared by _____ Date _____			

FIGURE 13—5. *Example of task planning form.*

Activity identification (see Figure 13–7)	Activity name	Activity duration
1,2	Draft budget preparation instructions	5 days
2,3	Make revenue projections	5 days
2,4	Department heads prepare expenditure projections	15 days
4,5	Manager reviews estimates with department heads	20 days
3,5	Dummy activity	0 days
5,6	Calculate millage requirement	1 day

FIGURE 13—6. *Example of preparations for developing a PERT schedule.*

interdependent activities be organized into a workable system. As with analyzing city information flows, the key to a workable schedule is identifying the relationships between interdependent and independent activities.

CONTROL

Control measures are established to identify and correct plan and schedule deviations. Control measures consist principally of report forms and review procedures that are developed during the planning phase and become an integral part of the entire project. As indicated earlier, a review and evaluation frequency is associated with each task.

TOOLS FOR PLANNING,
SCHEDULING, AND CONTROL

Since computer systems are relatively new to cities, many urban administrators are understandably overwhelmed by the barrage of technical systems terms. For this reason, many administrators feel compelled to take a back seat to in-house data processing specialists or outside consultants in project management. Unquestionably, technical competence is essential in any successful system, but in many cases the most difficult systems problems are those requiring management expertise.

Several management tools developed in recent years can help the manager acquire the expertise necessary for participating effectively in the management of a complex systems development project. Understanding these fundamental tools does not require a technical background. The following paragraphs present some basic guide-lines for understanding and utilizing several planning, scheduling, and control tools.

PERT. In complex projects, powerful tools such as PERT (program evaluation and review technique) and CPM (critical path method) are useful in describing what effect the timing of any one task has on the overall project schedule. Urban administrators will find the principles of these tools useful, although the tools themselves may be overly sophisticated for all but the most ambitious urban systems projects.

PERT was developed in connection with the Polaris submarine program. The purpose was to project a probable project completion date based on the probable completion dates of the tasks and subtasks making up the entire project. For example, PERT could answer the question: "If task A slips its completion deadline by two weeks, how far will the total project deadline slip?"

The basic principle behind PERT is the definition of each project task in terms of its relationship to other project tasks. For example, task C might be defined as preceding task D and following task B. In addition, part of PERT is used to estimate a duration for each task. Task C in the above example might be estimated as requiring three man-weeks, task D five man-weeks, etc. To illustrate the application of PERT, let's begin with a simplified example of the annual budget preparation process. As a first step all tasks might be defined as in Figure 13—6.

PERT allows the user to measure the effect of a difference between planned and actual time for any one activity on the starting time for any

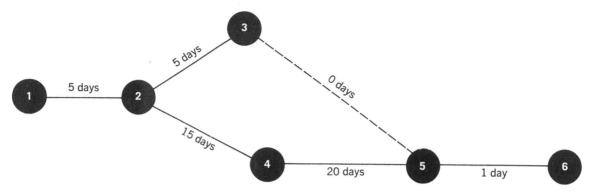

FIGURE 13—7. *Simplified example of PERT diagram.*

other subsequent related activity. Using the PERT concept, the activities in the budget example above could be arranged as depicted in Figure 13—7.

Each activity in Figure 13—7 is defined in terms of a beginning event and a completion event. For example, the budget preparation activity begins with node 1 (initial node) and concludes with node 2 (terminal node). The completion of the budget preparation task (task 1,2) triggers the beginning of two tasks: the revenue projection by the finance officer (task 2,3) and the preparation of expenditure estimates by the department heads (task 2,4). Activity 3,5 is a dummy activity that requires no time or manpower. Its function is simply to depict the link between the revenue projection task (2,3) and the millage rate calculation task (5,6).

A term associated with PERT is the critical path—in essence, the sequence of events requiring the longest time to complete and thus the path which is most critical to the timing of the entire project.

Finding the critical path requires summing the activity times in each path of the project network and selecting that path requiring the longest time. Returning to the budget preparation example, the critical path is immediately obvious. There are two paths. The path including activity 2,3 and dummy activity 3,5 requires five working days to complete, whereas the path including activity 2,4 and activity 4,5 requires thirty-five days.

If an activity is on the critical path, any dead-line slippage for the activity will delay the completion of the entire project. Slippage in an activity not on the critical path, however, would normally not affect the project deadline, since the difference between the lengths of the critical path and the noncritical path is slack time.

In actual application PERT greatly elaborates on the basic concepts of activity relationships and critical paths. Literally hundreds of activities can be specified, along with estimated durations, and a PERT computer program will quickly tell a project manager which the activities are critical to meeting a given completion date.

As a project progresses the original PERT program can be run repeatedly, each time with activity duration estimates revised according to actual project progress. From the new information, the PERT program will recompute the critical path and give a new estimated completion date.

PERT has also been adapted to assist project managers in cost accounting. PERT differs significantly from standard accounting systems in that costs are measured and controlled on a project basis rather than by organizational units. With PERT, each task, comprised of subtasks and activities, becomes a cost center. PERT costs can be broken down to the level of detail desired, although the difficulty of obtaining accurate input estimates increases as the level of detail increases.

In utilizing PERT/cost activity, costs are developed for each activity. Returning to the budget preparation example in Figure 13—7, only the addition of cost estimates is necessary to adapt the basic PERT to handle costs. Figure 13—8 shows cost estimates above activity estimates.

When PERT is used for cost control as well as activity time control, actual expenditures and time can be compared to planned expenditures and time. For any one activity it is possible to compare the percent of budgeted money spent. For example, if a PERT computation showed that 20 percent of the programming task was complete but 40 percent of the money budgeted for programming had been spent, the programming task obviously would be heading for a cost overrun.

The actual percent of cost overrun can be determined at any point in the project by using the following formula:

$$\left. \begin{array}{l} \% \text{ overrun} \\ \text{(or underrun)} \end{array} \right\} = \frac{\$ \text{ spent} - \$ \text{ budgeted}}{\$ \text{ budgeted}}$$

Suppose, for example, that midway through a systems development project a PERT computation showed that $50,000 out of a budgeted $40,000 had been spent. The percentage of cost overrun could be calculated as follows:

$$25\% = \frac{\$50,000 - \$40,000}{\$40,000}$$

PERT was originally developed as a tool for managing a research and development project in which there was great uncertainty regarding the completion times of individual tasks. Although our example has relied on single time estimates for a given activity, one of the advantages of PERT is that it can use three different time estimates for each task: an optimistic estimate, an average estimate, and a pessimistic estimate. Using statistical probability theory, PERT can take into account all activity time estimates, compute the critical path, and determine the most probable project completion date. Additionally, PERT can indicate the slack available in activities not on the critical path.

Programs to compute PERT, along with detailed texts and user manuals, are widely available. Although PERT techniques have not been widely used in urban project management, they certainly have some potential usefulness to urban administrators. Without using the more elaborate applications of PERT, a relatively simple project can benefit from the management exercise of applying the PERT concept. Better management understanding of the most elementary project can result from building a PERT activity network that describes activity timing and cost relationships.

CPM. Unlike, PERT, CPM (critical path method) was designed to operate in an environment of certainty. CPM was developed for application in industrial construction where time required to perform an activity is standard. PERT addresses the question, "How will the project completion date be affected by planned and actual time for individual activities?" CPM looks at the issue, "How will the allocation of ad-

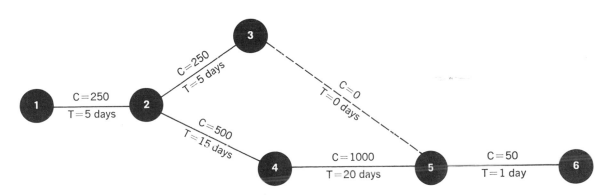

FIGURE 13—8. *PERT/cost model input.*

ditional manpower to an activity affect the project completion date?" CPM achieves its objectives first by indicating which tasks are on the critical path and second by computing the cost of shortening each critical task (and thereby the entire project) through allocating additional manpower to the tasks. The result of CPM is a least-cost schedule which gives the optimum length for a project. The optimum length reflects the pace at which money saved by shortening a project equally offsets the extra money for manpower required to shorten the project.

As with PERT, prepared CPM programs and user manuals are available. Unlike PERT, however, CPM has its greatest potential usefulness in public works projects such as street construction and repair.

Effective use of PERT and CPM requires a thorough understanding of their assumptions and limitations. Interested readers should refer to more specialized literature on these management techniques.[2]

Gantt Charts. The Gantt chart offers a straightforward method of diagramming the time sequencing of systems development tasks. It is a relatively simple way of relating tasks to one another as well as to the calendar. Figure 13—9 shows the application of the basic Gantt charting technique to a generalized systems development

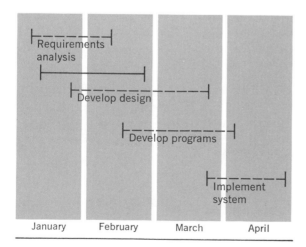

FIGURE 13—9. *Basic Gantt chart technique.*

project. Gantt charts are particularly useful in emphasizing areas in which tasks will be performed concurrently. For example, in Figure 13—9 it is apparent that requirements analysis will be about 50 percent complete when the initial design efforts begin. As the project progresses, Gantt chart estimates can be appended, as indicated, with the solid line below the broken line, to reflect the contrast between planned and actual time.

Description and Analysis

Once system planning has taken place and project scheduling and control measures have been instituted, the next step is to describe those activities that will be included in the system. The activities description and analysis task lays the foundation for all subsequent system efforts.

The purpose of the analysis phase is to determine which procedures and decisions can benefit from automation. Although this question has technical ramifications, it is ultimately a decision requiring managerial judgment. Consequently, although the analysis task must be performed with ultimate data processing considerations in mind, it needs to describe thoroughly all functions in clear, nontechnical terms.

To satisfy design requirements the description and analysis product must contain the following:

1. Description of data flow within and between functions to be automated
2. Current costs of manual activites
3. Description of file and form characteristics
4. Information requirements analysis of each decision.

The personnel assigned to perform the description and analysis tasks should be thoroughly familiar with the functional areas they are assigned to. They need not be computer systems experts. On the contrary, the function experts may well be better suited to the task if they possess a nontechnical systems background.

A frequent problem in systems projects is that the flow is shifted too early to the technical aspects of data, before a thorough understanding of information requirements has been acquired.

Throughout the description and analysis task the emphasis must be on information as opposed to data. Overlooking the distinction between information and data will result a system that does not really answer the important questions.

In order to visualize more explicitly the distinction, let us look at an extreme example. Suppose we are designing a computer system to meet the needs of the tax office. One possible approach would be to look at all the tax office forms and proceed to automate all the data we could identify. At the other extreme, we might disregard all available documentation and concentrate exclusively on the tax assessor's decisions, both as he perceives them and as they are described in appraisal literature. In examining each decision we must ask what information the assessor needs to (1) make a particular decision, and (2) evaluate his decision by testing the effect of decision alternatives.

If we simply computerize all existing data, the resultant system is a hodgepodge. Since little consideration has been given to essential decisions, a system inquiry will result in a mere visual display of the manual files in a different format. Any correspondence between the assessor's real decisional needs and the automated data file will be coincidental.

On the other hand, if decisional needs are emphasized in the analysis phase the resultant system will be able to interact effectively with the tax assessor in making key decisions. To illustrate further, a computerization of existing files and forms in most tax offices around the country would continue to tell the assessor the replacement cost new, less depreciation, of a property, for example. The decision-oriented system, however, may be able to tell the assessor the degree to which an individual property has been equalized to the neighborhood market values. In addition, the decision-oriented system may well be able to compute the extent to which the market value equalization of a property would be affected by raising or lowering the assessment.

The principal subtasks for accomplishing description and analysis task objectives are:

1. Survey of background information
2. Interviewing key personnel
3. Work observation
4. Documenting results of interviews using
   a) Activity flow diagrams
   b) File and data description forms
   c) Narratives
   d) Decision/information matrices.

The background information to be surveyed includes office procedure manuals, national organization handbooks, training guides, references such as *The Municipal Year Book* of ICMA, similar documentation such as the report of the Wichita Falls (Texas) Integrated Management Information System Consortium Phase I (which includes an evaluation of urban information systems research and development projects), and forms presently used by the functional departments.

Surveying background materials helps prepare the functional analysts to ask pertinent interview questions. As far as possible, background materials should serve to share two user perspectives with the analyst—namely, the current understanding that the user has of his information needs and decisions and an ideal, theoretical understanding of what the user's information needs and decisions should be.

The objective is to gain an accurate understanding of the functional decisions and information flows. To do this the analyst needs to prepare key questions and decide on methods of documenting the interview.

Key questions for any interview should be quite general. Normally, no more than six or seven should be necessary to lead into a thorough examination of a department's subject matter. Examples of key questions which can be used for an activities description interview are listed as follows:

1. What are the department's major activities?
2. What are the department's major decisions?
3. How does information pass through the department and on to other departments?
4. What are the major files, both formal and informal, and how are they used?
5. What decisions are associated with each department form, both formal and informal?
6. How are functional responsibilities divided among the department staff?

These general questions when supplemented by good background review should open the way to a detailed discussion of the department's activities. Inquiries into informal files and forms are particularly critical in determining a department's real information needs. No information system, automated or otherwise, can ever fully anticipate future information needs. Therefore, department personnel in time will often supplement the official forms and files with their own information sources. One of the keys to designing an information-oriented system as opposed to a data-oriented system is knowledge of the informal files and documents.

In addition to interviews and background surveys, direct work observation may be necessary to pinpoint certain procedural details. Effective work observation may require that the analyst actually walk through information processing procedures with departmental employees. In other cases, a user survey to obtain certain kinds of procedural data such as file access frequency may be the only way statistical data on departmental activities can be collected. An example would be a random sampling of the number of times water department clerks referred to the past due accounts file and how long each inquiry required. A compilation of these statistics will give a far more valid indication of activity frequencies than do interviews, since people tend to distort unintentionally their impression of activity frequency based on most recent events or peak activities. For example, a tax file may be heavily used during the peak tax collection period from October to January. An interview in February to determine the average number of inquiries to the tax file may produce strikingly different results from an interview in August.

The documentation process begins with interview preparation and concludes with a write-up of work observation, work surveying, and interview results. Each step in the analysis process should be self-documenting. To reduce the difference between what is said in an interview and what is written up, the analyst needs to give particular attention to methods for recording interview responses. Using an activity flow diagram to record interview responses serves the twofold purpose of permanently documenting the interview in an understandable form and

assisting the interviewee in describing his department's information flow. The effectiveness of the activity flow technique can be increased by using oversized paper and sitting alongside the interviewee during the interview. Both the interviewee and the analyst should have felt tip markers. As the analyst diagrams responses to questions, the interviewee can indicate corrections. Supplementary data, such as report timing and decision criteria, can be written next to the appropriate decision block or document. Allowing the interviewee to participate in the documenting process not only serves as an accuracy check, it also acquaints the prospective user with system concepts in a way that provides him with an early sense of participation in system development.

The primary objective of the documentation process is to provide informative, accurate descriptions which assist the analyst in performing his key task—analysis. There are many ways of describing activities for analysis. Among the most commonly used are activity flow diagrams, narratives, file and data decription forms, and matrices.

As mentioned earlier, the first cut at an activity flow diagram should be made during the interview. There are a wide variety of conventions for flow diagram symbols. Most manual procedures and decisions, however, can be described using a few basic symbols. An example of an activity flow diagram is seen in Figure 13—10.

Normally, a brief narrative should supplement the flow diagram. To make reading and analysis easier, the narrative can be keyed to the diagram with numbers. For example, the narrative paragraph key to step [1] on Figure 13—10 might read as follows:

[1] The tax clerk determines from the type of statement whether it is a delinquent statement. Current statements are on data processing cards. Delinquent statements are large forms completed by hand.

Each activity should be documented with a flow diagram and a narrative. In addition, a generalized flow diagram showing the interrelationships between all activities should be prepared.

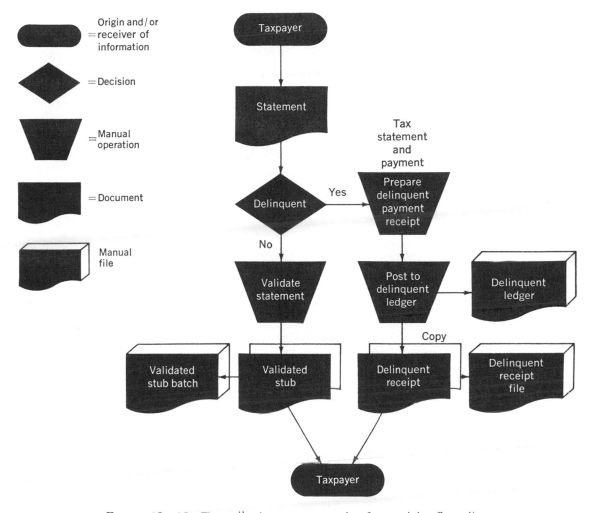

FIGURE 13—10. *Tax collection as an example of an activity flow diagram.*

File and data description forms are another self-documenting tool that can be used during the interview process. These are forms for recording the following kinds of information:

1. File name
2. Primary index (e.g., alphabetical)
3. Secondary index (e.g., address)
4. File size (number of documents)
5. Average number of times file referred to per day
6. File purge frequency.

In describing documents, a blank description form might provide space for collecting the following kinds of information:

1. Document name
2. Purpose of document
3. Major data elements
4. Document distribution (including internal files).

Based on a background survey, the document names and perhaps even the file names can be filled in prior to the interview and work observation. In the course of diagramming the information flow during the interview, as documents and files are mentioned the corresponding description forms can be filled in.

Flow diagrams and narratives assist the analyst in understanding the information processes. To analyze effectively the information/activity relationships, however, the analyst needs a broader look at system interaction than that offered by a detailed description of individual activities. Matrices are useful tools in arranging information and activities so that key relationships can be identified. One kind of matrix particularly helpful in relating decisions and information is the decision/information matrix, depicted in Figure 13–11.

Once a matrix such as Figure 13–11 has been prepared, the decisional information relationships that need to be addressed in the new system can be analyzed. The relative importance of various kinds of information becomes apparent.

Decision / Information	Sales data	Historical appraisal data	New deed abstract boundary description	Appraisal record description of boundary	Sales ratio calculation	Building permit data	Appraisal record description of land plus improvements	Classification of neighborhoods by value	Building cost schedule	Depreciation schedule
Does a reported sale reflect true market value?	●	●								
Have parcel boundaries changed in a transaction?			●	●						
Which properties should be revalued?	●	●			●	●				
What is the market value of a house that hasn't sold?	●	●				●	●	●	●	
What is the replacement cost of a new building?						●	●		●	
How much depreciation should be allowed?		●							●	●
Are property assessments equalized?	●	●			●			●	●	

FIGURE 13–11. *Decision/information matrix.*

For example, sales data (first column) and historical appraisal data (second column) are required by four and five different decisions respectively, whereas deed abstract boundary data (third column) and appraisal record boundary data (fourth column) assist in only one decision each.

The relative importance of the decisions identified in analysis must also be made clear. Preparing a matrix orients the analyst to a better understanding of the decision and information relationships within a function. Once this has been done the analyst, in cooperation with the user, needs to determine which decisions are most critical to achieving the functional objectives. The exercise of establishing decision priorities forces the analyst to orient systems design toward decisions and information as opposed to simply automating activities and data.

Systems analysis documentation must be prepared taking into account varying levels of analytical requirements. The documentation should provide summary information which will enable the steering committee members and upper management to participate in the analysis. At the same time, the level of detail needs to be such that systems analysts can prepare program specifications.

The final documentation might be arranged in a format similar to that given in the following outline:

I. Table of contents
II. Index of exhibits
III. Introduction. This would be generalized at the subsystem level, describing the principal exchanges of information between the subsystem activities and the activities of other subsystems. If analysis effort is restricted to one functional area within a subsystem, the relationship between that area and other areas should be identified. In addition, the Introduction should summarize the key decisions and information requirements within the subsystem or functional area.

    A. Function. General description of function and graphical display, such as

matrices which summarize decision data relationships. If the project is restricted to a single function then the function description will be contained in the introduction described above.

    1. Component. General description of component
      a) Activity. Brief summary of who performs the activity and what its objective is
        (1) Activity flow diagram
        (2) Narrative keyed to flow diagram
        (3) Statistics and cost data on the activity
    2. Component.

Note that the documentation outline is directly compatible with the system structure identified in the first section of this chapter, on systems approach.

Concluding appendices should contain the completed document and file analysis forms discussed earlier.

The importance of systems analysis-oriented documentation cannot be overemphasized. All too frequently activities are analyzed and a system designed and implemented without the preparation of adequate documentation. Well-organized and thorough documentation can be produced if documentation standards are established at the outset and project personnel are well oriented. Periodic review by the project manager will be necessary to maintain documentation consistency.

In systems analysis documentation it is easy to overemphasize data as opposed to information. There are cases in which documentation has been performed for its own sake. In such cases, formidable quantities of indigestible descriptive data have been produced which do not materially assist systems analysis. Structuring activity descriptions in a systems format and conscientiously using such tools as flow diagrams and decision/information matrices will help to ensure that analysis efforts will contribute significantly to the design of an information-oriented system that can be integrated into user activities.[3]

Design

The purpose of this phase is to design a system that will satisfy the information requirements identified by analysis. Design begins with the conceptualizing of an information flow interaction between the computer and the organization. Initially, the focus in design should not be restricted to obviously automatable activities but should describe the proposed automated and manual information flow. This description will contain the following elements:

1. Proposed automated files
2. Proposed microfilm or microfiche files
3. Existing files which will continue after the new system has been implemented
4. Input and output documents associated with the proposed system
5. Existing documents that will be maintained under the proposed system
6. Manual and automated data handling procedures.

The conceptual design description, like the systems analysis document, will be prepared at varying levels of detail to satisfy different management and technical needs. The design document should contain a systems level flow chart and narrative describing the major functional interfaces within the system. In addition, expected benefits of the new system should be summarized.

The design document must also address technical development and implementation needs. Proposed files need to be described in detail, specifying index keys, individual data elements, file organization, and maximum number of records.

Data processing steps must be specified in detail during the design. Too often the detailed specification of programming steps is left until the development and implementation phases. It is only when detailed specifications on a generalized system flow have been worked out that many system inconsistencies show up.

The outlining of user procedures should proceed concurrently with development of detailed data processing specifications, to help assure that the user-need approach followed in systems analysis will not be sacrificed in favor of a machine-oriented system in technical design.

To maintain a user-need orientation throughout the design phase, the user committee must be actively involved. New system user procedures that may appear perfectly feasible to an observing analyst may appear quite the opposite to a person who has performed the task daily for ten years.

The design document should be constructed according to the system structure developed in analysis. The proposed system design can be classified into subsystem, function, components, and activities. Where current manual activities described in systems analysis are to be replaced or altered by automation, a reference to the change is necessary.

Once a new system has been designed, a cost-benefit comparison between the present and proposed systems can be made. (The cost-benefit comparison technique is discussed in the final section on system evaluation.) In summary, the elements of the design document are:

1. System description
2. Forms descriptions
3. File description
4. Program specifications
5. User procedures
6. Cost-benefit analysis.

The documentation should be sufficiently detailed to enable the project staff to devote the rest of the project time to writing programs, converting files, and training users.[4]

Evaluation

Evaluating the system begins with the initial feasibility study and ends with the postimplementation review. The feasibility study is built on cost-benefit analysis, which is a useful approach for establishing criteria for evaluating the progress of a project throughout the development and implementation period, and for determining the processes that should be automated. The basic objective is to identify both measurable and unmeasurable costs and benefits. Any administrator involved in computer systems development needs to understand the principles of cost-benefit analysis. EDP system enthusiasts are frequently guilty of quite sincerely underestimating measurable costs (particularly personnel costs) and overestimating unmeasurable benefits. Many a system has been sold on the basis of such phrases as "improved efficiency," "better decision making," and "lower costs." The project administrator should require systems personnel to spell out in numbers just what is meant by the above terms.

Performing a cost-benefit analysis involves identifying measurable and unmeasurable costs and benefits of both the present and the proposed systems. To facilitate a useful comparison, costs and benefits must be projected. Many times a proposed system will cost more initially, but in the course of two or three years will cost less than if no change were made.

The principal measurable costs of both the present and proposed systems can be broken down into the following categories:

Computer lease/purchase
Computer operation: computer time; terminal
Clerical
Keypunch, maintenance, data conversion
Maintenance programmers
Administration.

Normally, unmeasurable costs vary, but usually they assume the form of potential disadvantages. Some examples of unmeasurable costs are: personnel resistance to innovation; confusion of transition period; and increase in status and power of the central data processing department at the expense of the line department.

Measurable benefits are predicted cost reductions resulting from improved performance. The following kinds of benefits are typical: reduction in inquiry response time; fewer clerks required to answer telephones; and less professional staff time spent on handling routine tasks.

In some cases a very pronounced ratio between costs and benefits may be observed. In most instances, however, a costs versus benefits comparison produces inconclusive evidence in support of a final decision. A valid and useful rule of thumb is to consider cost-benefit analyses only peripherally in making a systems decision,

since a clever analyst can easily derive a cost-benefit ratio to suit his bias.

In a city where growth is projected, annual operating costs will increase because of cost-of-living increases for current personnel and the necessity of hiring additional personnel to handle the increased work load. The growth trends of the city needs to be considered in projecting costs of continuing with the present system.

Seldom can a system be justified purely on the basis of cost reduction. Actually, the analysis of measurable costs and benefits (for anything other than large-volume, finance-oriented systems) may well indicate that a good many years of improved performance are necessary to recapture the initial systems investment. Therefore, when considering the measurable cost-benefit implications special attention must be given to unmeasurable benefits (and costs). In a political environment, especially, the unmeasurables are apt to be far more significant.

An example of the unmeasurable cost-benefit trade-off is the effort on the part of several jurisdictions to develop automated tax assessment systems. These systems provide the field appraiser with several precomputed estimates of market value based on cost-depreciation schedules and an analysis of sold properties. The appraiser chooses a precomputed value or substitutes an independent value. Such a system enables the appraiser to reappraise all properties each year to keep up with the market. The key costs and benefits of such a system are impressive and to some degree unmeasurable. The system claims to provide greater equalization of property assessments by allowing yearly reappraisals. On the cost side, however, there may be marked political resistance to annual assessment changes.

The cost-benefit analysis is a key element in the ongoing monitoring and evaluation phase of a systems project. Careful consideration of measurable and unmeasurable costs and benefits at this point helps to determine overall project feasibility. In theory the cost-benefit analysis should be used as a guide in deciding whether a project should be continued or whether the scope should be revised. Also in theory, the cost-benefit analysis should explore costs and benefits of alternatives such as the difference between a batch system and an on-line system with terminals, or even the difference between a computer system and a microfilm retrieval system. In practice, however, cost-benefit analyses are frequently used to justify a foregone conclusion. Consequently, in practice cost-benefit analyses are rarely used as a basis for discontinuing or drastically revising a project.

In addition to evaluating project objectives from a cost standpoint, an objective of the monitoring and evaluation task is to be sensitive to relations between project staff and users. It is important throughout the project to ensure that the systems project personnel, whether consultants or city personnel, develop a good working rapport with user personnel. The isolation of systems project personnel in an inaccessible clique of technical elites will do irreparable damage to project objectives over the long run. One method to induce effective interaction is to require individual analysts to "borrow" office space in user departments. If dispersing analysts throughout target departments is impracticable, some regular opportunities for analysts and users to work together should be provided.

Throughout the project review sessions should be held with key personnel to evaluate the project. The evaluation sessions should measure progress to date against stated objectives as well as measuring project money spent against estimated costs.

Once the system has been implemented it is necessary to conduct a final review session to evaluate the completed project. In the final review, the monitoring and evaluation process ties together all phases of the management process—planning, scheduling, and control. It is particularly useful to review the cost-benefit summary developed in the initial project phases with the implemented system.

In addition to measuring actual costs against estimated costs and actual benefits against anticipated benefits, the final review should involve users in a qualitative identification of problems and reactions. Any unanticipated benefits or problems should be recorded as the concluding part of the total systems documentation.

---

[1] For a candid appraisal of three projects undertaken in the late sixties, see International City Management Association and U.S., Department of Housing and Urban Development, APPLYING SYSTEMS ANALYSIS IN URBAN GOVERNMENT: THREE CASE STUDIES (Washington, D.C.: International City Management Association, 1972). Report prepared by the International City Management Association for the Department of Housing and Urban Development.

[2] For a thorough exposition of PERT and CPM on a management level—together with an extensive bibliography—see Jerome D. Wiest and Ferdinand K. Levy, A MANAGEMENT GUIDE TO PERT/CPM (Englewood Cliffs, N.J.: Prentice-Hall, Inc., 1969).

[3] For a comprehensive discussion of problems in urban systems analysis, see THE WICHITA FALLS CONSORTIUM PHASE I REPORT VOL. I: SYNTHESIS OF PHASE I CONCLUSIONS (Springfield, Va.: National Technical Information Service, 1970).

[4] For a thorough nontechnical treatment of project design tasks, see John C. Shaw and William Atkins, MANAGING COMPUTER SYSTEM PROJECTS (New York): McGraw-Hill Book Company, 1970).

14

Management Information Systems

THE MOVEMENT AND EXCHANGE of information has become a vital part of modern organizations, and municipal organizations are no exception. The prompt and accurate flow of data and feedback is essential to the effective management of a city, town, county, or other local government. Record systems for the quick, complete retrieval of data, including financial and performance aspects, have become organizational priorities. These record systems include legal necessities such as title deeds, as well as management information.

Many reporting systems are joined with public records and are designed to collect, summarize, and analyze information from the records as well as from other sources. Municipal agencies are typically well endowed with such reporting systems, covering current needs of financial control, preservation of legal documents, routine financial administration, police records, traffic statistics, and other ongoing data on municipal operations. Many of these record and reporting systems grew up at a particular time to meet a specific need. Thus, they have little relationship to other systems or to current priorities and overall information needs. Instead of a single integrated system, therefore, most cities and other local governments have many unrelated ways of reporting and recording information.

What Is an Information System?

The availability of sophisticated information technology, including, but not limited to, the computer, has changed management thinking about information. Integrated data collection, reporting, and analysis systems, which give logical consideration to information needs, flows, and users and which attempt to get the right kinds of information to the right people at the right time with a minimum of effort and cost, are now under development in a number of cities.

Two related developments are of particular interest: the Management Information System (MIS), the principal subject of this chapter, and the Urban Information System (UIS). These developments are frequently discussed together, but this is confusing, because an Urban Information System is by far the more ambitious of the two in that it provides intelligence on the physical and social municipality, often on a regional basis, rather than being limited to the technological information needs of the municipal organization. A UIS may in theory be designed to accommodate the purposes of one or more Management Information Systems. Thus, in practice, these two could and should interlock.

A Management Information System provides the information needed to manage the day-to-day operations of the organization and to help with policy analysis and other long-range efforts. MIS requires rational procedures for the collection, recording, flow, and retrieval of data on the operations of an agency, and the availability of that data for planning and decision making. An MIS is not a system solely for the chief administrator; on the contrary, it should be of considerable use to supervisors, department heads, councilmen, citizens, and others who are a part of decision processes. The primary goals of an MIS are to improve the organization's ability to deal effectively with decisions; to improve the ability to decide on, evaluate and control work;

and to meet more economically many of the purposes served by traditional records and reporting systems.

An Urban Information System, on the other hand, has its roots in areawide planning and policy processes. It is oriented to the effective coordination of the resources and efforts of the various agencies of an urban area rather than to the management and output of a single agency. An ideal UIS collects data from a number of agencies and, in return, provides summaries and analyses useful for current as well as long-range management. Typically, a UIS is concerned with the information needed for decisions on land use, areawide health planning, and transportation.

In a Los Angeles research project, William H. Mitchel and Kenneth L. Kraemer developed the following definition of an urban information system:

An urban information system consists of people, computer equipment and related programs, a dynamic data base, and institutional procedures interacting in a prescribed systems pattern. It is designed to collect, store, update, and facilitate the automated use of data on a continuing basis. Such data and [their] processing and analysis are related to both the internal affairs of government and the external environment. The manifold purposes of such an information system are to meet operational requirements; to facilitate various summarizing or analytical techniques relevant to the definition of community problems; to assist the search for program goals; to generate cybernetic flows for evaluation and control; and to permit the exchange of information among governmental units and with the public.[1]

It can be seen from this definition that a UIS is an ambitious undertaking requiring a great deal of sophistication.

The Management Information System is a more limited undertaking. An MIS is the orderly collection, indexing, and storage of data and records. It is one of the first major attempts to place problem solving and decision making on a systematic, informed basis.

It is desirable for an MIS to be developed with an eye to the prospect that it may eventually become part of a regional Urban Information System. In this case, just as a particular city is a subsystem of a larger urban complex, so the MIS becomes a subsystem of an areawide UIS. Figure 14—1 shows the kinds of organizational and community data which might be included in such an MIS.

There are a number of different objectives in collecting and using such data, and each objective has different implications for the technology of data collection, storage, and use and for the appropriate organizational location of the hardware and the skills. Four different types of objectives have been identified by the city of Sunnyvale, California.[2] These are reporting, measuring (for routine control and management decisions), planning, and predicting and controlling (of nonroutine situations). The matrix in Figure 14—2 shows the development and application of the Sunnyvale MIS.

One of the assumptions of an MIS is that a properly organized data system will provide better information faster to the right decision points in the organization. There would be reason to assume, therefore, that as an aid to rational decision making an MIS should be a major contribution to the organization.

Charles E. Lindblom presented the following decision-making model indicating that a rational manager, when making a decision, would:

1. Identify his problem;
2. Clarify his goals, and then rank them as to their importance;
3. List all possible means—or policies—for achieving each of his goals;
4. Assess all the costs and the benefits that would seem to follow from each of the alternative policies;
5. Select the package of goals and associated policies that would bring the greatest relative benefits and the least relative disadvantages.[3]

An MIS is a step in the *direction* of Lindblom's model, but a variety of factors stand in the way of the use of such a rational decision-making model; these are: cause—effect relationships that cannot be sorted out; the numerous goals or policy choices; the high costs of gathering information; the variety of backgrounds of the people involved in making the decision, and of their attitudes, beliefs, training, and interests; and the structural and personal relationships within the organization. In reality, the decision-making process is "the science of 'muddling through.' "[4] It is a process of compromise: instead of finding the best way, the procedure is to find a way that will both work and be accepted by all the parties affected.

One point must be made clear: an MIS is not a decision-making device, although it should, if properly established, provide decisive information for the decision-making process. Figure 14—3 outlines some general traditional and modern decision-making concepts. Between these traditional and modern techniques, however, there is an interface composed of human, political, and professional people. This interface must still encompass crucial decision-making elements such as judgment, interests, ideals, bias, prejudice, politics, common sense, and experience in a cultural-economic environment.

Potential Contributions of an MIS

The categories of data shown in Figure 14—1 and the objectives outlined in Figure 14—2 give an initial picture of some of the purposes that an MIS can serve. Here are some major uses.

1. Records storage and retrieval. Records are one of the crucial components of an MIS. They represent the foundation of most other information products.

2. Budget information and control. An MIS helps budgeting in at least two ways. First, budgetary *computation* has historically cost much in terms of human, physical, and time resources. An MIS can be used to compute the budget, freeing that time and effort for analysis work. Second, an MIS can improve the ongoing budget functions of control and evaluation. The purpose of control is to compare "actual performance against the plan as it proceeds."[5] Evaluation, in contrast to control, is after the fact. One of the most important payoffs from good control and evaluation is that the information becomes more readily available where it does the most good—close to the work and the worker.

3. Decision making. One of the most dramatic potentials of an MIS may be its support for decision making, where projections of needs and simulations of results represent some of the most exciting administrative frontiers. While 100 percent accuracy cannot be guaranteed, projection can provide the kind of information required for multiyear planning.

Data about the municipal government		Data about the community	

Management
  Planning
  Programming
  Budgeting
  Controlling
  Evaluating
		Physical	Public safety

			Housing
			Education

Housekeeping
  Staffing
  Personnel administration
  Purchasing
  Warehousing
  Accounting
  Payroll
  Revenue
		Environmental	Transportation

			Economic performance
			Health
		Economic	Environmental quality
			Demography

Operations
  Public safety
  Justice
  Transportation
  Health
  Education
    etc.
			Social welfare

		Social	Recreation

FIGURE 14—1. *Systematic relationships of organizational and community data.*

Objective	Hardware	Information system base	Measurement	Mechanism for control	Types of personnel	Organization
Reporting	Mechanical accounting and office machines	Systemized record keeping	Expenditures ($) cost	Line-item budget	Clerks	Department
Measuring	EDP equipment	Work measurement (efficiency)	Expenditures in terms of output (cost/unit)	Program budget	Cost accountants	Centralized record keeping and analyses
Planning	Computers (2nd generation)	Effectiveness	Production and results related to costs (productivity)	PPBS	Systems analysis, operations research specialists	Program is basis of organization structure
Predicting and controlling	Large time-shared computers plus advanced communications devices and peripheral equipment	Goals and objectives	Event-oriented system with exception reporting keyed to modeling and correlation (trend analysis, effectiveness measures)	Inter-governmental analysis to individual impact analysis	Economists, mathematicians, behavioral scientists	New inter-governmental organizations (data centered)

FIGURE 14—2. *Management information system development and application.*

4. Data processing. MIS provides cheap processing of routine data *if* they have been properly programmed and clustered.
5. Program information. MIS helps show the city council that the manager has a handle on things (control function) and a feel for the implications of his new proposals (planning and policy).
6. Internal communications. The quality and effectiveness of internal communications can be positively affected so that offices needing information receive what they need—and without masses of extraneous material.
7. Interdepartmental coordination. Finally, an MIS can contribute to interdepartmental coordination. An MIS can demonstrate mutual dependence on the same kinds of data and on common use of data which one department develops from the other. An MIS that is realistically accessible to the middle management and supervisory levels also offers the possibility of organizational growth.

Supervisors need to learn the same MIS skills as middle and top management.

When an MIS Is Set Up

One of the first steps in developing the actual system is to identify activities, users, and sources—a major task in complex governments. Activities must also be ranked in order of importance and according to their relationship to other activities.

The organizational structure is of little consequence in this first step, but a complete inventory of activities is required department by department. Many activities are handled by more than one department. For example, animal control can be carried out by the health department, which is responsible for rabies detection and tests; the community services department, which operates the animal shelter; the public works department, which grants licenses and verifies innoculations; and the police department, which kills reported rabid animals. The interrelationships of every activity of government must be identified as they relate to each other, to the entire system, and to the appropriate management processes. This is a difficult task that requires a total systems analysis of the organization.

In addition to functional overlap, it is likely that various departments will maintain records within different time parameters. For example, one unit will emphasize daily data, another weekly, another monthly, and another all of these. The result is that when different departments need to use the same information it may not be transferable. Thus, the standardized collection of data becomes an initial imperative.

Geographic differences in areas covered cause duplicate data gathering. One agency or department may collect data on a city-wide base, another on a neighborhood base, another using census tract boundaries, and still others precinct boundaries, special district boundaries, or other boundaries. As a result, the information does not fit the framework.

The factors of departmental overlap, time frame, and geographic coverage all mean that, even in the absence of the more sophisticated components of an MIS system, most organizations could accomplish important cost reductions by cutting down on duplication of data collection and establishing uniform data boundaries. An MIS helps identify specific areas in which such action can be taken.

Related to the problem of data collection is the accuracy of information. For example, does driving past a construction site on the way to another site constitute an inspection? Does writing down a serial number constitute an inspection? These are old problems amplified by a new system. Cost accounting systems have been weakened by failure to allow for such tactics. An effective MIS requires valid information. GIGO, the computer slang word meaning "garbage in, garbage out," is the watchword for any user of any information system.

TYPES OF DATA

Some general ideas about types of data are applicable. It is likely that an MIS would include the following types of data within some geographic and time parameters:

1. Administrative
2. Operational
3. Budgetary
4. Accounting
5. Social
6. Economic (including geographic data)
7. Political.

	Decision-making techniques	
Types of decisions	**Traditional**	**Modern**
Programmed		
Routine, repetitive decisions (organization develops specific processes for handling them)	1. Habit 2. Clerical routine: standard operating procedures 3. Organization structure: common expectations, a system of subgoals, well-defined informational channels	1. Operations research: mathematical analysis, models, computer simulation 2. Electronic data processing
Nonprogrammed		
One-shot, ill-structured, novel policy decisions (handled by general problem-solving processes)	1. Judgment, intuition, and creativity 2. Rules of thumb 3. Selection and training of executives	Heuristic problem solving technique applied to: a) training human decision makers b) constructing heuristic computer program

FIGURE 14—3. *Traditional and modern techniques of decision making.*

Administrative, operational, budgetary, and accounting data are the internal data which allow managers from the supervisory to the very top levels to better understand the workings of their respective units. The benefits are fewer shotgun decisions and the ability to resolve many problems before they become crises. Administrative data include more than just numbers. For example, letters and memos in what computer people call "natural language" contain vital factors which need to be considered, or very bad decisions can result. These factors may include the latest quantitative information about a piece of heavy equipment or a perceptive but unquantifiable evaluation of the prevailing attitudes in a segment of the community. Both types of data could have far-reaching implications.

Operational data refers to the work-related information that every department keeps, though usually in many different ways. These data are usually more quantifiable and refer to volumes of work, time/cost quantities, work priorities, and who does what, and when.

Budgetary and accounting data are closely related, as both are critical control points in most organizations and represent a core of information on human and monetary resources. In addition, the judgments of the top budget and accounting staff often make the difference between an accurate projection of revenues and expenditures and a useless exercise. It is at this point that information is often withheld in the name of competition so that "our projection will be more accurate than theirs." When any information system is used for such games, one key person can make a costly system unreliable.

The preceding types of data reflect the decision-making process by which ideas and demands become action. Social, economic, and political data, on the other hand, represent the environment in which the municipal government operates. Social and economic data come from census information, citizen attitude studies, and other special studies. The regional planning commission or council of governments should have data to contribute to these environmental subsystems. Political data would include election returns. (While governmental collection of political data could be an explosive issue, it should be remembered that, when analyzed in the context of the various other data, such information would be invaluable in planning bond programs, financial innovation, and approaches to state and national legislative programs.)

Another key point related to system design is that cities are becoming increasingly concerned with neighborhood information. Different functions are being organized on a neighborhood base, and proposals are being made for poverty area programs and other neighborhood-based programs. Many city managers and other administrators give a top priority to working with neighborhood and citizen groups. These efforts would be enhanced if the manager could support them with specific data relating to the neighborhood.

Moving from the neighborhood to the metropolitan region, the question of MIS compatibility with UIS or with the information needs of other governments cooperating on joint activities is important. Joseph C. Honan has pointed out a significant design element:

The relationship between the data in a local information system with other levels of government can be seen in the growth of information exchange between them. The growth of information exchange between the various levels of government, and the attendant Federal and state regulations thereon, make it the most important relationship to consider when designing a local information system. Ultimately the growing intergovernmental information exchange requirements may prove to be the decisive factor in shaping local information systems now in operation or in the development stage.[6]

Special attention should be given to the policy analysis and resource allocation uses of an MIS during its design. These are areas in which traditional record and reporting systems have often been of least help and, therefore, where the greatest improvement is possible with an MIS.

The essential questions being answered with an MIS analysis are: Are we committing manpower, equipment, and money as effectively as possible to attain the goals and objectives we have established? What alternatives or mixes of alternatives are available to improve delivery systems?

The kinds of data that must be reported are similar to production records: meters read per hour, letters typed per hour, federal grants obtained per year, holes patched per day, health visits per day, and inspections per day.

The information generated from the MIS being established in Wichita Falls, Texas, is affecting such programs as street construction, maintenance, and repair priorities, as well as scheduling and critical path programming of construction projects.[7] The Kansas City, Missouri, Police Department is generating patrol information on the basis of incidents and demand, again a specialized subsystem requiring a variety of data. While these are particular subsystems, it is apparent that all types of data, from legal to operational, would have impact on the decisions that must be made on priorities and programming.

Albert Mindlin describes four types of data systems which are needed by local governments to aid in effective resource allocation. These are:

1. Real property data system which identifies every lot in the city and assists in manpower distribution and programming for housing inspectors, policemen, or civil defense shelters;
2. Geographic system, reflecting social events (such as welfare families) that occur by areas, and [providing] ecological data for research, planning, programming, and evaluation;
3. Person system where the basic unit is the individual and the data includes information such as motor vehicle ownership, health or welfare usage; and
4. The family system reflecting known family relationships.[8]

Of the four systems, only real property and geographic systems have come into practical use in cities. The person and family systems are not being developed rapidly, owing to a lack of basic records, rapid turnover of information, and questions of confidentiality and invasion of privacy.

CENTRALIZATION VERSUS DECENTRALIZATION

When starting an MIS system, attention must be paid to centralization and decentralization for both the organization and the data. The growth of citizen participation and the emphasis on neighborhood-related groups has provided a new requirement for collecting data and making decisions on a neighborhood basis. In the long run however, much more attention will be paid to the regional data base as opposed to the single-city data base as metropolitan planning commission and councils of governments develop. Therefore, we are faced not with a choice between centralization and decentralization, but with a necessity to develop both.

Managers will also be faced with the question of where to house the MIS center. Centralization should be emphasized where there are clear and accepted objectives, but decentralization is preferable where there is a changing environment and where there is extensive interaction among departments. In both situations the manager must monitor effectiveness of the MIS.

Regardless of where the MIS is located, tight management controls will be needed for all data collection. Centralization provides the necessary authority for eliminating the duplication of efforts and enforcing the standard coding that is required in the efficient use of the data. The control methods used in data collection can be largely standardized through control of forms design, since forms are the major document for the collection of raw data.

Computers in the Design of an MIS

The introduction of new management tools presents a variety of problems (as will be outlined later in this chapter). Should an organization decide to move to more sophisticated computerized levels in its MIS, the availability of technical training in the requirements and uses is critical. Further, such a new tool will inevitably have unanticipated side effects, some favorable and some unfavorable. In addition, the special environment and culture of each organization presents new challenges to the application and installation of an MIS tool as far-reaching as a computer. The key word in the introduction of new technology is adaptation: of people, of systems, and of hardware and software approaches.

Because of all these variables, as well as unpleasant cost implications often discovered after the computer salesman has left, most organizations have introduced computers on a gradual basis. The first applications normally are for repetitive clerical operations, where speed and standardized responses of the computer will be an asset. Utility billing and inventory management are prime candidates for initial computer applications.

As city data processing departments have gained confidence, efforts have been made to extend computer use to other areas, where simple cost calculations are not as easy. Some examples are: deployment of police patrol cars for more effective coverage at peak crime hours; allocation of fire pumpers and other fire fighting apparatus for better coverage of new commercial centers; and analysis of traffic accident statistics as an input to improved traffic engineering.

The computer is not simply a new management tool. Organizations learn quickly that, to achieve a net saving (as opposed to a mere increase in speed which they may not be able to afford or may not need), they must seek full use of the computer by expanding the kinds of problems on which it may be used. Cities, therefore, should use computers to speed up their servicing of public needs, but they must also use them for sufficient numbers of management functions to make the use economically feasible (although the introduction of the time-sharing option in addition to the old options of buying or leasing hardware takes off some of the pressure to expand automated information processing into marginal areas just to use up expensive capacity).

Some of the most complex applications of the computer deal with decision making. Policy questions are complex because they involve so many variables and so many possible combinations of variables. The computer is an excellent tool for processing data useful for such decisions, but it will be effective only if adequate time has been devoted to data selection, analysis, and programming. This requires the direct involvement of line management.

The computer cannot: set the boundary conditions for any problem; define a problem; say how worthwhile it is to explore a particular problem in the first instance; hence it cannot indicate the rational use of resources of money or persons in work on an original problem; imagine the variables or other information which might be relevant to a consideration of a problem; decide what to include or exclude in the initial operations on a problem; select the functions to be explored; make decisions regarding the range to be covered by an included variable; construct a model; select the criteria to be explored (although we may program a

computer to select the "most predictable" criterion from the number which we have previously noted for inclusion); decide how to collect the basic data; decide upon a strategy of operations, such as deciding what proportion of resources should be devoted to different stages of a problem or the means for its solution; design or evaluate a sensitivity analysis.[9]

One of the problems in establishing an MIS which is computer based lies in "domesticating" the computer specialists. Secure in the knowledge that they have the key to the new technology which management needs, computer specialists may rush ahead with "their" system. The computer specialist must be incorporated into the training and education process along with all potential users and suppliers of information in the organization. In other words, "ownership" and effective use of the system is spread across the organization. If the computer specialist, the managers, and the supervisors do not develop common goals the result will probably be unfortunate. A dedicated systems designer wants nothing but the best for "his" system, to prove how great a system can be put on line. Computer managers are often not overly interested in settling for less than the best systems components. This can skyrocket the costs. The computer manager also may be uninterested in considering other objectives which could be accomplished with the same resources.

Conflict is not unusual between the computer specialist, who is a man with a technique in search of a problem, and the managers and supervisors, who are more generalist-oriented, have the problems, and are seeking techniques to help solve them. They have an ample community of interests, but the interests goals of the two groups tend to obscure the potential.

Human Barriers to MIS

Evidence gathered from attempts to introduce new technologies, including the computer, suggests that the appeal to rationalism has not succeeded in most organizations. In addition to the understandable resistance to change which MIS can provoke, MIS can lead to some special behavioral problems.

First, the people responsible for installing the

system are generally highly mission-oriented and may not have the interpersonal skills necessary to sell themselves or their system to the managers whose values and behavior they are trying to change. In addition, a computer-based MIS may be a radical departure from forms and procedures painstakingly developed over many years. Managers and supervisors are also astute enough to know that the changeover will involve a lot of hard work, frustration, and delay.

The specialists, usually consultants who come in from the outside to install the new system, must always be aware of the inherent threat represented to the managers and supervisors at all levels. The outsider is independent of management control and has access to privileged information as well as to the political leadership. These fears generate assumptions that consultants are fundamentally arrogant to even presume to tell a man who has been doing a job effectively how he should change his system or style.

Second, there is a certain amount of skepticism among managers, who know that sometimes the problem is not a shortage of information but too much information. No manager is able to read and digest all the information he considers appropriate to his operation or system. Managers and supervisors must be trained to know what data they need and how to use it. Further, there must be a willingness to use the information and the system before a financial commitment is made for expensive talent and equipment.

Third, even if an MIS would do a better job of providing necessary and valid information to decision makers, some managers might consider it threatening to their current decisions and past behavior. Few organizations operate with the kind of openness among managers or between departments which will enable them to be totally frank. This means that most organizations have a considerable amont of data which is kept within the various departments and knowingly withheld from decision makers. An MIS is a threat because it prevents departments from withholding such information from the total decision processes of the organization. It is a threat which will induce irrational reaction to the introduction of a more rational system.

Speaking on this point, Chris Argyris has written:

Concern and fear about what MIS will do to managers—what it will reveal about the way they have been operating all this time—is what creates the basic resistance. Naturally, this is not easily admitted or spoken about. However, to make sense of this emotional block to rationality, to see both the human potentials and the human problems in MIS and other rational technologies, you should face the issues squarely.[10]

The MIS will make basic information available to more management levels of the organization so that each manager will be held more directly accountable. His excuses for failure to meet goals and objectives will have less chance of convincing others than before. The resisting manager sees that he is being asked to place in the hands of his superiors the ability to second-guess him in areas where he has survived before by asserting his expertise. Obviously, this can be very threatening.

In addition, MIS tends to play down the traditional organization politics and, in fact, the efficacy of power in the organization. In an MIS-dominated organization, managers and supervisors with good information and the ability to use it for problem solving will find that this is a greater source of power than some of the traditional power bases. Interdepartmental politics, which often rob an organization of its effectiveness, should decline with an MIS. The transfer of information and the determination that certain types of information are the basis of operations for several departments helps to break down the walls which have been built up between departments. Isolationism among departments must give way to interdependence and openness.

There is the question of whether many organizations can really absorb such changes. Lengthy arguments about the rationality of the system and how it will improve decision making will do very little to reassure insecure executives. While the organizational impact of an MIS often raises problems, accentuates conflicts, and represents a significant commitment of resources, the payoffs of a soundly conceived and executed MIS in fact more than offset some temporary organizational discomfort.

PLANNING-PROGRAMMING-BUDGETING

Similar charges have been leveled against planning-programming-budgeting systems (PPBS). Aaron Wildavsky has cited PPBS for overlooking several types of political and behavioral realities:

1. Exchange costs—the costs of calling favors owed and the costs of making threats in order to get others to support a policy;
2. Reputational costs—the losses of popularity with the electorate, the loss of esteem and effectiveness with other officials, and the subsequent loss of one's ability to secure programs other than those currently under consideration; and
3. The costs of undesirable redistribution of power—those disadvantages that accrue from the increase in the power of individuals, organizations, or the social groups who may become antagonistic to oneself.[11]

PPBS is an interrelated system of cost-benefit analysis, systems analysis, and cost-effectiveness analysis, which could be included initially or added as a major subsystem of an MIS. It assumes that a rational effort toward budgeting and resource allocation is essential for decision making. PPBS guides the decision makers through the following stages:

1. Defining the major programs in each area of public service;
2. Defining the principal "outputs" (goals) of each program;
3. Identifying the "inputs" that generate "outputs" (inputs include various combinations of personnel, facilities, and techniques for rendering service);
4. Computing the costs of alternative combinations of inputs and the value of the outputs likely to be produced by each combination;
5. Calculating the cost-benefit ratio associated with each combination of inputs and outputs.[12]

As municipal administrators talk increasingly about the application of systems such as PPBS, it becomes increasingly clear that such systems can be most effective if supported by the use of a computer. On the other hand, the real use of PPBS is not possible unless technical and professional personnel capable of engaging in analytic functions are available. Clearly, all cities need these people, but, just as clearly, many cities do not have them and cannot afford them. Nevertheless, an MIS should be designed so that it can facilitate the introduction of a PPBS system.[13]

DATA CRITERIA

Some basic factors to be considered, then, in the development of an information system would include the following:

1. Data collection must be such that it permits both aggregation and disaggregation of data for specialized purposes.
2. There must be adequate protection of privacy. Some kinds of data collected by governments are of interest to commercial users and would in no way harm the privacy of the persons about whom the data were provided. Other kinds of data are more sensitive. Some means must be found of both fulfilling the legitimate information needs of government departments and protecting the privacy of the information from unauthorized users.
3. The system should be designed to facilitate compatibility and linkages with broader information systems such as a regional UIS or the reporting systems of state and federal granting agencies.
4. The philosophy of the system must be determined. Decisions must be made as to: (a) the extent to which regular operations and strategic planning data will be collected and maintained, separately or in some way integrated; (b) whether the system will contain both social and physical planning data or whether social planning will be deemphasized; and (c) the extent to which departmental data will be centralized or decentralized.
5. Data selection must anticipate the potential development of other systems which will be intrinsically related, such as PPBS and social indicator systems.

One of the major problems to be avoided with an MIS is the development of a system based on a volume of undigested routine data relating to employees, pay systems, inventories, and other overhead items. Such a system would generally not provide the information which is necessary for planning and policy purposes although it may be very essential for operations. If planning and policy information is to be derived from operations data, then it is essential to have full involvement of the users of planning and policy data in structuring the inputs to the system. Only in this way will the system include those types of data most likely to be usable in the planning and policy process. Failure to do this will make MIS a kind of security blanket for those who make decisions without providing the necessary decision support. Figure 14—4 shows the relationships that should obtain between data collection, processing, and use in an MIS.

COMMUNICATIONS

Organizations which have undertaken an honest study of their communications systems invariably conclude that there is a greater need for top management to communicate policy positions to lower level people so they understand the why of management decisions. An automatic corollary is

that lower level employees and managers should have enough confidence in top management to provide upward feedback when they see something they think should be changed. The third side of the triangle is that there must be adequate lateral communication. Obviously, none of these conditions is likely to develop unless the total environment of the organization—employees and their complex relationships—shows that openness and mutual trust are predominant characteristics.

For example, the National Aeronautics and Space Administration (NASA) was an organization in which the potential for misunderstanding existed because of the differing goals of professional engineers and scientists in a

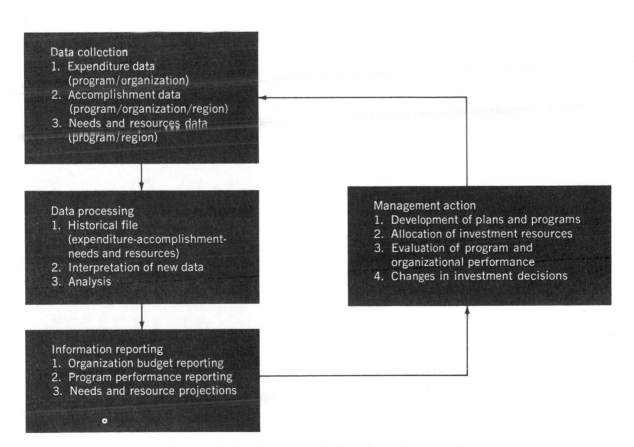

FIGURE 14—4. *Management information systems concepts.*

politically visible and attractive agency. An evaluation of staff communications systems in NASA illustrates this point:

It seems to be a truism that large organizations tend to grow extremely uncommunicative. Yet the ability to establish useful data source points predetermines whether any future staff actions are going to have a chance for success. The problem really is that most of the information which the chief executive needs is sensitive—not because of security but because it tends to reveal the effectiveness or lack of effectiveness of the subordinate officials or because it can raise questions for which no answer is readily available.

In attempting to establish these necessary preconditions for good completed staff action the thing which stands out most is the need to make the communication process a two-way street. That is, unless information is passed from the top down, unless there is good top-to-bottom communication, there is unlikely to be good bottom-to-top communication. By passing on to the line and staff offices guidance received from the NASA Administrator on various questions, a mutual confidence was established. Key officials in large organizations cannot do an effective job unless they know what the top man is thinking and why. It gives them a chance to clarify their understanding of his policies and goals.[14]

A special problem for public agencies is that written communications must be disseminated with the assumption that even items marked for restricted consumption can end up in the newspapers. This limits the freedom of top management to say many things which it might like to say to its employees. It requires that different techniques such as word of mouth, either in person or by telephone, be used to transmit certain information. In such cases the value of open communication becomes a critical element.

One related problem is that top management in a public organization has the same problems in interaction with the political body as the middle managers have with top management. Both withhold information from their superiors at various times which the superiors would like to have but which the withholding agent believes can be withheld until the situation is corrected, so that negative reactions will be minimized. An MIS tends to reduce the likelihood of top management and middle management withholding information, since the very presence of the system creates an expectation in the minds of the political leadership that management can

provide more information than it could in the pre-MIS system.

Impact of an MIS on the Organization

An MIS will have considerable impact on organizational styles, values, and systems which in the past provided guidance and security. The specific organizational changes generated by an MIS depend on a long list of variables, including size, structure, type of government, intergovernmental relationships, etc.

The effects of an MIS on organizational structure are usually apparent. Not so apparent are the subtle shifts in power that move with the data. To date, politicians have not been involved in the design or utilization of information systems. This lack of political involvement is causing some shifting of power within urban governments. City administrators and operating officials can gain power from data systems at the expense of legislators and old-style political advisers. Perhaps the final outcome will be to shift the advisory role to men who possess *both* technical knowledge and political wisdom.[15]

Designing a Management Information System involves more than merely introducing another procedure. It involves a reevaluation of who is doing what, why, and how, and the impact this has on what others are doing. In addition, a total Management Information System must concern itself with planning and policy questions. The producers and consumers of the data for operations decisions may be oblivious to the needs of those who are working at the policy level.

In many functional areas it is possible for top management to turn over the implementation of a new idea to consultants and specialists. This cannot be done with Management Information Systems, where only top management may know what kinds of data need to be collected and processed.

The analysis involved in developing an MIS helps point out the relationships within the organizational structure. The reduction of this structure to subsystems provides insights into such variables as authority; resources; monitoring, coordinating, and controlling; and contraction, extension, or deletion of activities. Evaluation of these variables can lead to a clustering of like activities into a single program and a clustering of programs into an organizational unit. Programs deemed needed or useful but too costly may become candidates for automation, process control, simulation, or other computer-related operations.

This brings us to the reality that the municipal government is not a collection of independent departments working in isolation on urban problems, but is in fact a dynamic and continuously interacting system. In short, any organizational format developed will be in some sense artificial in that it requires the drawing of artificial jurisdictional boundaries. As Mayor John Lindsay pointed out in his book *The City,* a complaint call related to water may go to the buildings department, the health department, or the public works department, depending on whether the call relates to the absence of water, the absence of hot water, or the absence of sufficient hot water,[16] An MIS would draw these various common elements together for programming purposes.

Urban Information Systems

Earlier in this chapter it was pointed out that a UIS provides broad physical and social information. The data draw heavily on census and other demographic indicators, on land use records, and on social indicators, and are often areawide or are part of a regional planning effort. The UIS approach is so broad that almost any kind of recorded data can be built in.

The UIS is a valuable framework for information covering several local governments or even an entire metropolitan area, but it also can be delimited to one city or society or even a subsystem within one local government. But a UIS is a large and costly undertaking, and the payoff may be several years away. The following paragraphs present some background on UIS and the alternative approaches to data bases.

Edward Hearle argues that the basic decision is what kinds of data should be contained in the system. He states that there are two major approaches:

The first, or "comprehensive data base" approach, involves placing into the system those basic data elements which analysis or judgment indicate are "required" by the system's users. While some of these data elements may be derivatives such as percentages, the bulk of the data items in urban systems are basic descriptors; for example: land use, family income, building condition, or assessed evaluation. Such data elements are generated either through the ongoing operations of governmental or private agencies or through field surveys following structural questionnaires, such as the census. Typically, the data are used not only for analysis but also in performing the regular operating activities of the municipal agencies.[17]

Hearle points out that the comprehensive data approach can be very costly, because the volume will be higher than anticipated and agencies will be tempted to enter all the data which come into their hands. This could lead to a system snarled with junk data and a call for more selective collection of data.

One outcome of a search for selective data has been an attempt to develop a system of social indicators—that is, efforts are being made to identify types of data which indicate broad trends in relation to such goals as reduction of poverty and improvement of housing. Thus, most social indicator theorists are asking for much more than economic indicators which "measure phenomena without any connection to the goal."[18] Goal definition has turned out to be much more difficult than anyone anticipated. We are a long way from agreement on social indicators which would be sufficiently reliable to help make major resource decisions.

Hearle argues that the only approach which makes sense at this time is the development of a comprehensive data base in which data relevant to operating functions can be emphasized. If such data are properly collected they can be aggregated and disaggregated by area, time, and subject matter so that management planning and policy analysis are facilitated. Hearle argues for using the comprehensive data base as a building block of basic data elements from which social indicators and other data may later be derived. Another consideration in is that operational data are clearly needed locally, whereas social indicator data, by their very nature, are more likely to develop as a national rather than a local system.

An MIS must serve the operating departments that generate the data as well as the management and planning staffs who use information outputs but do not make major data inputs. Again, Hearle comments:

One of the major lessons to be drawn from the experience of the past decade in the design of urban data systems is that they cannot be sustained if they serve planners alone. The cost of creating and maintaining such systems appears too great in relationship to the perceived value of the data they present for planning purposes alone.[19]

In the earlier days of information and systems (the mid- and late sixties) much discussion revolved around the data bank—the nerve center, so to speak, of all relevant operational and

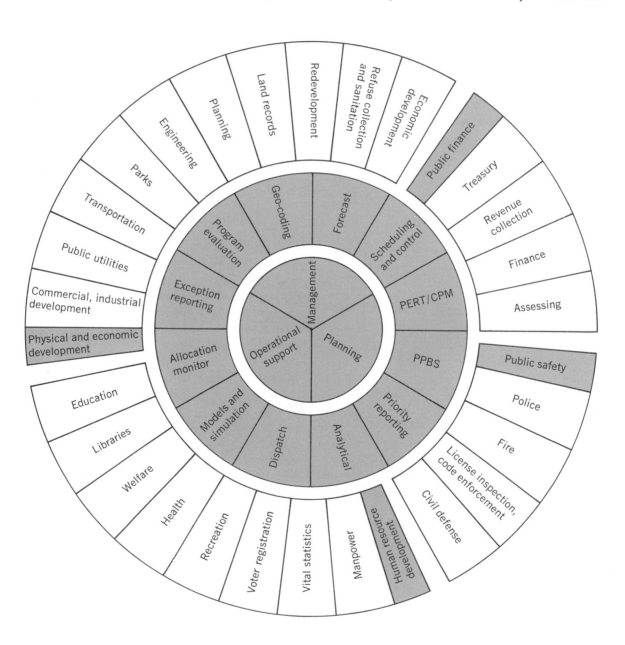

FIGURE 14—5. *Integrated municipal information system.*

environmental data needed for decision making. On the basis of experience and of demonstration projects, this ambitious and somewhat simplistic concept has been recast toward an integrated approach to information. In part, the emphasis has shifted from a banking (deposit, storage, withdrawal) approach to the process approach described in this chapter for ongoing operations.[20]

It is not possible at this time to recommend a single data base that will meet the needs of all comers; nor is there a definitive answer to the standing professional dispute of comprehensive versus indicator data bases. The answers to these questions must be resolved by those who will use the MIS or UIS. Ideally, such decisions follow a goal-setting undertaking, since goals and objectives provide the framework for decision making.

The USAC Project

Further insight into Urban Information Systems can be gained by looking at the Urban Information System research undertakings under the sponsorship of a federal umbrella agency called the Urban Information Systems Inter-Agency Committee (USAC). Six cities were selected as prototype UIS centers. Charlotte, North Carolina, and Wichita Falls, Texas, are to set up total information systems. The four other cities are to develop specialized information subsystems: Dayton, Ohio, in public finance; Long Beach, California, in public safety; Reading, Pennsylvania, in physical and economic development; and St. Paul, Minnesota, in human resource development. Each project involves a private systems firm and a university or research center.[21] The U.S. Department of Housing and Urban Development (HUD) and eight other agencies are participating in putting up 50 percent of the funding. USAC is charged with

... the primary objective of improving the information and decision-making capabilities of municipalities.

The projects also will encourage the standardization of data and data inventories at the local level as well as through successive levels of government. Also systems will be designed and developed in a way that will permit them to be transferred to other municipalities.[22]

The timing for establishment of these systems

was appropriate, since it coincided with the 1970 Census, which is providing new kinds of data. At the same time, new and more effective ways of providing access to the data have also been developed. A model of the integrated Municipal Information System program sponsored by USAC is shown in Figure 14—5. Essentially, it divides all the work of the city government into four major subsystem areas: (1) public safety; (2) human resource development; (3) physical and economic development; and (4) public finance.

All of the activities of local government are then classified into one of these four categories for which the subsystem grants have been made (see Figure 14—5). The functional and activity categories, which often represent organizational units of the city government, are classified by the four major subsystem areas. The different approaches to analysis, management, and control (program evaluation, exception reporting, allocation monitoring, etc.) can be used to improve management, planning, and operational support (Figure 14—5).

The USAC contract awards were the culmination of much work done during the sixties in universities and in county and city governments to explore computer applications to local government. The project has been very carefully developed to test hypotheses in the real world of six local governments.

The basic concepts of the USAC approach are now being tested in the six R&D projects currently underway. While there are already indications that research will verify these concepts, it will most probably take several years before they are fully substantiated. These concepts are, however, receiving continued widespread acceptance by cities concerned with more effective use of the computer technology for municipal purposes.[23]

Conclusion

This chapter is not intended to develop an MIS do-it-yourself kit but is rather intended to introduce managers and supervisors to a problem-solving approach which can provide effective information for program planning and implementation.

Just as an MIS is but one part of problem solving, so the role of the organization in setting up an MIS does not end with signing a consultant contract. An MIS is not a commodity: it is an organizational process for delivering services to the public. To make it a success, the allegiance and participation of all segments of the organization is necessary.

Like every management approach or method, MIS has both costs and benefits.

The costs include: the financial outlay for hardware and software (systems designs and computer programs); payroll costs (systems and computer people are well paid); the danger of neglecting highly important information because it cannot be programmed and built into the system; the inability of the system by itself to respond to changing conditions or to some data variations that may be danger signals; and the "reduced sensitivity" to the opinions and interpretations of midlevel people who may be bypassed in the system.

The benefits include: lower costs for data processing; faster availability and wider distribution of data; generation of new data as a result of the systematic process; better data reporting from the standpoint of consistency and accuracy; and feed-in to larger information systems. Above all, the MIS provides timely information to management on a process basis.[24]

The future of the MIS is bright. As managers and supervisors initiate such processes and interlock them with those of other governments, the values will become more evident. Organizations are continuously generating decision-making information. The question is whether they can do it in an appropriate form at the time it is required. Each attempt to reach a decision on MIS in a specific agency provides some indication of the need, usefulness, and potential of such a system. Successful implementation will take a long time, but it will ensure that there is no turning back to disparate and single purpose information gathering.

[1]Kenneth L. Kraemer, "The Evolution of Information Systems for Urban Administration," PUBLIC ADMINISTRATION REVIEW 29 (July–August 1969): 394–95.

[2]John E. Dever, "A Comprehensive Management Information System," PUBLIC MANAGEMENT, May 1973, pp. 11–13.

[3]Charles E. Lindblom, THE POLICY-MAKING PROCESS (Englewood Cliffs, N.J.: Prentice-Hall, Inc., 1968), p. 13.

[4]Charles E. Lindblom, "The Science of Muddling Through," PUBLIC ADMINISTRATION REVIEW 19 (Spring 1959): 79–88.

[5]James C. Emery, ORGANIZATIONAL PLANNING AND CONTROL SYSTEMS (London: Macmillan & Company, 1969), p. 140.

[6]Joseph C. Honan, "Information Systems for Local Government," paper delivered at the annual conference of the American Society for Public Administration, Denver, Colo., 20 April 1971, p. 3.

[7]Gerald G. Fox, "Municipal Information Systems," NATION'S CITIES, April 1970, pp. 32–33.

[8]Albert Mindlin, "Confidentiality and Local Information Systems," PUBLIC ADMINISTRATION REVIEW 28 (November–December 1968): 510.

[9]Leslie Wilkins, "Computer Impact on Public Decision Making," PUBLIC ADMINISTRATION REVIEW, 28 (November–December 1968): 510.

[10]Chris Argyris, "Resistance to Rational Management Systems," INNOVATION 6 (August 1970): 30.

[11]Aaron Wildavsky, "The Political Economy of Efficiency: Cost-Benefit Analysis, Systems Analysis, and Program Budgeting," PUBLIC ADMINISTRATION REVIEW 26 (December 1966): 292–93.

[12]Ira Sharkansky, PUBLIC ADMINISTRATION (Chicago: Markham Publishing Co., 1970), p. 66.

[13]A notable PPBS research effort in the late sixties, known as the 5–5–5 Project, involved five cities (Dayton, Denver, Detroit, New Haven, and San Diego), five counties (Dade, Florida; Nashville-Davidson, Tennessee; Los Angeles, California; Nassau, New York; and Wayne, Michigan), and five states (California, Michigan, New York, Vermont, and Wisconsin). The project was sponsored by the State-Local Finances Project of George Washington University (Washington, D.C.) with funding from the Ford Foundation.

[14]Thomas P. Murphy, "What Is Completed Staff Action?" SYSTEMS AND PROCEDURES JOURNAL 17 (March–April 1966): 10.

[15]Anthony Downs, "A Realistic Look at the Final Payoffs from Urban Data Systems," PUBLIC ADMINISTRATION REVIEW 27 (September 1967): 208–209.

[16]John Lindsay, THE CITY (New York: W. W. Norton & Company, Inc., 1970), pp. 83–84.

[17]Edward F. R. Hearle, "Designing Urban Information Systems," NATION'S CITIES. April 1970, p. 17.

[18]Ibid.

[19]Ibid., p. 18.

[20]For an explicit statement on disappointing experiences with data banks, see Kenneth L. Kraemer et al., INTEGRATED MUNICIPAL INFORMATION SYSTEMS: THE USE OF THE COMPUTER IN LOCAL GOVERNMENT (New York: Praeger Publishers, Inc., 1974), pp. 3–4.

[21]The Editors, "Info Systems Research Advances," NATION'S CITIES, February 1970, p. 66.

[22]Ibid.

[23]Kraemer et al. INTEGRATED MUNICIPAL INFORMATION SYSTEMS, pp. 31–32.

[24]Based largely on Downs, "A Realistic Look at the Final Payoffs from Urban Data Systems," p. 205.

15

Work Analysis
and Work Environment

THE MORE EFFECTIVE DELIVERY of services, when needed and where needed, is the constant concern of management. Work analysis helps managers and supervisors to develop and carry out programs, to adjust the work unit and the flow of work to changing requirements, and to adapt and change programs as goals and objectives change. Stated more precisely, work analysis is a process of management improvement for:

1. Clarification of needs and objectives
2. Increased performance
3. Increased effectiveness
4. Increased efficiency

The organization's work is done in a format that includes the layout and flow of work, forms design, space planning, and furniture and equipment. Together, these elements make up the work environment.

Since these two subjects, work analysis and work environment, are so interrelated, both are covered in this chapter. They appear under the major subject heads of Work Distribution, Work Flow, Operations Analysis, Work Layout, Forms Design, and Space Planning, Furniture, and Equipment.

Work Distribution

Work distribution is the first step in work analysis. The logical method of procedure is to prepare a list of activities—which are rather general—and tasks—which are more specific. The activities and tasks are then identified by specific employees. Figure 15—1 is an example of a work distribution chart for a personnel department, which combines activities and tasks and shows how much time each employee takes for each activity.

In preparing the work distribution chart, two types of data are needed: (1) an activity list and (2) a tasks list. An activity list is a general inventory of the principal activities of the office being studied. Listing of detailed activities should be avoided. A "miscellaneous" category can be used to group many secondary activities which do not directly contribute to the main objective of the unit. Tasks lists are prepared by each employee in the office to show jobs or duties performed and the estimated number of hours spent on each one. The form used should show the employee's name and position title as well as the unit being studied.

From the above information the work distribution chart is prepared, showing in a consolidated form the activities performed by both the unit and individual employees, and the total time spent on the activity both by the entire unit and by each employee. . . .

An analysis of the chart should be made to determine:

1. What activities take the most time?
2. Is there misdirected effort?
3. Are employees' skills being used properly?
4. Are employees' doing too many unrelated tasks?
5. Are tasks spread too thinly among employees?
6. Is work divided evenly among employees?[1]

This leads up to a discussion of work flow.

TASK LIST

DIVISION _____
DEPARTMENT Personnel
TITLE Clerk-Typist

Wilma Jackson

Task Number		Hours Per Week
		8
1	Wait on counter	2
2	Check old employee file	1
3	Stamp in Requisitions	3
4	Type	15
5	Operate PBX	10
6	Handle Pxxx xxxxx xx	
	TOTAL HOURS PER WEEK	40

ACTIVITY LIST — PERSONNEL DEPT.

1. Solicitation and recruitment of applicants.
2. Processing personnel requisitions.
3. Examining applicants.
4. Maintaining eligible lists.
5. Giving promotional examinations.
6. Answering inquiries.
7. Handling xx xx xxx xx x
8. XXX   xxx xx xx xxx

WORK DISTRIBUTION CHART

ACTIVITY	TOTAL MAN-HOURS	Wilma Jackson Clerk-Typist	MAN-HOURS	Jack Moody Personnel Assistant	MAN-HOURS	H. Melody Principal Clerk	MAN-HOURS	M. Dickson Clerk-Typist	MAN-HOURS	Daisy Hahn Clerk-Typist	MAN-HOURS	Mrs. Stern (Record Room) Principal Clerk	MAN-HOURS
Solicitation and Recruitment of Applicants	39	Wait on counter / Check old employee file	8 / 2	Write want ads / Wait on counter / Check old employee file	1 / 8 / 2	Write want ads	2	Type want ads / Wait on counter / Check old employee files	1 / 1 / 3	Wait on counter / Check old employee file	7 / 3		
Processing Requisitions	32	Stamp in Requisition	1	Check Requisition / Keep Requisition Register / Maintain Suspense File	2 / 2 / 2	Check requisition / Allocate / Keep Requisition Register / Certification	2 / 10 / 2 / 5	Assist Miss Melody	3	Assist Miss Melody	3		
Examining Applicants	1					Make request for needed examination to provide names for certification	1						
Fingerprinting New Employees	16	Type Fingerprint form	3	Fingerprint new employees / Maintain fingerprint file	10 / 2					Type fingerprint forms	1		
Giving Promotional Examinations	1					Request needed promotional examination	1						
Maintaining Eligible Lists	21					Supervise maintenance of Eligible and Promotional Lists	8	Maintain Eligible and Promotional Lists		Maintain Eligible and Promotional Lists			
Answering Inquiries	32	Operate PBX	15	Answer inquiries	5	Answer phone, letter, and personal inquiries	2	Answer Inquiries	2	Answer Inquiries / Relieve on PBX	6 / 2		
	240		40		40		40		40		40		

FIGURE 15—1. *Work distribution chart.*

Work Flow

Work flow begins with a graphic picture of the steps involved in a procedure or other activity. A work process chart will show how a job is being done and will highlight areas for improvement. The purpose of work flow analysis is to break down the job or procedure in detail, so that one can see clearly just what is being done, what activities need further study, and what improvements might be made. In addition, it can be: the "convincer" for obtaining approval of changes in procedures, assignments, or equipment; a means of obtaining employee participation in management; and a systematic method for reviewing ongoing activities.

THE FLOW PROCESS CHART

The flow process chart is the heart of work flow analysis. The basic elements are shown in Figures 15—2, 15—3, and 15—4. Little instruction is needed for individual employees to prepare a chart listing in detail the actions each takes in his portion of a procedure. With a little more orientation in work simplification techniques, an employee will be ready for the second phase of charting—the proposed method—eliminating, combining, or otherwise changing existing procedures.

Supervisory employees should prepare the more complex flow process charts that may be necessary when several employees are involved in a procedure. Such charts may be essentially a consolidation of single-column charts prepared by individual employees or the multicolumn or other types required for a specific purpose.

Management analysts or other top management representatives should prepare or participate in the preparation of charts covering procedures that cross department or division lines.

HOW IS THE FLOW PROCESS
CHART PREPARED?

Flow process charts are pictures of the procedure charted. To obtain the most useful picture we must use the right chart. A single-column process chart will serve satisfactorily in most instances. It will usually identify activities that require more complex types of charting. The chart may follow a procedure through several organizational elements, or it may be limited to a part of the procedure. The chart should show in detail just how the job is being done—not the way someone thinks it is being done or the way the office manual says it should be done. For this purpose, the chart must be completed by the employee actually doing the work or by someone observing the employee doing the work. In some instances the flow process chart may be attached to a form with entries made by persons involved in processing the form when they handle it.

The symbols needed for the flow process charting will vary according to the complexity of the study, but the symbols shown in Figure 15—2 are adequate for most charts.

The flow process chart must show every step that takes place in carrying out a procedure. When distance, quantity, or time may have some significance, such information should be entered on the form. Forms, form letters, and individuals

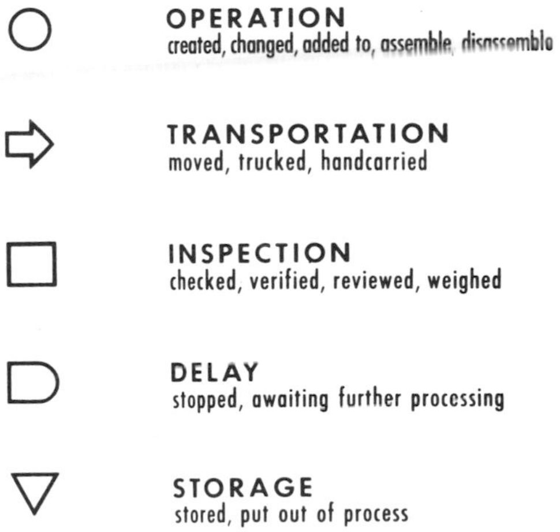

○ **OPERATION**
created, changed, added to, assemble, disassemble

⇨ **TRANSPORTATION**
moved, trucked, handcarried

□ **INSPECTION**
checked, verified, reviewed, weighed

D **DELAY**
stopped, awaiting further processing

▽ **STORAGE**
stored, put out of process

FIGURE 15—2. *Flow process chart symbols.*

FLOW PROCESS CHART
WORK SIMPLIFICATION PROGRAM

SUMMARY

ACTIVITY	PRESENT NO.	PRESENT TIME	PROPOSED NO.	PROPOSED TIME	DIFFERENCE NO.	DIFFERENCE TIME
◯ OPERATIONS	19	7½ min	9		10	7½ min.
⇩ TRANSPORTATIONS	4	1½ min	1		3	1½ min.
☐ INSPECTIONS	3	½ min	2		1	½ min.
D DELAYS						
▽ STORAGES	1		1			
DISTANCE TRAVELLED	75 FT.		0 FT.		75 FT.	

PROCESS Patients Control Clerk's handling of mailed VA Form 10-P-10 (Application for Hospitalization)—non-emergent, waiting list cases.

☐ MAN OR ☒ MATERIAL

CHART BEGINS 10-P-10 received by Patients Control Clerk
CHART ENDS After filing 10-P-10 with authorizations to report.

CHARTED BY John Doe (Patients Control Clerk)
DATE Jan. 26, 1960
PAGE NO. 1 OF 1

DESCRIPTION OF EACH STEP ☒ PRESENT ☐ PROPOSED METHOD	OPERATION	TRANSPORT	INSPECTION	DELAY	STORAGE	DISTANCE IN FEET	QUANTITY	TIME	NOTES	ELIMINATE	COMBINE	CHG. SEQ.	CHG. PLACE	CHG. PERSON	IMPROVE
1. Take 10-P-10 from in-basket	●								10-P-10 previously processed by Eligibility Unit						
2. Check to see if legal and medical eligibility established	◯		■												
3. Determine that 10-P-10 must go on waiting list	●														
4. Prepare 3×5 card for alphabetical index kept on my desk	●						1 min		Record to assist in quickly locating 10-P-10	X					
5. Prepare 3×5 card for chronological and priority file on my desk	●						1 min		Record used in selecting applicants to authorize	X					
6. Enter tally mark on waiting list report record I maintain	●						½ min		Running record of waiting list cases.	X					
7. Enter Veterans name on waiting list roster.	●						½ min		Handy reference for telephone inquiries	X					
8. Prepare waiting list letter to veteran and place in out-basket	●														
9. Attach copy of waiting list letter to 10-P-10	●														
10. Carry 10-P-10 and related material to file drawer	◯	●				25 Ft.		½ min		X					
11. Place 10-P-10 in file drawer	●								Filed Alphabetically						
12. 10-P-10 remains in file drawer until bed is available.	◯				▼										
13. Pull 3×5 chronologically filed index card.	●							½ min	when bed is available	X					
14. Go to file drawer—match 10-P-10 and index card.	●							1 min		X					
15. Carry 10-P-10 back to desk	◯	●				25 Ft.		½ min		X					
16. Review file—to see if any pertinent correspondence added.	◯		■												
17. Remove name from waiting list roster.	●							½ min		X					
18. Indicate change on waiting list report record.	●							½ min		X					
19. Select reporting date and note bed control record	●														
20. Remove 3×5 card from waiting list alphabetical file	●							½ min		X					
21. Prepare memorandum to travel clerk	●							1 min		X					
22. Send 10-P-10 and instructions to travel clerk	◯	●													
23. Take 10-P-10 and travel authorization out of basket	●								When returned to my desk from travel clerk						
24. Check travel authorization	◯		■					½ min		X					
25. Attach copy of T/O to 10-P-10 Place original T/O in out-basket	●							½ min		X					
26. Carry 10-P-10 and related papers to file drawer	◯	●				25 Ft.		½ min		X					
27. File 10-P-10 with other authorized cases according to reporting date.	●														
	◯														
	◯														
	◯														
	◯														
	◯								Note: Time has been estimated only for steps that may be eliminated						

ANALYZE - QUESTION EACH STEP. ASK *WHAT? WHERE? WHEN? WHO? HOW?* and follow each with *WHY?*

FIGURE 15—3. *Flow process chart, old procedure.*

affected by or that affect any step in the procedure should be identified on the chart. Attach copies of the forms or form letters involved. As each action is recorded, think about the following questions:

What is being done? . . . . *Why?*
Where should it be done? . . . . *Why?*
When should it be done? . . . . *Why?*
Who should do it? . . . . *Why?*
How should it be done? . . . . *Why?*

If the "Why?" questions raise any doubt about the procedure, appropriate notations should be made for possible action. Analyzing the data collected should be a pleasant and interesting task. It is an opportunity for the employee preparing the chart to show his ability and creativeness and to make his constructive ideas a matter of record. Everyone will find an exhilarating challenge in trying to eliminate, combine, simplify, or otherwise change a procedure in a manner that will provide the desired result in an easier or better way. We are all improvers at heart, and process charting is a good way to get recognition for our useful ideas.

The flow process chart shows you the sequence of work. It gives you a step-by-step account of what actually happens to your unit's activities. There are many types of flow process forms which may be used in process charting. Some are more elaborate than others, permitting the administration of the extremely detailed procedures to be found in accounting, data processing, engineering drafting, etc. In most instances, however, such detail is unnecessary. A simple form calling for analysis of procedure by requiring checks of each step has been developed by different federal government agencies. An illustration of the form, a single-column process chart, is shown in Figure 15—3. This lists the old procedure of twenty-seven steps which is ultimately reduced by the new proposed method of thirteen steps, as shown in Figure 15—4.

Flow process analysis is always focused on a reference point—individuals going through certain steps, some type of product being fabricated, or a form being completed or processed. In Figures 15—3 and 15—4 this reference point was the 10-P-10 form, Ap-

plication for Hospitalization. It in important that a supervisor always follow through on a person, item, or form around which the process turns. If this reference point is not rigorously kept in focus, the supervisor finds very shortly that he is not sure what he is studying, and his analysis beings to lose its meaning.

The budget office or the administrative analysis staff has no monopoly on the simplification of office work. The staff actually engaged in the office work usually is in the best position to develop simplification; they have a wide field of knowledge and experience which can be very fruitful if explored under proper guidance. A suggested method of handling this is to form each section of the office into a work group for reviewing of major procedures.

Operations Analysis

Work distribution and work flow are parts of analysis which normally involve several people. When, however, a number of employees are doing the same kind of job and the operation recurs frequently, there is an opportunity for savings by increasing the speed and ease with which each of these operations is accomplished. On the whole, this type of analysis, termed "operations analysis," is not so applicable to a municipality, where each job tends to be unique and not as susceptible to a specified routine. In a factory, on the other hand, where many jobs are exactly the same, the work cycle is repeated over and over again. In such situations detailed study of operations is most useful.

There are two occasions in which operations analysis is of particular value in the municipality. The first is when jobs conform to the pattern described above. Such studies have been made in refuse collection operations, for example, where the cycle of work, size of the lift, height of the lift, and other factors affect in marked degree the amount of work performed.

The second is when a single job is creating particular problems. The job may be causing a bottleneck; it may be causing difficulty in holding employees on the job; or it may be of critical importance to the success of other operations.

FLOW PROCESS CHART
WORK SIMPLIFICATION PROGRAM

SUMMARY						
ACTIVITY	PRESENT		PROPOSED		DIFFERENCE	
	NO.	TIME	NO.	TIME	NO.	TIME
○ OPERATIONS			9			
⤳ TRANSPORTATIONS			1			
□ INSPECTIONS			2			
D DELAYS						
▽ STORAGES			1			
DISTANCE TRAVELLED ___ FT.		___ FT.		___ FT.		

PROCESS Patients Control Clerk's handling of mailed VA Form 10-P-10 (Application for Hospitalization) — non emergent waiting list cases

☐ MAN OR ☒ MATERIAL

CHART BEGINS 10-P-10 received by Patients Control Clerk

CHART ENDS After filing 10-P-10 with authorizations to report

CHARTED BY John Doe (Patients Control Clerk)   DATE Jan. 27, 1960   PAGE NO. 1 OF 1

DESCRIPTION OF EACH STEP ☐ PRESENT ☒ PROPOSED METHOD	OPERATION	TRANSPORT	INSPECTION	DELAY	STORAGE	DISTANCE IN FEET	QUANTITY	TIME	NOTES	POSSIBLE ACTION (ELIMINATE / COMBINE / CHG. SEQ. / CHG. PLACE / CHG. PERSON / IMPROVE)
1. Take 10-P-10 from in-basket	●	⇨	□	D	▽					
2. Check to see if legal and medical eligibility established	○	⇨	■	D	▽					
3. Determine that 10-P-10 must go on waiting list.	●	⇨	□	D	▽					
4 Prepare waiting list letter to veteran and place in out-basket	●	⇨	□	D	▽					
5 Note 10-P-10 to indicate waiting list letter sent	●	⇨	□	D	▽				Save preparing copy of waiting list letter.	
6. Place 10-P-10 in file drawer (file chronologically)	○	⇨	□	D	▽				File cabinet for this purpose to be relocated by my desk.	
7. 10-P-10 remains in file until bed becomes available.	○	⇨	□	D	▼					
8. Pull 10-P-10 when bed is available.	●	⇨	□	D	▽				10-P-10's are filed chronologically — come up in turn	
9. Review file — to see if any pertinent correspondence added	○	⇨	■	D	▽					
10. Select reporting date — Stamp date on corner of 10-P-10 *	●	⇨	□	D	▽				Stamped info. for Travel Clerk — replaces memorandum	
11. Send 10-P-10 to Travel Clerk	○	⇨	□	D	▽				Travel Clerk prepares authorization — forwards orig. for mailing	
12. Take 10-P-10 from in-basket	●	⇨	□	D	▽				following its return from Travel Clerk	
13. File 10-P-10 with other authorized cases — by reporting dates	●	⇨	□	D	▽					
	○	⇨	□	D	▽				Notes:	
	○	⇨	□	D	▽				1. The number of steps will be reduced from 27 to 13	
	○	⇨	□	D	▽				2. I will just turn around in my chair to file applications	
*and on bed control record.	○	⇨	□	D	▽				3. Carrying 10-P-10's a distance of 25 feet on three occasions will be eliminated. (I walk 50 feet going and returning)	
	○	⇨	□	D	▽				The proposed changes are to some extent made possible by the	
	○	⇨	□	D	▽				reduction in applications placed on the waiting list since the	
	○	⇨	□	D	▽				present procedure was installed. Very little time will be required	
	○	⇨	□	D	▽				to make a physical count of applications on the waiting list,	
	○	⇨	□	D	▽				or to locate an application for telephone or other inquiries	
	○	⇨	□	D	▽					
	○	⇨	□	D	▽					
	○	⇨	□	D	▽					
	○	⇨	□	D	▽					
	○	⇨	□	D	▽					
	○	⇨	□	D	▽					
	○	⇨	□	D	▽					
	○	⇨	□	D	▽					

ANALYZE — QUESTION EACH STEP. ASK *WHAT? WHERE? WHEN? WHO? HOW?* and follow each with *WHY?*

FIGURE 15—4. *Flow process chart, new procedure.*

MOTION ECONOMY

Much of what has been said constitutes the rationale for the scientific management movement. It is based on the assumption that there is one best way of doing every job. The body of principles which has emerged from this striving for the the one best way is generally known as motion economy.

The essential rationale of motion economy is that there are three parts to work:

1. Getting ready: such steps as assembling materials, setting up equipment, and arranging for personnel to do the work are examples.
2. Doing the work.
3. Cleaning up after the job: such steps as unloading, disposing of unused materials, storing materials, and a general cleanup are examples.

It is apparent that the only truly productive time is in the phase of actually doing the work. The less time taken to get ready and to clean up, the more time available for the job and the greater the production. In any analysis of the job, then, primary attention should be given to the amount of time spent doing the work itself.

Motion economy assumes that the human body, the work place, and tools and equipment control the level of performance.

Motion economy has particularly emphasized the importance of making maximum use of the human body in the work cycle. There are some things that the human body does more easily and more naturally than others. A person can walk forward, backward, or sideways, but it is easier and more natural to walk forward. Motion economy lays great stress on gearing the human body to the work process in its most natural movements. Some of the questions that may be asked in order to make these determinations are:

1. Is the work within easy reach? When a person has to stretch, stoop, or bend, his fatigue will of course be greater.
2. Are the simplest motions being used? In general finger motions are, for example, simpler than those requiring the use of the entire arm. They require less effort and are therefore less fatiguing, and normally mean faster work.
3. Can both hands be used in performing this task? This is a particularly important point, since it is quite typical to use only one hand while the other remains idle. If the operation can be structured in such a fashion as to occupy both hands simultaneously, it is apparent that the amount of production can be greatly increased.
4. Can circular rhythmic motions be used? Here, again, we see the influence of natural ways of doing things. Circular sweeps of the hand are more natural, less fatiguing, and more easily learned than are zigzag or direct forward motions.
5. Can the motions be made continuous? Ideally the motions should be rhythmic, requiring as little erratic interruption as possible. Less fatigue results when the movement flows smoothly and unbrokenly.

THE ESSENTIALS OF CHARTING

As data are summarized for a process involving a number of people, so may they be summarized for a sequence of operations. Because this is a different level of analysis, with much more detailed steps, the analysis of the individual job motions is typically called an operations chart.

In this type of chart the points of focus are the two hands, left and right. The things each of these hands does during a cycle of motions are minutely identified and classified into three major categories: doing, transportation, and idle. It is typical, for example, for one hand to be doing nothing while the other is performing work. In such a case the effort in motion economy would be to get the idle hand to work.

The normal work area is shown in Figure 15—5, and Figure 15—6 is a sample of a right-and-left-hand (operator) chart, which is similar to the flow process chart but permits recording of the motion in action of the right and left hand movements.

As suggested in the discussion of motion economy, the principal points of analysis of the operations chart are (1) elimination of all unnecessary steps, and (2) elimination of those steps which do not contribute directly to the performance of the job, notably transportation and idle time.

Work Layout

Space layout tools are closely tied to the analysis of steps for any procedure or operation. As a consequence, it is highly desirable that you add another dimension to your analysis by making a layout chart to accompany the process or operations chart. This is simply a sketch or drawing of the work place, preferably indicating the flow of work. The layout chart should:

1. Make it possible to plot the walking distances involved in getting work done
2. Show the flow of work from one location to another

3. Identify poor arrangements of work stations in relation to one another
4. Show improperly located equipment and facilities, such as files, telephones, and machines.

The particular advantage of the layout chart, like the floor plan for a house, is that it shows the relationships of a physical situation without one's having to go through the burdensome task of creating that situation. Normally, a layout chart will include office partitions which are not movable, all equipment which occupies floor space, all major parts of the building, such as heating equipment, doors, and windows, and

FIGURE 15—5. *Normal work areas.*

SUMMARY	PRESENT		PROPOSED		DIFFERENCE		SUBJECT CHARTED	METHOD
	LH	RH	LH	RH	LH	RH		
◯ OPERATION								☐ PRESENT ☐ PROPOSED
▷ TRANSPORT							NAME OF OPERATOR	
▽ HOLD								
◗ DELAY							CHARTED BY	DATE
TOTAL								

WORK AREA LAYOUT

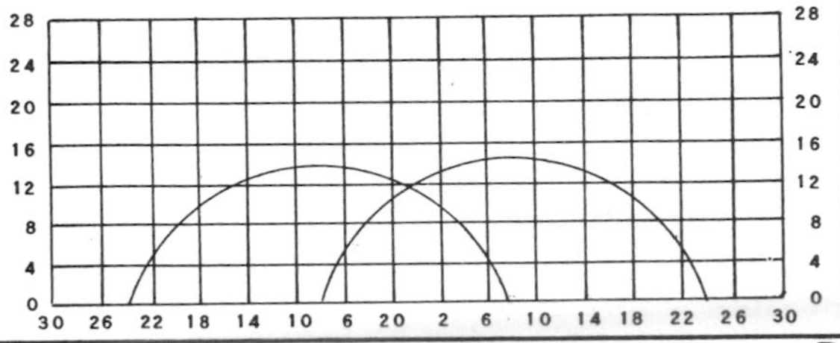

(Sketch of Parts)

SYMBOLS: ◯ - Operation; ▷ - Transport; ▽ - Hold; ◗ - Delay.

NOTES	LEFT HAND	RIGHT HAND	NOTES
	◯▷▽◗	◯▷▽◗	
	◯▷▽◗	◯▷▽◗	
	◯▷▽◗	◯▷▽◗	
	◯▷▽◗	◯▷▽◗	
	◯▷▽◗	◯▷▽◗	
	◯▷▽◗	◯▷▽◗	
	◯▷▽◗	◯▷▽◗	
	◯▷▽◗	◯▷▽◗	
	◯▷▽◗	◯▷▽◗	
	◯▷▽◗	◯▷▽◗	
	◯▷▽◗	◯▷▽◗	
	◯▷▽◗	◯▷▽◗	
	◯▷▽◗	◯▷▽◗	
	◯▷▽◗	◯▷▽◗	
	◯▷▽◗	◯▷▽◗	
	◯▷▽◗	◯▷▽◗	
	◯▷▽◗	◯▷▽◗	
	◯▷▽◗	◯▷▽◗	
	◯▷▽◗	◯▷▽◗	
	◯▷▽◗	◯▷▽◗	

FIGURE 15—6. *Right- and left-hand (operator) chart.*

many other components which may affect the conduct of work.

The design of a layout chart is done by drawing the floor plan to scale, including all permanently and semipermanently placed objects. Then each item of movable equipment is inserted. Templates (patterns) for all the standard types of office equipment, including files, desks, and chairs, are available in local stationery stores. Templates, generally based on a scale of one-quarter inch equals one foot, are significant time savers for layout work.

Obviously, there can be innumerable arrangements for space and equipment. When a very large police department moved into a new building, each unit within the department had to design its own layout. To facilitate this work the department had all the commonly used pieces of equipment made up as scale model blocks. Each block had a small magnet, and the board on which the space diagram was drawn was of metal (thus reducing the risk of someone's accidentally upsetting the labor of several hours). Sets were furnished to each of the units of the department, and generally satisfactory space arrangements were rapidly developed. A minimum of rearrangement was required when the new building was occupied.

CONSTRUCTING A LAYOUT CHART

It is first necessary to get a picture of present layout arrangements, which normally means drafting a scaled drawing of the present floor area. Then the equipment (in the form of templates) is inserted in the drawings or, if blocks are used, on the space board. When an attempt is made to relate the space layout to a particular procedure such as the application for a building permit, it is highly desirable to draw lines showing the path of that document from one desk and office to another. Figure 15—7 shows how such lines provide a useful picture of distance relationships in various steps of this process.

In developing space improvements, many of the principles of process analysis are applicable, especially to develop a system where work flows forward in as straight a line as possible, with backtracking held to a minimum. Other points to be considered in developing space improvements are:

1. Placement of work materials and equipment.
2. Provision for effective supervision. Requirements for supervision and proximity to subordinates are important in determining what arrangement will best aid in directing, controlling, and reviewing the work performed in a unit.
3. Comfort and safety of workers.
4. Attractiveness An attractive office layout obviously enhances the public relations of a municipality.
5. Economy. Every effort should be made to keep space requirements to a minimum and thus to release any unneeded floor space.

Basic standards for office layout have been developed on the basis of years of experience that provide some guidelines. These are:

1. Each person should be provided with an area of at least eighty to one hundred square feet.
2. Main aisles should be four to five feet in width; side aisles, three to four feet in width.
3. The seating space between desks should be approximately three feet.
4. Large open spaces should be provided for light and ventilation.
5. Persons doing close work should be placed in the best light.
6. No one should be placed in a position facing the light.

In a shop situation, criteria will depend primarily on the kind of work done, the machinery being used, and the nature of the building in which the work takes place.

EVALUATING LAYOUT PROPOSALS

When a new layout plan has been developed according to the guidelines above, it may then be evaluated in terms of two criteria. The first is square footage of space. If the proposed layout contains all the required equipment, conforms generally to standards, and at the same time reduces the total amount of space necessary for the operation, it can be presumed to be desirable.

The second criterion may be used when lines of flow for a particular process have been identified on the layout chart (Figure 15—7). These lines of flow may be measured, and if the

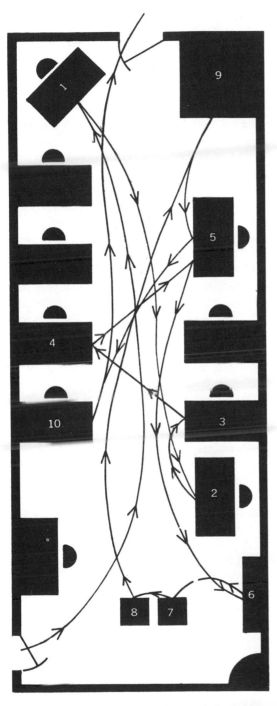

Before study   After study

FIGURE 15—7. *Layout chart.*

distance required to complete the procedure is less than in the present method it may again be presumed that the proposed change is desirable.

The supervisor should recognize the value of space analysis in the preparation of his budgetary requests. Where sincere efforts have been made to plan carefully for space usage, analysis can prove an important aid in securing necessary extra space. In other words, the typical rejoinder to a request for additional area is: "How do we know that the present space allocation is used at maximum efficiency?" Analysis provides the answer to this question and effectively states the need for an increased allocation.

Forms Design

Forms and documents are important aids to the conduct of municipal business, but any particular form or document must be *proved* necessary. It should be clear that the material which it contains cannot be found in an acceptable form elsewhere, e.g., in a letter or in another form. And a necessary form will only justify itself if it reflects the most efficient means of obtaining, storing, or disseminating useful information.

Most offices have to use a great many forms, and the resulting work occupies a significant part of the time of their staff. It is therefore essential that office forms be designed to require minimum effort on the part of those who have to fill them out and use them—whether municipal employees or members of the public.

Even the best forms can usually be improved on from time to time, if only because needs and circumstances change. Thus, systematic review of forms is generally worth the time. In one federal agency, for example, examination of 1,613 forms over a period of fifteen months resulted in major changes affecting about 10 percent of them (61 abolished or combined with other forms, 42 reduced in size, and 60 redesigned); many others were slightly amended, and a few new ones were introduced.

Many defects in forms are the result of designing forms without paying sufficient attention to the beginnings and ends of work (e.g., concentrating on information required without considering the sources from which it will be drawn or the way in which it will be used.

COLLECTING, ASSEMBLING, AND ANALYZING DATA

Ideally, forms should always be studied within the context of the whole procedure for which they are required and in relation to associated work that may be done in other branches or departments. The beginnings and ends of the work should be considered as well as the main processes. It is particularly important to see the complete process when other processes, e.g., copying or recording, may be undertaken before or after the main process reflected on the form. Therefore, before a form is designed or redesigned one must seek up-to-date facts about: the procedure; the purposes for which the form is required; the circumstances in which it will be completed, dispatched, filed, sorted and handled; and, where relevant, a variety of other information, such as the cost and effectiveness of arrangements and operations, the incidence of errors in completion, queries and difficulties, and the scope for possible change.

Review of forms begins with consulting: (1) employees responsible for the form or work (and examining completed samples of the forms and any associated documents); (2) staff whose work is or will be associated with the form at any stage, in all branches of the office; (3) persons who complete or may have to complete the form at any stage, inside or outside the department; (4) any departmental committee established to advise on forms used by the public; and (5) any other departments or organizations known to use similar forms.

Collecting Data. The collection of all the data needed as a basis for designing a form demands thoroughness and an inquiring and challenging attitude. It will also require some imagination and inventiveness, because the questions to be raised should help produce information which will show better ways of doing the job.

The questions used in collecting data will vary, of course, but the following should invariably be asked: (1) *What* causes the work (and therefore gives rise to the form)? What are the purposes of the form, the operation, and the procedure? What are the essential needs or unalterable limitations? (2) *How* is the work done? What are the processes, operations, and documents involved? (3) *Why* is the work done in the manner prescribed? (4) *Who* does the work and to what extent? (5) *Where* is the work done and what limitations does this impose? (6) *When* is the work done and what limitations does this impose? (7) *Which* related activities need consideration with the form or work being studied?

Whenever practicable, figures should be obtained on: the number of operations undertaken and of forms completed; volume of arrears at selected points in time; time taken to do work or complete forms; costs of the various stages of work; and number and nature of errors and other indications of ineffectiveness.

Assembling Data. A record of the procedures involved in the use of the form, setting out in sequence all the operations concerned, will establish the facts and aid in analysis. Usually a narrative step-by-step record is adequate, but sometimes other forms of records or charts are valuable. Where a series of forms has to be studied, it may be of advantage as an alternative to mount specimens on a large sheet of paper or linen or on a blackboard and record the associated actions alongside them. Various devices such as connecting lines to indicate movement, and colors and symbols to represent kinds of data, may then be used.

Analyzing Data. All the data should be examined and challenged. This applies not only to the actions or procedures with which the form is associated but also to the entries and explanatory notes on the form itself. Look for items that can be eliminated or reduced in length and complexity; check sequence of items carefully. In addition, question such costly features of the form as carbon patching, multicolor printing, and snapouts, which could be replaced by cheaper alternatives.

When these points have been reviewed, the way is clear to start designing the form.

Preliminary Design Factors

The process of assembling and analyzing information relating to a proposed form should make its purpose clear and establish its essential content. Various general factors likely to influence the design should then be considered.

Is a new form necessary? An existing form can sometimes be modified slightly, so that it can be used on a number of occasions. In some instances, stock items can be overprinted to meet small departmental requirements.

Should there be a new conception of the form? Can the number of forms used in a particular operation be reduced by designing a multi-purpose document? For example, a form might serve as an application for the public; it may serve both as a record of internal processing and as a notification of the action taken. Or an envelope or pouch may be designed to serve as both a file container for correspondence and an action record.

How should the needs of those using the form influence its design? Forms which are hard to understand and fill out will almost certainly cause more work in receiving departments.

How will working conditions influence design? If the form is to be used out of doors or in a dirty working area, for example, design may be influenced by these factors. The use of a form may be facilitated by such design factors as a special layout to speed up key punching, a particular shape or color to facilitate sorting, prescribed line spacing for office machines, and fixed sizes and shapes for filing equipment.

Layout and Style

The layout and style of the material included in a form merit careful consideration. This is not a question merely of the appropriateness of detail but is a question of the psychological impact of the form as a whole. Various factors contribute to acceptance and effective use of the form. These include: the apparent reasonableness of the demand for information; the choice and format of the heading; the location and content of notes and instructions; continuity from left to right and top to bottom; and the demands of machines, ranging from vertical spacing for forms filled out on a typewriter to coded rectangles and circles that are filled by pencil for a machine reading input to data processing.

Instructions. The instructions needed for an entry on a form are most likely to be effective if they are placed immediately before and adjacent to the entry. The use of asterisks or other symbols involving frequent reference to footnotes or to instructions overleaf can be irritating, especially if the form is in a typewriter, and greatly increases the possibility of errors.

General instructions concerning regulations, the number of copies, the disposal of the document, etc., can be confusing if they are scattered about in different places on the form. The users of a form do not always read the whole form before starting to complete the entries; they generally start at the top and work through to the bottom. Generally, any important instructions seen too late will be ignored.

Care is needed to avoid asking for what is difficult or impossible. For example, a request "Please do not fold" is irritating if the document cannot be enclosed in the average pocket, envelope, or handbag.

All notes and instructions should be classified (notes about entries, background information, notes about regulations, general notes about the number of copies, notes about disposal of the form enclosures, etc.). The layout and grouping should then be decided on, using the following guidelines:

1. Bring all general instructions together and place at the top of the form.
2. Write the instructions clearly, concisely, and courteously.
3. Place notes about specific entries above or at the side of entry spaces so they can be read before the entry is made.
4. Pretest the instructions (as part of a pretest of the entire form) by asking a sampling of employees and citizens to fill out the form.

Simplifying Entries. The work of completing a form may be simplified if a series of likely answers to a question is given and the means of choosing the appropriate answer indicated. Another advantage is that answers are usually obtained with precision and consistency. The methods adopted to indicate a choice may be: (1) boxes alongside the stated answers, requiring an X or a check to be entered opposite the chosen answer; (2) words or phrases to be ringed by the person completing the form; or (3) words or phrases not applicable which are to be deleted.

Mixed methods of indicating a choice on the same form can be confusing and can cause errors. Changes in method of indicating choice should be avoided, especially if they involve a complete reversal of thought.

Spacing Allowance for Entries. Adequate space must be provided for easy completion of entries; spaces which are too small (a common fault) slow down completion of the form. It is best if each entry is considered separately and given the space it needs.

The spacing proposed for a new form should be tested by making a range of specimen entries with any of the writing instruments likely to be used for completing the form, allowing for variations in sizes of handwriting and for differences in spacing required for different kinds of typewriter characters. The spacing should cater to entries of normal length.

The size of the entry space or column should be determined by the size of the entry, not by the size of the caption. When the caption is too long to fit the width of a column, the following methods may be useful: abbreviating; coding or numbering; dividing long words over two lines; and printing sloping or vertical headings.

Entries by Keyboard Accounting Machines. The advice given for typewritten entries applies in a general way to entries made by accounting and bookkeeping machines—i.e., the form should be designed to reduce carriage and platen movement.

Documents providing information for posting into accounts by machine should be designed to be used easily by the machine operator. For example, items identifying the account should be placed prominently at the top of the form, and other information should be arranged to reduce eye movement. Entries on related documents should be arranged in a sequence convenient for copying.

There are often substantial space limitations on the design of forms for accounting machines, since certain entries may be tied to particular print positions. Therefore, it may be desirable to consult a machine company's representative if the most is to be made of the equipment available.

Input and Output Documents for Punched Cards. In most punched card systems a number of preliminary operations are needed to prepare information. These operations vary from job to job, depending on the type of source document, where and how it is completed, the amount of checking necessary, and whether some of the information is required for uses other than punched cards. The design of output documents turns largely on the characteristics of the tabulator or printer employed.

Although there is a gradual increase in the use of mark sensing, character reading, and other techniques for preparing "machine language" data as a by-product of other operations, most systems still involve the transcription of fresh data from source documents into punched cards or punched paper tape.

GRAPHIC DESIGN

Concurrently with the above steps, consideration should be given to the graphic structure and other design elements involving layout, selection of type faces and sizes, use of rules and boxes, size of the form, kind of paper, and use of color. Design elements are integrated to aid effective communication and rational gathering of data in a process known professionally as "graphic design."

On the basis of experience with corporate identity programs (which include office forms along with letterheads, signs, and many other visual materials), some standards have evolved for office forms. These include: a standardized grid system to make it easier to add new forms from time to time within a uniform format; a minimum of rules and boxes, with careful use of space to provide emphasis; restrained typography with limited use of oversized type, words in all capital letters, boldface, and italic type, so that emphasis is made by contrast; and consistent placement and use of the organization name and address and other identifying information.

Graphic design usually calls for professional help. It is a good investment if done on a programmed basis as part of an overall review of forms and procedures.

Space Planning, Furniture, and Equipment

Office space has been discussed earlier in relation to work flow and placement of desks and other office furniture and equipment to facilitate operations.

Another kind of space planning is involved when a new municipal or county building is on the drawing boards. This is the time when major decisions are made about location of departments, provision of private offices, use of certain floor coverings, lighting standards, etc. Space planning on a major scale also is involved when a department or other unit moves into an existing building; in this case, of course, the total dimensions are fixed and the task is to allocate personnel, furniture, and equipment within that area.

In either case, many of the space planning tasks are similar: deciding on who gets private offices; setting square footage standards by types of jobs; locating reception rooms and other public areas; consulting with the telephone company representatives on number, location, and types of telephone extensions and stations; studying the perennial problem of centralized versus decentralized files, etc.

If the project involves new construction or major alterations, the work may be included in architectural services. Interior designers often work side by side with municipal personnel during the entire process. Under some circumstances it can be a do-it-yourself operation.

No matter how space planning is conducted, however, a few features are increasingly seen in contemporary office interiors:

1. The "office landscape," a system of modular and easily assembled partitions, provides great flexibility, economy, and good appearance. Its principal advantage is recognition that most offices, and other work sites as well, are constantly changing to meet changing job and program requirements. Therefore, the office plan must combine a modular system with open space to meet these needs. It is much too expensive to knock out and rebuild conventional floor-to-ceiling partitions.
2. A reduction in the number of private offices is a trend that is highly visible in banks and in savings and loan associations. The trend is spreading to other organizations. Private offices are expensive, and they also can be a barrier to the kinds of organizational relationships stressed in this book.

3. An attractive appearance is considered an investment in employee morale as well as a part of good public relations. Hopefully, the day of dreary government offices with regimental rows of desks and chairs is passing.

4. Careful attention is given to built-in features: air conditioning, floor coverings, building exits, and lighting.

OFFICE FURNITURE

The range of office furniture seems almost endless, and the claims and counterclaims for style, durability, and prestige are confusing indeed to the person who enters this arena for the first time. This is an area, however, where competition is keen, and competitive bidding can bring substantial savings—provided certain general guidelines are followed.

1. Look for modular pieces, especially chairs, sofas, and benches for reception areas. Most manufacturers now offer them. Modular pieces provide flexibility and economy.

2. Consider metal and plastic instead of wood for some applications. This may not be a popular point of view—some people do hold strong views on this—but cleaning and custodial costs may be lower.

3. Consider vinyl and other synthetic fabrics. Although they are not necessarily cheaper to buy, the cleaning costs are lower.

4. Use carpet on floors. Although initial costs may seem high, substantial savings in custodial and cleaning costs have been reported by libraries and many other institutional users.

5. Avoid anything that is permanently built in—files, storage cabinets, bookcases, and coat closets are examples.

With space at a premium and with insufficient areas to store chairs, particularly for reception rooms, waiting rooms, auditoriums, and training rooms, consideration should be given to purchase of chairs that stack and interlock. These are easily rolled away when stacked on heavy steel dollies.

Executive chairs should be comfortable and should be of heavy steel frame with swivel casters. Typist and stenographer chairs should have fingertip control for adjusting seat heights with a comfortable, upholstered seat. Most new upholstered pieces look and feel comfortable, but long-lasting comfort can result only from careful selection of materials and insistence on high standards of workmanship.

OFFICE EQUIPMENT

Desks, files, and equipment should be placed where they are most convenient to the person or persons who must use them. This means that less time will be wasted in rerouting forms, filing, looking up files, borrowing manuals, and searching for reference materials.

Following are some examples of office equipment and materials that have been tested by experience.

Acoustical Materials. Efficiency is promoted by the balanced use of acoustical ceiling, wall, and post materials as well as carpeting, draperies, and fabric-covered acoustical partitions. Acoustical materials offer efficient, highly individualized methods of balancing sound levels. Acoustical ceiling tile, for example, will trap up to 70 percent of excess sound. A large open floor plan reducing the spread of sound is a prime design consideration. Foot noise can be reduced by carpeting in hallways and corridors. Carpeting is also desirable in high traffic paths within the office area.

Another basic step is to cut noises at their source. Quiet operation should become a prominent requirement for office machines. Noisy machines should be isolated, where possible. Typewriters can be strategically placed so that their sound can be minimized by nearby sound-absorbing materials.

Carpeting. Economic and psychological factors combine to justify carpeting an entire office complex. In a typing pool or machine room, for example, the sound deadening properties of carpeting eliminate distraction and increase efficiency. In a file room or mail room, the soft underfooting reduces fatigue. Carpeting also has an enormous effect in raising employee morale.

Another major factor in the increased use of carpeting is low maintenance cost. Tests of the costs of building cleaning services show, on a daily basis, that maintenance is about the same between hard and soft surface floorings. Running a vacuum cleaner over a carpet takes about the same length of time as dry mopping of a floor, but there the similarity ends. Hard surface floors require additional care at least once a month, when the floor must be washed thoroughly, allowed to dry, and then waxed and polished. Carpet in the same office needs only complete shampooing once a year.

Telephones. Even small offices whose requirements are relatively uncomplicated should be aware of the various kinds of telephones available. The local telephone company will be able to advise on each problem; independent communication consulting firms can also be used.

Some telephone systems currently in use by many public agencies and private companies include: Centrex, a system of direct dialing to extensions in large offices, thus reducing the load on the switchboard and cutting down the number of operators needed; WATS (Wide Area Telephone Service), an open lease line for high-traffic corridors; and conference calls, a network for large organizations with field offices for rapid dissemination of information.

Picturephone equipment, on the threshold of communications technology, should, with its potential for bridging time, distance, and visibility, be of significant future help to management in making more effective use of key personnel.

Typewriters. Here, again, choose equipment wisely. Take one simple example of obvious savings. Although an electric typewriter costs $250 to $300 more than a manual machine, including maintenance and electricity, the cost is quickly recaptured in the increased productivity of the typist. Therefore, the days of manual typewriters for offices are almost over.

The same kind of calculation can tell you whether a piece of equipment is too expensive for your needs. It is obviously uneconomical to pay for a copier with a capacity of 500 copies an hour when you use only 1,000 copies a month.

Summary

Much of this chapter has described some management tools for work simplification which are relatively simple to adopt and use. At the same time, limitations must be recognized. You must still identify your problem, obtain your facts, and draw your conclusions. These tools, namely the work distribution chart, the work process chart, the operations chart, and the layout chart function principally as a means of summarizing data graphically. Thus, you have a better chance to see the problem as a whole and to make sure you have all relevant data.

The work process chart (Figures 15—3 and 15—4) is perhaps the most important of the tools suggested in this chapter. Its purpose is to help trace a person, an item, or a form from the beginning of its travel to the end. It shows who comes in contact with the processing of a form, what each does, in what sequence these contacts occur, and how each contributes to accomplishment. Unnecessary steps, backtracking, duplication of effort, excessive time consumption, and poor layout for the flow of work can be identified.

The operations chart (right and left hand) (Figure 15—6) is similar in theory to the process chart. The scale of its interest is the primary difference. Instead of being concerned with the relationships between steps of a procedure, it tends to focus on the way in which a single step is handled. Thus, a process chart is normally drawn before an operations chart. The former would identify general areas of improvement; if a single job is the problem, the operations chart would be utilized.

Operations charts are most useful where the work is repetitive, where large numbers of people do the work, or where a single job occupies a strategic place in the flow of a great volume of work. Industry has found greater use for such detailed analysis. Nonetheless, supervisors in a number of municipal operations will find this technique highly useful.

The layout chart (Figure 15—7) is designed primarily to provide a picture of physical relationships. How is the space being used? Can physical rearrangements improve efficiency in the work situation? Can they improve safety? Can they make surroundings more pleasant? The layout chart is particularly helpful in obtaining a sense of the physical situation and its relationship to flow of work without actually going through the burdensome business of moving things. Templates and scale model cutouts and blocks are particularly helpful.

These tools are not new in the literature of administration. In the hands of specialists they often become highly detailed and complicated, but the basic ideas remain the same. Remember, they are only tools. If you find yourself confused rather than aided, forget them and make a commonsense study of the work situation. Never make the mistake of becoming overly attached to a pretty graph or chart. It is important to recognize that there is never really a permanent "solution" to the systems problem.

A part of this chapter has dealt with the work environment as reflected in forms design and space planning and equipment.

Although seldom considered "environmental," office forms do provide a significant means of communication and a framework of the internal and external procedures and facts that guide work in process.

A form is a means of getting a job done with maximum efficiency. Once forms are established, their design may govern a procedure for a long period; unfortunately, there are many examples of quite unsuitable forms continuing in use for years. A good manager checks to see that all relevant factors are considered before a new form is designed and brought into use, and he insists that existing forms be regularly and critically reviewed. He regards a good form as a valuable tool of administration, a good workman inside the organization, and a good ambassador outside the department.

Physical space, furniture, office machines, and special equipment make up the more visible environment for work analysis. The most important trend in the past generation has been the integration of space planning, work programming, and interior design into a systems approach. The approach is useful in most applications, even for small offices, because it stresses operations and movement of work, traffic patterns of employees and the public; and flexibility to meet changing needs. Change is taken as a constant assumption that conditions all planning. The idea of systematic adaptability to change is certainly not new, but its emphasis in office space planning is a notable recent development.

The range of furniture, typewriters, desk calculators, file cabinets, and other office products is so large that it would be futile to even attempt to summarize it here. Fortunately, a great deal of testing has been done, comparative experience data often can be located, competitive bidding often is feasible, and sources of expert help are readily available. Computer technology—a term that includes not only hardware and software but also correlative applications in photography, television, telephone, radio, printing, archives, and other forms of information processing—is the area that will be of greatest interest, concern, and value for work analysis in the future.

---

[1]John K. Parker, "Administrative Analysis," in MANAGING THE MODERN CITY, ed. James M. Banovetz (Washington, D.C.: International City Management Association, 1971), p. 264.

Part Five

Employee Relations and the Public

Introduction

If you're not part of the solution, you're part of the problem.

ELDRIDGE CLEAVER

THE ENVIRONMENT, the area outside the municipal organization, is the primary subject of the last four chapters of this book. This is the world of the mayor and city council, the citizens residing in the municipality, the labor unions, and the many citizen groups and associations, structured and unstructured, that interact in the governmental process. This is the more political part of management in the sense of the formulation, adoption, implementation, and modification of policies that directly affect services. Several aspects of the environment could have been added—intergovernmental relations, economic development, federal grantsmanship, and the role of public education—but for purposes of this book the most important subjects are labor relations, public information, and citizen participation.

Unionization of government employees was a trend widely noted during the sixties and early seventies. The introductory pages of Chapter 16 indicate some of the reasons for this recent trend. One especially important reason from the management point of view is the breakdown, both legally and operationally, of the distinction between employment in the private and public sectors. Organized labor sees little if any difference between public and private employment, and it is increasingly difficult for managers and supervisors to maintain that "governmental soverignty" or some other legalistic concept precludes recognition and collective bargaining. Chapter 16 will help you understand the implications of these developments in the discussions on collective negotiations, strikes, arbitration, and grievance procedures.

Specific guidelines for labor relations management are set forth in Chapter 17 which explains the step-by-step procedures that take place before the union arrives, during the time when the union is seeking status, preparing for negotiations, conducting negotiations, handling impasse procedures, and administering labor contracts.

Public information, the subject of Chapter 18, is a very broad subject, and only a few suggestions can be provided here. Perhaps the most important parts of the chapter deal with relationships with the public and the press.

The public, as writers on public relations and public information constantly point out, is made up of many publics representing a variety of interests and values. Some are well organized and identifiable associations like the local chamber of commerce or the local ministerial society; others are amorphous but permanent groups like senior citizens; still others come and go on the basis of issues like groups that may spring up in favor of or in opposition to a referendum on a bond issue.

In dealing with the press, specific suggestions can be offered that benefit both the municipal government and the journalists who are covering governmental affairs. In dealing with newsmen an attitude of trust and respect goes a long way toward building beneficial relationships.

It seems appropriate to close this book with a chapter on the encouraging start that has been made in redefining citizen participation as part of municipal government. Citizen participation always has been an ideal, but it can be irritating, upleasant, and even disruptive when citizens decide to go outside the normal electoral processes to make themselves heard. Predictions always are hazardous, but it does seem likely, given long-term trends in this country in technology, education, economic development, and social mobility, that citizen participation outside normal institutional channels is here to stay. We still have a great deal to learn in this area. Chapter 19 of this book provides some tentative guidelines which are based on the limited experience that is at present available. If the ideals of the social process of the organization as described in so many parts of this book meet your values, then the ideals of citizen participation should be equally worth while.

16

Development, Status, and Procedures for Labor Relations

THE APPROPRIATENESS of collective bargaining in the public sector is a value question. Those who deny its usefulness generally are officials and administrators of public government, while its advocates are the representatives of certain groups of employees. Rightness or wrongness can be defined as a power equation that until very recently has been heavily weighted to deny collective bargaining. Legitimacy for the position that collective bargaining in the public sector is inappropriate has a long history of support through law, administrative rules, generalized statements of sovereignty, the idea that authority cannot be delegated, and the position that public employees are servants of the public trust.

Since 1962, when Executive Order 10988 was put into effect in the federal government, the power equation has shifted toward a relatively more balanced position. The extreme forms of unilateral policy making and administration have gradually given ground to a more broadly based process. Evidence is reflected in growth trends in public employee organizing.

In 1956 membership in government unions numbered 915,000, or 5.1 percent of total union membership of 18.1 million. By 1968 union membership among government employees was 2.2 million or 10.9 percent of total union membership.[1] The U.S. Bureau of Labor Statistics reported that union and association membership in government had increased from 3.86 million in 1968 to 4.08 million in 1970. At least one third of all public employees were members of unions and associations in that year. While federal employee organization membership continued to represent a greater proportion of total employment in public government than state and local membership, growth was greater at the state and local levels.[2] Employee associations, now generally adopting the same approaches to organizing, representation, and bargaining as unions, continue to play a significant role in public employee organizing. The National Education Association, with its one million plus membership, is predominant among teachers. The state associations affiliated with the Assembly of Government Employees continue to show increased membership along with the increased membership of municipal associations.

It can be concluded as a generalization, then, that increasing numbers of public employees are organizing into unions and associations. Why this is so is not so easy to ascertain. Recently assigned causes have included a progressively inflationary economy, wage inequities between the private sector and the public sector, and a growing militancy in our society generally.[3] It is possible that such causes are in reality only manifestations of deeper, more basic reasons. Over the years there have been a number of scholarly efforts to explain employee organizing. Let us briefly examine some of these.

Assumptions on Employee Organizing

The Division of Labor Studies at the Yale Institute of Human Relations has for years sought answers to the question of why employees join or do not join an organization such as a union. From these inquiries a major theoretical hypothesis has been developed:

The worker reacts favorably to union membership in proportion to the strength of his belief that this step will reduce his frustrations and anxieties and will further his opportunities relevant to the achievement of his standards of successful living. He reacts unfavorably in proportion to the strength of his belief that this step will increase his frustrations and anxieties and will reduce his opportunities relevant to the achievement of such standards.[4]

Robert F. Hoxie approached organizing from a sociopsychological framework. Hoxie felt that man is primarily concerned with his standard of living. Man's hopes and fears center primarily on such issues as employment, wages, hours, and conditions of work, in short, the most vital concerns which touch his present and future well-being. In attempting to comprehend and deal with these matters individuals develop an interpretation of the situation as viewed from their particular needs and experiences. Hoxie stated:

It is evident that under these circumstances workers similarly situated economically and socially, closely associated and not too divergent in temperament and training, will tend to develop a common interpretation of the social situation and a common solution of the problem of living. This may come about gradually and spontaneously, or it may be the apparently sudden outcome of some crisis in the lives of the men concerned. It may, for example, result immediately from some alteration for the worse in the conditions of living; or an interference with what are considered established rights and modes of action, of which cases in point would be wholesale discharges from employment or the discharge of favorite individuals, a lowering of the wage rate, the requirement of more onerous or more dangerous conditions of work, a sudden rise in the prices of necessities, some police action or legal decision which touches the workers on the raw with respect to modes of action or their assumed dignity and rights as men. Or this crystallization of sentiment may come about as the result of the appearance from without or the rise from within the group of a purposeful agitator and leader . . . who is capable of offering a positive solution of their difficulties. But whatever the immediate cause, the result is the same. A social group is thus constituted, marked off by a more or less unified and well-developed but effective viewpoint or group psychology. . . . As soon as this state of affairs has been reached group action is a natural consequence.[5]

Frank Tannenbaum addressed himself to the restoration of social status, the union or association providing group norms around which employees could establish fellowship and share in a common system of beliefs about work and its environment.[6] John R. Commons, writing about the early American shoemakers, stated that it was the widening of the markets for shoes that destroyed the community of interest and trust between employer and employee and split them into the alignment of employers' association and trade union.[7] Commons's thesis was that as markets for shoes expanded journeymen were increasingly forced to make shoes at lower wages. As a result they combined to protect themselves.

More recently, a report of the U.S. Advisory Commission on Intergovernmental Relations focused on a number of issues that may be creating an environment of public organization discontent. One of these is the failure of administrators, either through carelessness or ignorance, to consult with their employees about policies and procedures that affect their lives. The study pointed out that many public administrators continue to be wedded to an absolutist management ethic.[8] In all fairness, these observations must be tempered by the knowledge that frequently the administrator himself has little influence in making policy. Caught between commissions, legislators, city councils, and the employees, he lives in a state of frustration.

Finally, federal Executive Order 10988, issued in 1962, has also stimulated employee organizational growth at the state and local levels.[9] Certainly there is considerable merit to that assumption. The order (together with subsequent orders) has undoubtedly acted as a catalyst for public employees seeking relatively greater control over organizational activities that so vitally affect their lives. It should be recognized, however, that these executive orders and other public policies providing the right to organize frequently follow de facto attempts by employees.

At times, significant time lags exist between attempts to organize and the initiation of policy. It is in these periods that considerable conflict can and frequently does occur. It is at these critical times that public administrators, legislators, a conservative press, and many unknowledgeable citizens can overreact to employee organizing efforts and connect such behavior to conspiracy, to an extension of the alleged contemporary revolt against authority, or to various protest efforts by groups involved in direct confrontation with governmental power. From this perspective, attempts to organize may be seen by some administrators as attacks on governmental sovereignty, threats to public service, and illegal and antisocial behavior that must be stopped at any cost.

These are dangerous views that oversimplify actual events and transfer the complex causes of unrest to convenient scapegoats, thus relieving public leadership of any responsibility for the conflict. Failure of the public administrator to see these issues clearly can lead to increased organizational strife.

Labor Relations and Public Policy

Two primary legislative approaches have emerged as policy guides at the state and local levels. One is the meet-and-confer approach and the other is collective bargaining. The Advisory Commission on Intergovernmental Relations in its 1969 report formalized these two approaches by outlining the distinctive provisions of each.[10]

The basic difference rests with the status accorded the public employer regarding wages, hours, and working conditions. The employer under a meet-and-confer approach retains the right to make policy unilaterally with the employee representative's role primarily confined to discussion of issues. With collective bargaining, the employer and employee representatives meet more nearly as equals. Policy is formulated side by side and management's rights are more restricted. The latter approach resembles the labor relations pattern found in the private sector, although the right to strike has generally been prohibited.[11]

STATE AND LOCAL DEVELOPMENT

At the beginning of 1971, forty states had enacted legislation authorizing some form of collective activity by public employees; eight states had no legislation, and two prohibited any such activity. In twenty-five of the forty states, mandatory negotiations of either the meet-and-confer or collective bargaining type were required. In the other fifteen states the option to meet and confer or to bargain was left to the discretion of the employer. In 1970 Pennsylvania and Hawaii enacted comprehensive legislation, as did Minnesota in 1971. Seventeen states now have comprehensive mandatory collective bargaining legislation on the books.[12]

PROPOSED LEGISLATION

As significant as the rash of new public policy is the AFL-CIO public employee unions proposals for attaining uniform legislation governing state and local employees. In 1971 these unions were successful in lobbying for the introduction into Congress of a National Public Employee Relations Act. Further, they have drafted a model state bargaining law for the public sector. The statute, if enacted, would provide for a National Public Employee Relations Commission to administer the law. It also would permit exemption of state or political subdivisions that enact legislation reasonably equivalent to the proposed national labor law. The state model, like the national proposal, calls for a state board for administrative purposes. Both the national and state proposals would provide for: protection of the right to organize; machinery for determining representation rights; procedures for handling unfair labor practices; negotiation on the agency shop; and fact finding in the event of an impasse in collective bargaining. Supervisors would be excluded from bargaining units.[13]

The National Education Association has introduced into Congress a bill entitled the Professional Negotiations Act for Public Education which, if enacted, would cover professional employees of boards of education, excluding superintendents. The provisions of the bill include the establishment of a Professional Education Employee Commission in the U.S. Department of Health, Education, and Welfare (HEW) to administer the act. The commission would conduct hearings in recognition disputes and provide for runoff elections. Either party could call on the commission for mediation and, if agreed to by the parties, advisory arbitration. The arbitrator's recommendations would be binding only if both parties agreed. Strikes would be permitted, but injunctions could be issued where the start or continuance of a dispute would pose a danger to the public health or safety or where the employee representative had failed to utilize all other available means to settle the conflict. Unfair labor practices would be made explicit, with the commission authorized to issue complaints, hold hearings, and, if necessary, issue orders. States with statutes essentially equivalent to the proposed legislation would be eligible to apply for exemption from the federal act.[14]

IMPLICATIONS FOR MANAGEMENT

Although we may be a long way from being certain how to handle the problems and issues raised by collective negotiations in the public sector, their presence is an established fact. The enactment of new legislation in many states plus the amending of established law and executive orders all signal the institutionalizing of the process. Management at all levels of public government must prepare to meet the challenge. The supervisor at every level of management must be prepared to understand the emerging law as well as the bargaining and administrative processes. These are not episodic events but are bound together so that one impinges on and critically affects the other.

It is reasonable to assume that emerging labor law will influence the development of organization policy. It can be further assumed that the supervisor will be deeply involved in administering and possibly helping to develop that internal policy. Without at least a working knowledge of the legal framework, serious miscalculations and costly errors could occur.

The emerging patterns suggested above are particularly important at the municipal and county levels of government. A 1969 survey of all cities in the United States of over 10,000 population (undertaken by the Advisory Commission on Intergovernmental Relations and the International City Management Association) revealed that approximately two-thirds of 1,357 municipalities had not enacted any laws dealing with unions or associations.[15] What this means is that municipal and county labor relations will most likely reflect state-enacted legislation.

State legislation appears to move in two direc-tions: (1) requiring recognition and negotiation by local government; and (2) leaving the option of negotiation to local government while protect-ing the right to organize. The positions are fur-ther complicated by the extent to which state law is comprehensive or partial in its construction.

State mandating provides additional com-plexities. States that have comprehensive legisla-tion requiring governments to recognize and negotiate with employee representatives can be expected to provide a negotiation structure that will tend to reduce conflict between the parties. Incomplete policy, coupled with local option to bargin while protecting the right to organize, will lead to increased strife. Conflict tied to organizing will be particularly critical in those states that continue to prohibit union recognition as well as bargaining.

Regardless of the approach taken, ad-ministrators at the local levels, particularly in the smaller municipalities, will experience confusion and increased conflict unless there are educational opportunities in labor relations areas. Further, to the extent that local ad-ministrators are tied to state or civil service per-sonnel policy without clear definition of their roles with respect to employee organizations, they may suffer role ambiguity, a technical term that encompasses tension, anxiety, confusion, reduced motivation, and defensive behavior.[16]

Collective Negotiations

It is in the negotiation process that the interface between employee organization and local gov-ernment as employer actually takes place. We shall limit our discussion to the two dimensions that appear to have the greatest influence, relatively speaking: (1) the kind and extent of the labor law itself, and (2) leadership patterns.

For purposes of clarity, these points will be discussed within the following framework: scope of negotiations, personnel systems, management and employee rights, good faith negotiations, and the negotiation process.

SCOPE OF NEGOTIATIONS

In fashioning amendments to the private sector National Labor Relations Act, Congress in 1947 added Section 8(d) which sought to define the obligation to bargain collectively. Section 8(d) states:

To bargain collectively is the performance of the mutual obligation of the employee and the representative of the employees to meet at reasonable times and confer in good faith with respect to wages, hours and other terms and conditions of employment, or the negotiation of an agreement, or any question arising thereunder, and the execution of a written contract incorporating any agreement reached if requested by either party, but such obligation does not compel either party to agree to a proposal or require the making of a concession.[17]

In controlling and defining the scope of bargaining, Confress, the National Labor Relations Board, and the courts have regulated what the parties can bargain about. The content of bargaining has been classified into three categories: mandatory subjects, nonmandatory but lawful subjects, and prohibited or illegal subjects. Bargaining with respect to wages, hours, and other conditions and terms of employment has been placed in the mandatory classification. The phrase "other terms and conditions of employment" has been interpreted broadly by the NLRB and the courts to include almost anything affecting the employee in work.

In the federal government service, Executive Orders 10988 and 11491 state that the parties

shall meet at reasonable times and confer in good faith with respect to personnel policies and practices and matters affecting working conditions, so far as may be appropriate under applicable laws and regulations, including policies set forth in the Federal Personnel Manual, published agency policies and regulations, a national or other controlling agreement at a higher level in the agency, and this Order. . . . In prescribing regulations relating to personnel policies and practices and working conditions, an agency shall have due regard for the obligation imposed by paragraph (a) of this section. However, the obligation to meet and confer does not include matters with respect to the mission of the agency; its budget; its organization; the number of employees; and the numbers, types, and grades of positions or employees assigned to an organizational unit, work project or tour of duty; the technology of performing its work; or its internal security practices. This does not preclude the parties from negotiating agreements providing appropriate arrangements for employees adversely affected by the impact of realignment of work forces or technological change.[18]

At the local government level the scope of negotiations is controlled and defined by the kind and extent of state labor relations policy. In states with meet-and-confer legislation management retains the right to control the emergence and maintenance of personnel policy unilaterally. Although agreement might be reached between the employer and employee representatives, the government need not abide by the agreement unless it so desires. There is, however, informal pressure to honor such aggrements even though the local requirements may be weak or lacking. It should be noted that state mandating and civil service regulations (where applicable) can have the effect of placing constraints on collective negotiations.

In those states where labor relations public policy specifies a collective bargaining approach between government and its employees, a number of relevant questions arise about the scope of negotiations. Are the merit system (where it exists) and collective negotiations compatible? Should the employee representative attempt to negotiate with an independent civil service or merit system commission if it has control over certain personnel policies? Is all merit system personnel policy off limits for purposes of negotiation?[19]

PERSONNEL SYSTEMS: PATRONAGE, APPOINTEE, AND MERIT SYSTEMS

Considerable debate and deliberation have gone on regarding the compatibility of the merit system and collective negotiations.[20]

Patronage. The patronage personnel system is still extensively used in state and local government, and, while less so at the federal level, its presence is still felt there. Many public administrators, whose positions are influenced by politics, cling to the patronage system. It provides a procedure for rewarding party loyalty; further, it leaves relatively great control over employees in the hands of individual people. Considerable resistance is generated when attempts are made to replace the patronage system with a merit system.

The Appointee Approach. With the appointee system the employee is theoretically hired on qualifications rather than on the basis of reward for party loyalty. Personnel policy, rather than being decentralized and controlled by each agency or department head, is centralized to a large extent, although individual administrators may retain some authority over final decisions on hiring and discharge. Very infrequently is there any due process or appeal machinery beyond the immediate supervisory-subordinate relationship. The appointee personnel system may have such advantages as providing relatively more qualified employees and standardizing the employment process, but it has the disadvantage of diminished individual administrator control over personnel policy formulation compared with the patronage system.

The Merit System. The Advisory Commission on Intergovernmental Relations has stated:

"The merit principle" is a concept of public personnel administration which holds that an employee's selection, assignment, promotion, and retention should be based upon his ability to perform his duties satisfactorily rather than upon his political affiliation, race, religion or other considerations extraneous to ability to perform. The "merit system" seeks to implement this concept typically through the establishment of a civil service commission having rule-making authority over such personnel matters as recruitment, examination, selection, position classification, promotion, and discipline. Frequently, these commissions also perform personnel management functions not directly relevant to the merit principle, such as grievance resolution, training, salary administration, attendance control, safety, and morale.[21]

It can be seen from the above that a merit system seriously challenges traditional authority and control over personnel policy by department heads. It transfers that authority to an independent commission. The point at which a merit system comes into conflict with collective negotiations is in bilateral determination of personnel policy as opposed to unilateral control by the merit system commission. The commission, in a very real sense, resists sharing authority over personnel policy formulation with the union, just as some administrators resist sharing it with a merit system commission. The major difference is that the commission is generally seen as an extension of management.

In the opinion of this writer, civil service personnel systems can survive along with collective negotiations. Perhaps the most meaningful approach is for employee organizations to negotiate with civil service commissions directly on personnel policies under commission authority. Once an agreement has been reached between the civil service commission and the employee representative, it would be put in writing and submitted to the legislative body for approval.

MANAGEMENT AND EMPLOYEE RIGHTS

In the public sector management rights have found protection and rationalized legitimacy in the doctrine of sovereign immunity. This doctrine was deeply embedded in the English Common Law and was followed assiduously by American courts. It is the courts that have provided the base of authority and power for protecting the doctrine against frequent challenges. The doctrine was a logical necessity in the days when England was an absolute monarchy and the king claimed to rule by divine rights. As Blackstone explained to the lawyers and intellectuals of his day:

Besides the attribute of sovereignty, the law also ascribes to the king in his political capacity absolute perfection. The king can do no wrong. . . .

The king, moreover, is not only incapable of doing wrong, but even of thinking wrong: he can never mean to do an improper thing: in him is no folly or weakness.[22]

Stripped of the shrouds of legitimacy, management rights are power created by man to control other men in organizational endeavor. Once we see this, we can explain why the working man until very recently had little or no claim to employee rights. He lacked the power, made legitimate by authority, to make any such claim stick. As Arthur Goldberg so aptly puts it:

Too many spokesmen for management assume that labor's rights are not steeped in past practice or tradition but are limited strictly to those specified in a contract; while management rights are all-inclusive except as specifically taken away by a specific clause in a labor agreement.

This view of the history of rights is not accurate; nor is it reasonable. Labor always had many inherent rights, such as the right to strike, though its exercise could lead to varying consequences; the right to organize despite interference from management, police powers, and even courts; the right to a fair share of the company's income even though this right was often denied; the right to safe, healthful working conditions with adequate opportunity for rest. Failure of management to recognize such rights does not indicate they did not exist. . . . Collective bargaining does not establish some hitherto non-existing rights; it provides the power to enforce rights of labor which the labor movement was dedicated to long before the institution of arbitration has become so widely practiced on labor relations.[23]

To the extent that the public administrator assumes unilateral right over organizational issues that affect the employee's welfare, it can be expected that he will be challenged by collective negotiations. Presently many public organizations are using legal constraints to prevent what they see as incursions into areas reserved for management.[24] In those states with meet-and-confer legislation, management rights, and thus management, are not as threatened as in states where bilateral collective bargaining legislation has been enacted. It is highly unlikely that legal attempts to place constraints on bargainable issues will be successful, particularly if those issues directly impinge on the employee's life in the organization. It would seem far more realistic to make all legal issues that directly affect the employee's welfare subject to negotiation.

Good Faith Negotiations

Negotiating in good faith is a most complex and elusive concept. It has been a constant subject of controversy in the private sector since passage of the National Labor Relations Act in 1935. Where the rights of public employees to organize and to negotiate have been made legal, federal and state legislation frequently include provisions to protect these rights and encourage good faith negotiations. These provisions are generally identified with unfair labor practices or prohibited practices and consist of obligations imposed upon employee organizations, employees, and employers.[25]

State unfair labor practices, where spelled out, tend to parallel those of the National Labor Relations Act and those of Executive Orders 10988 and 11491. As the Advisory Commission on Intergovernmental Relations points out:

The two most common statutory obligations found in all the mandatory public employee labor relations laws are preventing interference with the right of employees to organize and requiring both the employee organization and the public employer to meet and confer or bargain in good faith. Where unfair practices are listed in the statutes of States following the collective negotiation route, they may include the following items.

For Employers:

- Interference with employee rights under the law (13 States);
- Domination of employees by organizations (8 States);
- Discrimination against employees for union or concerted activities (12 States);
- Retaliation against employees for invoking their rights to participate in organizational affairs (4 States);
- Refusing to bargain in good faith with a majority representative of the employees (10 States); and
- Blacklisting any employee organization or its members to deny them employment (1 State).

For Employees:

- Refusing to bargain with the employer (10 States);
- Striking, or inducing others to strike (1 State);
- Inducing the employer to perform an unfair practice (1 State);
- Interfering with, restraining, or coercing public employees in the exercise of any rights granted of them under the terms of the law (11 States);
- Discriminating against an employee who has filed an unfair labor practice charge (1 State); and
- Blacklisting any public employer to prevent the filling of employee vacancies (1 State).[26]

The basic question is not whether unfair labor practice procedures are needed. Ample evidence is available to suggest that they are essential to meaningful negotiations between public employer and employee organization. To expect the public administrator to negotiate with an employee organization based on enlightened leadership is probably unrealistic. The concept of leadership normally does not include doing something voluntarily that will be perceived as eroding power and authority. This has been the case time and again with protective labor legislation that has weak enforcement powers. Without unfair labor practice procedures applicable to both parties, it is doubtful that much negotiation will take place. This is particularly true when one party has considerably more power than the other.

The Negotiation Process

To the extent that successful negotiations are identified by the parties as winning, the probability is high that the process will be surrounded by endless conflict before, during, and after negotiations. For the union, this may mean success in forcing all of its demands; for the employer it may mean thwarting the union effort. Walton and McKersie refer to this as the distributive win-lose model.[27] Its roots lie in the beliefs and values of the organization's (both union and management) leaders. To the extent that public administrators lobby for meet-and-confer legislation, resist employee organizing, use their power and authority to thwart bargaining, discipline employees for organizing, and the like, they are participating in a win-lose approach. For union leaders, encouraging illegal behavior, threatening slowdowns and strikes, and putting forth unreasonable demands are examples of this win-lose posture.

Unfortunately, in the public sector many aspects of the legal framework at the federal, state, and local levels encourage a win-lose context. A typical example can be seen in the International City Management Association—Advisory Commission on Intergovernmental Relations survey. Some two-thirds of the 1,357 municipalities responding had enacted little if any labor relations public policy.[28] Further evidence may be seen in the states with meet-and-confer laws. None have enumerated unfair labor practices or established comprehensive procedures for dealing with negotiational disputes. Many states have enacted no labor relations legislation, which means that attempts by employees to organize and bargain must confront all of the traditionally held power and authority of the public employer. Expensive conflict is inevitable.

The results of the above approach to negotiations by either or both parties are distrust, suspicion, and defensive behavior. One manifestation of defensive behavior is to aggressively strike out at the other party, which in turn precipitates a like response.

A number of scholars and researchers in the labor field have suggested ways of minimizing conflict in collective negotiations.[29] Walton and McKersie have proposed an integrative bargaining model, where negotiations are built on information sharing and trust. Instead of trying to win, the parties work together to find common or complementary interests and attempt to solve problems confronting both parties.[30] The authors see possible limits to the approach, particularly where economic considerations such as wages are involved. With these kinds of issues, there may be little solid ground for a problem-solving approach. Recalcitrant value positions by both parties, however, may have much to do with perceiving the bargaining environment as one where a win-lose approach is the only way out.

Who Negotiates? Negotiating a collective agreement is a complex technical process requiring professional negotiators for both union and employer. School board and city council members, department and agency heads, mayors, and commissioners may not be qualified, on grounds of time and expertise, to serve as negotiators for the public employer. This position does not imply that attorneys be used as negotiators. Lawyers with training in win-lose theory and behavior should probably be used in the limited capacity of assisting in the writing of the agreement. Further, the use of part-time consultants is discouraged, since they, like lawyers, have little commitment to the organization beyond negotiations. They will certainly not be around during the difficult period of administering the agreement. It is well to remember that the contract is only a skeletal framework; the administration of the agreement provides the flesh.

Regarding the question of decision-making responsibility, clearly defined responses are not so easy to come by. As Milton Derber has pointed out, decision-making responsibility is not easily defined for at least six reasons:

1. Decision-making responsibility of public agencies is shaped, in the first instance, by federal and state constitutions and by the manner in which constitutional provisions are interpreted and implemented. . . .
2. Few public agencies are autonomous units with the legal authority to generate their own economic resources. . . .
3. Public agencies are increasingly deriving their revenues from a multiplicity of sources rather than from a single source. . . .

4. When one agency depends upon another governmental body (whether legislative or administrative) for operating funds, it can usually expect some constraints on the use of the fund....
5. Quite apart from the revenue raising and spending question, the legislature may either retain authority or assign it to some other agency for the formulation of specific working rules which would be negotiated in the private sector.
6. Finally, rule-making in the public sector is heavily weighted by political considerations. Political power may be distributed in a wide variety of ways, ranging from nearly total concentration in a single political leader to a sharing of power by a diversity of competing power groups.[31]

It can be seen that there is frequently a problem of ascertaining who has the decision-making responsibility. Even when it is clear which departments, agencies, units, and administrative officials have a legitimate interest in and responsibility for particular terms and conditions of employment in a specific negotiating unit, it may be far from clear as to how the total package which an agreement covers can best be put together. Although municipalities are not generally legally autonomous units, but instrumentalities of a state, under normal circumstances they are responsible decision-making bodies for labor negotiations. The negotiator for the employer may be a personnel or labor relations specialist, a city department head, or a negotiating team. (This is discussed in Chapter 17.) Final authority for formulating policy and approving the agreement resides with the city council. In those municipalities with strong mayors and a political party structure, final authority could very well rest with the mayor instead. It is also possible to have a division of authority between mayor and council.[32]

Techniques of Negotiation. Where and when meetings are held, use of tape recorders, order of business, who chairs the negotiation sessions—these kinds of procedural issues and problems are best left to the parties. In some instances legislation or executive orders may specify procedures or limitations, but generally these items are best resolved by agreement among the negotiating members. If certain procedural issues are not resolvable, it is generally possible to have the state or local labor relations administrative board decide the issue. Sometimes procedures of this nature are built

into the public policy or are formulated as administrative rules to provide guidelines for behavior. Whatever procedures are followed, it should be kept clearly in mind that these prenegotiation patterns of activity will significantly influence the tone of the negotiations and their outcome.[33]

Interest Disputes

Impasse procedures revolve around two primary concerns: interests and rights. Disputes involving interests become manifest in collective negotiations, while conflicts over rights arise from interpretation of the labor agreement. The area of gravest concern presently is interest disputes. It is here that the administrator perceives his traditional management rights as being eroded away by the requirements of collective negotiations. It is here also that we find the increasingly frequent discussions, research, and writings about the strike and alternatives. It will be fruitful to look at interest disputes initially; not only is it this area which is creating more conflict, but it logically precedes discussion and analysis of disputes over rights which emerge from the language of the collective agreement itself.

Statistics on work stoppages by government employees during the sixties suggest that employees are no longer willing to accept unilateral control over organizational activities that seriously affect their lives. Between 1958 and 1968 the frequency of government employee strikes per year rose from 15 to 254, and the number of employees involved rose from 1,720 to 201,800. Man-days of idleness increased from 7,510 to 2.5 million. These strikes included eight federal government disputes involving 5,870 employees.[34]

In 1958 public employee disputes constituted 0.4 percent of all strikes, 0.08 percent of all employees involved, and 0.03 percent of total idleness. By 1968 this had risen to 5.0 percent, 7.6 percent, and 5.2 percent respectively.[35]

DISPUTE ISSUES

Wages and supplemental benefits are the most frequent strike issues; job security, the least frequent. Government employees, however, are much more likely to strike over official union recognition than are private sector employees. This is to be expected, since the legal right to organize in the private sector has been a reality for many years. From 1962 to 1968 almost 22 percent of the work stoppages in government involved union organization and security. During this same period in the private sector just under 14 percent of all strikes resulted from organizational attempts.

From 1962 to 1965 wage and supplementary benefits issues accounted for 54 percent of government disputes.[36]

SOME DEFENSIVE RESPONSES

Some public managers attempt to isolate government employees from other employee groups and convince them that they should be willing to work for the community good at the expense of rights guaranteed employees in private industry. On moral grounds, employees may be reminded of their responsibility for continued service to all citizens regardless of cost or sacrifice. On economic grounds, it may be pointed out that all governmental functions are carried on within the strict limitations of budgets, available funds, and administrative responsibility. It can be argued that conditions of employment are fixed and beyond the authority of the employer to change, therefore, they are beyond bilateral collective negotiations. In the political realm, one may support the traditional ban on employee protest and rely on court rulings, attorney general opinions, outright prohibitions on unionization, and the unwillingness of many state legislatures to enact enabling legislation. This political view may be reinforced by the rationale that the state legislature is unable to delegate authority to establish wages, hours, and other conditions of employment.[37] All of these responses tend to set up a win-lose situation and increase the probability of dysfunctional conflict as opposed to problem solving and serious negotiation.

THE LEGAL FRAMEWORK

While most federal, state, and local labor relations policies condemn the right of public employees to strike or engage in strike-related activities, experience increasingly indicates the impracticality of this approach. Cyrus F. Smythe,

associate professor of industrial relations at the University of Minnesota, points out that such a prohibition is not an effective solution to public employment collective negotiations problems from at least five standpoints:

1. Prohibition is based on weak theoretical groundwork.
2. Prohibition often cannot be enforced effectively.
3. Employee groups may utilize alternatives which prove more disruptive than a strike.
4. The public employer may use a prohibition to justify a lack of bargaining on his part.
5. Public employees are often limited by the prohibition in utilizing an adequate range of strategies in contract negotiation.[38]

More public employee strikes will encourage some of those directly affected to argue for more severe prohibitions and penalties. It can be predicted that this will precipitate increased conflict. What is needed is research on why strikes are occurring with increasing frequency and emphasis on finding alternatives to the strike. Those who seek absolute guarantees against strikes in the public service will find this possible only in a police state. Hopefully, there are alternatives which are more meaningful and which manifest concern for democratic ideology.

The Search for Alternatives

In the search for alternatives to the strike, the most productive and immediate results can come from the establishment of comprehensive state and local labor relations policies which recognize the right of public employees to organize and negotiate with the public employer. This, of course, means bilateral negotiations in good faith. It does not mean reliance solely on a meet-and-confer approach[39] based on a philosophy of continued unilateral authority, power, and control. It can be argued that meet-and-confer has little to do with bilateral negotiation in good faith—that it has much more to do with extending past practice. It can be assumed that greater numbers of strikes will occur with those governments which fail to develop comprehensive labor relations policies. Alternatives to the strike will be most needed in those governmental areas. Let us look at some of the possibilities.

COMPULSORY ARBITRATION

Employers and employees in both the private and public sectors have had relatively little experience with compulsory arbitration[40] of interest disputes. Major exceptions include private sector experience during World War II and the Korean War, when the National War Labor Board in the former case and the Wage Stabilization Board in the latter served as courts of last resort. Limited experience exists in the railroad industry, where resort to compulsory arbitration has occurred since 1963, when nationwide rail strikes threatened and fact finding and emergency boards failed to resolve the conflict.

At the state level, experience in the private sector has occurred primarily in intrastate industries. For the most part, compulsory arbitration has been a little-used procedure since the Supreme Court found a Wisconsin law unconstitutional.[41] In the public sector, at least four states have recently legislated compulsory arbitration as the final step in dealing with impasses in collective negotiations between employers and certain groups of public employees. These include Michigan (1969), Pennsylvania (1968), Rhode Island (1968), and Wyoming (1965).[42]

Contrary to the views of many labor relations partisans, compulsory arbitration played a significant role in collective negotiations between local governments and their police and fire fighting employees. Loewenberg reports that at least sixty-six arbitration awards covering conditions of employment for Pennsylvania police and fire fighters resulted from compulsory arbitration proceedings implemented during the first year in which Pennsylvania legislation was in force. In a minimum of an additional twenty cases, arbitration proceedings were initiated but suspended when the parties successfully negotiated an agreement. The availability of compulsory arbitration did not terminate or seriously hinder collective negotiations between police and fire employees and their respective employers. Two-thirds (132 of 198) of the municipalities which negotiated with their safety employees arrived at a negotiated agreement.[43]

Despite such relative success, some labor relations experts believe that compulsory arbitration would destroy free collective negotiations as we have come to think of them historically.[44] They do not think it would be effective in encouraging collective negotiations because of the penchant of arbitrators for achieving "perceived equity." This tends to encourage the parties to resist modifying their demands in hopes that the final split will favor them.

If state legislatures continue to resist legalizing the strike and the public employer uses the ban to sidestep bilateral negotiations, employees will probably force compulsory arbitration on the public employer.

It is highly doubtful that the public employer would desire this. From the point of view of governmental administrators, arbitration threatens their control, particularly where an independent, neutral third party assumes responsibility for policy and wage determination. On the other hand, if the arbitrator is an agent of the local government the employees may well feel that they cannot expect equity and reasonableness. Finally, there are those who believe that compulsory arbitration is a faulty approach to dispute settlement because the parties have almost totally withdrawn their participative commitment and, out of desperation, have been forced to accept the arbitrary judgement of a third party.[45]

VOLUNTARY ARBITRATION

In voluntary arbitration the employer and employee representative jointly agree without compulsion to submit specific issues to a third party for a final and binding decision. Further, the parties are free to choose their own arbitrator—a person in whom both have confidence and who they feel will understand their particular issues and problems.

Since the arbitration of contract negotiation impasses can be voluntarily agreed to, there is no need to give the arbitrator unlimited powers to settle a dispute. Further, there is no need to necessarily allow an unlimited range of issues and unlimited scope.[46] One could well argue, however, for the broadest possible range that the parties can agree upon. The scope of arbitration has generally been restricted to interpretation of the contract language. Certainly, the parties would want to spell out carefully these procedural requirements.

Staudohar has pointed out that possibilities for the expansion of voluntary arbitration into the public sector are enhanced by access to the services of the American Arbitration Association (AAA), which permits the parties to choose arbitrators from its National Panel of Arbitrators. To some extent the AAA has already moved into public labor relations disputes. The AAA currently provides names of arbitrators on request. Further, the Labor-Management Institute was established to assist public management and labor to improve negotiation procedures and to set up dispute settlement systems that are appropriate for varying governmental jurisdictions. Finally, the AAA has created the National Center for Dispute Settlement. This center has as one of its primary purposes the developing of special panels of arbitrators and neutrals who will be available for mediation, fact finding, and arbitration.[47]

The state of Maine provides an excellent example of how the AAA can assist in dispute settlement. Maine, in its Municipal Employment Relations Law, has chosen voluntary arbitration of negotiation impasses. Arbitrators are chosen by the parties. If the parties fail to agree on an arbitrator they may request that the American Arbitration Association use its own procedures to select the umpire.[48]

MEDIATION

Mediation[49] in interest disputes is one of the oldest of the tried and accepted procedures. This is particularly true in the private sector and is increasingly becoming the case in public labor-management relations. Harold W. Davey, labor relations expert at Iowa State University, stated in 1969:

The principal need in the public sector is for qualified mediators, fact finders and advisory arbitrators rather than for conventional arbitrators accustomed to the "judicial" approach in private sector grievance arbitration.[50]

Edward B. Krinsky believes that every state should have a list of highly qualified mediators available to assist in settling public government disputes.[51] Mayors, judges, governors, and other

governmental administrators should not be included among neutral candidates. Krinsky suggests consideration of New York City's tripartite approach as meaningful. Further, he advocates mediation prior to the use of other procedures but does not recommend mediation based on a law requiring the use of such procedures a specified number of days prior to a budget deadline:

A mediator entering a dispute at the behest of a statute because a certain date has been reached may enter the bargaining prematurely and adversely affect the development of the bargaining relationship. The parties may reach their own settlement as the pressures of the advancing budget deadline are felt and they may be better off having the experience of reaching agreements themselves.[52]

Although mediation may fail to resolve the impasse completely, there is little doubt that it can narrow the scope of the dispute and contribute to the effectiveness of other procedures.

FACT FINDING

Fact finding[53] as a procedure for dealing with disputes raises such questions as the following:

1. Where does it fit into the dispute-solving process?
2. Should fact finding be adjudicatory, that is, determining what the correct settlement should be, based on facts, evidence, and argument?
3. Should the fact finder's initial role be one of mediation?
4. What are the facts in a dispute?
5. Who should be the fact finder?
6. Who should pay the cost of fact finding?
7. Should both parties be required as a condition of good faith negotiations to act on the recommendations of the fact finder?

Krinsky believes that if mediation fails fact finding should be the next logical step in public employment interest disputes.[54] He bases much of his argument on Wisconsin's success with fact finding, utilizing the mediation approach.[55]

Connecticut and New York have also emphasized mediation as a first step in fact finding. In a three-year period, under the Municipal Employees Act, the Connecticut Board of Mediation and Arbitration (either through board staff or through a fact finder) settled two-thirds of the disputes referred to it without the need for formal fact finding.[56]

In New York, under the Taylor Act, some 316 disputes were referred to the Public Employment Relations Board. Over half of these impasses were resolved by mediation alone. Some 150 disputes were referred to formal fact finding. Twenty-two percent of these were settled by mediation and 45 percent by acceptance of the report of the fact finder. The fact finder's report was not accepted completely in 33 percent of the cases. In two-thirds of this last group, settlement was achieved by intense mediation following the fact finding report. In one-third, the recommendations were modified by the employer. A total of nine strikes occurred, two in New York City and seven out of it.[57]

Michigan, in contrast to Wisconsin, Connecticut, and New York, emphasizes the separation of mediation from fact finding. The Michigan Labor Mediation Board, which administers the law, has suggested divorcing mediation from fact finding, thus making fact finding more adjudicatory in procedural form. The board has, however, recommended that mediation be exhausted before fact finding is invoked. Other groups, such as the Advisory Committee on Public Employee Relations, have suggested that a timetable related to budgetary submission dates be established to encourage more orderly and planned fact finding. In part, this recommendation grew out of Michigan's experience with urgent strike situations, where fact finders found themselves engaged in what has been called "instant fact finding."[58]

FACTS AND FACT FINDING

The complex problem of assessing hard facts in labor disputes is well known. Facts are one thing; interpretation is another. Further, the fact finder, although hopefully neutral, will influence the fact finding process and the facts gathered. Consciously or subconsciously his values and beliefs will make their presence felt.[59]

The difficulty of gathering and interpreting facts objectively would appear to argue for emphasis on mediation rather than on settlement procedures that assume that facts are objective

and that correct judgments can be made equitably.

FACT FINDING AND GOOD FAITH NEGOTIATIONS

As with the strike, if employers or union leaders feel little or no responsibility to act on the report of the fact finder then one or both may ignore the recommendations. This would be particularly true in those states with legislation—usually the meet-and-confer approach—protecting the employer from the requirement and responsibility of negotiation. This would also be true in those states operating under common law, since the employer retains great unilateral grants of authority and power. Unless unfair labor practices are clearly present, the employer or union does not have to consider the consequences of refusal to discuss and act on a fact finder's recommendations. This is definitely an advantage for the employer, because he retains so many residual rights.

If fact finding is to be an effective method for handling interest disputes it must be backed up with enforcement machinery making failure to recognize, discuss, and act on fact finders' recommendations an unfair labor practice, subject to penalty.

THE FACT FINDER

It is probably unrealistic to believe that a fact finder can be neutral and make recommendations only on hard facts and evidence. Many writers in the field of labor relations lay stress on the neutral third party. The concept operationally defined does not imply that the mediator or fact finder comes to the impasse without any personal values or beliefs on the subject. It is assumed that he will make his judgments after the facts have been ascertained, much as is done or attempted in our courts of law. The history of court decisions in labor law does raise the question of neutrality of court decisions (which are frequently value laden).[60]

It would seem safer and perhaps more equitable if fact finding procedures required the appointment or selection of a panel of investigators sufficiently diversified to reflect considerable deviation from a dominant point of view.

THE PARTIAL STRIKE:
THE CANADIAN EXPERIENCE

Labor relations in the Canadian federal service have progressed from advisory consultation to comprehensive collective negotiations. The official position on negotiations and strikes has been to grant the same rights to public employees that their private sector counterparts receive. Without doubt, the bargaining procedure section of the Canadian labor law is most controversial.

The act requires that before notice to bargain may be given, the bargaining agent must specify which of two disputes settlement procedures it will follow—referral to arbitration or referral to a conciliation board, followed by the right to strike. If the agent elects the arbitration route, it cannot call a strike and the employees may not engage in a strike. If the conciliation route is elected, and if the conciliation board's recommendations are rejected, a strike may be called. The decision as to which route will be followed is exclusively that of the bargaining agent. The choice of routes may not be changed during negotiations, although the bargaining agent may change its election before the next round of negotiations.[61]

When the conciliation alternative has been chosen, either party to a dispute may request that the labor relations administrative board establish a conciliation panel. This panel is composed of one member appointed by each party and a chairman selected by the parties. Such a conciliation board will be established only after the parties have agree on, or the Federal Labor Relations Board has determined, which employees or classes of employees are designated as essential and are thus prohibited from striking. If the conciliation board's recommendations are rejected a strike may lawfully occur seven days after receipt of the conciliation board's report.[62]

Denial of the right to strike to specified employees is central to other union members' having that right. The parties initially attempt to work out the essential classes of employees on their own. If they are unsuccessful the board will make the final determination. The primary danger here is in designating which employees will be seen as essential to the safety and security of the public. Great care must be taken to ensure that those so designated are without question essential and cannot be allowed to strike. Fur-

ther, some way must be found to deal equitably with those individuals or classes of public employees who are prohibited from striking.

Variants to the federal experience can be seen in provincial approaches to impasses. Saskatchewan, for example, grants public employees all rights accorded employees in the private sector. British Columbia, Ontario, and Nova Scotia, while allowing bargaining, prohibit the strike and use various forms of mediation, fact finding, and arbitration. Quebec and New Brunswick follow the federal government pattern, but have somewhat different procedural rules regarding the designation of essential employees. In Quebec the designation is made immediately prior to a strike. In New Brunswick the individuals or classes are determined after the conciliation stage but prior to the appointment of a fact finder.[63]

Grievance Procedures

As an assumption, almost all administrators sincerely feel they are fair, equitable, considerate, and sensitive to their employees. Further, many feel that the open door approach to employee complaints is adequate and point to a minimum of grievances[64] to prove that all is well. What they fail to point out, however, is how the authority and power of administrators keep employee grievances from surfacing directly. Frequently the effects of unresolved grievances can be seen in turnover figures, union organizing, and other indirect ways.

In the absence of labor contract provisions, grievance appeals procedures can take one or more of the following forms: (1) no procedures; (2) informal procedures, generally called the open door approach; (3) formalized procedures using the open door approach and the chain of command; (4) formalized procedures using the chain of command at the first step but substituting the personnel department if the complaint is not settled; (5) formalized procedures allowing use of the chain of command or the personnel department at the first step; and (6) civil service procedures.

All of the above forms maintain the judicial function within the same group (management).

Further, all but alternatives 5 and 6 maintain the integrity of the classical organization concept of chain of command. Alternative 5 alters this slightly by allowing the aggrieved employee the right to go to the personnel department initially. Alternative 6 alters this somewhat more by allowing for a civil service board hearing. These boards, however, are still part of the governmental machinery, and so are not perceived as neutral by many employees.

The major weakness with most of the traditional procedures is that they don't work. Employees are so frightened of the potential use of discipline by their supervisors that they rarely lodge complaints of a personal nature. Management thus has created a self-fulfilling prophecy: no complaints, no problems.

Appeals procedures in government organizations stand or fall on employee rights. Until recently, it has been felt by government management that employees had few rights. This concept is gradually changing through employee pressure for reform. Organizing into unions is one manifestation of this pressure. While it is difficult to say to what extent absence of meaningful due process procedures has encouraged employee organizing, it can be estimated as substantial.

NEGOTIATED APPEALS PROCEDURES

In a study on appeals procedures in state and local government, Ullman and Begin analyzed 304 contracts negotiated by the American Federation of State, County and Municipal Employees, the Building Service Employees, the Laborers' International Union of North America, and the International Brotherhood of Teamsters. The researchers estimated that approximately 21 percent of employees in state and local government are covered by bilaterally negotiated contracts and that about 19 percent of these employees have access to jointly determined grievance procedures.[65]

Ullman and Begin found, surprisingly, that over half of the grievance procedures at the state and local levels allowed binding arbitration; specifically, 159 of 282 contracts provided for binding arbitration of grievances as the final step. An additional 25 provided for advisory arbitration only. This contrasts with a 94 percent

figure having binding arbitration in the private sector in 1966. In the federal service, experience under Executive Order. 11491 is just beginning to be felt since the signing of the new order allowing binding arbitration.[66]

The issues that can be brought to grievance arbitration in state and local government may lie somewhere between those of the private sector and those of the federal sector. In the private sector there are few specific exclusions. The federal government restricts the scope of grievance arbitration by including a strong management rights clause and by making all agreements subject to applicable laws and Civil Service Commission and other government agency rules and regulations.

At the state and local levels, data on inclusions and exclusions from the grievance arbitration process are practically nonexistent. Ullman and Begin found that 60 percent of the state and local agreements contained no specific exclusions while also finding that the other agreements varied widely in extent of specific exclusions and in subject matter.[67]

It can be argued that some overlap of appeal procedures generally exists even where collective bargaining has a long history. Overlapping procedures can and sometimes do create confusion. In the case of open door policy versus bilateral procedures the problems are minimal. Primarily, the government employee uses the union-management negotiated procedure. Where civil service procedures exist relatively more problems of overlap and confusion occur. In the federal service both civil service and agency procedures can be used to appeal adverse actions. Over 40 percent of the 282 agreements examined by Ullman and Begin contained both agency and negotiated procedures covering the same issues.[68]

At the local government level overlap of civil service and negotiated procedures would be most likely to occur in the larger municipalities. The reluctance on the part of the employer to give up established unilateral procedures in lieu of bilateral procedures can be traced to a number of factors. In the first place there is a strong feeling that such procedures, when they were established, were right, fair, and meaningful for solving employer-employee problems. Second, in many governmental units negotiated grievance procedures cover limited subject areas and issues. The employer has reserved for himself certain areas of personnel policy that fall within management rights clauses. Third, it can be assumed that civil service boards have garnered considerable authority and power by centralizing government personnel policy, including appeals procedures. Last, there is potential for over-lapping of state-mandated personnel policy with local unilateral procedures and negotiated procedures.

Time will assist in solving some of the overlap or potential overlap. As the parties learn to live within the framework of bilateral relations they will also learn how to make their systems for due process more meaningful and effective. Employee use of different procedures will provide valuable feedback.

THE SCOPE OF ARBITRATION

The scope of arbitration can be as broad as that of the grievance part of the appeals process, or it can be more restrictive. Ullman and Begin's analysis of appeals procedures for public employees found, at state and local levels, that 40 to 50 percent of the contracts examined in their sample admitted all complaints to both the grievance procedure and to arbitration. Twenty-three percent of the agreements with all-inclusive grievance provisions restricted the scope of arbitration, but only 11 percent of the agreements limiting the scope of the grievance procedures further restricted the arbitrator.[69]

If the arbitration process is to be made more restrictive than the grievance procedure, this should be decided by the parties rather than by a group of legislators sitting in a distant state capitol. Decisions imposed from outside will only lead to further conflict.

If the grievance process is to work effectively it must not be deprived of arbitration. Short of this final step, the governmental employer retains the right to decide unilaterally.

When this happens the entire process loses something of its meaning in that the procedures which allow for challenge to a unilateral position are diminished.

[1]Harry P. Cohany and Lucretia M. Dewey, "Union Membership among Government Employees," MONTHLY LABOR REVIEW 93 (July 1970): 15.

[2]U.S., Department of Labor, Bureau of Labor Statistics, "Labor Union and Employee Association Membership 1970," press release, 13 September 1971.

[3]Cohany and Dewey, "Union Membership among Government Employees": 18.

[4]E. Wight Bakke, "To Join or Not To Join," in UNIONS, MANAGEMENT AND THE PUBLIC, ed. E. Wight Bakke, Clark Kerr, and Charles W. Anrod (New York: Harcourt Brace and world, 1967), p. 85.

[5]Robert F. Hoxie, "A Socio-Psychological Interpretation" in UNIONS, MANAGEMENT AND THE PUBLIC, pp. 53—54.

[6]Frank Tannenbaum, "The Restoration of Social Status," in UNIONS, MANAGEMENT AND THE PUBLIC, pp. 57—61.

[7]John R. Commons, LABOR AND ADMINISTRATION (New York: The Macmillan Company, 1913) pp. 210—64.

[8]U.S., Advisory Commission on Intergovernmental Relations, LABOR-MANAGEMENT POLICIES FOR STATE AND LOCAL GOVERNMENT, Report of the Commission (Washington, D.C.: Government Printing Office, 1969), p. 12.

[9]Ibid., p. 11.

[10]Ibid., p. 12.

[11]Joseph P. Goldberg, "Public Employee Developments in 1971," MONTHLY LABOR REVIEW 95 (January 1972): 60.

[12]Ibid.: 63.

[13]Ibid.: 60—61.

[14]Joseph P. Goldberg, "Changing Policies in Public Employee Labor Relations," MONTHLY LABOR REVIEW 93 (July 1970): 11—12.

[15]U.S., Advisory Commission on Intergovernmental Relations, LABOR-MANAGEMENT POLICIES, p. 36.

[16]Alan C. Filley and Robert J. House, MANAGERIAL PROCESS AND ORGANIZATIONAL BEHAVIOR (Glenview, Ill.: Scott, Foresman and Company, 1969), p. 247.

[17]Herbert R. Northrup and Gordon F. Bloom, GOVERNMENT AND LABOR (Homewood, Ill.: Richard D. Irwin, Inc., 1963), p. 113.

[18]U.S., Advisory Commission on Intergovernmental Relations, LABOR-MANAGEMENT POLICIES, p. 225.

[19]It should be noted that in those state and local governments with no labor relations public policy the employer remains in control of the process for establishing personnel policy.

[20]For discussion on the compatibility of unions and merit systems, see, for example, David T. Stanley, "What Are Unions Doing to Merit Systems?" PUBLIC PERSONNEL REVIEW 31 (April 1970): 269—72.

[21]U.S., Advisory Commission on Intergovernmental Relations, LABOR-MANAGEMENT POLICIES, p. 77.

[22]Blackstone's Commentaries 246, in Wilson R. Hart,

COLLECTIVE BARGAINING IN THE FEDERAL CIVIL SERVICE (New York: Harper & Brothers, Publishers, 1961), p. 41.

23Arthur J. Goldberg, "Management's Reserved Rights: A Labor View," in UNIONS, MANAGEMENT AND THE PUBLIC, p. 237.

24See, for example, Federal Labor-Management Executive Orders 10988 and 11491. Many of the inclusions under the management rights section are subjects vital to the welfare of the employee. These include hiring, promotion, transfer, assignment of work, suspension, demotion, discharge, and disciplinary action. It can be expected that employees will make every effort to surround these alleged rights of management with rules and regulations emerging from collective negotiations.

25It will be remembered from previous discussion that of the 1,357 municipalities over 10,000 population that participated in the 1969 Advisory Commission on Intergovernmental Relations—International City Management Association survey, some two-thirds had not enacted legislation dealing with employee organizing; nor did they have legal provisions for signing of negotiated agreements, dispute settlement, or matters such as unfair labor practices and negotiating in good faith.

26U.S., Advisory Commission on Intergovernmental Relations, LABOR-MANAGEMENT POLICIES, pp. 80—81.

27Richard W. Walton and Robert B. McKersie, A BEHAVIORAL THEORY OF LABOR NEGOTIATIONS (New York: McGraw-Hill Book Company, 1965).

28See U.S., Advisory Commission on Intergovernmental Relations, LABOR-MANAGEMENT POLICIES. p. 37.

29See, for example, Robert R. Blake, Jane S. Mouton, and Richard L. Sloma, "The Union-Management Intergroup Laboratory: Strategy for Resolving Intergroup Conflict," JOURNAL OF APPLIED BEHAVIORAL SCIENCE 1 (January—March 1965): 25—57; Robert R. Blake and Jane S. Mouton, "Union Management Relations: From Conflict to Collaboration" PERSONNEL 38 (November—December 1961): 38—51.

30Walton and McKersie, A BEHAVIORAL THEORY OF LABOR NEGOTIATIONS p. 4.

31Milton Derber, WHO NEGOTIATES FOR THE PUBLIC EMPLOYEE? (Champaign, Ill.: University of Illinois Institute of Labor and Industrial Relations, 1969), pp. 52—53.

32Ibid., pp. 52—50.

33For a good basic introduction to the operational aspects of public employer negotiations, see Kenneth O. Warner and Mary L. Hennessy, PUBLIC MANAGEMENT AT THE BARGAINING TABLE (Chicago: Public Personnel Association, 1967).

34Sheila C. White, "Work Stoppages of Government Employees," MONTHLY LABOR REVIEW 92 (December 1969): 29.

35Ibid.: 30.

36Ibid.: 31.

37Arnold M. Zeck, "Why Employees Strike," ARBITRATION JOURNAL 23, no. 2 (1968): 75—76.

38Cyrus F. Smythe, Jr., "A Pragmatic Approach to Public Employee Legislation," PUBLIC PERSONNEL REVIEW 31 (October 1970): 265.

39"Meet-and-Confer. A process of determining wages, hours, and conditions of public employment through discussions between representatives of the employer and employee organization with a view toward reaching a non-binding agreement to be presented to the employer's governing body or statutory representative for final determination." Allan W. Drachman, MUNICIPAL NEGOTIATIONS: FROM DIFFERENCES TO AGREEMENT (Washington, D.C.: Labor-Management Relations Service, 1970), p. 45.

40"Arbitration. A method of settling disputes through recourse to an impartial third party. The primary use of arbitration involves the interpretation of the terms of an existing contract. Occasionally, arbitration involves disputes over what the contract terms ought to be. Arbitration is usually based on voluntary agreement by both parties, and occasionally is compulsory, i.e., required by law. Arbitration involving the interpretation of the terms of an existing contract is usually final and binding, which means that the award is enforceable in court. Arbitration may also be advisory, i.e., with recommendations but without a final and binding award." Ibid., p. 42.

41Amalgamated Association v. Wisconsin Employment Relations Board, 340 U.S. (1951).

42J. Joseph Loewenberg, "Compulsory Arbitration for Police and Fire Fighters in Pennsylvania in 1968," INDUSTRIAL AND LABOR RELATIONS REVIEW 23 (April 1970): 367.

43Ibid.: 377. Compulsory arbitration and the resulting awards were resisted by public employers in the form of court suits. In June 1969 the Pennsylvania state Supreme Court upheld the constitutionality of Act III in Harvey v. Russo et al., 435 Pa. 183 (1969).

44Harold S. Roberts, "Compulsory Arbitration," in CRITICAL ISSUES IN LABOR, ed. Max S. Wortman, Jr. (New York: The MacMillan Company, 1969), pp. 403—408.

45Thomas H. Patten, Jr., "Compulsory Arbitration: A Third-Rate Concept in Employment Relations," in NEW HORIZONS IN PUBLIC EMPLOYEE BARGAINING, ed. Public Personnel Association (Chicago: Public Personnel Association, 1970), pp. 18—28.

46Paul D. Staudohar, "Voluntary Binding Arbitration in Public Employment," ARBITRATION JOURNAL 25, no. 1 (1970): 36.

47Ibid.: 37—38. It should be noted that the National Center for Dispute Settlement has assumed the functions previously handled by the Labor-Management Institute.

48Ibid.: 38.

49"Mediation (Conciliation. An attempt by an impartial third party to help in collective negotiations or in the settlement of an employment dispute through suggestion, advice, persuasion or other ways of stimulating agreement, short of dictating its provisions (a characteristic of arbitration). Mediation in the United States is undertaken through federal and state mediation agencies, or by a person selected by the parties to act as mediator." Drachman, MUNICIPAL NEGOTIATIONS, p. 45.

50Harold W. Davey, "The Use of Neutrals in the Public sector," in Industrial Relations Research Association, PROCEEDINGS OF THE ANNUAL SPRING MEETING (Des Moines, Iowa: n. p., 1969), p. 529.

51Edward B. Krinsky, "Avoiding Public Employee Strikes: Lessons from Recent Strike Activity," in Industrial Relations Research Association, PROCEEDINGS OF THE ANNUAL SPRING MEETING (Albany, N.Y.: n. p., 1970), pp. 464—72.

52Ibid., p. 466.

53"Fact-Finding. Investigation of a labor dispute or bargaining impasse by an individual, panel or board. The fact-finder assembles and reports the facts, after a hearing, and may make recommendations for settlement." Drachman, MUNICIPAL NEGOTIATIONS. p. 44.

54Krinsky, in Industrial Relations Research Association, PROCEEDINGS OF SPRING MEETING (Albany, 1970), p. 466.

55Ibid.

56Jean P. McKelvey, "Fact Finding in Public Employment Disputes: Promise or Illusion?" INDUSTRIAL AND LABOR RELATIONS REVIEW 22 (July 1969): 535.

57Ibid.: 538.

58Ibid.: 534—35.

59James A. Gross, "Value Judgments in the Decisions of Labor Arbitrators," INDUSTRIAL AND LABOR RELATIONS REVIEW 21 (October 1967): 55—72.

[60]Even a cursory examination of U.S. Supreme Court decisions regarding labor relations clearly points out the value orientations of the judges.

[61]J. Douglas Muir, "Canada's Experience with the Right of Public Employees To Strike," MONTHLY LABOR REVIEW 92 (July 1969): 54.

[62]Ibid.: 55.

[63]Ibid.: 56.

[64]"*Grievance.* Usually a complaint by an employee or employee organization concerning the interpretation or application of a collective bargaining agreement. Occasionally defined as any dispute over wages, hours, or working conditions." Drachman, MUNICIPAL NEGOTIATIONS, p. 44.

[65]Joseph C. Ullman, and James P. Begin, "The Structure and Scope of Appeals Procedures for Public Employees," INDUSTRIAL AND LABOR RELATIONS REVIEW 23 (April 1970): 326—28. The authors believe that their sample is reasonably representative of state and local agreements covering nonprofessional employees.

[66]Ibid.: 328.

[67]Ibid.: 332.

[68]Ibid.: 327.

[69]Ibid.: 333.

17

Labor Relations Management

GENERAL GUIDELINES for the management of labor relations—a frame of reference for the chief administrator, the department heads, the personnel agency, and other management people—are provided in this chapter. In more or less chronological order, we will follow the stages of unionization from the period before the union arrives up to and through the orientation of supervisors and others to the terms and conditions of the contract that has been accepted by both management and labor.

Chapter 16 provides a review of trends, policy considerations and implications for management, definitions and concepts, and procedural issues. Here we will carry the process to managerial operations, the bargaining table, and the major steps in negotiation.

A warning signal: labor relations law for government workers is relatively new, amorphous, and contradictory. While legal precedents are evolving, the process is slow, and some areas of rights and obligations are, in fact, uncertain. Therefore, any specific course of action that has not been taken before should be checked out by your city attorney or by other counsel against state statutes, court decisions, and administrative rulings.

Attitudes toward Unionization

Before the union arrives, management should develop its philosophy or policy toward unionization. There are three possibilities available—to discourage it, to promote it, or to remain neutral.

DISCOURAGING UNIONIZATION

In the absence of legal requirements cities have occasionally—not often—refused to discuss or recognize a union. In some of these situations the unions have taken the law into their own hands and have engaged in a work stoppage or slowdown to force attention to their interest in recognition for collective bargaining.

A more constructive approach being undertaken by some jurisdictions has been to create an atmosphere in which most employees do not feel the need to organize. A good beginning is to make sure, well before there is a union on the horizon, that the total package of wages and fringe benefits is fair and is comparable to that of other jurisdictions and to similar work in the private sector. It is important, too, that this not merely be achieved, but also that it be brought home to the worker and his family. A technique that is growing in popularity is the distribution each year of a statement of earnings plus the value (or cost to the municipality) of various fringe benefits such as pensions, medical insurance, life insurance, uniforms, and vacations.

Another useful step is to establish a well-organized and well-publicized grievance system, so that any unfairness—whether fancied or real—can be brought forcefully to the attention of top management. A worker has to feel he has some recourse for his rights other than having to go outside the government building and seek out a union organizer.

PROMOTING UNIONIZATION

Some local government officials think that if they help organize their own union or employee association they can dominate or control its actions. This, in addition to possibly violating state statute, is likely to be a pipe dream. It is quite likely that a real live union will capitalize with employees on the weak position of a kept union. The end result is likely to be the establishment of a particularly aggressive union, with members bearing a grudge for having been "taken" previously.

STAYING NEUTRAL

The practice in most communities has been to stay neutral. The public sector has not been characterized by the all-out legal and illegal opposition undertaken by some private sector employers when faced by unionization efforts. Some cities have considered it an obligation to make sure that employees understand that union membership involves payment of dues and other obligations. Most cities feel that they have done their duty when they have provided a chance for a secret ballot vote on whether employees in an appropriate unit wish to be represented by a particular union.

The choice of one of the three possible attitudes outlined above may well be conditioned by local attitudes toward unions in the private as well as the public sector, by the extent of union influence in local government politics, and by the presence or absence of unionization in neighboring jurisdictions.

Before the Union Arrives

An important step—sound at any time—is to develop an effective management team. Labor relations demands managers who are knowledgeable about the process and have joined in implementing the jurisdiction's labor policy. Top management should identify who belongs on the team, should bring members together frequently, should consult with them about policies affecting their employees, should communicate with them all (not with some on one question and others on a different one) and should involve them in long-range policy and program planning. In short, it is important that employees be actual participants in forging management policy.

Middle and first-line supervisors are part of the management team and should be given appropriate responsibilities and authority. Otherwise, they may have the titles but their hearts and support will lie with the rank-and-file employees. (In case of a battle over their inclusion or exclusion from a bargaining unit, their actual day-to-day duties would be far more conclusive than their job titles.)

The history of municipal labor relations is dotted with reports of long-enduring battles over whether or not certain employees were supervisors. Police and fire departments, where team spirit is a working principle, are particularly open to such debate. In Boston it took a five-year effort before an administrative agency and several courts could get deputy and district fire chiefs classified as management and excluded from a bargaining unit.

The failure to weld supervisors into the management team has resulted in unions being created of police or fire officers, as in New York City, or of school principals and department heads, who have a national union chartered and operating. The problem is not an easy one, for some unions have evolved from social organizations in which everyone—high and low—held membership. In some cases unions are headed by the officers in the government department, and this, of course, poses some difficult problems (if not outright conflict of interests) in resolving grievance issues, in preparing and carrying out bargaining, and in providing minimal services in departments struck by work stoppages or slowdowns.

One problem which relatively few municipalities have faced up to is that many supervisors welcome the arrival of unions, feeling that as benefits improve for the personnel they supervise so will their own—a tandem relationship. A few farsighted communities have initiated a special package of management benefits that differs from benefits for the rank and file and have treated pay separately, not as part of a lock-step tie-in with rank-and-file workers.

Clearly, the employees who were given a pay raise and the title of supervisor and never again brought into the management circle are hardly likely to take management's side in a labor-management confrontation. The avoidance of this depends on an alert and active management.

Another must is to improve communications with employees. New employees, and a lot of old ones as well, need orientation on how they fit into the government, what is expected of them, and what they may expect of the government. They also need opportunities for promotion, training, travel or conferences, and a detailed explanation of their pay and fringe benefits. Surveys show that employees frequently don't know about their job opportunities and working conditions. This means that the municipality does not get the benefit of the advantages it provides—a wasted asset. It also means that some employee dissatisfaction which could be averted is left to grow and flourish, particularly in the hands of a skilled union organizer.

Handbooks and written policy statements on personnel matters are necessary, and their distribution should not be limited to the looseleaf binder on the supervisor's desk.

Annual reports can be developed for a few cents each by computerized data centers, and their benefits are far-reaching. They don't have to be as fancy as corporate annual reports to stockholders, but they should be good enough for the employee to want to take them home, share them with the family, and put them away in a safe place.

Personnel policies should not be chiseled in stone—they have to change as people change. Changing views about grooming or dress have caused some managements to ask whether good taste is a real job requirement or whether it reflects an attitude of a predecessor manager. What is good taste? Yesterday's version is not necessarily today's. Even job hours have undergone reexamination—is 8:00 to 5:00 really required by the job? Or is it tradition? Some enterprising city managements have found that such new techniques as flextime give employees some appreciated latitude in arriving and departing and also, since preferences differ, permit an extension of hours of service to the public.

In examining personnel practices, take a look at the grievance file: what grievances are about, where they are centered, and which supervisor's name keeps turning up. Watch for patterns, because favoritism is a rallying cry for organizers and a unifying force for unhappy employees.

Involve employees in the review process. They are the group most affected, the consumers, in effect. And, of course, if they take part in the promulgation they have a special responsibility to honor the end result. This participation can be an influence, too, in deciding any grievance arbitration which may ensue.

Work practices and rules are also good areas for reexamination. Here the opportunity for involvement of workers is especially important, since they should know their tasks better than anyone else. They may have some very useful suggestions on revision of work processes, staffing, hours of service, and new equipment. And there are dividends in higher morale and a feeling of significance.

The Union Seeks Status

Assuming that a union or employee association is formed and seeks management recognition, the response, if this is to be considered seriously, should include insistence on a statement of exactly which categories of workers are to be represented and specific exemptions—in short, a clear definition of the bargaining unit.

Efforts may be made to persuade you and other management representatives that a clear majority of the group has indicated a desire to be represented, but this should not be taken for granted. An election should be held in every case. Employees have a right to feel that management will give them a chance to cast a secret ballot, and they will feel better about the outcome—whichever way it goes—if they have had this chance. The National Labor Relations Board (NLRB), which has held elections for more than 25 million workers in industry and commerce, has found that in some cases, where more than 50 percent of the unit signed membership cards or a petition for an election, when the actual election was held the union failed to win a majority. A secret ballot insulates an employee from pressure and a bandwagon spirit.

During the preelection campaign, following private sector precedents, managements are generally expected: (1) *not* to form a company union or dominate an existing union; (2) *not* to discipline employees for organizational activity in nonwork hours; (3) *not* to make promises or threats, or coerce employees into influencing election results; (4) *not* to question employees about union preferences; and (5) *not* to spy on employees. While most top management people would automatically respect these prohibitions, it is important to alert lower level supervisors, who may turn out to be zealots—for or against the union.

Management may take certain steps during the unionization effort to protect work processes during work hours. A management attorney has pointed out that the city may adopt and enforce a no-solicitation and no-distribution rule in the work place; may publicize its opposition to union organizational efforts, including a presentation of specific reasons; and may notify all employees of their legal rights—the right to refuse to sign a union authorization card, for example. Management may, in the absence of legal prohibitions, question employees concerning problems at work, individual desires, and union strength where a claim of majority representation has been advanced. Management can also make unilateral improvements in wages, hours, and working conditions as a result of the employee discussions.[1]

In deciding whether to take essentially a hands off position or a "hard-line opposition" position, management will want to consider the possible effects carefully. Will the hard line be effective or will it have a reverse effect? Is it worth risking a hostile start on labor-management relationships? What would be the political consequences of the hard line?

UNIT DETERMINATION

A crucial aspect of the election, indeed of the whole labor-management relationship, is defining the bargaining unit. This is a group of employees recognized by the voluntary action of an employer or designated by a labor relations agency (state, local, or ad hoc) as appropriate for representation by a union or employee organization for purposes of bargaining or of meeting and conferring.

Obviously, the determination of who is in and who is outside the unit can determine whether the union wins or loses the election. In a contest among unions, defining the bargaining unit can tilt the election toward a particular union. As

one officeholder has suggested, it is as important in labor relations as redistricting is in politics. A poorly defined unit can cause all kinds of grief for a negotiator, for a chief executive, for a city; there is sufficient aggravation for them all to join in the suffering.

In the absence of a state law, management has much more power to influence the definition of the unit. It may choose to insist on a particular type as the price for granting an election or according voluntary recognition. In general, cities and towns have sought the largest practicable unit in order to avoid fragmentation and a generally "can-you-top-this?" atmosphere among competing bargaining units. Cities also seek to exclude from the bargaining unit all members of management, including supervisors, and confidential employees, those whose information might be injurious to the management position in the labor relations process.

A bargaining unit should include employees with a "community of interest." This is a rather esoteric term used by labor relations professionals. Although few would draw the community perimeters exactly the same way, professionals do look at whether the proposed unit employees have similar job duties, skills, training, working conditions, supervisory structure, organizational structure, and method of wage payment—hourly, annual, cash, or check. They will also be interested in any bargaining history. What kind of unit did exist? Did it work? What is the extent of organization? All of these elements will be weighed, with some given higher values than others, and out comes an appropriate unit. Some management people will hold out for the most appropriate unit; most union people will settle for an appropriate unit.

In cities with long bargaining experience there is a consensus that the more than two hundred units in New York City and the more than one hundred in Detroit are a grave threat to negotiator sanity and city treasury liquidity. Both cities are trying to undo the errors of earlier administrations and cajole or crowd unions to decrease the number of units. Numerous units have a deleterious impact on public administration, since they usually produce differing working conditions, constant vying for best place, and never-ending comparisons of job classifications having nearly the same content but represented by another bargaining agent.

In some cases skillful negotiators, faced with dozens of units, have managed to develop two-tier bargaining in which they bargain on wages, hours, and some fringe benefits with each unit representative. They then meet only with the largest union to work out the fringe benefits requiring uniformity, and the smaller unions abide by the result.

THE ELECTION PROCESS

The National Labor Relations Board has had extensive experience in conducting union recognition elections under widely varying conditions over the past generation. From this experience, tested in employment situations and scrutinized by the courts, policies have evolved that are legal, workable, and generally acceptable to management and labor. A practical example is the rule requiring a showing of interest by at least 30 percent of the bargaining unit before NLRB will spend government money to hold an election. Most of the state boards have the same rule. The NLRB policies have a strong influence on the laws and regulations that are likely to control an election in your city.

In the public sector an election may be run by a state board, if it exists; if not, a contract can be drawn up for the services of the U.S. Labor Department, the National Center for Dispute Settlement of the American Arbitration Association, or the Honest Ballot Association of New York City. If management and labor representatives agree, a group of local persons, such as ministers, professors, or other neutrals, may conduct the election. Election procedures must be set forth specifically in a written agreement covering hours and location of polling places, number of observers, determination of voter eligibility, notices of election, posting of results, etc. In general, polling booths on work premises and voting during working hours encourage the largest possible participation.

Preparing for Negotiations

Assuming the union wins the recognition election, the next step is preparing for negotiations.[2]

Among the first decisions to be made is who will lead the bargaining, who the other members of the team will be, and how the team will relate to other interested parties, such as the mayor, the city council, and the city manager. Some public officials like to think of themselves as apart from labor relations, but labor unions will rarely permit them to enjoy such isolation. To union leaders everybody on the management side, elected and appointed, is "the boss."

Another notion to be dealt with sometimes held by elected officials is that working out a labor agreement is a simple matter, essentially little different from developing a highway construction contract or hiring a firm of architects. On the contrary, collective bargaining is a very demanding procedure requiring infinite patience, great ability in human relations, technical skill, and even some luck. It is no area for the novice—there are many disasters around the country where first agreements have resulted in the union virtually capturing city hall lock, stock, and dome.

Some municipal officials, still living emotionally in the era when they unilaterally set wages, hours, and conditions of employment, would like to deal with bargaining on a simple take-it-over-leave-it basis. This has failed in the industrial-commercial world and has had no success in the public sector either. The usual result is either an impasse or improvements in the offer that are higher than if normal procedures were followed.

On the other hand, inexperience has hurt some public management representatives in that they have approached the bargaining table unprepared and have wound up working merely to keep union demands within bounds. A well-prepared team has proposals of its own and looks on bargaining as a two-way street rather than as an uneven give-and-take relationship in which the city gives and the union takes.

One of the first decisions is whether to engage such outside help as an experienced negotiator, attorney, management consultant, or a nearby municipal official who can moonlight as a negotiator or adviser to the negotiators. The first choice is to develop in-house capability—that is, to train appropriate management personnel so they can provide continuing expertise in administration of the contract after signing and continuity of relationships with union leaders.

In hiring outside assistance, a problem may be encountered in setting an appropriate fee. Some practitioners like to be paid by the hour; the city then worries about consultant-made, dragging-out procedures. Some practitioners propose a flat rate; then the city worries about whether the settlement comes too quickly, at the expense of municipal interests.

It may be necessary, if unionization comes on suddenly, to begin with outside aid and gradually build up internal capability. There are numerous courses offered by public interest groups and universities, and some self-training is possible also through reading publications prepared by various organizations. One of the best ways is to involve a promising staffer in the intern program of the Labor-Management Relations Service so that he or she can receive on-the-job training in a city or county government working directly with full-time labor relations professionals.

In selecting a chief negotiator, officials should look for someone with empathy, patience, articulateness, and knowledge of labor relations and laws.

The chief negotiator's integrity and candor are mandatory for successful negotiations, because these traits create a climate of trust for all parties. Without integrity, candor, and trust, negotiations can easily slide into confrontation, impasse, and other acts of hostility.

The chief negotiator may be someone in the manager's office or in the personnel or finance department, the city attorney, or some other qualified person. The chief negotiator is the city's principal spokesman, but he will need the assistance of others, particularly the head of the agency involved in negotiations. He will have to keep the mayor and manager informed, first getting from them an understanding on how far he can go in contract terms, what he should be seeking, how firmly they feel about these matters, and how willing they are to take the heat if favorable terms are not forthcoming. He will have to deal frankly with the city council, directly or through others, on the same matters, so that a unified management position is clear and will persist even in the face of attack.

Some department heads will discourage offers to take part in the bargaining, since they don't want to be the "bad guys" with their own employees, but they do have the first-hand experience to understand the significance and possible hazards of seemingly "little" changes proposed by the union. Department heads who have taken part in the process can better administer the contract provisions resulting. It also helps weld them into a management team, rather than leaving them in command of independent sovereignties. Their participation also makes it more likely that they will have a positive contribution to make when departments are asked for suggestions on contract changes in the next round. At a minimum, they will better understand why they couldn't have their own way exclusively at the bargaining table.

Some city managers, mayors, and councilmen thirst for the thrill of bargaining. A few may be very good at it, but as a general rule they are well advised to leave this to others. When they take part, negotiations tend to focus on them and on their political vulnerability. Discussions become personality-oriented rather than issue-oriented. It is better for them to stay in close contact with the negotiators, advising and consenting as much as possible.

Top city officials may also be importuned by union heads to overturn the city negotiators, but elected officials have a responsibility to their colleagues, city management, and city taxpayers generally, as well as to the union members who are constituents.

Some officials have suggested that they sit in on the bargaining sessions, but there are dangers because any visit may become the focal point of the discussions. If city officials want to see the process, films of simulated sessions are readily available from professional groups, state municipal leagues, and other sources. In addition, many public interest group workshops include simulated sessions in their programs.

In the prenegotiating period the management team should try to anticipate union demands and prepare possible responses and, at the same time, gather and reinforce management demands for presentation.

Starting first with the analysis of possible union demands, management should:

1. Review contracts of comparable, nearby jurisdictions. Review wages and benefits accorded

without contract as well. Such data can be obtained directly from the communities involved or often from the contract files maintained at the U.S. Department of Labor. Other sources are *The Municipal Year Book* of the International City Management Association, wage surveys carried out by state municipal leagues, and U.S. Bureau of Labor Statistics comparisons of private and municipal pay in various cities. Data indicating trends and rates of improvement should be culled as well as the current status.

2. Internally, a review should be made of unmet union demands hanging over from previous negotiations in your city. Grievances and grievance arbitration awards should be examined for subject, frequency, and unit involved, to see if they can be reduced significantly through contract language changes. Perhaps most important of all, supervisors at all levels should be solicited for suggestions on contract language that will help them carry out their responsibilities.

3. Review of cost-of-living data for current costs and for trends.

In addition, the well-prepared negotiating team will assemble a great deal of data about the work force involved, so that it can assess and calculate the impact of various union proposals which may arise during negotiations. Included should be age distribution charts; length of service distribution charts; pay step distribution charts showing the number at each step; pay escalation charts showing improvement over various numbers of years; data on turnover, absenteeism, and average overtime; and the average wage rate for hourly employees. These could all be very handy in an uptight, right-on-deadline session. A tabulation of the dollar value of fringe benefits is a crucial ingredient for adequate negotiation of total compensation, yet many cities fail to compile this elementary information.

Negotiators will want to have in handy form all applicable personnel policies, executive orders, labor laws, and court decisions governing employment indexed and ready to take to negotiations in case they are needed.

When the union proposals are received they should be examined thoroughly before acceptance or counterproposals are made. Union negotiators should be expected to explain and justify each union proposal. In the process, management members will begin to separate those proposals which are really meant from those which are "eyewash" to placate only a few employees or to be used as trade-offs.

Union proposals should be routed by management negotiators to line managers for their reactions, particularly on how the right to manage is affected. Those with legal implications should be the subject of city attorney comment.

Proposals with cost implications—those regarding wages, benefits, new positions, new equipment—should be priced thoroughly by the personnel and budget departments, keeping in mind not only direct cost but also impact on overtime, fringe benefits, and overhead. Then negotiators should estimate possible effects on other parts of the work force, which are likely to insist on similar treatment (this is known as the "ripple" effect). Several detailed formulas for such calculations have been prepared by Drachman.[3]

The cost effect of the union proposals on tax rates is a traditional bargaining tool, but it should be used sparingly. It could boomerang if figures are not proven out and the union challenges future credibility. Even if your cost figures do check out, taxpayers may feel their representation at the bargaining table was not as effective as it should have been. Contract settlements are usually difficult for voters to understand, but tax rates are understood immediately.

Now we come to management's proposals. They should focus on language designed to improve operations, make employees accountable for their role in achieving city objectives, and eliminate ineffective work practices. Many slipshod practices have crept into municipal procedures and have been hallowed by years of practice without challenge. In some cases, traditional private sector policies of minimum crew requirements and maximum quotas have been transplanted to the government service. Productivity may be hampered. Contract language can help turn these things around.

In addition, thought must be given to counterproposals to union demands. This may take the form of a first-line position and then a second, retreat, position. On crucial issues the alternatives may be even larger in number.

Both parties will settle the ground rules for time, place, and perhaps length, for negotiations. There may be discussion over whether negotiations should be on work time or not. This is a delicate matter, involving union proposals for paid time for their negotiators, although many union representatives value their independence and prefer to "pay their own way." There may be concern about how big the union negotiating committee should be. One approach is to ask the union how many are coming and attempt the keep the number reasonably small in terms of available physical facilities.

The Negotiations

The initial session is likely to be crucial, setting the tone of the whole relationship. Management negotiators cannot lose by being sincere, calm, and courteous, although sometimes this is difficult in the strange new bilateral relationship. Be patient but persistent in confirming that all the union proposals are on the table and are not being dribbled in piece by piece, prolonging and exacerbating negotiations.

Discussion may be attempted, in the absence of a state statute to the contrary, on how any deadlocks that may occur are to be resolved. Agreement on mediation, fact finding, or arbitration may condition conduct at the bargaining table. Another option is to face the impasse when and if necessary.

Agreement should be reached at the start on the right to caucus. If possible, agreement should be reached that there will be no statements to the press, except joint ones, until either agreement or clear impasse has been reached. This avoids bargaining through the press and averts "spitting contests."

At the early stages of bargaining sessions should be spaced so that there is adequate time to consult with affected departments, gather facts, and analyze and prepare responses, as well as carry out other assigned municipal duties. Later, as the climax approaches, sessions tend to be more frequent and occasionally go around the clock. A good general rule is to bargain as long as progress is being made and recess when it is not. Tired people tend to become hostile people, and that is not the road to agreement.

Be prepared for disruptionists who try to take you off your guard or grandstanders who put on a show for union members. Negotiations provide opportunity for employees to let off steam, particularly in the first session, so try not to be offended by vulgarity, even name calling. You are not the first boss to be so addressed.

Hear people out, but don't be too quick to agree. You will be respected all the more for your caution and insistence on clarity for both sides. As matters are agreed upon, it may be desirable to initial each, making it clear that each provision is approved conditionally, subject to agreement on the entire contract.

One frequent error in negotiating is to yield on language which, without being so labeled, infringes on management rights. The argument is made that this doesn't cost the city anything, but in truth it may be even more expensive than the wage improvement clause. Management rights are easy to give away and hard to recover. One way to protect rights is to include a management rights clause.

There is respectable argument for a short clause which says essentially that management reserves to itself all rights not given up in the contract. There is also vigorous support for a long clause which includes a list of specific rights which management reserves to itself. As James Baird has pointed out, the long form does help in winning a grievance case, but it can also hurt if through oversight or changing conditions something is left off the list. Baird prefers the short form.[4]

As a general philosophy, many negotiators believe the shorter the contract the better—there is less ground for contention, less area to build upon in the next contract, less argument at the bargaining table, and more rights reserved to management.

The timetable for negotiations usually involves union submission of its complete set of proposals with oral explanation and justification of each item. After time for study a second session is scheduled at which management proposals are unveiled, accompanied by oral explanation and justification. Actual give-and-take bargaining may start then or at a subsequent session.

In bargaining, it is useful to think through an overall plan with possible trade-offs of major items (insisting on a quid pro quo) based on an analysis of your own and the union's priorities and then possible compromises on key issues where trade-offs are not likely. This should give you a view of the ultimate contract and a chance to decide whether the package is fair and acceptable. If not, some early revision of prospective positions is essential.

During negotiations keep a wary eye on each member of the union negotiating committee to assess weaknesses, power, and importance attached to particular issues. Any information available on the background of the negotiators, specifically how they would be affected by the outcome on key issues, is helpful in these assessments.

Avoid being pressured into developing provisions on the spot. Seek time out or another session, for haste does make waste; if nothing else, it creates fertile markets for grievance arbitrators. If you are going to compromise, get the goodwill benefit from the union by indicating the influence of its arguments.

Obviously, don't misrepresent facts or make commitments you are unwilling to keep. The contract lasts a long time, and the parties have to live with each other for every single day of it.

It is important to keep accurate and detailed notes, for memories falter and occasionally prove erratic. The chief negotiator may keep sketchy notes, but one member of the negotiating team ought to have the principal responsibility for complete notes on agreements and disagreements.

Some novices seek a model contract or want a contract clause checklist. Both have limited value, since the first tends to be utopian and misleading to the beginner and the second may open up paths which wiser negotiators would forego.

In general, it is important to get into the contract language dealing with problems that are present or are likely to develop but not to try to cover every possible contingency. Some troublesome areas management negotiators focus on include work assignments, overtime, seniority, definition of a grievance, and prohibitions against a strike or slowdown.

Most union negotiators concentrate, of course, on economic terms, but they also emphasize their desire for union security. Any union, but particularly one with a shaky hold on the membership, is likely to seek a dues checkoff and union shop, maintenance of membership, or agency shop.[5] Some management negotiators, overwhelmed by the union showing at the polls or in membership cards, have assumed the dues checkoff is an automatic right. Others have managed to salvage various clauses in a trade-off for such union-sought provisions. Agency shop is a much more controversial provision that still is being tested in the courts. In these and other union security areas, the crucial point is that management should not give anything away for free.

At some point management may decide to make its final offer. This is a significant step, not one to be abused by amateurs hoping to grab a bargain. When made it should represent the united view of the management side, both elected and appointed officials, and a willingness to stand behind it. There still may be more give and take based on the offer, but the proposal should represent essentially the final position.

The proposal may not be accepted, not because it is unreasonable but because of considerations on the other side of the table: a first-time union that has to prove itself, a union leader challenged for continuation in his post, or a feeling by the union committee that more may be available. Thus, substantial yielding after the final offer is an invitation to similar scrabbling over the last penny next time.

If management stands firm, there are likely to be charges of failure to bargain in good faith. What is good faith? Boards and courts have wrestled with this one since the first labor laws were enacted. In general, it is a willingness to sit down at reasonable times, to confer about appropriate matters, and to put into writing any agreement reached. The obligation to bargain, however, does not compel either party to agree to a proposal by the other, nor does it require either party to make a concession to the other.

Failure to bargain in good faith in the industrial-commercial sector is an unfair labor practice, and in those states with comprehensive statutes this approach has been followed. But whether there is a statute or not, both parties will have to stand before the bar of public opinion and demonstrate that they have been reasonable and, indeed, eager, to reach a fair agreement.

Timing is important in the art of negotiating. Allan Drachman, an experienced negotiator, has commented:

There is no identifiable set of uniform procedures which, if followed, will insure successful negotiations. Sometimes a gracious YES rendered early will reap handsome dividends. At other times a hard line will likewise have a salutary effect. If the negotiator determines that saying yes to an item will not result in any meaningful union concession, he may be forced to continue to say no until a "tradeoff" becomes timely. Indeed, there are times when a management negotiator is compelled to engage in oral argument in order to probe the genuine union sentiment about a proposal.

There are also times when an issue can be settled immediately. Under these circumstances it is critical that the management negotiator should have sufficient authority or discretion to make the decision on the spot with confidence that his decision will be backed up by the chief executive officer. In the alternative, he must be able to promptly confer with the chief executive by phone. Caucuses during the negotiations are frequently useful so that parties can adapt quickly to settlement possibilities which develop during the give and take of negotiations and which, if not dealt with promptly, may be lost.

Since the basic feature of negotiation is communication, a management negotiator's choice of technique may depend on how well the other side is communicating. If the union negotiating committee is realtively sophisticated and under the control of an experienced professional, communication is likely to be more clearly effective. If, on the other hand, the union negotiating committee is a leaderless group of individuals, each seeking to outmilitant the other, the likelihood of reaching a mutually agreeable settlement is significantly reduced. Regardless which approach the negotiator is taking at any particular moment, he should be retaining the essential flexibility of mental attitude and settlement options to be effective when the time is ripe.[6]

Impasse Procedures

In the event that negotiations, no matter how well prepared and carried out, wind up in impasse, there are three principal methods of resolution:

1. Mediation. An impartial third party works between the parties to offer advice, persuasion, and alternatives in hopes that they will help the parties come to agreement. He is not concerned with the fairness of the result and he cannot direct a result. Both parties retain final control.

2. Fact finding. An impartial third party gathers data on the issues in controversy and makes a report on his recommendations, perhaps privately to the parties, perhaps publicly, perhaps both. Both parties retain final control over whether to accept his recommendations.

3. Arbitration. An impartial third party takes evidence on the issues in contention and hands down an award, a decision binding on both parties. It can be advisory, if the parties desire, in which case it is not much different from a fact finder's recommendations, since the parties can accept or reject.

In either fact finding or arbitration, the choice of the third party neutral is important. Participants will be interested in his background and experience. Another important aspect is adequate preparation, since neutrals come to the issue without the earlier dialogue and must be adquately briefed if a party's interests are to be well represented.

Another form of impasse resolution is the strike, illegal though it may be in most jurisdictions. Publications are available on contingency plans for continuing standby operations during strikes.[7] In general, nobody gains by a strike. The sooner the parties get the fire out of their speech and get their persons back to the bargaining table the better both their interests will be served. A strike in the public sector, some believe, does not have nearly the economic impact as in the private sector and is really a vying for public opinion. This is something different from a private sector economic endurance contest in which each side tries to outlast the other. A sound position, effectively articulated, and an appeal to the courts in illegal actions, reinforced by as much service as can be rendered by supervisory personnel, is probably the best stance in such difficult situations.

CONTRACT ADMINISTRATION

Hoping for the best, contract signing, the next step is effective contract administration. The new agreement should be carefully and fully explained to supervisors—top, middle, and bottom—and, where appropriate, connection should be made between contract language adopted and suggestions offered in the prenegotiation period by supervisors.

The first-line supervisor is the key man in day-to-day labor relations. He is often up from the ranks, associates intimately with his workers, feels the heavy constraints of civil service and headquarters personnel policies, and is usually inexperienced in dealing with unions. He may turn out to effectively undercut management's hard-won provisions or he may turn out to be a born grievance provoker, resenting bitterly any rights given in the contract to individual employees. His education is, therefore, vital.

This may require a lot more than mere training in labor relations; it may suggest the need for supervisory training, to show him how to be a supervisor in more than title and pay only and how to deal with employees in a collective bargaining atmosphere. A good supervisor can avert or solve grievances. A bad one may cause an endless drain on middle and top management time and create an antimanagement atmosphere throughout a work unit. The stakes are large.

Al Leggat, former director of labor relations for the city of Detroit, has outlined a formula for supervisors in grievance handling:

1. *Know your tools—the provisions of the labor-management agreement.*

   Be well acquainted with the grievance procedures and City policies. These are your special tools. They will help you do the job only if you become skillful in using them.

2. *Know your power to adjust grievances.*

   You are the front line of management to your employees and make your own determinations. A supervisor who openly relies on the judgment of others—or who says he is making a decision because someone else told him to do so—quickly loses the respect of those he supervises. Of course, in many cases you will want to discuss the matter with your immediate supervisor. You are entitled to this advice—often you must have it!

3. *Get all of the facts, restate them and then settle grievances informally and quickly.*

   Be prompt in making whatever settlements you are able to make. If you need advice, get it as quickly as possible.

4. *Be sincere, sympathetic, fair and understanding.*

   You will enjoy the respect of all your work force if impartiality and unprejudiced thinking is obvious. Your conduct should always merit the approval of the workers.

5. *Do not "bargain" grievance adjustments.*

   Be a fact-getter, a decision-maker, and not a negotiator. Judge each case on its individual merits.

6. *Avoid the use of underhanded methods to "outsmart" grievants.*

   Be above any trickery. You are going to live a lifetime and your long-range reputation means a lot more than any temporary adjustment which smacks of deceit. Don't adopt questionable expedients. . . .

7. *Always have a justifiable basis for your decisions.*

   It is your responsibility to ascertain all the facts and to review all relevant records. Usually this can't be done without asking questions. Remember, the aggrieved employee and the Steward want to air their difficulties. You should ask question after question to help do so and to get all of the facts. Then, ask questions concerning the records and concerning the way in which to handle this kind of case of your supervisor. Don't hesitate to ask for advice when circumstances require. Ask for advice based upon the facts you have developed.

8. *Your decision making must be clear and definite.*

   Be tactful, especially in the event of a grievance denial. It is natural to resent the denial of an alleged right or to be told that one is wrong. Personalize the things that are good—de-personalize those that are bad.

9. *Don't be afraid to admit when you are wrong.*

   This attitude encourages employees to admit their own errors. Also, don't blame others for your own mistakes.

11. *Adjust all grievances so that Union representatives have a knowledge of all the facts and a thorough understanding of the reasons for the decision.*

   Prejudice against Union representatives is irresponsible. Union officials can be, and often are, of genuine assistance in adjusting troublesome grievance problems.

12. *Keep well informed as to the outcome of grievance cases on appeal.*

   Be acquainted with grievance disposition at all levels. Keep informed: Remember, at all times that personnel or labor relations and *your* immediate supervisor are anxious to help you; but, they may not know what tools you need unless you ask for them.[8]

Municipal management, while encouraging resolution of grievances in individual departments, will want to create a central repository for review so that uniformity is developed and inequities are discouraged. The personnel department may be the appropriate spot.

Conclusion

While collective bargaining is a very demanding vehicle, requiring wearying hours upon hours of preparation, discussion, and confrontation, it is a proven way of reconciling employee interests with that of management and provides an outlet for strong feelings which might otherwise become explosive.

Archibald Cox, former solicitor general of the United States, has made this comment:

Participating in debate often produces changes in a seemingly fixed position either because new facts are brought to light or because the strengths and weaknesses of the several arguments become apparent.

Sometimes the parties hit upon some novel compromise of an issue which has been thrashed over and over. Much is gained even by giving each side a better picture of the strength of the other's convictions.[9]

And so, good luck in gearing up for labor relations.

The author of this chapter gratefully acknowledges the research, thought, and reassurance of Roger Dahl, assistant director, Labor-Management Relations Service.

[1]James Baird, Management Rights: Little Understood, Little Used, Quickly Lost (Washington, D.C.: Labor-Management Relations Service, 1973), pp. 11–12. No. 17 in series Strengthening Local Government through Better Labor Relations.

[2]A useful guide is Allan W. Drachman, Municipal Negotiations: From Differences to Agreement (Washington, D.C.: Labor-Management Relations Service, 1970). No. 5 in series Strengthening Local Government through Better Labor Relations.

[3]Ibid., pp. 29–34.

[4]Baird, Management Rights, pp. 7–8.

[5]Drachman, Municipal Negotiations. p. 47, provides these definitions; *"Union Shop.* The employer may hire anyone, but all employees must join the union within a specified time period after hire, often after 30 days, and must remain members as a condition of employment. A modified union shop may exempt those already employed at the time the provision was negotiated but who had, until then, not joined the union.

"Agency Shop (Agency Service Fee). Requires all employees who do not join the union to pay a fixed amount, usually the equivalent of union dues to the union treasury as a condition of employment, to help defray the union's expenses as bargaining agent. Some clauses provide for payments to be allocated to the union's welfare fund or a charity rather than to the union's treasury.

"Maintenance-of-Membership Provision. Employees who are union members at the time the provision is negotiated, or who thereafter voluntarily join the union, must maintain their union membership for the duration of the agreement as a condition of employment."

[6]Ibid., pp. 12–13.

[7]See, for example, Carmen D. Sasso, Coping with Public Employee Strikes: A Guide for Public Officials (Chicago: Public Personnel Association, 1970).

[8]Al Leggat, The Supervisor: Key Man in Labor Relations (Washington, D.C.: Labor-Management Relations Service, 1970). Supplement to No. 6 in series Strengthening Local Government through Better Labor Relations.

[9]Archibald Cox, "The Duty To Bargain in Good Faith," 71 Harvard Law Review 1401, 1412.

18

Public Information

WITH MANY DIVERSIFIED INTERESTS competing for citizen attention, administrators should realize that systematic effort must be made to communicate and create positive relations with citizens. But most administrators continue to follow a reactive role in communicating with their publics. They answer questions as they arise and respond to developments as requested. By using professional information assistance, the administrator may help turn the reactive role of government communications to a proactive role.

The trained public information officer, with his knowledge of the media and of what interests the public, can help improve communications with the public. He can sense a story, he knows which media will use it, and he can gather the information the reporter needs.

The information officer can also help develop such avenues of communication—internal and external—as newsletters, direct mail pieces, reports, and directories.

The Nature of Public Relations

A question of definition arises in any discussion of public relations programs. Because the citizens we communicate with often have a stereotype of the PR man (as popularized by motion pictures) as glossing over events and pushing clients, we hesitate to use this term. People can, however, accept such a term as "information programs," because they understand and accept many kinds of messages as part of daily living.

The task of the information officer is more than a mere presentation of information. Since communication is a two-way street, public ex-

posure alone will not suffice. Through communication, as a much broader process than publicity, the practitioner is charged with sensing what is going on in the total pattern of activity—listening, analyzing, working to obtain constructive associations with citizens, and communicating through appropriate media.

Public relations programs are geared to keeping citizens informed about the overall administration of government affairs. Ideally, this will prompt them to participate more fully in the government of the community.

The actual public relations program is in three parts.[1] The first is the negative portion where we find out what the city is doing that annoys citizens. Often overlooked, this process of seeking and correcting sources of irritation can go a long way toward improving government-citizen relations. Something as simple as better wording of a form letter can be a significant improvement.

The second, or passive, portion of the program means saying or doing nothing. It is very difficult to bring off this approach successfully.

Relating most directly to the information officer is the third, or positive, part of the program, which involves building good relations with the media and developing various forms of communication with the citizens.

Despite the fact that it has been established longer in government than in any other field, public relations continues to be a difficult and controversial task for government. Two reasons for this are ambiguous public expectations of government and confusion about the meaning of public relations. Ambiguity is evident when legislators enact governmental programs and yet resist attempts to make these programs widely known. Complicating the ambiguity is the mistaken perception of public relations as advertising, which it is not, or as publicity, which is only one part of public relations.

In addition, many citizens apply a double standard to government versus private enterprise. Generally, people will accept the right of business to publicize and advertise even though the customer pays for it in the long run. But the same citizenry often regards a similar expenditure of funds for government information as frivolous or a waste of the taxpayers' money.

Public officials often feel that local media complicate information to the extent that the daily business of good public administration is lost in the clamor of inconsequential issues "blown up out of all proportion."[2] Sometimes this feeling is justified.

While we would like to think that all newspapers and all television and radio stations are fair and unbiased, we know they aren't. Introduction of the human element makes such an expectation unrealistic. It may be comforting to note, however, that omissions and unwarranted emphasis catch up with the media, as well as with public officials in the form of a credibility gap. Public trust is lost.

Objectives

Primarily, the public relations process of the municipality should enable management to understand the government's nature and purposes thoroughly, to communicate this understanding to others, and to observe and evaluate the effect.[3]

The objectives of the information program must take into account the growing complexities of all levels of government. These complexities are what have increased the importance, as well as difficulty, of effective communication. When establishing the position of community information officer the city of Saginaw, Michigan, outlined the following objectives, which can serve for most cities and towns:

1. To assist in the translation of public opinion into concrete programs by passing on to the city administration and city council citizen opinions, suggestions, and complaints, so that they may become the basis for building realistic new programs and for making necessary modifications in ongoing programs
2. To clarify and explain the policies of the city government
3. To make information available to citizens about various services provided by the city so that they may fully utilize and gain the greatest benefit from the services
4. To educate citizens by providing them with the facts relating to the government activities, policies, and procedures, as well as with an understanding of those facts.

Community Publics

In meeting the objectives outlined above, two broad groups of publics must of necessity be identified.

One group is the internal public—the people who work for the government. The activities of the government and its policy changes affect these employees, and they expect to be consulted and kept up to date.

The quality of communication between the administration and its employees will determine how they relate to the citizens of the community. The overall image of the municipality hinges on these day-to-day contacts.

The other group, the external public, is the one to which the information officer directs most of his attention. Ultimately, the administration must answer to these diversified groups of citizens. Therefore, their part in the process of forming and implementing policy must be completely understood.

The groups of citizens may be identified on the basis of social, political, generation, income, or other characteristics. Although they are groups with sufficient cohesiveness to be identified in the flow of influence and opinion, they lack any formal institutionalization.[4]

External groups (or publics) with common interests include minority groups, age groups, religious groups, income groups, and occupational groups.

Personal observation tells us that most of these groups are not categories. Any of us may be in two or more groups and may, so to speak, switch our membership upon occasion from one group to another. Thus, groups are constantly changing as people's preferences change, along with their ages, incomes, educational levels, etc.

Once these groups have been identified, they may be linked with formal groupings such as clubs, associations, or other organizations.

It is important for the information officer to be alert to the viewpoints of the various publics. In order to mobilize specific groups on specific issues, he must put himself in their shoes.

To analyze a proposed government policy for the citizen, the information officer should be a character actor. First he must understand the background from which the idea grew and the needs and objectives of the sponsors. He should walk all around the subject, imagining himself a member of the various publics affected by the new policy. Sometimes he must think of himself, for example, as a member of a leading religious or patriotic group, a farmer, a factory worker, a bookkeeper, a housewife, or a garage mechanic.[5]

He must also recognize that there are certain segments of the population which are more civic-minded than others and are better informed on local government activities because they make an effort to obtain information. These groups can provide invaluable assistance by channeling information to citizens, as well as to the municipality, as feedback for evaluating procedures.

Finally, the information officer must recognize, regretfully but realistically, that interest groups can exert pressure far beyond the size or importance of the people they speak for. Usually a minority, sometimes a minority within a minority, their recommendations may be beneficial, neutral, or harmful. The astute mayor, city councilman, city manager, or other public official learns quickly to differentiate and to consider the wider interests of the silent majority.

The Practitioners

It has become increasingly apparent that the information process should be a team effort. Returning to the theory that the employees constitute an internal public, further segmentation must be mentioned. Working for the government are the city council, the chief administrator, the department and division heads, and the regular employees. These people determine the relationship of the municipality to the citizens it serves. Their roles are not identical in the information process, but these initial relationships must be in top order to assure that communications with the citizens are fair and complete. Strengthened interaction and understanding between the internal groups is integral to positively reaching the public.

This is why it is important for the city to issue a written information policy. Suggested guidelines for such a policy are that department and division heads should answer questions within the framework of their knowledge and responsibility and should avoid guessing or speculating about things that are not within their immediate sphere of responsibility.

The information officer serves as a pipeline. With his general understanding of government activities, he is able to steer a media representative in the right direction if further details are required. He fills the reporter in on background information and answers questions which might unnecessarily tie up the department head or other administrator. To do this job, the information officer must know what is going on.

Department and division heads should consult with the information officer on matters which require public relations considerations. This certainly would apply to letters or notices mailed to a substantial number of citizens explaining policy changes (for example, a water rate increase). The information officer can sometimes help ward off negative response by the mere changing of a word or phrase. He won't magically eliminate the unhappy citizen, but he can help make him more receptive to change.

Periodically, the information officer should review form letters used to notify citizens of street construction projects, removal of diseased parkway trees, noncompliance with zoning ordinances, and other routine matters.

THE ROLE OF THE CITY COUNCIL

As the legislative and policy-making body, the city council sets the tone for the municipal government. The councilman is in the center of the cross-currents of influence and opinion. For many citizens he is *the* representative of the city government, the one to whom they turn with grievances and questions.

It is usually a particular climate of public opinion which has put a councilman into office in the first place. He responds by formulating the policies and legislation which the citizens favor. Public attitudes may be determined by public opinion polls, public meetings, questionnaires, or tabulated data on inquiries and complaints received at city hall.

For example, the city of St. Louis set up a $110 million improvement program as a result of a study by a "leading citizen" committee named by the mayor. With the department heads, the committee surveyed city needs and then decided which were urgent. On a smaller scale, a citizen committee appointed by the village board in Oak Park, Illinois, studied the need for a street lighting program and made specific recommendations for proceeding with a $6 million project. Appointment of the committee was made when a public opinion survey showed that 72 percent of the citizens favored a street lighting improvement program.

City objectives often have the best chance of realization when they are set by the city officials and citizens with the help of a public relations counselor.[6] Objectives, in final form, are precise. They should be practical, considering time, money, personnel, public attitudes, and general economic and social conditions.

The importance of responding to public opinion is impressed upon the councilman as soon as he announces that he is seeking public office. Once he assumes this position, he begins to learn about the interplays of publics in government activity.

To be objective the councilman must weigh how his action will affect various citizens and then try to vote in the public interest. The public interest may be viewed in several ways, but the most widely held concept is that of consensus—the position in which there is sufficient community support to represent either a majority or a substantial minority with majority acquiescence.[7]

Fortunately, the city councilman will find that he is not as a practical matter seeking the public interest as if it were clear, unified, and ascertainable. Rather, he is seeking an adjustment of a mélange of interests competing for the time and attention of elected officials.[8]

One of the functions of the city's information officer is to help bridge the gap between the elected officials and the citizens. The citizen must be shown how the council is accomplishing what he (the citizen) wants, and how he may participate in the government. Methods of participation which may be suggested include:[9] (1) reading and discussing city reports with family, neighbors, and associates; (2) suggesting city activities on which more information is needed; (3) recommending improvements in municipal reporting techniques; (4) advising city hall of conditions that need correction (street lighting, fire hazards, pavement breaks, etc.); (5) serving on city, neighborhood, school, or community committees; and (6) voting in all city elections and urging others to vote.

The council members should be prepared to speak with reporters and community leaders regarding their positions on issues which affect the community.

In some municipalities a communications committee of the council has been formed. By working with the information officer on a regular basis, this committee can be certain that the council's actions are correctly explained and that public reports are factually correct.

THE ROLE OF THE CHIEF ADMINISTRATOR

The chief administrator is the key figure in the communications process.

The city manager has an inescapable obligation for public relations, an obligation that is just as compelling as his responsibilities for sound public finance, effective personnel systems, and other areas of management. He must instigate training for employees in all areas of public relations....It is the city manager's job to deal with the press on a knowledgeable basis....It is the city manager's job, using all means available to him, to fashion improvement in the image of the city. He sets the pace for the entire municipality.[10]

The formal structure for public information ranges from a department of information (found in the largest cities and counties) to the assignment of information duties to an administrative assistant, a common practice in places with city managers or other appointed chief administrators.

A word of caution is in order about assigning an administrative assistant to information in addition to other responsibilities. If the assistant is loaded with other duties, and news development happens in spare moments, the job won't get done. The person with this responsibility should be allowed plenty of time in which to uncover interesting stories buried within the organization.[11]

The chief administrator, however, is the person ultimately responsible for public relations and public information. The city council sets the tone; the administrator sets the tempo.

The top executive must keep everything in balance. He must help to bridge the information gaps between elected officials and citizens and between municipal employees and citizens, as well as between municipal employees and elected officials. Increasingly, administrators are relying on information specialists to assist in keeping in touch with the various publics and to plan, execute, and measure specific proposals. There is a fine line here. The administrator can be assisted, but he cannot divorce himself from the information process, because it is "fundamental to and nonseparable from the administrative process."[12]

Ideally, the information officer should be included in major decision-making meetings, should have an office located close to the chief administrator, and should be in constant contact with him. He is then in a good position to advise.

It is prudent to have someone at the conference table whose job it is to consider the press and public reaction. Such a safeguard, when pointed out, seem obvious. But public administrators, with their minds keyed to city issues, programs, and projects, often don't think in terms of public relations hazards until it's too late.[13]

The information officer who is fully aware of the inner workings of the government can assist reporters when they call in a routine check to see if there are any new developments.

As long as the reported knows he can get to the top man when he wants to, the system works well. The information officer, however, should not become the official mouthpiece for the ad-

ministrator. If he even attempts to be the only spokesman for the government, the information officer is producing more problems for himself and the administration by fostering a climate of suspicion and misunderstanding. If the media and the citizens cannot reach the chief administrator when they feel they need to, their gripe will be: "We can't even get an answer from that so and so." To put it as plainly as possible, don't dodge the reporter; keep your door open; be accessible.

THE ROLE OF THE EMPLOYEE

The role of the employee in municipal government relations must not be underestimated. Constantly in the public eye, the municipal employee personifies the municipal government. Many citizens rarely see personally the chief administrator, the department heads, the planners and other professional personnel, the members of the city council, the mayor, or the members of boards and commissions. Their perception of municipal government is the license clerk, the policemen in the patrol car, the chargeout clerk at a branch library, the playground supervisor, and the refuse collector. These are the people who decisively influence the image of government.

These employees are the rank and file—the troops—who get the daily routine done. To do it well they need a good understanding of their government—what it is and what it does. This is provided through orientation training and through briefings as needed to keep everyone up-to-date. Employees who understand and take pride in their government are able to answer many questions and to refer others to the appropriate sources.

A courteous and correct referral scores points for the city. Only negative feelings are generated with the dreaded runaround. Employees should be instructed to take the citizen's name and phone number if they are in doubt about where to refer a query. They should then follow through by having the proper person return the call as soon as possible.

Such factors as the tone of voice of a switchboard operator, the attitude of a housing inspector, and the manner of collecting fees by a cashier can confirm or nullify any well-planned public relations project. Schedule periodic meetings with these and similar employees to discuss public relations.

The information officer's role in this process is to work to promote understanding between the employee and the administration. Channels for an upward flow of employee opinion must be created and utilized.[14] Employee papers, bulletin boards, and suggestion systems may be employed to supplement, but not supplant, the working communication system.

A news capsule of city council meetings is a useful device for establishing a communication link between employees and elected officials. A concise statement of action taken on each agenda item can be used to summarize the meeting. The information officer should prepare the capsule as soon as possible, so that distribution to employees directly follows the meeting, and employees thus have an accurate account of council action.

Communicating with the Public

Bringing information to public attention is by far the most familiar part of the public information process to the average citizen. His daily newspaper, his morning news on his car radio, his evening news on TV, and an occasional encounter with an annual report or city hall newsletter make up much of what he thinks of as "information." The various ways of transmitting this information are known collectively as news media; of these, the most important is the newspaper.

The Press

The newspaper reporter's concern is to provide a fast, lively, and informative account of what goes on at city hall (a term newspaper people use to cover just about everything a municipal government does). He is concerned with "the people's right to know"; therefore, he is zealous in pursuing stories that are in his judgment of wide interest, even if such stories are embarrassing to city officials.

Reporters may not resent it if they are asked to hold back on such matters as reporting on a crime, which might jeopardize apprehending a criminal. They may well resent it if you withhold information because, in your opinion, the public won't be interested.

The information officer is usually a former news or public relations man. With this background he has a valuable understanding of the requirements of local media: time limitations and deadlines; the need to "translate" professional and technical terms into words that are commonly understood; the relative news value of developments; and the uses and limitations of news releases, interviews, and press conferences.

A bureau chief has put it this way: if these three things are available at city hall—open doors, a road map to find them, and all the necessary printed material along the way—then the media's only remaining question in terms of doing its job is its own efficiency.

Perhaps the most helpful step for promoting sound press relations "is to employ on the city manager's personal staff an assistant or aide who possesses a skill and a liking for working with newspaper reporters."[15]

Each department head should be aware that this assistant represents the manager with the press. Without this understanding and cooperation the aide cannot give valid assistance to the press.[16] Instead of viewing the press assistant as an information source, the reporter will take a path around him.

The News Release. Some newsmen regard the press release as an insult. They don't want the information officer to do their job. Nonetheless, the release has proven a valuable reference tool in that it gives the reporter background data, proper spelling of names, correct figures, and the administration's interpretation of an event. However, the information officer should never expect the newspaper to use his release exactly as written.

Always have a name and phone number— usually the information officer's—at the top of the release, so that newsmen can call for more details or for clarification, if necessary.

News releases are particularly useful for smaller newspapers, where smaller staff prohibits complete coverage of city hall.

Advance Information. Important municipal reports (such as budgets, committee studies, new ordinances, or program proposals) should be given to the reporter as soon as possible. A copy of the city council meeting agenda should be forwarded to city hall reporters a day or two in advance of the meeting. This alerts them to news which may be breaking and also tells them if there are subjects to look into prior to the meeting.

It is unfair to expect complete coverage if the news media have not been given sufficient advance information. The reporter is dealing with deadlines and limited space allowance. He will pick up the meat of the report, but he cannot possibly give in-depth coverage if he hasn't had an opportunity to digest the report or ask questions about it. He won't have an opportunity to expand his coverage later, because the report will quickly become old news.

Time for clarifying questions from the media should be a part of the presentation of the report. Doubts and questions can be erased, and the result may be a good, reasoned presentation which will head off substantial opposition.[17]

Government policy should emphasize fair and impartial dissemination of information. An advantage should not be given to one newspaper over another or to one medium over another. If a reporter spots a story first, and you promise to fill him in on details if he can wait until these are available, this commitment must be honored as an exclusive. Advising other reporters at the same time would not be fair.

There is an important and delicate exception also to be considered:

Let's say the reporter for the morning paper has faithfully covered the entire meeting (where a major news break occurred) while the other media chose not to "staff" it. Is it fair for the information officer to get on the phone and give the story to the television man who didn't cover the meeting, thus allowing him the break on his late news program?

The answer depends on a number of other circumstances and frankly, the self-interest of the administration. However, it is a serious question rising from the growing resentment of newspaper men who complain that while they get out on the line and cover the news, public information officers are doing much of the work for their electronic competitors.

As a general rule of thumb, it can be rationalized that if there is a reporter from a major media outlet present when the news happens or is announced, the public's information rights are protected; and,

therefore, your obligation to notify the other media as soon as possible is modified. To be fair, the game surely must provide some rewards for the man and the media who work hard to get the news as opposed to those who don't.[18]

The Press Conference. The press conference provides a format for the administrator to speak with all newsmen at the same time. While it is a convenient device for the administrator, it also can put him on the spot; he is the moving target for hard questions. Mistakes can—and will—be reported. A private interview is more relaxed. In the atmosphere of a conversational interview a reporter probably won't take advantage of a temporary slip if one is made.

Definitely avoid the hazard of a weekly press conference. News isn't that regular, and you will quickly turn off a willing press by gathering them together for "no news." Only "big" news warrants an organized press conference. More than one or two a year would be unusual for all but the largest cities.

If it is necessary to limit the conference to a certain amount of time, be sure that this is clear to reporters when the meeting is convened. Otherwise you leave yourself open to the criticism that they are being cut short because of the type of questions that are being asked, or the fear that something unfavorable to the administration will be uncovered.

OTHER MEANS OF COMMUNICATION

The Electronic Media. Radio and television, by their nature, do not lend themselves to local news coverage in most cities. Time allotted to local news is very brief and, in fact, with the exception of the larger cities, is almost nonexistent.

However, the possibility of some coverage for smaller communities should be explored. A radio or television interview or panel program may have a spot for a community expert whose prestige would attract positive attention to the municipality. For example, A new or unique approach to a community problem or an all-out citizen effort to complete a project may be featured. Also, radio and television can often donate brief time spots for public service announcements of community events.

Personal Contact. One of the best ways to inform citizens is to take the government to the people by means of neighborhood forums, listen-in sessions, or speakers' bureaus.

City officials can meet with citizens on an informal basis to develop understanding of a particular proposal or of the government in general. A distinct advantage of these sessions is that the citizens are made aware in a direct way of the fact that the administration is interested in their problems and in their uncertainties about local government as it pertains to them. Citizen feedback is also readily available and may prove invaluable for revision of proposals, etc.

The municipality must also consider how it will reach groups of citizens that do not belong to the civic clubs or service organizations that provide the natural forums for speakers. One approach might be to schedule periodic visits of a minibus of officials to various areas of the city. The citizens would be invited to visit the mobile unit to discuss community issues.

In addition, area meetings might be scheduled at schools or churches. Officials should seek out representatives of various segments of the community so that bridges for communications can be established and maintained.

Annual Reports. Basically, two types of annual report are prepared. One is a financial report, aimed primarily at bankers, bondholders, or buyers. The other, which is the responsibility of the information office, is a factual summary of city operations. It delineates specific accomplishments of the various departments, outlines future problems and prospects, and translates financial data in terms of overall expenditures and income sources.

The format for the report may be a booklet, a newspaper supplement, or a calendar which also notes dates of city meetings and special events.

Data for the report are collected and edited by the information officer working with the various department heads. A conversational tone should be used. Professional photographs and design help provide an attractive and readable report.

Distribution ideally should be to every household in the community. This may be accomplished by mailing or by house-to-house delivery. If the report is incorporated as a supplement to a local newspaper, copies should also be available to citizens who do not subscribe to the paper. They should be available at the libraries, the municipal offices, and other public buildings. Some cities incorporate municipal directories of staff and department phone numbers and responsibilities in the annual report.

Another approach is to work jointly with other government agencies to prepare a handbook or directory of community services. The community handbook provides a source of information on all phases of community life, including government, schools, churches, hospitals, and other agencies.

Bulletins and Newsletters. Information bulletins may be prepared to cover topics which are of interest to a specific group of citizens. Examples include such topics as a checklist for guarding against burglaries, rules for dog owners, hints for house repairs, or fire safety rules. They may also be written to explain specifically how a comprehensive planning program will affect a particular neighborhood.

Some bulletins may report activities of appointed boards and commissions and cover city beautification, environmental protection, community relations, or zoning matters. These reports are mailed to a list that includes community leaders who are in a position to help disseminate the information further.

In some suburban communities, where local press coverage is inadequate or nonexistent, a general newsletter covering municipal activities is published and mailed to every household on a monthly or quarterly basis.

Other Approaches. Other methods of disseminating information are limited only by a municipality's ingenuity and financial resources. All but the smallest cities can develop a modest slide show if a talented amateur photographer is on the city payroll. Film strips with color and sound are quite effective and are relatively inexpensive to prepare. Audiotapes and videotapes are gaining acceptance, particularly when professional help is available from a state university.

Cities, towns, and other local governments have for years sponsored many kinds of activities and special events. Carefully planned and timed, these can be quite popular and informative. These activities and events include tours of municipal facilities, youth days at city hall, personal invitations to city council meetings, dedication ceremonies, art festivals, classes in city government, open houses, and historical commemorations.

EVALUATION

The time to start an evaluation of public relations activities is when you begin building the overall public relations program.[19]

Readership surveys should be conducted to find out if communications are understandable and if they generate response. Surveys of this kind can be conducted in various ways—by telephone, by direct mail, by personal interview, or by recording votes through various techniques from postcards to suggestion boxes.

Evaluation and feedback never stop, because people change, and their attitudes and needs change as well. The information officer works in a circle, not a straight line: defining objectives, defining policy, defining central themes or ideas to be communicated, determining audiences, selecting media or kinds of action to be taken, scheduling activities and evaluating results.[20]

[1]Peter F. Starrett, MASS COMMUNICATIONS FOR LOCAL OFFICIALS (Tempe, Ariz.: Arizona State University Institute of Public Administration, 1970), p. 6.

[2]Ibid., p. 2.

[3]Howard Stephenson, ed., HANDBOOK OF PUBLIC RELATIONS (New York: McGraw-Hill Book Company, 1960), p. 11.

[4]Theories and concepts of public opinion, particularly on the reciprocal effects of the flows of influence and opinion, are summarized in Garth N. Jones, "The Multitudinous Publics," in MUNICIPAL PUBLIC RELATIONS, ed. Desmond L. Anderson (Chicago: International City Managers' Association, 1966), pp. 65—76.

[5]Philip Lesley, PUBLIC RELATIONS HANDBOOK, 3rd ed. (Englewood Cliffs, N.J.: Prentice-Hall, Inc., 1967), p. 43.

[6]Stephenson, HANDBOOK OF PUBLIC RELATIONS, p. 711.

[7]David S. Arnold, "Public Relations," in MANAGING THE MODERN CITY, ed. James M. Banovetz (Washington, D.C.: International City Management Association, 1971), p. 384.

[8]Ibid.

[9]Stephenson, HANDBOOK OF PUBLIC RELATIONS, pp. 712—13.

[10]Desmond L. Anderson, "Public Relations and the Administrative Process," in MUNICIPAL PUBLIC RELATIONS, p. 33.

[11]Starrett, MASS COMMUNICATIONS, p. 7.

[12]Anderson, in MUNICIPAL PUBLIC RELATIONS, p. 34.

[13]Starrett, MASS COMMUNICATIONS, p. 9.

[14] Scott M. Cutlip and Allen H. Center, EFFECTIVE PUBLIC RELATIONS, 3RD ED. (Englewood Cliffs, N.J.: Prentice-Hall, Inc., 1964), p. 232.

[15] E. Frederick Bien, "Needed: A Reliable Press Assistant," PUBLIC MANAGEMENT, December 1970, p. 8.

[16]Ibid.

[17]James J. Cook, "Needed: Putting on Reporter's Shoes," PUBLIC MANAGEMENT, December 1970, p. 9.

[18]Starrett, MASS COMMUNICATIONS, p. 33.

[19]James B. Strenski, "Guidelines for Evaluating a PR Program," MANAGEMENT REVIEW, March 1970, p. 35.

[20]Ibid., pp. 35—36. Defined as the seven key elements that provide stepping-stones to efficient public relations.

19

Institutionalizing Citizen Participation

Cᴵᴛɪᴢᴇɴ ᴘᴀʀᴛɪᴄɪᴘᴀᴛɪᴏɴ has become a familiar term to almost every municipal administrator. In theory, the concept of citizen participation has widespread acceptance, but practically it may raise the specter of innumerable administrative roadblocks to "efficiency" in municipal management. The participation of the non-elective, nonappointive citizenry in public decision making has become a fact of modern life, yet the number of alternative combinations and degrees of participatory activity remains bewildering. Who should participate? In what programs? When? With what expected results? How will it affect "good" management?

The answers to these questions are extremely complex; consequently, many administrators have refused to deal with these matters. However, be it a human right or a political expediency, citizen participation is a factor to be reckoned with in municipal administration.

Citizen participation is a nuisance. It is costly, it is time consuming, it is frustrating; but we cannot dispense with it for three fundamental reasons. . . .

First, participation, in and of itself, constitutes affirmative activity—an exercise of the very initiative, the creativity, the self-reliance, the faith that specific programs . . . seek to instill. . . .

Second, citizen participation, properly utilized, is a means of mobilizing the resources and energies of the poor—of converting the poor from passive consumers of the services of others into producers of those services. . . .

Third, citizen participation constitutes a source of special insight, of information, of knowledge and experience which cannot be ignored by those concerned with whether their efforts are fulfilling their aims.[1]

The fact that this significant element in local decision making has generally been neglected is evident in results ranging from inappropriate programs accompanied by citizen mistrust in the abilities and motives of their local government to malfunctioning or nonexistent programs accompanied by citizen violence. Given this condition, it is increasingly necessary for every municipal administrator to address the participation issue in his programs. It is the aim of this chapter to aid in that process by setting forth some guidelines for the equitable inclusion of the citizenry in the public decision-making process.

Philosophical Approaches to Citizen Participation

Underlying any guidelines for including citizens in decision making must be some philosophical foundation. Citizen participation has been studied thoroughly enough to permit a categorization of the basic philosophies that might underlie its adoption in public programs. There are four fundamental theories:

1. The cooptation theory
2. The consultation theory
3. The education/social therapy theory
4. The community power theory.[2]

The cooptation theory is at the base of those programs which provide for participation largely as a means of appeasement.

[T]his theory aims to keep the projects from being killed because of opposition within the target area through building a constituency ... the professional staff reasons that the residents are not likely to make a positive contribution to the program.[3]

The consultation theory is based on the idea that the middle class value concept of "the public interest," which traditionally guided policy makers, is no longer valid, especially in dealing with low-income citizens. Therefore, communication with citizens becomes a requisite for equitable decision making.

Consultation relies on three processes: informing area residents about the options available to them, marshalling citizen opinion, and incorporating community ideas into the final plan or program.[4]

The education/social therapy theory has deep roots in democratic theory. It says that participation is a training ground for good citizenship.

[The education/social therapy theory] is based on the assumption that only by actively involving the residents of the target area in programs affecting them can they actually gain the ability to improve their conditions.[5]

The community power theory is a dramatic departure from the others, because it provides for a fundamental redistribution of power. Those who have previously been shut out (for many reasons) are given access to the policy-making process.

Within the community power strategy, two basic approaches can be identified. One approach aims at making local governmental institutions more responsive and democratic. This approach usually involves the inclusion of citizens on joint policy boards. A formally negotiated sharing of power takes place between the community and those officially responsible for the program.

The other approach aims at establishing independent political power bases in low-income areas. ... The establishment of independent neighborhood corporations and citizen control is the goal.[6]

Only recently have efforts been made to achieve this final concept in public programs. Often it must be sought from outside the established decision-making system. Only in the newest federal domestic programs has it even

been suggested in part. A brief account of the participation concept will help shed light on the development of these theories and the organizational forms they have taken.

The Recent History of Participation

The emergence and development of citizen participation as an integral part of municipal management covers three distinct periods.[7]

The first of these (1949—63) was that of the *nonindigenous citizen as adviser-persuader.* Federal programs during this period included urban renewal and workable programs for community improvement. The citizens involved were largely white businessmen, planners, and civic leaders. They were *not*, as a rule, residents of the affected areas. The instrument of their activities became known as "blue ribbon" citizen advisory committees (CAC). By and large they were mayoral appointees; they were also consensus builders and persuaders.

The second period (1964—68) was that of the *indigenous citizen as partner-adversary.* Included here were the Community Action and Model Cities type of programs. Participation came from the poor minority group members of the affected neighborhood. This was the time of "maximum feasible participation" and other such nonspecific federal guidelines. Neighborhood representatives were elected or appointed to such bodies as Community Action Agencies (CAA) or City Demonstration Agencies (CDA). They were often accountable to a nieghborhood constituency. Powers included both policy making and advice. The results varied. The problems that the participants had experienced earlier appeared here as well: representatives were not always from the neighborhood; technical problems hindered review and decision making on plans and programs.

The third period (from 1969 onward) can be called *regionalism and decentralization.* While many programs have moved toward the consolidation of governmental activities on a level that can provide increased economies of scale (i.e., savings in or more optimal provision of services because of the size or scope of the area serviced), others have moved even more strongly toward the neighborhood. Several administrative responses have been developed to placate an alienated citizenry including: town hall meetings, neighborhood councils, community ombudsmen, special telephone lines to city hall, and "little city halls."

The response from city and county officials, according to a 1971 survey, has been quite favorable. In evaluating "decentralization of services—citizen participation," responses from 232 of 362 cities (64 percent) indicated that it was a "difficult but very worthwhile experience." Seventy-five out of 101 responding county governments made the same response.[8]

The obvious suggestion from this brief account is that there is no pat formula for citizen participation. Some of these divergent efforts have been successful where others have not. It is impossible to devise the model which the administrator has merely to put into effect in order to gain the optimum amount of citizen participation in policy- and decision-making processes. In short, citizen participation cannot be standardized.

Who Participates?

Before citizen participation can be adequately planned and developed, it is necessary to identify those who are likely to participate. Often this is a difficult task, because many individual citizens most directly affected by municipal programs may not be identifiable in advance. It is possible, however, to anticipate those who want to participate by learning about those organizations with an interest in public programs and a strong appeal to residents.

Citizens' organizations may be divided into three general groups: federally initiated groups (required by federal statute); groups organized or assisted by local government (advisory to the mayor and the local governing body); and voluntary organizations (locally recognized by the political process).[9]

These groups pervade the history of the participation concept. The federally initiated and local government assisted groups are the newest and have dominated most of the recent activity noted in the preceding section.

Nongovernmental (voluntary private groups)

Patriotic and historical groups
Women's groups—civic and business-oriented
Fellowship and fraternal groups
Religious sponsored groups
Veterans and military groups
Health, welfare rights, and legal aid groups
School PTA's and other educational groups
Business and professional groups
Labor organizations
Merchants and trade organizations
Homeowners and tenants associations
Economic improvement organizations for the disadvantaged
Youth organizations
Ethnic groups
Partisan political organizations

Federal statute groups
Human resources corporations
    (citizens assemblies, neighborhood boards)
Model Cities boards
Urban renewal groups

Local government assisted groups
Community councils
City block clubs
Mayors' advisory groups

FIGURE 19—1. *Citizen participation groups.*

Voluntary citizens' groups have existed for some time. They are "by far the oldest, largest, and most diversified category in our inventory. Here are private associations expressing enduring interests such as home ownership, business, unionism, education, religion, welfare, patriotism, civil rights."[10] It is in these "established "citizen groups that:

We find the least and the most politically conscious groups; the most conservative and traditionalistic on the one hand and most radical (be it Left or Right) on the other. . . . They show relatively most grass-roots initiative. But at the same time these organizations make better use of administrative fiscal and operational expertise, unhampered by political constraints or ideological inhibitions.[11]

The more recent federally initiated and locally assisted groups have not yet become so institutionalized. The federal groups have grown as the result of massive national efforts in poverty and urban-related problem areas. For this reason they are "typically composed of the lowest socio-economic strata. . . . The organizations are structurally volatile. Their operational effectiveness is problematic."[12]

The local government initiated groups are not so narrow in scope. They may cover an entire jurisdiction as well as all socioeconomic strata.

Overall there is much more of a racial balance here than in the "Federal" groups. As areas and communities are more settled here the organizational structure of the "City" groups is more stable. Ideologies and strategies are more conservative. There is less overall friction, though tensions between the regularly elected city politicians and these groups do exist. There is plenty of rank and file apathy.[13]

These three groups, then, provide us with a general typology of the organized citizens' groups to be encountered at the municipal level. A listing of kinds of organizations likely to be found within each appears in Figure 19—1. With this knowledge of who is likely to want to have a hand in municipal policy making (at least in the aggregate), we can consider when the input of such groups is appropriate and to what degree.

The Participation Problem in Municipal Government

To make the abstract ideal of citizen involvement a real part of the public policy process, the municipal administrator must determine who should participate in a given program; in doing this he must set the boundaries (jurisdictionally and functionally) of the effort and must estimate the feasible depth of participation.

Much of the conflict between citizens and government has been created by a condition of *remoteness*. It has become increasingly difficult for the individual citizen to find responsiveness. To many, even the act of voting has become frustrating. Government at all levels seems to have become a monolith beyond reasonable control.

The administrator is charged with the responsibility of carrying out his program despite such conditions. This leads many to avoid sharing power with individual citizens or citizen groups. If any participation is permitted it will be of the

cooptation, the consultation, or the education/social therapy sort. In many cases this may be sufficient. Certain municipal programs do not lend themselves to actual power sharing. For these programs, the adoption of a consultation strategy may be sufficient to remove the appearance of governmental remoteness.

These techniques may also be used to eliminate a further, related, cause of conflict. This is the *lack of responsiveness* felt by many individual citizens. Governmental solutions to individual problems are often slow in coming. A change in this condition is often sufficient to resolve the citizen's feeling of helplessness.

The remoteness and unresponsiveness of government may be both physical and administrative. The seat of government may well be physically removed in terms of time and distance from the individual citizen. Likewise, government may be administratively remote owing to excesses of red tape and the inaccessibility of the administrator and his staff. Reduction of the remoteness of government through physical or administrative alterations aimed at the inclusion of affected citizens may go far to reduce the amount of conflict present in today's community and may produce the well-managed "efficient and effective" government that we all like to talk about. The benefits of this approach can affect all areas of municipal administration.

Basic Guidelines for Effective Citizen Participation

Three recommendations are basic to change in both the physical and administrative areas. First, regardless of the program or programs involved, the administrator should endeavor to make the opportunity for *citizen access* as fundamental as possible in the decision-making process. Many factors may bear upon this, but, ideally, access permits the citizen to determine whether there is to be a program at all. This recommendation has both physical and administrative ramifications. It may mean a physical change in the location of the seat of power, and, administratively, a total change in practices and procedures.

The second basic recommendation is for the

creation of a *continuous information flow* to the community as soon as possible in program consideration, and frequently thereafter throughout the decision-making process. Much of the conflict between citizens and government at the local level is generated by the suddenness and finality with which municipal or municipally supported programs appear and go into effect. Usually, by the time an individual citizen hears of a program that will affect him directly, it is too late to do anything about it. It has already been planned, developed, and scheduled for implementation before he is aware of its existence. If the affected citizenry were genuinely informed (not merely through a newspaper advertisement) as soon as a new program was being considered, however distant its implementation date, much of the surprise which leads to conflict could be eliminated.

In the physical sense this may mean the creation of neighborhood offices for certain units of the municipal government, or at the very least the addition of a well-staffed department to make the information task meaningful on a community-wide basis. Administratively, this implies much emphasis on the coordinative function, between departments as well as between the governmental machinery and the community.

The information flow must be continuous; it must be incremental; it must reach the affected citizen by whatever means necessary. One cannot rely on the "constructive knowledge" achieved by filling the minimum requirements for hearings and advertisements. Continuous contact with citizens affected by the program must be maintained, even if it means supplementary mailing lists and extensive personal contact. Actual knowledge rather than constructive knowledge of governmental intentions is what counts with people.

The third recommendation is for a process of *continuous research* that is to be conducted throughout the community, especially in areas immediately affected by governmental programs. Continuous research into community attitudes and conditions can provide every administrator with substantial information well in advance of his consideration of a governmental program for the area.

The citizen survey is an excellent example of the kind of technique that can be used. This is not a new idea by any means, but it has recently come to the fore as a way of obtaining citizen feedback. These surveys, which can be taken by mail, telephone, or in person, serve three essential purposes.

First, the surveys gather information about public opinion on major problems facing the community. . . .
Second, surveys can be used to obtain information on personal experiences related to local government services, such as use of public transportation facilities. Third . . . surveys can be used as a market research device for pretesting changes in existing programs or the introduction of new city services.[14]

Methods such as these can provide the administrator with the data he needs to make equitable program decisions.

Physically speaking, the information dissemination and research functions could be located side by side. Administratively, the research function is complex and requires skilled personnel in its management, but the rewards of doing one's homework in this area are great. (Even a street commissioner can avoid the embarrassment of having irate housewives blocking traffic on an unpaved or poorly paved street through the use of a proper research mechanism.)

These three basic recommendations should aid in removing the barrier of remoteness from government and should help set a firm foundation for effective citizen participation in the development of programs which affect them. Through making access as fundamental as possible, creating a continuous information flow, and conducting continuous community research, the administrator can not only build trust among the citizenry but can impart to them a certain amount of the technical expertise necessary in making planning and programming decisions in today's municipal environment.

A Decision Diagram

Given these basic recommendations, what further means can the administrator use to encourage effective citizen participation in his programs? The decision diagram in Figure 19—2 is intended to help.

Obviously, this diagram is an over-

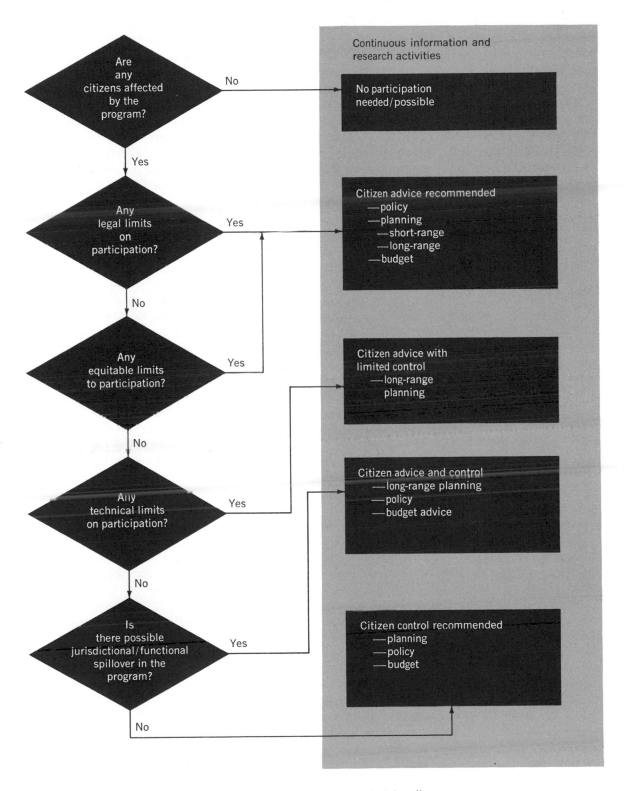

FIGURE 19—2. *Citizen participation decision diagram.*

simplification of the complex decisions involved in this problem, but it should provide the necessary framework for the intelligent use of administrative discretion. The large outer rectangle on the right represents the fundamental information and research activities already discussed. They must be performed regardless of the amount of citizen involvement decided upon for a given program.

On the left are representations of the decisions which administrators must make regarding their programs. The amount of possible citizen involvement builds, as a practical matter, on the outcome of each previous decision. The desirable magnitude of involvement is represented in the individual boxes opposite each decision point. The emphasis on the community power theory of participation increases as one moves from top to bottom through the alternatives.

The first question which must be asked is whether there are any citizens affected by the program at all. It is difficult to conceive of a situation in which there would not be. However, a consideration of this question is basic to the idea of participation. Internal matters of management such as interoffice paper flow and other minor operating matters may fall into this category. However, when the totality of any municipal program is considered, valid candidates for this category are difficult to find.

There may well be legal limitations or inducements imposed on the type and amount of citizen involvement in a program. This is the second consideration. They may be either positive or negative. In any case, they usually limit the scope of the administrator's decision-making discretion in some way.

Associated with legal limitations to participation are equitable limitations. Decisions on these are left almost totally to the administrator's discretion. In some instances it may be that total citizen control of a program would work an inequity on other portions of the community (for example, the residents of a totally white suburban area may make policy decisions which virtually ensure the exclusion of minorities from a program). It is the administrator's duty, then, to see that social equity prevails for all those affected by his program.

A further question to be dealt with by the

municipal administrator is whether there are any prohibitive technical limitations to the involvement of the citizenry. If the information and research functions of his program are operating effectively, this may not often be a problem. Indeed, there are many current examples illustrating the fact that members of the community can make rather complex sound policy and planning decisions. However, should a program be so technically complex that complete participation of community members is not feasible, citizens should at least be involved in the process to the point of advice on all operations and some control over those with long-range implications.

The final question in Figure 19−2 requires a close look by the municipal administrator. Is there any possible jurisdictional/functional spillover anticipated in the program? If there is, then citizen involvement may necessarily be restricted in the area of budgetary control. However, if all the previous questions have been satisfied and there is no anticipated spillover of costs or benefits, thus making the boundary identifiable, there is no reason why those citizens directly affected by the program should not have control over its planning, policy setting, and budget management.

Examples of this type of involvement are becoming increasingly evident in governmental programs (for example, in certain neighborhood development corporations). The charrette[15] concept of community facilities planning embodies the idea directly. Wherever it is being used the affected citizenry controls the planning, policy, and budgetary decisions, often overcoming technical limitations to do so. Furthermore, there is evidence, in the charrette concept at least, that the result of such heavy citizen involvement is cost effective in the sense that the job is done and the program objectives met at a lower cost and in less time than with traditional methods of performing the task.

Specific Suggestions for Participation

The decision diagram in Figure 19−2 may help the administrator decide on the magnitude of citizen involvement for his program, but what, specifically, can he do to encourage that involvement? Following are important suggestions for effective citizen participation:

1. Maintain a sincere desire to obtain genuine collaboration.
2. Select a skilled staff with the necessary authority and support to deal with citizen participation.
3. Work at the neighborhood level with organizations and leadership that neighborhood residents accept as representing their interests.
4. Provide opportunities for improving communication and coordination among government officials, staff, and citizens through social-educational training activities, starting with team building approaches.
5. Make technical assistance available to citizens and neighborhood representatives in a form agreeable and understandable to residents.
6. Employ neighborhood residents in governmental planning and operation activities.
7. Schedule meetings at times and locations convenient to residents.
8. Provide funds for the cost of individual participation (transportation, day care).

These specific suggestions, as well as the more general considerations discussed earlier, are empty without the proper structures and processes to carry them into effect. Let us turn now to an examination of these.

Organizational and Administrative Mechanisms

Suggestions for effective citizen participation in municipal programs can only be implemented through the use of proper organizational and administrative mechanisms. Numerous experiments have been conducted in this area by municipal governments (e.g., the neighborhood city halls and direct telephone lines mentioned earlier) and by citizens themselves (e.g., elected neighborhood groups and community advocates).

Of the techniques used by government, the most widespread has been that of organizational

and administrative decentralization. Neighborhood service centers, neighborhood city halls, and the like characterize this movement. Decentralization has been well received and is being increasingly implemented at the local level. Municipal offices in the neighborhoods can lead to the achievement of the basic research and information dissemination objectives, thus aiding in the elimination of governmental remoteness and unresponsiveness.

Five fundamental models of municipal decentralization have been suggested.

1. *The Exchange Model.* This mechanism is aimed at improving the communication process between local government and the citizenry. Methods used in achieving this are field offices, little city halls, local citizen advisory boards, ombudsmen, and multiservice centers.
2. *The Bureaucratic Model.* Functional form: municipalities decentralize municipal services such as police, fire, education, and public works. Usually a district superintendent is placed in charge. Territorial form: neighborhood managers are appointed. They derive their strength from the mayor and coordinate agencies in their area. Personnel are appointed by the existing structure.
3. *Modified Bureaucratic Model.* Here the neighborhood manager is responsible to both the mayor and the residents. There is a neighborhood council with decision-making powers.
4. *Development Model.* Here residents control policy making and administration through a neighborhood corporation. They can administer programs themselves or contract them out to the city or other agencies.
5. *Government Model.* Here totally new political units are created at the neighborhood level.[16]

Four patterns of decentralization currently in existence may fall within any or all of these models.

1. Traditional branch municipal facilities that place the usual city services in field offices for efficiency and convenience to citizens
2. Multiservice centers that provide social services and some municipal services in one location

3. Neighborhood city halls that emphasize communication, coordination, and personal involvement with citizens; some provide a minimum of services, others have multiservice functions

4. Mayor's outreach office; city hall aides work on special problems.[17]

Other techniques may be employed to ensure a participatory role for citizens in municipal decision making. Probably the most common is representative citizen participation, in which individuals or groups are identified as community representatives, either by election in the community or selection by those with program responsibility. This has traditionally been a difficult and often confusing and inequitable process. Whether the citizens selected are indigenous or nonindigenous, they are liable to form objectives of their own, or worse, to work at cross objectives. The Model Cities program has provided examples of this possibility.

Citizen participation can be an effective means of blocking progress. That is easy, particularly when the apparent spokesmen for the minority community are divided and contentious. It is more difficult for citizens and their government to develop a working partnership that will move from rhetoric to joint planning, to delivery of programs responsive to needs, and to changes in existing systems and institutions to make them more responsive.[18]

A further practical technique is the creation of some form of grievance response machinery for citizens. This directly addresses the fundamental requisites of information flow and research as well as the basic shortcoming of the remoteness of government. It is often difficult for members of the community to protest or even question administrative decisions. The operation of grievance machinery would alter this condition in three ways:

1. It would open channels of communication between the citizen and both low- and high-level municipal officials.
2. It would increase the visibility and accessibility of municipal agencies by bringing them closer to the people.
3. It would mitigate individual and community

opposition to agency policies and possibly neutralize it through explanation.

Many methods have been used to achieve this objective, including the community ombudsman, community advocates, and neighborhood city halls or service centers.

Finally, the established governmental framework provides a ready mechanism for citizen participation, as to some degree it always has. Boards of education, public health and planning commissions, and other agencies are enhanced by careful selection of citizens *directly* affected by their programs to serve as members.

The Use of Discretion

We should frankly recognize and acknowledge the fact that the depth and breadth of citizen participation is a function of the outlook of the administrator, of his values and of his perceptions of how government works best. Structures such as the charrette, the ombudsman, and little city halls are a means of working toward the participatory goal, but they necessitate some fundamental changes in the traditional bureaucratic outlook. In short, the citizen cannot be viewed as subordinate to governmental machinery or goals, or as a categorized problem. The administrator can no longer hide behind such things as structure, lack of discretion, or demands for economy and efficiency. All of these concepts must change if participation is to be truly effective

How must they change? What can the administrator do to facilitate that change? What behavioral alterations might he make, even within the prevailing structure? The following maxims describe an administrative philosophy which might help answer these questions.

1. Service is not at a distance—it means personal involvement with people.
2. No person or problem is beyond . . . concern or attention.
3. . . . Interests or personal feelings are not of any importance as we serve.
4. We must individually assume that we are responsible. . . .[19]

As these guidelines suggest, responsibility is the important issue. The administrator must not base his decisions solely on the book if equity and fairness are to be achieved. Instead, he must assume responsibility for the client, taking affirmative, compensatory action to achieve equity where necessary. In this view the client must be treated as the peer of the bureaucrat. They solve problems together. Further, the client is viewed as a total person, not merely a part of a larger problem.

Summary

The preceding pages have not provided concrete answers to the question of citizen participation in municipal administration. Indeed, as we have noted, the kind and degree of participation cannot be standardized. However, recent history has shown us that the factor of citizen involvement in programs that affect them directly has become an unavoidable fact of modern municipal life.

The administrator's dilemma in determining answers to the fundamental questions involving the complex issue of citizen participation can be eased by creating basic *information* dissemination and *research* collection activities in the community. These aid in removing the stigmas of remoteness and unresponsiveness from government.

The issue can be further resolved by following a simple decision process which traces the entire spectrum from no participation to total control, and ensures equitability in the process. This can be supplemented by some fairly concrete suggestions for participatory mechanisms. All, however, are limited by the complexity of the total issue.

Final answers can be found only through the administrator's individual reappraisal of his and the citizen's relationship to the governmental structure. With such a change in outlook, the answers to the questions of who should participate, in what programs, when, and with what expected results, can be made much less troublesome. The true importance of citizen participation in municipal programs can then be grasped and the concept more readily implemented.

[1] Edgar S. Cahn and Jean Camper Cahn, "Citizen Participation," in CITIZEN PARTICIPATION IN URBAN DEVELOPMENT, ed. Hans B. C. Spiegel, vol. 1 (Washington, D.C.: National Training Laboratories Institute for Applied Behavioral Science, 1968), pp. 218–20.

[2] U.S., Department of Housing and Urban Development, THE ADMINISTRATIVE ASPECTS OF MODEL CITIES CITIZENS ORGANIZATIONS, Model Cities Management Series, Bulletin No. 6 (Washington, D.C.: Government Printing Office, 1971), pp. 1–2.

[3] Ibid., p. 1.

[4] Ibid., p. 2.

[5] Ibid.

[6] Ibid.

[7] Carl W. Stenberg, "The History and Future of Citizen Participation: An Overview," report for the Advisory Commission on Intergovernmental Relations, Washington, D.C., 1971. (Mimeographed.)

[8] Carl W. Stenberg, "Decentralization and the City," in THE MUNICIPAL YEAR BOOK, 1972 (Washington, D.C.: International City Management Association, 1972), p. 96. The complete wording of the item in the survey questionnaire was: "A difficult but very worthwhile experience resulting in increased trust and understanding between citizens, city hall or county courthouse officials, and public administrators."

[9] Gerhard W. Ditz, ORGANIZED CITIZEN PARTICIPATION IN KANSAS CITY, MISSOURI (Kansas City, Mo.: University of Missouri/Mid-America Urban Observatory, 1971), p. ii.

[10] Ibid., p. iii.

[11] Ibid.

[12] Ibid., p. ii.

[13] Ibid., p. iii.

[14] International City Management Association, "Obtaining and Using Citizen Feedback: The Citizen Survey," PUBLIC MANAGEMENT, January 1972, p. 30. Remarks made by Harry Hatry at the 1971 ICMA Annual Conference, cited in special conference issue of PM.

[15] The charrette is a community planning idea in which the residents of the affected neighborhood do all their own planning with the assistance of lawyers, architects, and planners retained by them.

[16] George J. Washnis, "Municipal Decentralization and Other Neighborhood Facilities," THE MUNICIPAL YEAR BOOK, 1971 (Washington, D.C.: International City Management Association, 1971), pp. 9–10. Paraphrased from Henry J. Schmandt, in a paper prepared for the Center for Governmental Studies, Washington, D.C., in May 1970.

[17] Washnis, "Municipal Decentralization," p. 9.

[18] Ralph Taylor, "Citizen Participation in the Model Cities Program," in CITIZEN PARTICIPATION IN URBAN DEVELOPMENT, ed. Hans B. C. Spiegel, vol. 2 (Washington, D.C.: National Training Laboratories Institute for Applied Behavioral Science, 1969), p. 109.

[19] Orion F. White, Jr., "The Dialectical Organization: An Alternative to Bureaucracy," PUBLIC ADMINISTRATION REVIEW 29 (January–February 1969): 36–37.

Selected Bibliography

This bibliography is highly selective and is based primarily on recommendations of the chapter authors for this book. It represents informed judgments about basic materials in management areas in which thousands of books, reports, and articles have been published.

In addition to the books and other references listed, certain basic periodicals are recommended for keeping up-to-date on developments in management, organization development, leadership, and other areas covered in this book. These are listed immediately below.

The Municipal Year Book. Annual. Published by the International City Management Association. A compendium of trends and developments in cities, with articles and survey reports on a wide range of subjects, many covering different aspects of management. All volumes through 1972 carry a Selected Bibliography covering major areas of local government administration. Of particular interest are the subject headings for Professional Development, Management and Decision Making, Personnel and Supervision, and Manpower. The 1975 *Municipal Year Book*, and subsequent editions, will again carry this Selected Bibliography.

The American City. Monthly. Buttenheim Publishing Corporation. Features short articles on city government activities, mostly in public works. Occasional articles on management subjects.

Nation's Cities. Monthly. National League of Cities. Articles and short news items on local government activities, including some management subjects. Occasional book reviews and publication notices.

Harvard Business Review. Bimonthly. Graduate School of Business Administration, Harvard University. Articles in broad fields of marketing, finance, labor relations, motivation, management, and related areas. Every issue contains at least one or two articles close to the interests of this book.

Management Review. Monthly. American Management Association. Articles and article digests on management subjects in the field of business. Brief news items on management trends. Publication notices.

Public Management. Monthly. International City Management Association. Written and edited primarily to serve the local government administrator. Each issue covers a major subject of current interest, with topics ranging from broad policy questions to many kinds of immediate management issues. Occasional book reviews and publication notices.

Public Personnel Management. Bimonthly. International Personnel Management Association. Articles cover the entire range of interests in public personnel administration; many of the articles deal with organization development, leadership, training, career development, motivation and morale, and other subjects of direct interest to users of this book. Includes publication notices.

Public Administration Review. Bimonthly. American Society for Public Administration. This journal serves administrators at all levels of government with articles covering almost every area of public administration except public education. Each issue features a symposium, together with articles on other subjects. Other features include brief reports on administrative developments, indepth book reviews, and extensive coverage, through short notices, of new publications.

1. The Realities of Local Government

BANFIELD, EDWARD C., ed. *Urban Government: A Reader in Administration and Politics*. 2nd ed. New York: The Free Press, 1969.

BANOVETZ, JAMES M., ed. *Managing the Modern City*. Washington, D.C.: International City Management Association, 1971.

BENNIS, WARREN G.; BENNE, KENNETH D.; and CHIN, ROBERT, eds. *The Planning of Change*. 2nd ed. New York: Holt, Rinehart & Winston, Inc., 1969.

BOLLENS, JOHN C., and REIS, JOHN C. *The City Manager Profession: Myths and Realities*.

Chicago: Public Administration Service, 1969.

BOLLENS, JOHN C., and SCHMANDT, HENRY J. *The Metropolis: Its People, Politics, and Economic Life.* 2nd ed. New York: Harper & Row, Publishers, 1970.

BROWN, F. GERALD, and MURPHY, THOMAS P., eds. *Emerging Patterns in Urban Administration.* Lexington, Mass.: Lexington Books, 1970.

EAST, JOHN P. *Council-Manager Government: The Political Thought of Its Founder, Richard S. Childs.* Chapel Hill: University of North Carolina Press, 1965.

KENT, FRANK R. *The Great Game of Politics.* Garden City, N.Y.: Doubleday, Doran & Co., 1930.

NATIONAL ASSOCIATION OF MANUFACTURERS OF THE UNITED STATES, INDUSTRIAL RELATIONS DIVISION. *What's Wrong with Work? How To Release Human Potential and Improve Productivity.* New York: National Association of Manufacturers, 1967.

RIDLEY, CLARENCE E. *The Role of the City Manager in Policy Formulation.* Chicago: International City Managers' Association, 1958.

STONE, HAROLD A.; PRICE, DON K.; and STONE, KATHRYN H. *City Manager Government in the United States.* A Review after Twenty-Five Years. Chicago: Public Administration Service, 1940.

2. Management Concepts and Organization Models

BECKHARD, RICHARD. *Organizational Development: Strategies and Models.* Reading, Mass.: Addison-Wesley Publishing Co., Inc., 1969.

BLAU, PETER M., and SCOTT, W. RICHARD. *Formal Organizations: A Comparative Approach.* San Francisco: Chandler Publishing Company, 1962.

BOBBIT, H. RANDOLPH, JR.; BREINHOLT, ROBERT H.; DOKTOR, ROBERT H.; and McNAUL, JAMES P. *Organizational Behavior: Understanding and Prediction.* Englewood Cliffs, N.J.: Prentice-Hall, Inc., 1974.

ETZIONI, AMITAI. *Modern Organizations.* Englewood Cliffs, N.J.: Prentice-Hall, Inc., 1964.

GULICK, LUTHER C., and URWICK, LYNDALL. *Papers on the Science of Administration.*

New York: Institute of Public Administration, Columbia University, 1937.

HICKS, HERBERT G. *The Management of Organizations: A Systems and Human Resources Approach.* 2nd ed. New York: McGraw-Hill Book Company, 1972.

LIKERT, RENSIS. *The Human Organization: Its Management and Value.* New York: McGraw-Hill Book Company, 1969.

MASLOW, ABRAHAM H., ed. *Motivation and Personality.* 2nd ed. New York: Harper & Row, Publishers, 1970.

MAYO, ELTON. *The Human Problems of an Industrial Civilization.* New York: The Macmillan Company, 1933.

NATIONAL COMMISSION ON URBAN PROBLEMS. *Building the American City.* Washington, D.C.: Government Printing Office, 1969.

PRESTHUS, ROBERT. *The Organizational Society: An Analysis and a Theory.* New York: Random House, 1962.

ROETHLISBERGER, FRITZ J., and DICKSON, WILLIAM J. *Management and the Worker.* Cambridge, Mass.: Harvard University Press, 1939.

SIMON, HERBERT A. *The New Science of Management Decision.* New York: Harper & Row, Publishers, 1960.

TAYLOR, FREDERICK W. *The Principles of Scientific Management.* New York: W. W. Norton & Company, Inc., 1967.

WEBER, MAX. *The Theory of Social and Economic Organization.* Translated by Talcott Parsons. New York: The Free Press, 1967.

3. The Human Side of Organization

ADLER, ALFRED. *Social Interest: A Challenge to Mankind.* New York: Capricorn Books, 1964.

AITKEN, HUGH G. J. *Taylorism at Watertown Arsenal: Scientific Management in Action.* Cambridge, Mass.: Harvard University Press, 1960.

CAPLOW, THEODORE. *Principles of Organization.* New York: Harcourt Brace & World, Inc., 1964.

COPLEY, FRANK B. *Frederick W. Taylor: Father of Scientific Management.* New York: Harper & Brothers, Publishers, 1923.

HABER, SAMUEL. *Efficiency and Uplift: Scientific Management in the Progressive Era, 1890–*

1920. Chicago: University of Chicago Press, 1964.

HOXIE, ROBERT F. *Scientific Management and Labor*. Clifton, N.J.: Augustus M. Kelley, Publishers, 1966.

LEAVITT, HAROLD J. *Managerial Psychology*. 3rd ed. Chicago: University of Chicago Press, 1972.

McGREGOR, DOUGLAS. *The Human Side of Enterprise*. New York: McGraw-Hill Book Company, 1960.

MASLOW, ABRAHAM H., ed. *Motivation and Personality*. 2nd ed. New York: Harper & Row, Publishers, 1970.

MAYO, ELTON. *The Human Problems of an Industrial Civilization*. New York: The Macmillan Company, 1933.

ROETHLISBERGER, FRITZ J. *Management and Morale*. Cambridge, Mass.: Harvard University Press, 1941.

TAYLOR, FREDERICK W. "A Piece Rate System: Being a Step Toward Partial Solution of the Labor Problem." Reprinted in *Scientific Management: A Collection of the More Significant Articles Describing the Taylor System of Management*, pp. 636–83. Edited by Clarence Bertrand Thompson. Cambridge, Mass.: Harvard University Press, 1914.

TAYLOR, FREDERICK W. *The Principles of Scientific Management*. New York: W. W. Norton & Company, Inc., 1967.

5. Management Styles and Working with People

BELLOWS, ROGER; GILSON, THOMAS O.; and ODIORNE, GEORGE S. *Executive Skills: Their Dynamics and Development*. Englewood Cliffs, N.J.: Prentice-Hall, Inc., 1962.

BLAKE, ROBERT R., and MOUTON, JANE S. *The Managerial Grid*. Houston: Gulf Publishing Company, 1964.

CATHCART, ROBERT S., and SAMOVAR, LARRY S., eds. *Small Group Communication: A Reader*. Dubuque, Iowa: William C. Brown Company, Publishers, 1970.

COOPER, JOSEPH D. *How To Get More Done in Less Time*. Rev. ed. Garden City, N.Y.: Doubleday & Company, Inc., 1971.

DALE, ERNEST, and URWICK, LYNDALL F. *Staff in Organization*. New York: McGraw-Hill Book Company, 1960.

EDDY, WILLIAM B.; BURKE, W. WARNER; DUPRE, VLADIMIR A.; and SOUTH, ORON., eds. *Behavioral Science and the Manager's Role*. Washington, D.C.: National Training Laboratories Institute for Applied Behavioral Science, 1969.

HAYEL, CARL. *Organizing Your Job in Management*. New York: American Management Association, 1960.

KAHN, ROBERT L., and CANNELL, CHARLES F. *The Dynamics of Interviewing: Theory, Technique and Cases*. New York: John Wiley & Sons, Inc., 1957.

LIPPITT, GORDON L.; THIS, LESLIE E.; and BIDWELL, ROBERT G., JR., eds. *Optimizing Human Resources: Readings in Individual and Organizational Development*. Reading, Mass.: Addison-Wesley Publishing Co., 1971.

McCAY, JAMES. *The Management of Time*. Englewood Cliffs, N.J.: Prentice-Hall, Inc., 1959.

McGREGOR, DOUGLAS. *The Professional Manager*. New York: McGraw-Hill Book Company, 1967.

METCALF, HENRY C., and URWICK, LYNDALL, eds. *Dynamic Administration: The Collected Papers of Mary Parker Follett*. New York: Harper & Brothers, Publishers, 1942.

NICHOLS, RALPH G., and STEVENS, LEONARD A. *Are You Listening?* New York: McGraw-Hill Book Company, 1957.

ROETHLISBERGER, FRITZ J., and DICKSON, WILLIAM J. *Management and the Worker*. Cambridge, Mass.: Harvard University Press, 1939.

SATIR, VIRGINIA M. *Peoplemaking*. Palo Alto: Science and Behavior Books, Inc., 1972.

TANNENBAUM, ROBERT; WESCHLER, IRVING R.; and MASSARIK, FRED. *Leadership and Organization: A Behavioral Science Approach*. New York: McGraw-Hill Book Company, 1961.

URIS, AUREN. *The Efficient Executive*. New York: McGraw-Hill Book Company, 1957.

6. Influencing Employee Behavior

ARGYRIS, CHRIS. *Personality and Organization*. New York: Harper & Row, Publishers, 1957.

FLEISHMAN, EDWIN A.; HARRIS, EDWIN F.; and BURTT, HAROLD E. *Leadership and Supervi-*

sion in Industry; An Evaluation of a Supervisory Training Program. Columbus: Ohio State University Press, 1955.

HERZBERG, FREDERICK. *Work and the Nature of Man.* Cleveland: World Publishing Company, 1966.

HERZBERG, FREDERICK; MAUSNER, BERNARD; PETERSON, RICHARD O.; and CAPWELL, DORA F. *Job Attitudes: Review of Research and Opinion.* Pittsburgh: Psychological Service of Pittsburgh, 1957.

HERZBERG, FREDERICK; MAUSNER, BERNARD; and SNYDERMAN, B. *The Motivation to Work.* 2nd ed. New York: John Wiley & Sons, Inc., 1959.

LESIEUR, FREDERICK C., ed. *The Scanlon Plan: A Frontier in Labor-Management Cooperation.* Cambridge, Mass.: The M.I.T. Press, 1958.

McCLELLAND, DAVID C.; ATKINSON, J. W.; CLARK, R. A.; and LOWELL, E. L. *The Achievement Motive.* New York: Appleton-Century-Crofts, 1953.

McGREGOR, DOUGLAS. *The Human Side of Enterprise.* New York: McGraw-Hill Book Company, 1960.

MASLOW, ABRAHAM H. *Motivation and Personality.* 2nd ed. New York: Harper & Row, Publishers, 1970.

MAYO, ELTON. *The Social Problems of an Industrial Civilization.* Boston: Harvard Business School, 1945.

SCHACHTER, STANLEY. *The Psychology of Affiliation: Experimental Studies of the Sources of Gregariousness.* Stanford, Calif.: Stanford University Press, 1959.

SKINNER, B. F. *Science and Human Behavior.* New York: The Free Press, 1965.

WHITE, ROBERT W. "Motivation Reconsidered: The Concept of Competence." *Psychological Review* 66 (September 1959): 297–333.

7. Making Decisions

COOPER, JOSEPH D. *The Art of Decision-Making.* Garden City, N.Y.: Doubleday & Company, Inc., 1961.

DALE, ERNEST, and MICHELON, L. C. *Modern Management Methods.* Cleveland: World Publishing Company, 1966.

DRUCKER, PETER F. *The Effective Executive.* New York: Harper & Row, Publishers, 1967.

FOLSOM, MARIAN B. *Executive Decision Making: Observations and Expenses in Business and Government.* New York: McGraw-Hill Book Company, 1962.

GORE, WILLIAM J. *Administrative Decision-Making: A Heuristic Model.* New York: John Wiley & Sons, Inc., 1964.

KEPNER, CHARLES H., and TREGOE, BENJAMIN B. *The Rational Manager: A Systems Approach to Problem Solving and Decision Making.* New York: McGraw-Hill Book Company, 1965.

KRAEMER, KENNETH L. *Policy Analysis in Local Government: A Systems Approach to Decision Making.* Washington, D.C.: International City Management Association, 1973.

LIKERT, RENSIS. *The Human Organization: Its Management and Value.* New York: McGraw-Hill Book Company, 1969.

LINDBLOM, CHARLES E. "The Science of Muddling Through." *Public Administration Review* 19 (Spring 1959): 79–88.

McDONALD, JOHN. "How Businessmen Make Decisions." *Fortune,* August 1955, pp. 84–87.

MILLER, DAVID W., and STARR, MARTIN K. *The Structure of Human Decisions.* Englewood Cliffs, N.J.: Prentice-Hall, Inc., 1967.

SIMON, HERBERT A. *Administrative Behavior: A Study of Decision Making Processes in Administrative Organization.* 2nd ed. New York: The Macmillan Company, 1957.

SMITH, DAVID S. "Making Decisions." In *Managing the Modern City,* pp. 134–50. Edited by James M. Banovetz. Washington, D.C.: International City Management Association, 1971.

8. Groups and Meetings

ALBANO, CHARLES. "A Conference Isn't a Meeting." *Supervisory Management* 18 (April 1973): 11–16.

CONNELLY, J. CAMPBELL. *A Manager's Guide to Speaking and Listening.* New York: American Management Association, 1967.

GULLEY, HALBERT E. *Discussion, Conference, and Group Process.* 2nd ed. New York: Holt, Rinehart & Winston, Inc., 1968.

MEAD, MARGARET, and BYERS, PAUL. *The Small Conference: An Innovation in Communication.* New York: Humanities Press, Inc., 1968.

MORGAN, JOHN S. *Practical Guide to Conference Leadership.* New York: McGraw-Hill Book Company, 1966.

NATHAN, ERNEST D. *Twenty Questions on Conference Leadership.* Reading, Mass.: Addison-Wesley Publishing Co., Inc., 1969.

ZELKO, HAROLD P. *The Business Conference: Leadership and Participation.* New York: McGraw-Hill Book Company, 1969.

9. Administrative Communication

ALBERS, HENRY HERMAN. *Organized Executive Action: Decision Making, Communication and Leadership.* New York: John Wiley & Sons, Inc., 1961.

AMERICAN MANAGEMENT ASSOCIATION. *Effective Communication on the Job.* 2nd ed. New York: American Management Association, 1963.

BARNARD, CHESTER I. *The Functions of the Executive.* Cambridge, Mass.: Harvard University Press, 1968.

BATTEN, J. D., and MCMAHON, J. V. "Communications Which Communicate." *Personnel Journal* 45 (July–August 1966): 424–26.

BORMANN, ERNEST G., et al. *Interpersonal Communications in the Modern Organization.* Englewood Cliffs, N.J.: Prentice-Hall, Inc., 1969.

CHERRY, COLIN. *On Human Communication: A Review, a Survey and a Criticism.* 2nd ed. Cambridge, Mass.: The M.I.T. Press, 1968.

DORSEY, JOHN T., JR. "A Communicative Model for Administration." *Administrative Science Quarterly* 2 (December 1957): 307–24.

PARRY, JOHN. *Psychology of Human Communication.* New York: American Elsevier Publishing Co., 1968.

REDFIELD, CHARLES E. *Communication in Management.* Rev. ed. Chicago: University of Chicago Press, 1958.

SCHOLZ, WILLIAM. *Communications in the Business Organization.* Englewood Cliffs, N.J.: Prentice-Hall, Inc., 1962.

SHANNON, CLAUDE E., and WEAVER, WARREN. *The Mathematical Theory of Communication.* Champaign, Ill.: University of Illinois Press, 1949.

SYBOLD, GENEVA. *Employee Communication: Policy and Tools.* New York: National Industrial Conference Board, 1966.

10. The Management of Change

BENNIS, WARREN G. *Changing Organizations.* New York: McGraw-Hill Book Company, 1966.

BENNIS, WARREN G.; BENNE, KENNETH D.; and CHIN, ROBERT, eds. *The Planning of Change.* 2nd ed. New York: Holt, Rinehart & Winston, Inc., 1969.

COSTELLO, TIMOTHY. "The Change Process in Municipal Government." In *Emerging Patterns in Urban Administration.* pp. 13–32. Edited by F. Gerald Brown and Thomas P. Murphy. Lexington, Mass.: Lexington Books, 1970.

DALTON, GENE W.; LAWRENCE, PAUL R.; and GREINER, LARRY E. *Organizational Change and Development.* Homewood, Ill.: Richard D. Irwin, Inc., 1970.

FRENCH, WENDELL L., and BELL, CECIL H., JR. *Organization Development: Behavioral Science Intervention for Organization Improvement.* Englewood Cliffs, N.J.: Prentice-Hall, Inc., 1973.

GOLEMBIEWSKI, ROBERT T. *Renewing Organizations: The Laboratory Approach to Planned Change.* Itasca, Ill.: F. E. Peacock Publishers, Inc., 1972.

GOODWIN, WATSON, ed. *Concepts for Social Change.* Washington, D.C.: National Training Laboratories Institute for Applied Behavorial Science, 1967.

NATIONAL TRAINING AND DEVELOPMENT SERVICE. *First Tango in Boston: A Seminar on Organizational Change and Development.* Washington, D.C.: National Training and Development Service, 1973.

11. Training

BRUNTON, ROBERT L. *A Manual for Municipal In-Service Training: Purpose, Method, Procedures.* Chicago: International City Managers' Association, 1960.

FISHER, FRED E. *The Art of Leadership Development.* Management Information Service Reports, vol. 3, no. LS–11. Washington, D.C.: International City Management Association, 1971.

FORDYCE, JACK K., and WEIL, RAYMOND. *Managing with People: A Manager's Handbook of Organization Development Methods.*

Reading, Mass.: Addison-Wesley Publishing Co., Inc., 1971.

FRENCH, WENDELL, and BELL, CECIL H., JR. *Organization Development: Behavioral Science Interventions for Organization Development.* Englewood Cliffs, N.J.: Prentice-Hall, Inc., 1973.

HEISEL, W. D.; PADGETT, E. R.; and HARRELL, C. A. *Line-Staff Relationships in Employee Training.* Chicago: International City Managers' Association, 1967.

INTERNATIONAL CITY MANAGERS' ASSOCIATION. *Post-Entry Training in the Local Public Service: With Special Reference to Administrative, Professional, and Technical Personnel in the United States.* Chicago: International City Managers' Association, 1963.

KIRKHART, LARRY, and GARDNER, NEELY, eds. "Organization Development." *Public Administration Review* 34 (March–April 1974): 97–140.

KNOWLES, MALCOLM. *The Modern Practice of Adult Education: Androgogy versus Pedagogy.* New York: Association Press, 1970.

LYNTON, ROLF P., and PAREEK, UDAI. *Training for Development.* Homewood, Ill.: Richard D. Irwin, Inc., and the Dorsey Press, 1967.

NADLER, LEONARD. *Developing Human Resources.* Houston: Gulf Publishing Company, 1971.

PATTER, THOMAS H., JR. *Manpower Planning and the Development of Human Resources.* New York: Wiley-Interscience, 1971.

POLLOCK, HARRY. *Cooperative Approaches to In-Service Training.* Management Information Service Reports, vol. 1, no. S-8. Washington, D.C.: International City Management Association, 1969.

PUBLIC PERSONNEL ASSOCIATION. *Employee Training and Development in the Public Service.* Chicago: Public Personnel Association, 1970.

SCHEIN, EDGAR H.; BENNIS, WARREN G.; and BECKHARD, RICHARD, eds. *Organization Development.* Reading Mass.: Addison-Wesley Publishing Co., Inc., 1969.

STOUT, RONALD M., ed. *Local Government In-Service Training: An Annotated Bibliography.* Albany: State University of New York, Graduate School of Public Affairs, 1968.

WYMAN, SHERMAN. *Training for Organization Development.* Management Information Service Reports, vol. 2, no. L-7. Washington, D.C.: International City Management Association, 1970.

12. Managing by Objective

BECK, ARTHUR D., JR., and HILLMAR, ELLIS D. *A Practical Approach to Organization Development through MBO-Selected Readings.* Reading, Mass.: Addison-Wesley Publishing Co., 1972.

GILL, J., and MOLANDER, C. F. "Beyond Management by Objectives." *Personnel Management* 2 (August 1970): 18–20.

GOODACRE, DANIEL M. "Management by Objectives Can Work." *Training and Development Journal* 24 (October 1970): 10–12.

HUGHES, CHARLES L. *Goal Setting: Key to Individual and Organizational Effectiveness.* New York: American Management Association, 1965.

HUMBLE, JOHN W. *How To Manage by Objectives.* New York: American Management Association, AMACOM, 1973.

———. *Management by Objectives in Action.* New York: McGraw-Hill Book Company, 1970.

KOONTZ, HAROLD O. *Appraising Managers as Managers.* New York: McGraw-Hill Book Company, 1971.

LEVINSON, HARRY. "Management by Whose Objectives?" *Harvard Business Review* 48 (July–August 1970): 125–34.

LOEN, RAYMOND O. *Manage More by Doing Less.* New York: McGraw-Hill Book Company, 1971.

McCONKEY, DALE D. *How to Manage by Results.* Rev. ed. New York: American Management Association, 1967.

MILLER, ERNEST C. *Objectives and Standards: An Approach to Planning and Control.* New York: American Management Association, 1966.

MORRISEY, GEORGE L. *Management by Objectives and Results.* Reading, Mass.: Addison-Wesley Publishing Co., Inc., 1970.

ODIORNE, GEORGE S. *Management by Objectives: A System of Managerial Leadership.* New York: Pitman Publishing Corp., 1965.

REDDIN, W. J. *Effective Management by Objectives: The 3-D Method of MBO.* New York: McGraw-Hill Book Company, 1971.

13. Systems Analysis and Urban Information

HANEL, RICHARD S. *Management, Systems Analysis and Urban Data*. Management Information Service Reports, vol. 1, no. L–2. Washington, D.C.: International City Management Association, 1969.

HARTMAN, W.; MATTHES, H.; and PROEME, A. *Management Information Systems Handbook*. 2nd ed. New York: McGraw-Hill Book Company, 1968.

HOOS, IDA R. *Systems Analysis in Public Policy: A Critique*. Berkeley: University of California Press. 1972.

KRAEMER, KENNETH L.; MITCHEL, WILLIAM H.; WEINER, MYRON E.; and DIAL, O. E. *Integrated Municipal Information Systems: The USAC Approach*. New York: Praeger Publishers, 1973.

LA PATRA, JACK W. *Applying the Systems Approach to Urban Development*. Stroudsburg, Pa.: Dowden, Hutchinson & Ross, Inc., 1973.

ORLICKY, JOSEPH A. *The Successful Computer System: A Management Guide*. New York: McGraw-Hill Book Company, 1969.

PARKER, JOHN K. *Introduction to Systems Analysis*. Management Information Service Reports, no. 298. Washington, D.C.: International City Managers' Association, 1968.

SCIENTIFIC AMERICAN, ed. *Information*. San Francisco: W. H. Freeman & Co., 1966.

SHAW, JOHN C., and ATKINS, W. *Managing Computer System Projects*. New York: McGraw-Hill Book Company, 1970.

WEIST, JEROME D., and LEVY, FERDINAND K. *A Management Guide to PERT/CPM*. Englewood Cliffs, N.J.: Prentice-Hall, Inc., 1969.

The Wichita Falls Consortium Phase I Report: Volume I. Synthesis of Phase I Conclusions. Springfield, Va.: National Technical Information Service, PB 206 789-1, 1970.

14. Management Information Systems

DOWNS, ANTHONY. "A Realistic Look at the Final Payoffs from Urban Data Systems." *Public Administration Review* 27 (September 1967): 204–10.

FORRESTER, JAY. *Urban Dynamics*. Cambridge, Mass.: The M.I.T. Press, 1969.

GEORGE WASHINGTON UNIVERSITY STATE-LOCAL FINANCES PROJECT. *PPB Pilot Project Reports from the Participating Five States, Five Counties, and Five Cities*. Washington, D.C.: George Washington University, State-Local Finances Project, 1969.

HANEL, RICHARD S. *Management, Systems Analysis and Urban Data*. Management Information Service Reports, vol. 1, no. L-2. Washington, D.C.: International City Management Association, 1969.

HATRY, HARRY, and COTTON, JOHN. *Program Planning for State, County, City*. Washington, D.C.: George Washington University, State-Local Finances Project, 1967.

HEARLE, EDWARD F. R., and MASON, RAYMOND J. *Data Processing System for State and Local Governments*. Englewood Cliffs, N.J.: Prentice-Hall, Inc., 1963.

HYSOM, JOHN, JR., and AHNER, RAYMOND P. *Computerized Urban Development Information System*. Urban Data Service Reports, vol. 4, no. 9. Washington, D.C.: International City Management Association, 1972.

INTERNATIONAL CITY MANAGEMENT ASSOCIATION. *Applying Systems Analysis in Urban Government: Three Case Studies*. A report for the U.S. Department of Housing and Urban Development. Washington, D.C.: International City Management Association, 1972.

KRAEMER, KENNETH L. "USAC: An Evolving Intergovernmental Mechanism for Urban Information Systems Development." *Public Administration Review* 31, (September–October 1971): 543–51.

KRAEMER, KENNETH L.; MITCHEL, WILLIAM H.; WEINER, MYRON E.; and DIAL, O. E. *Integrated Municipal Information Systems*. New York: Praeger Publishers, 1974.

PARKER, JOHN K. *Introduction to Planning, Programming and Budgeting Systems*. Management Information Service Reports, vol. 1., no. L-9. Washington, D.C.: International City Management Association, 1969.

————. *Introduction to Systems Analysis*. Management Information Service Reports, no. 298. Washington, D.C.: International City Managers' Association, 1968.

PAZOUR, JOHN. *Municipal Information Systems: The State-of-the-Art in 1970*. Urban Data Service Reports, vol. 4, no. 1. Washington, D.C.: International City Management Association, 1972.

SIMON, HERBERT A. "Applying Information Technology to Organization Design." *Public Administration Review* 33 (May–June 1973): 268–78.

SWEENEY, STEPHEN, and CHARLESWORTH, JAMES C., eds. *Governing Urban Society: New Scientific Approaches.* Monograph no. 7. Philadelphia: American Academy of Political and Social Science, 1967.

WILDAVSKY, AARON. "The Political Economy of Efficiency: Cost Benefit Analysis, Systems Analysis, and Program Budgeting." *Public Administration Review* 26 (December 1966): 292–310.

15. Work Analysis and Work Environment

BALLOWN, JAMES S., and MALONEY, JOHN F. "Beating the Cost Service Squeeze: The Project Team Approach to Cost Improvement." *Public Administration Review* 32 (September–October 1972): 531–38.

DENHARDT, ROBERT. "Alienation and the Challenge of Administration." *Personnel Administration* 34 (September–October 1971): 25–32.

FUHRO, WILBUR, J. "Work Simplification: Key to Greater Efficiency." *Supervisory Management* 16 (March 1971): 2–7.

GOLEMBIEWSKI, ROBERT T. "Organization Development in Public Agencies: Perspectives on Theory and Practice." *Public Administration Review* 29 (July–August 1969): 367–77.

HAYNES, W. WARREN, and MASSIE, JOSEPH L. *Management: Analysis, Concepts and Cases.* 2nd ed. Englewood Cliffs, N.J.: Prentice-Hall, Inc., 1969.

KOONTZ, HAROLD, and O'DONNELL, CYRIL. *Principles of Management.* 5th ed. New York: McGraw-Hill Book Company, 1972.

MILWARD, G. E. *Organization and Methods: A Service to Management.* London: Organization and Methods Training Council, 1959.

STEISS, ALAN WALTER, and CATANESE, ANTHONY JAMES. "Programming for Government Operations: The Critical Approach." *Public Administration Review* 28 (March–April 1968): 155–67.

TERRY, GEORGE R. *Principles of Management.* 6th ed. Homewood, Ill.: Richard D. Irwin, Inc., 1972.

U.S. EXECUTIVE OFFICE OF THE PRESIDENT. Office of Management and Budget. *Papers Relating to the President's Departmental Reorganization.* Washington, D.C.: Government Printing Office, 1971.

WILDAVSKY, AARON. "The Self-Evaluating Organization." *Public Administration Review* 32 (September–October 1972): 509–20.

16. Development, Status, and Procedures for Labor Relations

17. Labor Relations Management

AUSSIEKER, M. W., JR. *Police Collective Bargaining.* Public Employee Relations Library, no. 18. Chicago: Public Personnel Association, 1969.

CLARK, R. THEODORE. *Compulsory Arbitration in Public Employment.* Public Employee Relations Library, no. 37. Chicago: Public Personnel Association, 1963.

LABOR-MANAGEMENT RELATIONS SERVICE. *Arbitration: Last Stop on the Grievance Route.* Strengthening Local Government through Better Labor Relations, no. 14. Washington, D.C.: Labor-Management Relations Service, 1973.

———. *Facts about Fact-Finding.* Strengthening Local Government through Better Labor Relations, no. 8. Washington, D.C.: Labor-Management Relations Service, 1971.

———. *Municipal Negotiations: From Differences to Agreement.* Strengthening Local Government through Better Labor Relations, no. 5. Washington, D.C.: Labor-Management Relations Service, 1970.

———. *Public Employee Strikes: Causes and Effects.* Strengthening Local Government through Better Labor Relations, no. 7. Washington, D.C.: Labor-Management Relations Service, 1970.

———. *A View of the Public Employees' Unions.* Strengthening Local Government through Better Labor Relations, no. 4. Washington, D.C.: Labor-Management Relations Service, 1973.

NIGRO, FELIX A. *Management Employee Relations in the Public Service.* Chicago: Public Personnel Association, 1969.

SASSO, CARMEN O. *Coping with Public Employee Strikes: A Guide for Public Officials.* Chicago: Public Personnel Association, 1970.

STANLEY, DAVID T., and COOPER, CAROLE L. *Managing Local Government under Union Pressure.* Washington, D.C.: Brookings Institution, 1972.

STIEBER, JACK. *Public Employee Unionism: Structure Growth, Policy.* Washington, D.C.: Brookings Institution, 1973.

U.S. ADVISORY COMMISSION ON INTERGOVERNMENTAL RELATIONS. *Labor-Management Policies for State and Local Government.* Washington, D.C.: Government Printing Office, 1969.

WARNER, KENNETH O., and HENNESSY, MARY L. *Public Management at the Bargaining Table.* Chicago: Public Personnel Association, 1967.

WELLINGTON, HARRY H., and WINTER, RALPH K., JR. *The Unions and the Cities.* Washington, D.C.: Brookings Institution, 1972.

ZAGORIA, SAM, ed. *Public Workers and Public Unions.* Englewood Cliffs, N.J.: Prentice-Hall, Inc., 1972.

ZEIDLER, FRANK P. *New Roles for Public Officials in Labor Relations.* Public Employee Relations Library, no. 23. Chicago: Public Personnel Association, 1970.

18. Public Information

ANDERSON, DESMOND L., ed. *Municipal Public Relations.* Chicago: International City Managers' Association, 1966.

ARNOLD, DAVID S. "Public Relations." In *Managing the Modern City*, pp. 377–401. Edited by James M. Banovetz. Washington, D.C.: International City Management Association, 1971.

BURTON, PAUL. *Corporate Public Relations.* New York: Reinhold Publishing Corporation, 1966.

"Communicating with the Communicators." *Public Management,* November 1970, Entire issue.

CUTLIP, SCOTT M., comp. *A Public Relations Bibliography.* 2nd ed. Madison, Wis.: University of Wisconsin Press, 1965.

CUTLIP, SCOTT M., and CENTER, ALLEN H. *Effective Public Relations.* 4th ed. Englewood Cliffs, N.J.: Prentice-Hall, Inc., 1971.

NATIONAL ASSOCIATION OF REGIONAL COUNCILS. *Regional Council Communications: A Guide to Issues and Techniques.* Washington, D.C.: National Association of Regional Councils, 1973.

STARRETT, PETER F. *Mass Communications for Local Officials.* Tempe, Ariz.: Arizona State University, Institute of Public Administration, 1970.

VANCE, JOHN E. *Information Communication Handbook: Policies for Working with the Media for Public Officials, Citizens, Business and Community Groups.* St. Paul, Minn.: By the author, 1757 North Fry Street, St. Paul, 1973.

WALL, NED L. *Municipal Reporting to the Public.* Chicago: International City Managers' Association, 1963.

19. Institutionalizing Citizen Participation

ALMOND, GABRIEL A., and VERBA, SIDNEY. *The Civic Culture: Political Attitudes and Democracy in Five Nations.* Princeton, N.J.: Princeton University Press, 1963.

ALTSHULER, ALAN A. *Community Control: The Black Demand for Participation in Large American Cities.* New York: Pegasus, 1970.

CARMICHAEL, STOKELY, and HAMILTON, CHARLES V. *Black Power: The Politics of Liberation in America.* New York: Random House, 1968.

"Citizen Participation." *Public Management,* July 1969, Entire issue.

COMMUNITY PLANNING ASSOCIATES. *A Citizen's Handbook for Neighborhood Planning.* Tulsa, Okla.: Community Planning Associates, n.d.

FREDERICKSON, H. GEORGE. "Curriculum Essays on Citizens, Politics, and Administration in Urban Neighborhoods." *Public Administration Review* 32 (October 1972): Special issue.

GROSSER, CHARLES F. *New Directions in Community Organization from Enabling to Advocacy.* New York: Praeger Publishers, 1973.

KOTLER, MILTON. *Neighborhood Government: The Local Foundations of Political Life.* Indianapolis: Bobbs-Merrill Co., Inc., 1969.

LANE, ROBERT E. *Political Life.* New York: The Free Press, 1959.

MILLBRATH, LESTER W. *Political Participation.* Skokie, Ill.: Rand McNally & Company, 1965.

Mogulof, Melvin B. *Citizen Participation: A Review and Commentary of Federal Policies and Practices.* Washington, D.C.: The Urban Institute, 1969.

Moynihan, Daniel P. *Maximum Feasible Misunderstanding: Community Action in the War on Poverty.* New York: The Free Press, 1969.

Riddick, William L., II. *Charrette Processes: A Tool in Urban Planning.* York, Pa.: George Shumway Publisher, 1971.

Spergel, Irving A. *Community Organization: Studies in Constraint.* Beverly Hills, Calif.: Sage Publications, 1972.

Spiegel, Hans B. C., ed. *Citizen Participation in Urban Development.* 2 vols. Washington, D.C.: National Training Laboratories Institute for Applied Behavioral Science, 1968.

Stenberg, Carl W. "Decentralization and the City." In *The Municipal Year Book 1972.* Washington, D.C.: International City Management Association, 1972.

Sundquist, James L., and Davis, David W. *Making Federalism Work: A Study of Program Coordination at the Community Level.* Washington, D.C.: Brookings Institution, 1969.

Washnis, George J. *Municipal Decentralization.* Washington, D.C.: Center for Governmental Studies, 1970.

Zimmerman, Joseph F. *The Federated City: Community Control in Large Cities.* New York: St. Martin's Press, Inc., 1972.

List of Contributors

Persons who have contributed to this book are listed below with the editors first and the authors following in alphabetical order. A brief review of experience, training, and major points of interest in each person's background is presented. Since most of the contributors have written books, monographs, reports, and articles, information of this kind has not been included.

STANLEY PIAZZA POWERS (Editor, Chapters 2, 3, and 9) is Director of the Governmental Organization Development Division and Assistant Professor in the Department of Public Administration at the University of Nebraska at Omaha. His extensive background includes experience as a newspaper editor and publisher, and four years as a senior staff member with the International City Managers' Association. From 1966 to 1972 he was with the Industrial Relations Center, University of Chicago, serving from 1968 as director of the Governmental Management and Research Division. In addition to teaching and research, his current activities include organization development programs for several Nebraska and Iowa cities. His educational background includes a bachelor's from Kent State University, a master's in journalism and communication from the University of Florida, a master's in public administration from Roosevelt University, and work toward the Ph.D. in public administration at the University of Pittsburgh.

F. GERALD BROWN (Editor, Chapters 4, 5, and 11) is Assistant Professor and Coordinator of Public Administration Programs, Center for Management Development, School of Administration, University of Missouri—Kansas City. In addition to teaching and research, he has conducted and participated in workshops and other training programs for city managers and other municipal employees in areas of management development and human relations. He has had additional academic experience with the University of Pittsburgh, Contract Team, Institute of Administration, Zaria, Nigeria. Other

experience includes service with the College-Projects Program of the American Friends Service Committee, administrative assistant to the city manager of Saginaw, Michigan, and research associate on the staff of the International City Managers' Association. He holds a bachelor's degree from the University of Oregon, a master's in public and international affairs from the University of Pittsburgh, and is a candidate for the Ph.D. in public administration at the University of Pittsburgh.

DAVID S. ARNOLD (Editor, Introductions to Parts One, Two, Three, Four, and Five) is Director, Publications Center, the International City Management Association, and Editor, the Municipal Management Series. He has been with ICMA since 1949 with a variety of responsibilities in research, editing, writing, and publications production. From 1943 to 1949 he was on the field staff of Public Administration Service. He has been president of the Chicago Chapter, American Society for Public Administration, and served on the executive committee for the project on classification of cities jointly sponsored by ICMA and Resources for the Future. He holds a bachelor's degree from Lafayette College and a master's in public administration from the Maxwell Graduate School, Syracuse University.

HAROLD T. BUSHEY (Chapter 15) is Director, Pittsburgh Regional Office, U.S. Veterans Administration. He has been with the VA since 1946, having previously served as assistant director and personnel director. He also has been a personnel management consultant to the U.S. Agency for International Development and to the Veterans Administration Central Office in Washington, D.C. He is an adjunct professor in the Graduate School of Public and International Affairs, University of Pittsburgh, and has lectured at the Graduate School of Business Administration, Harvard University, and at Duquesne University. He has received the Outstanding Management award from the Veterans

Administration. He holds the master's degree in industrial management and relations from the University of Pittsburgh.

JAMES S. CRABTREE (Chapter 16) is Professor of Industrial and Labor Relations, School of Administration, University of Missouri—Kansas City. In addition to teaching and consultation, his research interests have been in personnel administration, labor market information, and labor relations. He holds bachelor's degrees from the University of Kansas and the University of Akron, the master's in business administration from the University of Missouri—Kansas City, and the Ph.D. in industrial relations from the University of Wisconsin.

WILLIAM B. EDDY (Chapter 10) is Professor and Director, School of Administration, University of Missouri—Kansas City. He has been with the university since 1962 with a variety of teaching and research assignments, including staff development programs, service with the Greater Kansas City Mental Health Foundation and the Institute for Community Studies, educational programs for business and public administrators, and consultation to community organizations. In 1971-72 he was on leave as Professor and Associate Director, Federal Executive Institute, Charlottesville, Virginia. He holds the bachelor's degree from Kansas State University. He hold the master's from Kansas State University in industrial psychology and the Ph.D. from Michigan State University in industrial psychology.

AGNES M. FOWLES (Chapter 18) is Public Information Officer for the village of Oak Park, Illinois. She has had prior marketing and public relations experience with the Oak Park Trust and Savings Bank and with Bozell & Jacobs, Inc., Chicago. She is completing work for the master's degree in public administration at Roosevelt University and holds the bachelor's degree in journalism and communications from the University of Florida.

PETER B. GILES (Chapter 13) is a consultant with the Government Services Group of Booz-Allen & Hamilton, Inc. He has participated in projects to design and develop information systems for several local governments, including a financial management information system for the city of Portland and Multnomah County, Oregon, and an integrated municipal information system for Wichita Falls, Texas. Prior to joining Booz-Allen, he was an urban systems engineer with the Systems Technology Group of Westinghouse Research Laboratories where he was involved with computer modeling and simulation techniques on urban growth patterns and public service delivery. He holds the bachelor's degree from Brigham Young University and the master's in urban affairs from the Graduate School of Public and International Affairs, University of Pittsburgh.

CLEMM C. KESSLER, III (Chapter 6) is Director of the Organizational Laboratory and Associate Professor of Psychology, University of Nebraska at Omaha. In addition to teaching and research activities, he is a consultant to several business concerns in the Omaha area. His bachelor's degree is from Bucknell University and his master's in psychology is from Western Reserve University. He holds the Ph.D. in industrial psychology from Case-Western Reserve University where he was an industrial mental health trainee with duties in personnel assessments, job evaluation, test administration, vocational counseling, attitude surveys, industrial mental health research, and related areas.

WALLACE G. LONERGAN (Chapter 8) is Director, Industrial Relations Center, and Associate Professor, Graduate School of Business, University of Chicago. He has overall management responsibilities for center activities concerned with organization improvement and management development programs for industry, schools, hospitals, governmental agencies, churches, and community organizations. Many of the projects deal with leadership, communication, problem solving, decision making and setting objectives. He also has served as a consultant to the Ford Foundation and other public and private organizations. He holds the bachelor's degree from the College of Idaho and the master's in business administration and the Ph.D. from the University of Chicago.

THOMAS P. MURPHY (Chapter 14) is Executive Director, Institute for Urban Studies, and Professor of Government and Politics, University of Maryland. He has been in his present position since 1971. From 1966 to 1971 he was Professor and Director of the Public Administration Program, University of Missouri—Kansas City. He has had extensive experience with the federal government, including the United States Air Force, the Federal Aviation Agency, and, from 1961 to 1966, the National Aeronautics and Space Administration. He holds the bachelor's degree from Queens College, the master's in political science from Georgetown University, and the Ph.D. in political science from St. John's University.

FRED PEARSON (Chapter 12) is Associate Training Specialist and Coordinator for Government Projects, Industrial Relations Center, University of Chicago. He works with a variety of IRC clients as teacher, consultant, program designer, and program materials writer. Clients have included municipalities in the Chicago area, the Chicago Housing Authority, four state police organizations (Illinois, Iowa, Minnesota, and Wisconsin), the Chicago Community Fund, and Illinois Blue Cross and Blue Shield. He also has been an editorial writer for the Lindsay-Schaub newspapers in Decatur, Illinois. He holds the bachelor's degree from Wheaton College and the master's in journalism from Northwestern University.

ROBERT J. SAUNDERS (Chapters 1 and 11) is Director, Center for Management Development, School of Administration, University of Missouri—Kansas City. He has been with the university since 1967 and has conducted and participated in a wide variety of seminars, workshops, and other kinds of training programs for local government officials as well as serving as consultant to several community groups. From 1968 to 1973 he served as director and co-consultant/trainer for the City of Kansas City (Missouri) Organization Development Program. Earlier experience includes service as City Administrator of Belton and Liberty, Missouri. He holds a bachelor's degree from the University of Kansas City and a master's in public administration from the University of Kansas.

DAVID C. SCOTT (Chapter 7) is Professor and Chairman, Department of Public Administration, University of Nebraska at Omaha. He has been a consultant to charter commissions and citizen groups, is a past president of the Missouri Municipal League, and served as mayor of Springfield, Missouri, 1959-62. He has been on the faculty at the University of Iowa and Southwest Missouri State College, has served as executive officer for business affairs at Southwest Missouri State College, and has been with the University of Nebraska at Omaha since 1965. He holds the bachelor's and master's degrees in political science from the University of Iowa and the Ph.D. in political science and public administration from the University of Iowa.

DANIEL H. STRAUB (Chapter 19) is Vice President, Mariscal and Company. He is responsible for three areas of specialization for this management consulting firm: urban policy analysis, health systems, and general business. Current projects include marketing studies, a site location study, and a model cities evaluation project. He has been a consultant with Theodore Barry and Associates and with the Institute for Urban Policy and Administration, University of Pittsburgh. In addition, he served for four years in the United States Air Force holding the rank of captain at the time of separation. He holds the bachelor's degree from Allegheny College, the master's in urban development administration from the Graduate School of Public and International Affairs, University of Pittsburgh, and is a candidate for the Ph.D. at the University of Pittsburgh.

SAM ZAGORIA (Chapter 17) is Director, Labor-Management Relations Service which is sponsored by the National League of Cities/U.S. Conference of Mayors and the National Association of Counties. From 1965 to 1969 he was a member of the National Labor Relations Board by appointment of President Lyndon B. Johnson. His extensive background also includes ten years of service as administrative assistant to U.S. Senator Clifford P. Case and ten years with the *Washington Post* as a reporter and editor. He was a Nieman Fellow at Harvard University, specializing in political science and labor relations.

Index

Page numbers in italics refer to illustrations.

MUNICIPAL MANAGEMENT SERIES
Developing the Municipal Organization

TEXT TYPE:
Baskerville

COMPOSITION:
Graphictype, Inc., Arlington, Virginia

PRINTING, AND BINDING:
Kingsport Press, Inc., Kingsport, Tennessee

PAPER:
Glatfelter Offset

PRODUCTION:
David S. Arnold and Emily Evershed